The Turnpikes of New England

"Dipping into the valley and then rising over successive hills."

NEW ENGLAND TRANSPORTATION SERIES

The Turnpikes of New England

FREDERIC J. WOOD

Abridged with an Introduction by
Ronald Dale Karr

Branch
Line
Press

Pepperell, Massachusetts

The Turnpikes of New England, and Evolution of the Same through England, Virginia, and Maryland, by Frederic J. Wood, was originally published by Marshall Jones Company, Boston, in 1919.

Cover design by Diane B. Karr

Frontispiece: *Norfolk and Bristol Turnpike in Wrentham, Massachusetts*

Library of Congress Card Number 96-85443

ISBN: 0-942147-05-7

Branch Line Press
13 Cross Street
Pepperell, Massachusetts 01463

10 9 8 7 6 5 4 3 2 1

Dedicated
to
Charles A. Stone, Edwin S. Webster, and Russell Robb
M.I.T. '88
In appreciation of the continuance of friendship of college
days

"When the Indian trail gets widened, graded, and bridged to a good road, there is a benefactor, there is a missionary, a pacificator, a wealth bringer, a maker of markets, a vent for industry."

Ralph Waldo Emerson.

"So, if there is any kind of advancement going on, if new ideas are abroad and new hopes arising then you will see it by the roads that are building."

Horace Bushnell.

Contents

Introduction

MORE THAN fifteen years ago while working in Northwestern University's Transportation Library, I came across *The Turnpikes of New England, and Evolution of the Same through England, Virginia, and Maryland,* by Frederic J. Wood. This beautiful old book, illustrated with pictures of a bygone era, I found fascinating. Wood brought to life an otherwise forgotten episode in New England's history. *The Turnpikes of New England* eventually became the model for my own book on the history of New England's rail lines.

When Wood completed his book in 1919, the heyday of the New England turnpike was a century past. Even before the coming of the railroad in the 1830s, turnpikes had already passed their peak, and the iron horse soon put most of the remaining companies out of business. Wood spent a decade tracking down the story of every turnpike company in the region, pouring through local histories in libraries, carefully examining maps, then attempting to trace the routes of forgotten pikes by asking older inhabitants if they remembered where the old turnpikes went a half century or more before. Sometimes the surviving records were scant, and he did not always succeed in establishing the complete history of every company. But his achievement, *The Turnpikes of New England,* comes as close to a definitive work on the topic as we are likely ever to have. Three quarters of a century later it remains unique.

New England's turnpike companies first appeared in the 1790s, reached their peak early in the next century, declined after 1820, and were largely gone by the 1850s. (Electric street railroads would follow this same sequence exactly a century later.) Turnpikes provided an obvious precedent for railroad corporations, and their meager profitability doubtless made the task of attracting investors to early railroads that much more difficult. The railroad undermined support for most long-distance roads, both toll and free, and it was not until the popularity of the bicycle at the end of the century that attention returned to road improvement.

In addition to recounting early history, *The Turnpikes of New England,* in both its photographs and text, also documents New England's roads as they were at the dawn of the automotive era in the first two decades of the twentieth century. There is frequent mention of trolleys and rail lines, which have become historical artifacts in there own right, and many of the photographs show streetcar tracks. The enormous increase in automobile traffic in the 1920s soon transformed many of the scenes that Wood so carefully recorded.

Little is known of the author, Frederic James Wood. He was born in London, England, March 3, 1867, the son of John Farmer and Ella Louise (Skinner) Wood. As he later claimed membership in the Sons of the American Revolution, it would appear that at least one of his parents was an American. Raised in Boston, he graduated from the Massachusetts Institute of Technology in 1888. He worked as a civil engineer, first in railroading and later in fire prevention. For two years he served in the U.S. Army Corps of Engineers, leaving with the rank of Major. In 1893 he married Susie E. Bowley. For many years he resided in the Boston suburb of Brookline. He retired in 1935. I have yet to learn when and where he died.

The Turnpikes of New England has been out of print for more than half a century and has never before appeared in paperback. In undertaking this abridgment I have tried to respect the integrity of Wood's work while making the book affordable and accessible to the modern reader. What has been left out? First, all footnotes and bibliographic references have been removed, except when integral to the text. A large section in the first chapter, which traced the history of turnpikes through England and into the colonial American South, has been dropped. I also selectively cut in places where Wood was repetitive or went into excessive detail, particularly in recounting the financial returns of Massachusetts turnpike corporations. (Omitted passages are indicated by an ellipse.) Some of the less interesting illustrations have been left out. Finally, I have removed most references to unbuilt turnpikes and have instead listed them at the end of each chapter. I have also assigned numbers to all of the lines and added these to Wood's maps. Otherwise, the author's lively prose has been left as first published in 1919 (thus when the text refers to "to-day" or "now," it always means as of the original publication date, not 1997).

With The Turnpikes of New England in hand the modern reader may set out to explore these old roads today. Many of them are still called "turnpikes" or "pikes" and can be readily identified on local maps or atlases. Some have become major highways; others are no more than paths through the woods. Although their heyday was brief, the old turnpikes left a legacy still visible on the New England landscape of our time.

RONALD DALE KARR

PEPPERELL, MASS., April 19, 1997

Author's Preface

IN 1908, in connection with a report on certain transportation facilities which I was preparing, I ventured into the historical side of the question, and soon ran into references to this and that turnpike. My efforts to gather data on that subject were fruitless; the extensive public library to which I had access yielding nothing but a work of fiction under the word "turnpike," and our most comprehensive index giving only five references, three of which were purely local. Gradually the search became a habit, no opportunity to learn more on the subject being neglected, and, as the data accumulated, the idea grew: first to prepare a brief magazine article, next a full story of some special road, then to cover Massachusetts, and finally all New England. Here and there in local histories brief articles were found; but in the main the facts presented in the following pages were gleaned from old records, in the perusal of which I soon acquired the habit of blowing the dust from each volume top as I took it from its long-undisturbed resting place. The labor has been long but full of interest. May its presentation prove interesting as well.

My employment in civil life taking me well over New England, and my subsequent two years in army service requiring travel over the entire eastern section of the United States, I was enabled to secure most of the pictures which are reproduced herein myself; but acknowledgment is due to George R. Groesbeck, official photographer at the Hog Island Shipyard, for the more than professional interest which he took in developing the same. Others to whom I am indebted for photographs are Miss Cora S. Cobb of Newton, Mass., for the artistic picture of the old Cook Tavern; A. Hutton Vignolles of Newton, for the views in Crawford Notch; Miss Ellen A. Webster of Cambridge, Mass., for the pictures of the Webster Tavern; I. Chester Horton of Canton, Mass., for the snow scene on the Stoughton Turnpike; Martin Baker of Marshfield, Mass.; William H. Blood, Jr., of Wellesley, Mass.; Professor Frederic W. Brown of Bowdoin College; Mrs. Irwin C. Cromack, Dorchester, Mass.; Allan W. Crowell, Washington, D. C.; Howard P. Fessenden, Newton, Mass.; C. Elmer Gane, Allston, Mass.; Jerome F. Hale, Wells River, Vt.; Miss Martha E. Knight, Camden, Maine; Arthur J. Shea, Dorchester, Mass.; Dana M. Wood, Belmont, Mass.; Walter S. Wood, Concord, Mass.; A. Stuart Pratt, manager of the Blue Hill Street Railway; Fairbanks Museum of Natural Science, St. Johnsbury, Vt.; National Museum, Washington, D. C.; Shorey Studio, Gorham, N. H.; and the Stone and Webster Engineering Department, Boston.

To Messrs. Edward W. Baird of Roslindale, Mass., William H. Blood, Jr., Wellesley, Mass., William A. Buck, Willimantic, Conn., George A. Carter, Jr., Brockton, Mass., Nelson H. Daniels, Bedford, Mass., Arthur W. Gates, Willimantic, Conn., Dr. Byron G. Ingalls and Francis M. Perry, Foxboro, Mass., George H. Wetherbee, Jr., Braintree, Mass., and Walter S. Wood, Concord, Mass., is due my personal acquaintance with many old turnpikes which I was enabled to acquire by the kind contribution of their time and automobiles.

Valued assistance has been had from Philip H. Borden, city engineer of Fall River, George A. Carpenter, M. Am. Soc. C. E., city engineer of Pawtucket, Samuel Hartshorn, town clerk of Franklin, Conn., William J. McClellan, historian, Baltimore, Howard G. Philbrook, Boston, Herbert E. Sherman, M. Am. Soc. C. E., Providence, Arthur C. Sprague, Wollaston, Mass., Irwin C. Cromack of the Boston Street Department, and a host of others, among whom I must include the officials of the many state, county, and town offices, especially the present clerk of Norfolk courts, Robert B. Worthington, whose patience was always proof against my attacks.

And, lastly, to my own home surroundings, to the two whose faith and confidence in my ability to pilot unknown fields always upheld me, whose sympathy and encouragement ever spurred me, is due the greatest debt of all.

FREDERIC J. WOOD

BROOKLINE, MASS., October 15, 1919.

The Turnpikes of New England

IN many New England towns will be found an old road locally known as "the turnpike," or the "old turnpike," over which are hovering romantic traditions of the glory of stage-coach days, while perhaps a dilapidated old building, standing close beside its now grass-grown pathway, is reverently pointed out as having occasionally been the temporary resting place of men great in our country's annals. But aside from the charm of such old stories the inquirer will be able to learn but little for, strange to say, those old roads have not found their place in history, and what little is known about them seems to be fast departing with an older generation.

In the hope of saving some of this information an effort has been made to compile such as is still available, and the result appears in the following pages.

Turnpikes, as distinguished from the ordinary roads of the same time, were those on which gates barred the progress of the traveler, at which payments were demanded for the privilege of using the road. Such payment was called "toll" and the gates were known as "tollgates." The privilege of building such "turnpikes" and of collecting toll thereon was conferred by the legislatures of the several states upon various individuals under the form of turnpike corporations, and the roads were constructed by private capital, were privately owned, and were operated for the revenue derived from the collection of the tolls.

In the eighteenth century the name "pike" seems to have been applied to anything terminating in a point and the form of gate now called a "turnstile," being made of four crossed bars sharpened at their outer ends and turning on a center, was called a "turnpike." As this was about the only form of gate in use the name was readily applied to the tollgates when they first appeared. A reversion to ancient form is thus found in the entrances to our elevated and subway systems and many places of amusement where we enter through such "turnpikes" or "turnstiles" paying our toll as we pass. The dictionaries still define "turnpike" as a gate, and the early charters allowed the building of "turnpike-roads" and the erection of "turnpikes" across them. But the longer word soon became shortened and as "turnpikes" the roads themselves were commonly known. . . .

New England Roads of the Colonial Period

For generations untold before the settlements at Plymouth and Boston, the Indians followed certain trails which were later adopted by the white men for their early roads. Many predecessors of Massasoit and King Philip had led their tribes along these trails on warlike expeditions or on annual trips to lakes and ocean to secure their supplies of fish and game, and consequently such paths, worn by the feet of countless braves and their Indian ponies, were well defined, often being depressed a foot or two below the adjoining ground. Many may be followed today, sometimes in comfort by automobile, but more often with jolting and shaking over little used country roads.

The "Coast Path" between Boston and Plymouth; the "Kennebunk Road" following the coast northerly; the "Bay Road" from Boston through Stoughton to Taunton; the "Old Connecticut Path," through Wayland, Marlboro, Worcester, Oxford, and Springfield, to Albany and thence over the "Iroquois Trail" to Lake Erie; and the "Old Roebuck Road" through Dedham, East Walpole, Foxboro, North Attleboro, and Pawtucket, to Providence, were the principal routes of through travel which centered in Boston. The last, connecting with the "Pequot Path" which connected Providence with Westerly, formed a link in the chain of paths which reached from Boston to New York, over which a monthly post was established about 1690. That it was a rough and narrow road we know from Madam Knight who, in 1704, made the trip overland from Boston to New York, and recorded all her trials and discomforts for future generations to read. At the site of South Attleboro Village, on the "Old Roebuck Road," another trail branched off, following down the easterly shore of the Seekonk and Providence rivers to the point where Bristol is now situated. This trail, with the "Old Roebuck Road," was one of the early colonial roads, a primitive ferry from Bristol completing the journey from Boston to Newport.

The restrictive policy of Great Britain toward her American colonies, by which she sought to prevent all intercolonial trade, reserving for her merchants at home the profits of such intercourse, almost entirely prevented the improvement and development of those early routes, and down to the outbreak of the American Revolution facilities for travel parallel to the seacoast were sadly lacking.

The early settlements were naturally on the coast, and water communication, being most convenient, was generally used. As the fertile fields of the inland districts gradually drew settlers away from the ocean it obviously became necessary to have roads or paths connecting the new homes with the older settlements, and a "hit or miss" arrangement of rough roads, radiating from central points on the coast, resulted. Until well into the nineteenth century each village was an independent community, having its own church, blacksmith, shoemaker, gristmill, and country store. The farmer's clothing for the day and his bedding for the night were spun and woven by the women of his own family from the wool of his own sheep. The grain of the fields was harvested into barns on the same premises, or ground into meal or flour at the mill but a few miles distant. From the cattle of his own raising he laid away his winter's supply of meat, and the hides, dressed nearby, were made into shoes by the local artisan, who boarded with his patrons as he performed their work. Little need was there then for many roads. The one fixed journey was the weekly trip to church, and the road which provided the facility for that generally led also to the gristmill and to the country store, where were kept the few article needed in the farmer's daily life, which his own labor did not produce and where also he could dispose of the surplus which his farm might yield.

Long distance freight movement was absolutely impossible. The charge for hauling a cord of wood twenty miles was three dollars. For hauling a barrel of flour one hundred and fifty miles it was five dollars. Either of these charges was sufficient to double the price of the article and set a practical limit to its conveyance Salt, which cost one cent a pound at the shore, would sometimes cost six cents pound three hundred miles inland, the difference representing the bare cost of transportation. It was on these cheap articles of common use that the charge bore most heavily. It forced every community to live within itself. [Hadley, *Railroad Transportation*]

Such were the facilities of transportation in the new United States of America about the year 1800. Each of the thirteen original colonies was still sufficient unto itself and contained within itself, but a new era was dawning, and such conditions were fast becoming intolerable. The ambitious growth of our country made men realize that duplication of labor, whereby each little community did everything that was done in all of the others, was wasteful, and that a geographical division, by which each section would perform the part assigned to it by nature, was inevitable.

Manufactures were just commencing on a larger scale, and the mill and factories were locating in situations convenient for the new method of doing business, and the transportation requirements were far in excess of the existing conveniences. Ohio, just freed by "Mad Anthony" Wayne from the perils of Indian warfare, was open for settlement, and a host of emigrants was hastening westward, bearing with them all their worldly possessions with which to furnish and maintain their new homes.

What facilities were offered to these factories and travelers by the older communities, many of which were, by that time, approaching their bicentennial? This question can best be answered by a brief recital of conditions of traveling and quality of roads previous to that time.

The *Boston News-Letter*, in its issue of April 4, 1720, contained the following:

These are to give notice that the stage coach between Boston and Bristol Ferry for once a fortnight the six ensuing months, Intends to set out the first time from Boston at Five o'clock on Tuesday Morning the 12th currant, and be at the said Ferry on Wednesday Noon, when those from New Port may then there arrive, and be brought hither on Friday Night. Such as have a mind to go for Bristol or Rhode Island, may agree with John Blake at his house on Sudbury-street, Boston, for their passage to the said Ferry, at 25s. each person, with 14 Pounds weight of carriage and 3d. for every pound over.

The route of that stage was over the "Old Roebuck Road," as previously described, as far as South Attleboro, and thence down the easterly side of the Seekonk and Providence rivers to what is now the city of Bristol; and the comfort of the ride and condition of the roads may be deduced from the time required: from 5 A.M. Tuesday to 12 M. Wednesday, for a journey of fifty-five miles.

That was the route to Newport, at that time the largest town in Rhode Island, and destined a few years later to overshadow New York as a commercial port.

The first regular stage between Boston and Providence was established by Thomas Sabin of Providence in 1767. This ran weekly through Pawtucket and South Attleboro to North Attleboro, whence it followed the route of the present state highway through Wrentham and Walpole to Dedham, and on to Boston over the "Neck." The section of road between North Attleboro and Wrentham was publicly laid out about 1751. Connecting with an old road which led from Dedham through Walpole and Wrentham toward Woonsocket, it soon replaced the "Old Roebuck Road," held its own against turnpike competition, and is today the favorite automobile route. The time consumed by Sabin's stage is not known, but an advertisement of a stage over the same route in 1800 gives us the running time then as ten hours.

A weekly stage from Boston to Portsmouth appears to have been established in 1761, making the trip in two days. McMasters tells us that the first stage between New York and Philadelphia was not "set up" until 1756, and made the run then in three days.

June 25, 1772, this advertisement appeared in the New York *Journal*:

THE STAGE COACH
between
NEW YORK AND BOSTON

Which for the first time sets out this day from Mr. Fowler's Tavern (formerly kept by Mr. Stout) at Fresh Water in New York will continue to go the course between Boston and New York so as to be at each of those places once a fortnight coining in on Saturday evening and setting out to return by way of Hartford on Monday morning. The price to passengers will be 4d. New York or 3d. lawful Money per Mile and Baggage at a reasonable price. Gentlemen and Ladies who choose to encourage this useful new and expensive Undertaking, may depend upon good Usage, and that the Coach will always put up at Houses on the Road where the best Entertainment is provided. If on Trial, the Subscribers find Encouragement they will perform the Stage once a week, only altering the Day of setting out from New York and Boston to Thursday instead of Monday morning.

JONATHAN and NICHOLAS BROWN.

These dates plainly show us that communication, by land at least, between the colonies was very infrequent down to the outbreak of the Revolution, and the conclusion is readily reached that neither roads nor vehicles were such as to produce comfort.

The large number of pleasure carriages in use in Boston in 1753 is accepted by some as evidence of the excellence of American roads at that time, but the author is inclined to make the deduction as local as the reason. Undoubtedly the roads in Boston and immediate vicinity we good although, as we realize to this day, very crooked, but the effective radius of the horses, handicapped by the crude old-time carriages, must have been short, and the evidence is strongly to the effect that the interior roads were very bad. The moderate requirement as to width found in the old Lancaster (Massachusetts) records, wherein it stipulated that the proposed road shall be wide enough to make "feasible to carry comfortably four oxen with four barrels of cider at once," suggests that it was necessary to spread the money out pretty thin. . . .

During that war the interior roads were much improved as a matter of military necessity, and because the safety of water travel was menaced by the British war vessels, but we have abundant testimony that our country started with a deplorable system of highways. Then the triweekly postriders between New York and Boston required six days in summer and nine in winter for the trip. During Washington's first term two stages and twelve horses were all that the business between those cities required, and they jogged along, covering forty miles a day in summer and twenty-five in winter. There were no bridges over the larger streams or many of the smaller ones, and the stage was "set over" by ferries propelled by oars or sails. . . .

So we will answer our question by saying that the facilities offered to the new factories and to the westward-bound travelers were practically none, and that extensive additions, amounting to practically the creation of a new system, were demanded.

But a country which had successfully waged an eight years' war for independence against the strongest power in the world, which had overcome the difficulties causing the Shay's Rebellion and the Whisky Insurrection, and had suppressed an instigated Indian uprising on its western frontier, was not to be daunted by any difficulties.

When Alexander Hamilton made his investigation of the manufactures of the United States in 1791, he found a small but creditable number of industries all eager to expand. Of cotton he found but few factories, one of which was at Beverly, for which the first Massachusetts act of incorporation for manufacturing was passed on February 3, 1789. That industry, however, owing to the then recent inventions of Hargreaves and Arkwright, was about to make phenomenal advances. Watt's steam engine was invented about seven years prior to Hamilton's census, and the tubular boiler was only a year younger than the engine; but the mechanic arts had not then sufficiently advanced to render the commercial production of either practicable, so the new factories were obliged to derive their power from the precipitous rivers such as abound in New England. Such powers being found only at suitable falls of the rivers, it obviously followed that the mill locations were often remote from any of the existing roads or, if near them, accessible by highways used previously for neighborhood communication only and utterly unsuited for the heavy teaming of raw and finished materials of manufacture. Then, too, the sale of the products demanded outlets to more than one of the small centers of that time, and roads of other destinations were required. But who was to pay for all these needed improvements?

Francis H. Kendall, writing in the *New England Magazine*, says:

To go back to the year 1800 we must imagine scattered villages within the territorial limits of most of the towns of to-day, with but little manufacturing, the inhabitants being usually farmers, depending largely on the products of their own acres for their sustenance and comforts. Very seldom indeed was a journey of much distance undertaken by these rural inhabitants to obtain things of a different sort to add to their comforts, and to barter and trade the products of their labor for "wet and dry goods," such as molasses, sugar, tea, rum, and cloths other than homespun woven.

And to those of us who have attended the New England country town meetings, it is not hard to go further and imagine the difficulty of persuading those same "rural inhabitants" to vote appropriations for the building of roads to accommodate those "newfangled factory people," for the towns on which fell the burden of providing those public necessities were too poor to stand the necessary expense. All of them were impoverished by their contributions of men, money, and supplies in the war for independence, and by the struggle of the next decade to maintain themselves against the commercial warfare waged by English merchants. The states were in no better condition, and it was simply out of the question for the public funds to provide for the increased transportation. In this dilemma relief was found by the willingness of private citizens to invest their funds and energies in the construction of the roads, provided the same might be done as a conservative business investment. How was this to be accomplished?

As individuals they possessed no power by which they could lay their roads in the best locations; they could not take over or improve any portion of an old road, nor even cross one. Their collection of tolls if they built a road, could not be enforced and, what was of more vital importance to them, any one of them would be personally liable for injuries or damages consequent upon any defect in the road, or action of their servants. Only from the state could they obtain such rights and desired immunity, and under conditions which would assure to the public the rights and privileges to it belonging.

Such undertakings required combinations of capital in excess of anything then known in private affairs, and a permanent form of organization was necessary for the maintenance of such roads. Out of these difficulties grew the turnpike corporations, organized to construct the roads and to derive revenue from the collection of tolls.

"Though the ownership is private the use is public," said one learned judge in deciding a turnpike case, and such public use involved the indiscriminate right of all individuals who paid the toll to travel over the roads in comfort and security at all times. On the other hand, in return for the tolls collected, the private owners were under obligations to maintain their roads constantly in proper and sufficient repair.

The First Public-Service Corporations

In earliest English law we find special obligations imposed on those engaged in occupations on which the welfare of the public depended. The surgeon, from the scarcity of men qualified for that position, had to serve a large number and enjoyed a monopoly in his territory. The consequences, should he discriminate against any individual and refuse to attend him, would be far too serious, and hence he was obliged by law to serve alike all who stood ready to pay him. In similar relations to the public stood the tailor, smith, victualler, baker, innkeeper, miller, carrier, ferryman, and wharfinger. By competition and increased numbers engaged in the occupations most of the above trades have been removed from the class of public service, but the obligation still rests upon the victualler and innkeeper; the carrier has been succeeded by the railroads, and the ferryman by the publicly maintained bridges.

The organization of corporations for business purposes began about this time, having been unknown previous to the Revolution, and by far the larger part of the first twenty years of such productions were for the purposes of turnpikes and toll bridges. In old English law a corporation could only be formed by charter from the Crown or by a special act of Parliament. Upon the severance of the ties to the mother country such powers of the monarch ceased and they were never bestowed upon any individual officer of the new government. General laws, by which corporations could be organized by complying with certain requirements and without a dispensation from some supreme authority, originated in New York in 1811, at which time laws for the formation of manufacturing companies were enacted, but it was many years before such privileges were extended to corporations for other purposes. So, at the opening of the turnpike era, there was but one power—the legislature or assembly of the state—which could grant a charter for a corporation; and as long as turnpikes were projected this condition continued in New England.

The charters for turnpike purposes thus granted bore a general resemblance to each other; in fact many paragraphs were exactly copied and in but few were special features contained. To avoid the weary repetition involved in the duplicate recital of routine sections of turnpike charters, the Massachusetts legislature, on March 16, 1805, enacted them all into a general law and provided that such should be the rights, powers, and privileges of all turnpike corporations thereafter created. By this procedure Massachusetts anticipated by forty years the famous "Companies' Clauses Consolidation Act" of Great Britain. The other New England states, however, continued the long-drawn-out repetition with each company formed, although Vermont, in 1808, formed eight corporations in one act with the routine sections enacted once for all of them. Otherwise throughout the turnpike history of New England we find a special act of a legislature creating each corporation.

As the turnpike corporations relieved the local governments of their obligations to maintain certain highways, it was but proper that some of the governmental powers should be conferred upon them. Hence they were granted the rights under the principle of eminent domain, that an obstinate landowner could not, by refusing to sell, block the great enterprise of such value to the public. They were further allowed to take over and incorporate into their roads various sections of what had long been public highways, freely open to all classes of travel but which, under the control of the turnpike corporation, became subject to the interruption of a gate and the demand for toll. Although the occasion for the last privilege was provided by the neglect or inability of the communities to keep the roads in proper repair, and the companies, in consideration, were bound to maintain properly such section of road, the diversion from public to private control caused much hostility on the part of the local population, and was the cause of much litigation, and several times, of acts of violence. Many acts of the legislatures have been found, usually in behalf of a special corporation providing penalties for damages done to the road or its gates. A popular form of road was the "Shunpike," which was a short section leaving the turnpike on one side of a gate and joining it again on the other. Special and general laws were enacted to discourage such enterprises and penalties were provided for evasions of toll by other means.

What now seem pretty severe restrictions were also imposed upon the corporations. They were limited strictly to the building and maintaining of a road, and were not allowed to do any other act or thing. The Rhode Island acts generally permitted the companies to acquire and dispose of a reasonable amount of land, but in the other New England states the acquisition of a few acres, that the keeper of a remote tollhouse might cultivate a garden, was only allowed by special legislative act. When the Torrington Turnpike was laid out in Connecticut, it entered the road of the Talcott Mountain Turnpike Corporation at a flat angle, and the locating committee saw fit to include the little triangle in the layout of the road. But the assembly of 1805 declared that the road was only authorized to be four rods in width, that the taking of such additional land was illegal, and that the land was still owned by the party from whom the committee had sought to take it.

Rates of toll were fixed in the charter, and the number of gates which the company was to be allowed to erect was also specified. The location of the gates was determined by the committee which was appointed to inspect the road after completion, and gates once located by such committee could only be moved by legislative consent. The location of the road was not intrusted to the judgment of those who were investing their money and who could best be depended upon to act conscientiously, but was delegated to a committee appointed either by the legislature or by the judge of the county court. Since the turnpike was to be for the public service, the representatives of the public fixed its location, as had previously been done in the laying out of public roads.

Corporations formed in the northern New England states did not have a charter provision fixing the amount of their capital stock. As the company was to be allowed to do only certain definite things, there seemed to be no need of limiting the amount of money which it might raise, and considering the difficulty experienced by nearly all the projects in getting financed there was no need. The later Vermont companies were chartered with a nominal capital which they were at liberty to increase to "any necessary amount."

There were two forms of turnpike franchises in New England. One form, that most commonly found in Connecticut, was that in which existing old road, badly in need of repairs and beyond the resources of the local authorities, was declared no longer a public highway and was presented to a turnpike corporation organized for the purpose of putting it in good order and thereafter maintaining it so. In the early Rhode Island corporations we find the same method, notably in the case of the first franchise granted there. In the petition for a charter for that company it was recited that the petitioners had raised a certain sum which they would expend in specified repairs, if they might have a designated highway to be by them maintained as a turnpike.

The second form of franchise was that in which the intention was to have an entirely new road built, cutting across fields and through forests hitherto untouched and shortening the distance between the terminal points. Naturally such a road often ran into some old road and not infrequently followed the course of one for a little way, but it was seldom that a deflection to one side was made to secure such a result.

The Connecticut practice in providing for such a road was for the assembly to pass an act describing in more or less detail the location, or route of the proposed road, to declare that a road was thereby laid out along such described route, and to decree that the same should be a public highway. Then the newly established public character of the road would be stripped from it, and a corporation would be formed for the purpose of building the road and operating it as a turnpike. Under this method the towns were required to acquire and pay for the land and to build the bridges, the corporation merely building the road itself, unless a bridge of considerable size was necessary, in which case the franchise might require the corporation to build it. Naturally such procedure, putting heavy burdens on the towns which they were not willing to assume, for conveniences which they themselves had not desired, caused much dissatisfaction, and in 1803 New Milford, at a town meeting, appointed a committee to confer with other towns in an effort to have the granting of such turnpike franchises stopped. But the effort did not succeed and many more such turnpikes were established. It can easily be conceived that after a lapse of several years some confusion arose as to the responsibility for different bridges, and a general act of the Connecticut assembly was needed to straighten out the difficulty.

In most of the early Massachusetts charters for roads of this class it was directed that the turnpike should be built in as straight a line as possible, and this was nearly always done with unfortunate results, as the resultant location led up and down hill regardless of grades, and, disregarding centers of population, usually rendered the road of little practical use. It does not appear, however, that this condition was imposed without the consent of the persons incorporated, for the one idea pervading the minds of turnpike promoters seemed to be to build in a straight line whenever possible. In fact the crookedness of existing roads was the chief argument used by petitioners for turnpike franchises, and hence they were more or less bound to build straight roads.

A quaint old book, published in 1806, entitled *Rural Economy*, by S. W. Johnson, contains some ambitious sections on turnpikes. Of their layout it says: "The shortest line, is a straight one and can not be rivalled, and as such merits the first consideration." The author advised laying out the route on the ground by that principle, and that it be abandoned only in the face of "innumerable obstructions." The maximum angle of ascent should be exceeded if thereby the straight line could be maintained.

Nearly all the Massachusetts turnpikes were of this latter class, of which the Newburyport, the Norfolk and Bristol, and the New Bedford and Bridgewater furnish striking illustrations.

Only two types of road were ever specified in the New England charters. There was the "turnpike-road," with no attempt to describe its character or quality, and the "plank road." In the former case the corporation was left free to choose whether it would build a high-grade macadam road or just clear away the trees and sod and make a common dirt road. Where plank-road franchises were granted some very simple specifications were generally included in the charter, requiring that the "track of the road" should be laid with plank "or some other hard material," and that it should present a smooth and even surface. Only about a half-dozen plank roads were ever built in New England, and those were in Vermont and Connecticut.

The modern public-service commissions were anticipated by Connecticut as early as 1803, when an act was passed providing that two commissioners should be appointed annually for each turnpike in the state, with powers to inspect and compel repairs. Vermont enacted a more practical law in 1806 by providing for the appointment of three turnpike inspectors for each county, with authority over all roads within their territory. In Massachusetts a provision by which a justice of the court of common pleas could order repairs and enforce his order appears in 1805, and in 1840 such powers were conferred upon the county commissioners. In all the states the turnpikes were liable to indictment for being in bad order, which rendered the corporation liable to a fine the same as in the case of the towns. But it would seem that it was often cheaper to pay a fine than to make repairs, so the officials mentioned above were given power to throw open the tollgates when their orders were not obeyed.

Rosy hopes were entertained in all the New England states of the financial success of turnpikes. No limit to the life of the franchises was thought necessary, other than the provision that, when the investors had been repaid their original investment plus interest at the rate of twelve per cent, the road should revert to the public. With the possible exception of the turnpike between Providence and Pawtucket, not one New England road ever came within gunshot of realizing such expectations, the best Massachusetts road, that of the Salem Turnpike Corporation, reporting an average net earning of three and one tenth per cent over a period of sixty years.

Under authority of these turnpike charters roads were built all over New England, except in Maine, where few obtained a footing. Every town of any importance, and many of none, had its turnpike connections often radiating in all directions, while the routes leading from the more populous centers were frequently paralleled and but a short distance apart.

The turnpike era began in New England in 1792, when the first turnpike was established between New London and Norwich, and it may be said to have ended about 1850, although at the opening of the year 1917 there were four companies still doing business in New Hampshire and one in Vermont. Contrary to the general impression the railroads were not usually responsible for the cessation of turnpike operation. In the few cases where favorable conditions had kept the old toll roads alive until the invasion of their territory by the locomotive, it was but natural that the competition should relegate the old-fashioned methods to the past; but in the majority of cases the turnpikes had given up the struggle before the appearance of the rival. It was simply a case of not enough business to make the investment pay.

There were three grades of turnpike roads as constructed in America but, owing to the rigors of the New England winters, one of them was not adapted for this section. Hence we had two grades within the scope of this volume:

First, those where the only improvement consisted in the reduction of hills, and in the formation of a convex roadbed with ditches on the sides, using the natural soil for making the road. By cutting the hills to a determined grade the angle of ascent was made much easier, enabling the horses to draw larger and heavier loads; and by the shaping and ditching of the roadway standing water was prevented and the road kept dry. Such roads cost, in Massachusetts, from six hundred to a thousand dollars a mile, but were expensive to maintain, as the wheels of passing vehicles made ruts in the soft material, in which the water would stand, softening the entire structure.

The second class, of which there were but few, comprised those roads where a substantial surface of gravel was provided, supposedly of sufficient depth to withstand the action of the frost. Such were known as "artificial roads" on account of the material for the surfacing being brought from some other place, and in distinction from the "natural roads," where the surface was made from the soil on the spot or thrown out in digging the ditches. The only roads in Massachusetts surely of this class were the Newburyport, the Salem, and the Norfolk and Bristol, or the Providence Road.

One of the great points gained by the construction of turnpikes was the establishment of easier grades than those previously maintained. The advantage thus obtained was thus expressed in the old days:

It is found that, upon a slope of one in forty-four or one hundred and twenty feet to the mile, a horse can draw three quarters as much as he can upon a level. On a slope of one in twenty-four or two hundred and twenty feet to the mile, one half as much, and on a slope of one in ten or five hundred and twenty-eight feet to the mile, one quarter as much. But these proportions vary with the condition of the road, the grade being virtually increased by its softness.

The comparative advantages of different kinds of surfacing was expressed in rather a back-handed way, for they said:

The greatest estimated inclination down which a horse can safely trot is one in fifteen on a gravel or dirt road, one in thirty-five or forty on a macadamized road, and one in sixty on roads paved with blocks.

In a report made in 1831 by the canal commissioners of Pennsylvania, the increased efficiency of teams resulting from turnpike construction was stated to be sufficient to enable four horses which would draw on a common road, in addition to the weight of the wagon containing the load, one ton a distance of twelve miles, to move on a turnpike with grades not exceeding five degrees (eight and seven tenths per cent) one and one half tons a distance of eighteen miles. In other words, the energy which was necessary to move one ton twelve miles on the old roads was sufficient to move the same ton twenty-seven miles on a turnpike—an increased efficiency of one hundred and twenty-five per cent. . . .

How the Work Was Done

In these days of labor-saving machinery and devices for performing enormous amounts of work, it is difficult to imagine the difficulties under which the turnpike constructors labored. There were no factories in which the ordinary tools of daily life were manufactured in quantities, and they were not to be found in larger amounts than probably half a dozen in the stores. If a man wanted a shovel, a pick, rake, or hoe, he might find one in a store, but more likely he would have to wait the convenience of the local blacksmith, who would hammer them out one at a time on his order.

From Bishop's *History of Manufacturing* we learn that the great shovel factory of the Ames Company, in North Easton, Massachusetts, was founded in the most primitive manner in 1804 by Oliver Ames, Sr. Procuring the material for about a dozen shovels, he would proceed to fashion them in his shop, after which he would journey to the town for the purpose of selling them. With the proceeds, stock for another dozen would be bought. So we can see that, during the period of turnpike construction, few shovels were to be had at short notice. Oziel Wilkinson, who had the contract for building thirteen miles of the Norfolk and Bristol Turnpike in 1805-06, was obliged to set up a shop of his own in Pawtucket, in which he manufactured the shovels and picks needed for his work.

Carts and wagons were no more easily obtained, each one being "custom made" by a local smith, who probably made no more than three or four in a prosperous year. Had it not been possible to hire as laborers the farmers along the route, with their horses, carts, and tools, it is doubtful if the work could have been accomplished at all.

The grading of the roadbed was accomplished, as it would be today, by shoveling the earth into carts and hauling it to its destination and shaping it to finished form by rakes or hoes.

Ledges were drilled by hand with locally made drills. The time fuse was unknown then, and the old method of laying a train of powder was used to explode the blasting charges of powder. The hole having been drilled and loaded, a long hollow quill was inserted in the powder with its upper end above the surface of the rock. The tamping was then placed around the quill which, filled with powder and connected with the train, carried the fire to the charge.

The line was staked out by means of a surveyor's compass like those in use today, or with a circumferentor, an instrument long forgotten. For work of the most exacting character there was available an instrument of greater precision, including a telescope with cross hairs; but such instruments were few and only to be had at great expense. The engineer's transit did not appear until after 1830. . . .

These instruments were operated by "mearsmen," and anyone who has motored over the Newburyport, Salem, Norfolk and Bristol, or New Bedford and Bridgewater turnpikes will join in a tribute to the skill with which those crude old-time instruments were made to project long straight lines. Johnson said, in his *Rural Economy*, that when the extreme points of a long line cannot be taken at one operation, that is, when the straight section is so long that its entire length cannot be seen from one position of the instrument, more accuracy than that of a quarter compass or circumferentor will be needed. Then would be required the use of a "telescope with intersecting hairs."

An anticipation of the present-day wye level, "a telescope with a spirit level," was used in connection with "station staves" in running the levels and determining the grades. Horizontal measurements were taken with a "Gunter's chain of four poles or perches, which consists of one hundred links." Thanks to old deeds any modern surveyor knows about Gunter's chain—that it was sixty-six feet long and each link, consequently, 7.92 inches.

Plank Roads

When the pioneer road builders had occasion to cross a swampy piece of ground they made a bed of tree trunks set transversely to the road and closely adjacent to each other. This form of road was called "corduroy," and over it the vehicles went in a succession of bumps, painful to the traveler and destructive to the running gear. Of such a piece of road, encountered between Columbus and Sandusky, Dickens wrote:

A great portion of the way was over what is called a corduroy road which is made by throwing trunks of trees into a marsh, and leaving them to settle there. The very slightest of the jolts with which the ponderous carriage fell from log to log, was enough it seemed, to have dislocated all the bones in the human body. . . . Never, never once that day, was the coach in any position, attitude, or kind of motion to which we are accustomed in coaches.

But crude and pain-productive as those old corduroy roads were, they were founded on scientific principles of economy and stable foundation in insecure places, and it is but natural that their use should have been continued after sawmills had made it possible to lay timbers of uniform thickness. Of the same class were the plank roads so popular in the interior states, but refined and made more endurable by the advance in mechanic arts. . . .

The first application of the plank principle in the western continent, and probably in the world, occurred in Toronto in 1835, when the northerly extension of Yonge Street was built in that way. The cost of the planks and labor of laying them was reported as five hundred and twenty-five pounds for one mile, besides which was the cost of ditching and the application of a coat of sand. During the next ten years about four hundred and forty-two miles of plank roads were laid in Canada.

Commencing about 1846 that form of construction was begun in New York, and in 1850 twenty-one hundred and six miles were either completed or in process of construction. They seem to have been built in radiating clusters around various important towns. One hundred and sixty-three miles centered in Utica, one hundred and forty-eight miles in Rome, ninety-nine miles in Syracuse, while Rochester, in 1850, had only two roads with a mileage of eleven and one half completed, but seven other roads, with a mileage of one hundred and thirty were being built.

Fifty per cent additional tractive efficiency was claimed for plank roads over the type of macadam road then in use, and a great saving in first cost and maintenance was shown. Of course the planks would rapidly decay, and it was considered necessary to figure that a road would have to be rebuilt at the end of every seven years. . . .

New Jersey had several plank roads, among the most notable of which was the one across the marshes between Newark and Jersey City. . . .

In Massachusetts the Plum Island Turnpike was at one time laid with plank. One corporation was formed in New Hampshire to build a plank road, but no reason has been found to believe that its purpose ever was realized. Vermont created fourteen companies, and Connecticut, during the years

1851, 1852, and 1853, granted incorporation to seven companies for that purpose.

Plank roads were particularly well adapted to the needs of regions possessing rich soils with a deficiency of gravel, and they are still found to be economical in the Central States. There the planked surface will be frequently met, but the tollgate has now become a part of the unregretted past.

The Vehicles That Used the Turnpikes

Although some form of wagon or cart was in use in very early days, no marked improvement in its form or construction was effected until the day of the turnpike, when a greater demand for wheeled conveyances arose. . . .

Chauncey Thomas has written that the volume of business done by American carriage manufacturers in 1795 was exceedingly small. Technical knowledge was not wanting, for there were many shops which had been established in colonial days where fine carriages were occasionally built and many imported vehicles repaired. But business languished for lack of customers. The hard times which followed the Revolution made simplicity a virtue, and the luxury of a carriage was not suited to the democratic habits which then prevailed. All parts of the largest towns were within walking distance of each other, and there was but little occasion to visit neighboring places.

But as the country grew prosperous a demand arose for vehicles for business, pleasure, and travel, and several varieties developed. Among them the principal were the chaise, curricle, chair, chariot, phaëton, whisky or gig, coach, landau, and many types of wagons and carts for working purposes.

The *chaise* was early in great demand, and down to 1840 it seemed that nothing could ever supplant it in popular favor. The earlier forms had enormously high wheels and the tops were stationary, being supported on iron posts. Curtains of painted canvas or leather covered the sides and back, and the vehicle was often unprovided with dasher or apron. In later years they were provided with folding tops which, with the dasher and cushioned seats, made it a carriage of luxury. The accompanying illustration clearly shows the details of such a carriage. The one pictured, now in the Fairbanks Museum of Natural Science in St. Johnsbury, Vermont, was long in service in and around Providence, carrying the well-known Doctor Brown on his visits.

The *curricle* was an ancient form of vehicle, having been in use in Italy for many years, where it was suspended on leather braces. Springs were added by the French, and the English altered the shape, giving the back a graceful ogee curve, improving the hood, and adding a spring bar across the horses' backs. It was a vehicle of easy draft and could be driven at great speed, but it was rather dangerous if the horse shied or stumbled. In Europe the horses were usually attached in a span, but in America they were driven tandem. It seems to have been an equipage of less luxury than a chaise, although generally closely resembling one. In the toll rates the curricle was commonly allowed to pass for a smaller sum. The curricle was drawn by two horses, the chaise by one.

The *chair*, commonly pronounced "cheer," was the only traveling vehicle

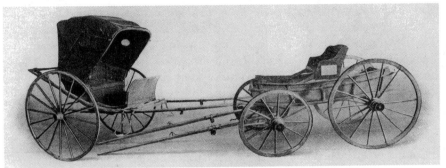

Dr. Brown's chaise and wagon made by Thaddeus Fairbanks

seen in the rural regions in 1800, according to Stratton in *The World on Wheels*, and the cost of one was no inconsiderable sum. It was hung upon springs made of wood, generally with rude bow or standing-tops of round iron, hung around with painted cloth curtains. The linings and cushions stuffed with "swingling-tow," sometimes with salt hay, were, in those primitive times of simplicity and innocence, deemed good enough for any American sovereign.

The *chariot* was really half a coach, having only one seat, while the coach had two. Each was hung high above the ground in order to clear the heavy wooden timbers which connected the two axles, which were far apart on account of the large size of the wheels. The bodies were inclosed and were hung by leather braces from scroll-shaped steel springs which inclined upward at an angle of about fifteen degrees from the perpendicular. The rear spring was called a "whip spring" and the front an "elbow spring."

Of *phaëtons* there were many varieties, none of which were driven by coachmen. Young England in those days delighted in very lofty phaëtons and fast driving. The style continued to develop until it culminated in an excessively high type which the witty Irish dubbed a "suicide." These were four-wheeled carriages. The one-horse phaëton had the body over the hind axle, where it was hung on grasshopper springs which were bolted to the axle and connected with the body by scroll irons. The body was joined to the front wheels, where there were no springs, by wooden stays, which were slightly goosenecked to allow the front wheels to cut-under. Naturally with all that space between the axles, and with the body set back far enough to clear the turning of the front wheels, the horse was a considerable distance in advance of its driver.

The *whisky*, or gig, has been perpetuated in the gig or racing sulky of the present day.

The *landau* was an improved form of coach in which the roof parted in the middle and folded back each way to an angle of fort five degrees, making a more agreeable carriage for pleasant weather.

Of the vehicles in use in 1790 Thrupp says in his *History of Coaches*, that the woodwork was heavier and the ironwork lighter than in later days. The iron frequently broke both on account of its insufficient proportions and its poor quality, but the axles being more carefully made gave little trouble. The wheels were very high and appeared light. The extreme height was five feet and eight inches, which size was made with fourteen spokes, and the smallest size, three feet and six inches, had eight. All bodies hung high in order to clear the perch, which was the name given to the heavy connection between the two axles. The larger wheeled vehicles were hung upon framed carriages which supported the upright springs.

In 1804 Obadiah Elliot invented the elliptic spring which, with the reduction in the size of the wheels, brought the bodies much nearer the ground. This was the most pronounced advance which had made in carriage development.

In the early years of the century business in the old carriage towns was done on what was called the "dicker" system, wrote Thomas. Woodworkers, blacksmiths, trimmers, and painters each did business on his own account and swapped parts, as they termed it, the final settlements being made in finished carriages. The dealer in materials took carriages in payment. The workmen were paid in orders for goods, and money was almost unknown. The old operators used to say that this plan was much safer than the cash system, there being fewer failures and less danger of getting involved in debt. But those old customs had their day, and gradually the business became concentrated, until now we have the enormous factories with their constant outpouring of finished products. . . .

The primitive form of stage described as in use in 1806 was soon superseded by the egg-shaped coach, which is the form commonly pictured on the old stage-coach bills. In this type the body was hung in leather braces high above the ground in order to clear the connection between the front pin and the rear axle, which was high on account of the large size of the wheels. There were three seats inside, as described by Abdy, with a seat and footboard in front on the outside. The base of the body and the roof curved symmetrically forming an oval from which the resemblance to an egg was fancied, while the boot for baggage on the rear was inclosed by curtains which made a tangent to the roof curve and fell behind the rear wheels. Such were the stages during the teens and twenties of the nineteenth century. With the easy entrance and exit by means of a side door, the easy motion due to the leather hangers, and the three large windows by which the entire upper half of the side was open to daylight, such a vehicle must have seemed the climax of luxurious traveling to those who had been accustomed to the crude "machines" described by Melish.

The well-known Concord coach was introduced about 1828 by Lewis

Concord Coach

Downing who, about fifteen years earlier, had founded the now well-known house of Abbot, Downing, and Company in Concord, New Hampshire. It seems that the full measure of success was attained in the design of these coaches, for hardly an improvement has been made in them since their first appearance, and those in use today are practically built on the same lines as were those of ninety years ago. The Concord coach at once leaped into popularity both on account of its excellence in workmanship and from its ease in riding and, wherever such vehicles are needed today, may be found still in service. They are too well known to need describing. In the construction of our first railroad cars the builders could think of nothing better, and Concord coach bodies, mounted on railway trucks, followed the first locomotive over the Mohawk and Hudson Railroad in 1831. . . .

Various forms of sleds and sleighs were in use, although it was an old saying that there was never any snow on a turnpike. The sleighs were of the pattern still to be found in northern New England and called "board runners" on account of a single piece of board being used for the runner, the same being shaped to a suitable form for running over the road. Probably all such sleighs

First train on the Mohawk and Hudson Railroad, 1831

and the sleds, too, were homemade or of local manufacture, as they could easily be made by one familiar with carpenter's tools.

Further romantic interest is found in the old wagons in which the large shipments of freight were carried, and all accounts of the Cumberland Road or of any of the turnpikes leading to the West, teem with references to the white-topped wagons with their strings of horses.

These splendid wagons were developed in Pennsylvania by topographical conditions, by the soft soil, by trade requirements, and by native wit. They were the highest type of a commodious freight carrier by horsepower that this or any other country has ever known; they were known as Conestoga wagons from the vicinity in which they were first in common use, as is told by Alice Morse Earle in *Stage Coach and Tavern Days.*

These wagons had a boat-shaped body with a curved bottom, which fitted

Conestoga wagon

them specially for mountain use, for in them freight remained firmly in place at whatever angle the body might be. The rear end could be lifted from the sockets; on it hung the feed trough for the horses. On one side of the body was a small tool chest with a slanting lid. This held hammer, wrench, hatchet, pincers, and other simple tools. Under the rear axle-tree were suspended a tar bucket and water pail. The wheels had tires sometimes a foot broad. The wagon bodies were arched over with six or eight bows, of which the middle ones were the lowest. These were covered with a strong, pure white hempen cover corded down strongly at the sides and ends. These wagons could be loaded up to the top of the bows, which was the object attained by having them high at the ends. Four to six tons was the usual load for such a vehicle.

The driver rode on the nigh-wheel horse or walked, no seat being provided for him. A board projecting from the side between the wheels afforded a precarious seat for the helper, who generally worked his way by such employment.

In 1783 Levi Pease, in company with Joseph Sykes, established a stage line between Boston and New York over the rough and crooked roads which then constituted the northern route, passing through Worcester, Palmer, and Hartford, and making the trip in a week. In later years Josiah Quincy described his experiences on a journey over the line in 1784 as follows:

I set out from Boston on the line of stage lately established by an enterprising Yankee, Pease by name, which at that day was considered a method of transportation of wonderful expedition. The journey to New York took up a week. The carriages were old and shackling and much of the harness was made of ropes. One pair of horses carried the stage eighteen miles. We generally reached our resting place for the night, if no accident intervened, at ten o'clock and after a frugal supper went to bed with a notice that we should be called at three the next morning, which generally proved to be half past two. Then, whether it snowed or rained, the traveller must rise and make ready by the help of a horn lantern and a farthing candle, and proceed on his way over bad roads, sometimes with a driver showing no doubtful symptoms of drunkenness, which good-hearted passengers never fail to improve at every stopping place by urging upon him another glass of toddy. Thus we travelled eighteen miles a stage, sometimes obliged to get out and help the coachman lift the coach out of a quagmire or rut, and arrived at New York after a week's hard travelling, wondering at the ease as well as the expedition of our journey.

We have already noted the starting of a stage line over the same route in 1772, but it did not continue long. After Pease's effort continuous service between Boston and New York was maintained by increasing numbers of coaches and then by trains.

Prior to 1806 such stages journeyed over two hundred and fifty-four miles of roads, the distance being reduced by road improvements in that year to two hundred and forty-six miles, and by 1821 a total reduction of forty-four miles had been made, leaving two hundred and ten miles, to be covered between Boston and New York. Such savings in mileage were the prime objects sought by turnpike construction, but it was too often attained at the expense of steep grades over hills which lay in the direct line. Still stage routes increased with the development of turnpikes and, as a rule, followed them over the hills.

One feature of the *Old Farmer's Almanac* was the publication of a list of the stages running from Boston, and from the issue of 1801 we note that one hundred and sixteen coaches arrived at and departed from that town weekly, there being twenty-six separate lines to as many places. Pease's stage by that time had two rivals, one going by way of Providence, and the running time had been reduced to thirty-nine hours, due doubtless to running all night instead of stopping for sleep at taverns by the way. These lines ran three times each week. There were two daily stages to Providence and the trip was made in eight hours. The service to Portsmouth had been improved from the weekly two-day trip in 1761 to a fifteen-hour journey three times a week, and a new route to Albany ran through Worcester, Brookfield, and Northampton twice a week, making the trip in thirty-eight hours. All this was before the turnpikes had become factors of influence.

When the Boston *Traveller* was founded by Badger and Porter, in 1825, its issue was accompanied once in every two months by a supplement called the *Stage Register*, in which it was sought to give a complete list of all the stage lines in New England, with distances, route followed, and rates of fare. The issue of September 6, 1825, shows sixty-eight lines leaving Boston, with three hundred and seventeen stages in and out each week, and a total of one hundred and twenty-five lines in New England. From Boston there were seven lines to Albany, each running three times a week. By way of Greenfield the trip was made in thirty-five hours, through Northampton in forty-one, with the same time by way of Springfield. Another route was through Brattleboro and Bennington, and forty-three hours were occupied on that journey. New York was reached by way of Worcester, Stafford, Hartford, and New Haven in forty hours, while the traveler who staged it to Norwich and voyaged thence to New York by the steamer *Fanny* spent the same length of time.

Travelers to Bristol Ferry had a much happier time than in 1720, for in 1825 the route was through Taunton, and the required time had been cut down from thirty-one to eleven hours. The Portsmouth line had disappeared, at least by that name, and those desirous of going there embarked on the Portland stage. That took nine hours to reach Portsmouth, gave its passengers fifteen hours for rest, and completed the journey in nine hours more. . . .

The Eastern Mail Stage, an anticipation of the modern limited train service, carried its passengers to Portland for eight dollars, with proportionate rates for way stations, requiring but eight hours to reach Portsmouth.

The regular time of departure for long-distance stages was 2 A. M., which was the hour for resuming the journey from resting places also.

A study of the routes followed by the different lines of stages shows that generally the turnpikes were followed, but it is seen that the Cambridge and Concord and the Union turnpikes were scrupulously avoided. The Union was not badly located, but it suffered from its associations, for the Cambridge and Concord was built straight without regard to centers along the route, and in one case, at least, with a fatal disregard for grades. The local stage from Concord could not afford to spurn the business of Lexington and West Cambridge (Arlington), so it kept off the turnpike and went over the public roads. And the stages from the northwestern part of the state, reaching the western end of the Union Turnpike, diverted over the short Lancaster and Bolton Turnpike and proceeded thence to Boston over the "Great Road" through Sudbury and Waltham. The Union and the Cambridge and Concord seem to have had little other business either, for each was very short-lived.

Between 1825 and 1832 the number of stage lines in New England was more than doubled, there being two hundred and sixty separate routes in operation in the latter year, with a proportionate increase in the lines from Boston. The New York Mail then left Boston at 10 P. M., reaching Worcester at 3.30 A. M.; Hartford by way of Stafford at 1.30 P. M.; New Haven at 8.30 P. M.; and New York at 10 A. M. the second day.

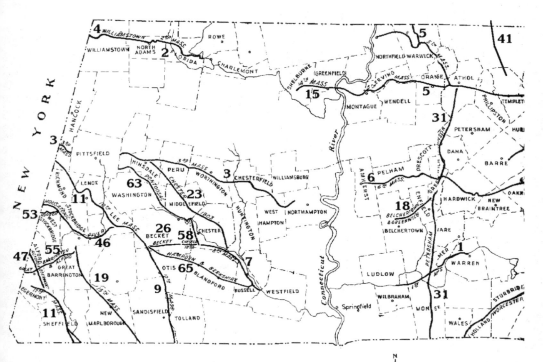

TURNPIKES
OF
MASSACHUSETTS

SCALE ~ MILES

1. First Massachusetts	23. Chester	45. Worcester
2. Second Massachusetts	24. Cambridge & Concord	46. Housatonic River
3. Third Massachusetts	25. Newburyport	47. Alford & Egremont
4. Williamstown	26. Becket	48. Lancaster & Bolton
5. Fifth Massachusetts	27. Essex	49. Wrentham & Walpole
6. Sixth Massachusetts	28. Wiscasset & Woolwich	50. Stoughton
7. Eighth Massachusetts	29. North Branch	51. Taunton & South Boston
8. Ninth Massachusetts	30. New Bedford & Bridgewater	52. Hingham & Quincy
9. Tenth Massachusetts	31. Petersham & Monson	53. Hudson
10. Third New Hampshire	32. Union	54. Douglas, Sutton & Oxford
11. Twelfth Massachusetts	33. Taunton & New Bedford	55. Great Barrington & Alford
12. Salem	34. Blue Hill	56. Mill Dam
13. Norfolk & Bristol	35. Hartford & Dedham	57. Barre
14. Quincy	36. Dorchester	58. Chester
15. Fourteenth Massachusetts	37. Bath (Governor King's)	59. Watertown
16. Camden	38. Brush Hill	60. Central
17. First Cumberland	39. Andover & Medford	61. Cambridge-Watertown
18. Belchertown & Greenwich	40. Middlesex	62. Gore
19. Fifteenth Massachusetts	41. Worcester & Fitzwilliam	63. Pontoosac
20. Wiscasset & Augusta	42. Ashby	64. Taunton & Providence
21. Medford	43. Worcester & Stafford	65. Hampden & Berkshire
22. Braintree & Weymouth	44. Plum Island	66. Granite

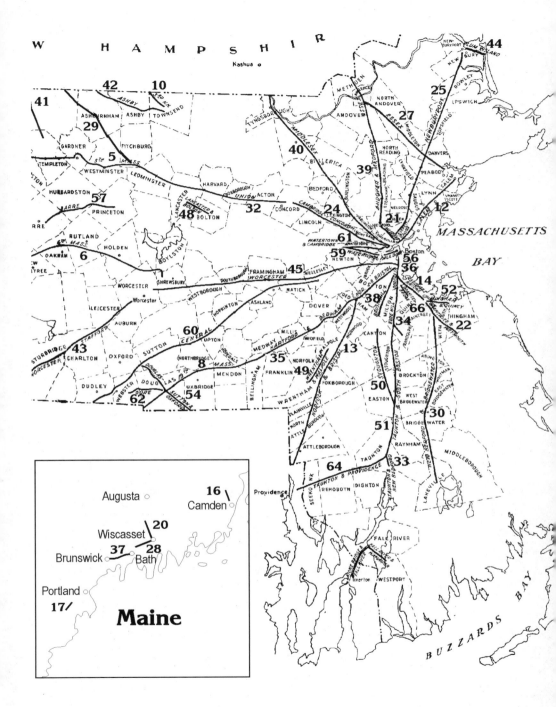

The Turnpikes of
Massachusetts

I Massachusetts the custom was almost general, in providing for turnpikes, to require the construction of an entirely new road, although
there were some notable exceptions in which the corporation was
allowed to take over an old established highway and incorporate the
same as a part of its toll road. The English custom was never followed in this
state, but each turnpike was the outcome of financial confidence in it as an
investment, or projected for the collateral benefits which were expected to
follow. Each was authorized by a special act of the legislature, and down to
1805 each act of incorporation went at length and in full detail into all phases
of the corporate formation, and the same was repeated, at what must have
been dreary length, with each successive company. The stereotyped form of
act was about as follows:

1. Certain persons incorporated under the specified name for the "purpose of
   laying out and making a turnpike-road."
2. Course of the road described.
3. Width of the same specified.
4. Number of gates to be erected when approved.
5. Rates of toll.
6. Exemptions from liability for toll.
7. Power given to commute tolls.
8. Sign to be erected displaying rates of toll.
9. Right to take land conferred.
10. Penalties provided for avoidance of toll.
11. Penalty on corporation for delaying travelers or for failure to keep road in repair.
12. Methods of procedure in organizing corporation.
13. Required filing of account of cost of road and annually thereafter a statement
    of receipts and disbursements.
14. Provided that the corporation might be dissolved when it had earned its original
    investment plus twelve per cent.
15. Charter void unless road was completed within specified time.

In 1805 the earliest general corporation law was passed in Massachusetts.
This applied only to turnpike companies and provided that thereafter no
charter should be granted until the proposed route had been viewed by a
legislative committee after public notice. Previously each route, after the

charter had issued, had been laid out by a committee, consisting generally of one senator and two representatives specially appointed for that purpose; but after 1805 that duty devolved upon five disinterested freeholders appointed by the court of sessions for the county in which the road was to be built. The act also recited the routine portion of the charters previously granted and provided that future charters should have the same powers without repetition. An additional provision was made that any corporation might be dissolved at the pleasure of the legislature, after twenty years, without reference to its earnings.

Upon the completion of a road application would be made to the court of sessions of the county in which the road was located for the appointment of a committee to view the new turnpike, and advise the court whether or not the same was constructed in a manner sufficiently safe for public travel. Such a committee was usually empowered to specify the location of the tollgates. The court of sessions, having received the report of its committee that the road was well built and safe for travel, would then declare the turnpike open for public use under the conditions imposed in the charter.

A great difference naturally existed in the earning powers of roads in different parts of the state, and it would manifestly have been unfair to allow the same rates of toll in the Berkshires on a road built under engineering difficulties and through sparsely settled districts as were granted to a route tributary to Boston and connecting several prosperous communities. Hence a variety of authorized charges may be found by detailed search, but a fair average can be given. The Massachusetts custom was generally to allow the erection of tollgates at intervals of about ten miles, and in the eastern part of the state the traveler would be apt to find displayed upon a signboard at each gate, in accordance with the charter requirement, "fairly and legibly written thereon in large or capital letters" the following:

RATES OF TOLL

For every coach, phaëton, chariot, or other four-wheeled carriage drawn by two horses	25 cents
And if drawn by more than two horses, for each additional horse	4 cents
For every curricle	17 cents
For every cart, wagon, sled, or sleigh drawn by two oxen or horses	10 cents
And if drawn by more than two, for each horse or oxen in addition	3 cents
For every chaise, chair, or other carriage drawn by one horse	10 cents
For every sled or sleigh drawn by one horse	6 cents
For every man and horse	4 cents
For all oxen, horses, mules, and neat cattle, led or driven besides those in teams and carriages, each	1 cents
For all sheep and swine by the dozen	3 cents

Adjacent to the New York line, in the town of Hancock, would have been found a signboard on which the rates would have run from twenty to fifty per cent higher than those just given; but the usual manner of giving relief to companies in receipt of insufficient tolls was not to allow an increased rate but to authorize additional gates, thus giving extra collections of the same amount.

For local reasons a company was often allowed to establish two gates within the limits of one, collecting one half the allowed rate at each. Such were significantly known as "half gates."

Certain persons were exempt from paying toll. Such were:

any person who shall be passing with his horse or carriage to or from public worship, or with his horse or team to or from any mill, or with his horse, team, or cattle to or from his ordinary labor on his farm, or on the common or ordinary business of family concerns within the same towns; or any person passing on military duty.

And if the toll gatherer was not at his post the gate had to be left open and everybody passed free. In special cases it was often provided that the inhabitants of certain districts should pass free because a section of the public road had been absorbed into the turnpike.

Each company was required to file a statement of the cost of its road and, annually, an account of its receipts and expenditures, but no penalty was ever provided for failure to do so. Consequently out of the sixty corporations which built roads in Massachusetts only eight made conscientious efforts to obey the rule. Twenty-seven others reported the cost of their investment, and some of them made desultory attempts to render the annual accounts, while twenty-five calmly ignored the requirement.

Under the law of 1805 any justice of the court of common pleas, upon complaint being made to him that a turnpike was in bad order, might give a hearing and, if he found the complaint well founded, order repairs to be made, the gate meanwhile to be open for free passage of all. In 1840 this power was transferred to the county commissioners.

An act passed in 1845 provided that the county commissioners might lay out any turnpike as a public highway, if they deemed it a public convenience and necessity, upon petition of the turnpike corporation or with the corporation's consent.

Generally, the corporation was allowed to do nothing beyond the acquisition of the strip of land four rods wide and the building and operation of a toll road on it. Prior to 1805 corporations were not allowed to run accounts with regular customers unless the legislature specifically authorized it, but under the general laws enacted in that year the privilege was extended to all. Very few general laws applying to turnpikes were ever passed, many of the acts providing penalties for evasions of toll and for damage to the road being enacted in behalf of certain specified companies, although ultimately such laws appeared upon the statutes applicable to all roads. . . .

No general provision was ever made for the organization of a turnpike corporation. Petition had to be made to the legislature which, if it saw fit, might create the corporation and allow it the privileges appertaining to such under the general provisions, with such special rights as could be obtained.

In each New England state every corporation was made subject to dissolution when its first investment plus twelve-per-cent interest had been repaid, and it may be interesting to consider how far short of realizing such hopes the actual performances were. Some reason has been found for inferring that it was expected that the life of a corporation under such terms would be about twenty years, and to fulfill that expectation a road would have to yield net earnings of twelve per cent for interest and five per cent for a sinking fund, or seventeen per cent in all. We will consider the two best roads in Massachusetts, the Salem Turnpike and the Dorchester Turnpike, taking the best single year's business done on each road . . . .

The best year on the Salem was 1835, when the net earnings of the road amounted to $12,330, or about six and eight tenths per cent of the cost of construction. The Dorchester's biggest year's work was done in 1838, when its net earnings were $4005, or about nine and two tenths per cent of the cost.

So it may safely be said that in only one year and on only one road did the earnings yield half enough to meet the expectations. And in nearly every case the road was finally given up at an almost total loss. . . .

And yet the investment in turnpikes was heavy. Considering only the corporations whose bridges were not the greater part of the cost, we find that thirty-two companies, owning five hundred and ninety-three and one half miles of roads, reported their investments, with a total of $1,230,823. We have outside information that three others expended $578,200. Taking the companies which failed to report their first costs, and placing an estimate on each according to the return for a similar road, we find it probable that $569,977 more was invested in turnpikes in Massachusetts, making a total of $2,379,000. As the population of the entire state in 1830, when turnpikes were at their prime, was 610,408, it is seen that the turnpike investment was in the proportion of about three dollars and ninety cents per capita. When it is considered that this investment provided only the road, with a few gates and tollhouses which seldom cost a thousand dollars apiece, and that the rolling stock and motive equipment was a further matter for individual investment, it is seen that the per-capita amount tied up in the turnpike utilities did not compare poorly with the later capital placed in railroads.

Why, then, were the turnpikes built? In a letter written by one of the incorporators of the First Massachusetts Turnpike, and dated in 1800, warning was given against too great expectations from such investments, as the First had proved a disappointment; and it seems to have been generally known long before the rush of construction subsided that turnpike stock was worthless.

It can be conceived that propositions to connect such cities as Boston and Providence, Worcester, Hartford, Salem, and Newburyport may have seemed to stand in a separate class and to hold hopes of remunerative business; but what encouragement could have been seen for roads in the rural districts connecting small towns? The conclusion is forced upon us that the larger part of the turnpikes of New England were built in the hope of benefiting the towns and the local business conducted in them, counting more upon the collateral results than upon the direct returns in the matter of tolls.

The turnpike era commenced in Massachusetts in 1796 when the first act of incorporation for a turnpike was passed, and generally it can be said to have ended by 1850, when railroads were in the ascendancy, although certain companies continued to do business through the sixties, and one did not surrender its corporate rights until 1905.

The early roads were in the western part of the state, as were some of the last ones, but those which collected their tolls well within the memory of men now living were on the eastern coast.

1. The First Massachusetts Turnpike

The first Massachusetts act of incorporation for a turnpike company was approved by Governor Samuel Adams on the eleventh day of June, 1796. As

First Massachusetts Turnpike: Not even a country road now

First Massachusetts Turnpike: Palmer Old Center

customary in those days, the act commenced with a preamble which read as follows:

Whereas the highway leading through the towns of Palmer and Western is circuitous, rocky, and mountainous, and there is much travelling over the same, and the expense of straightening, making, and repairing an highway through these towns, so that the same may be safe and convenient for travellers with horses and carriages, would be much greater than ought to be required of the said towns under their present circumstances, etc., etc.

Hence the First Massachusetts Turnpike Corporation was created and authority granted it to lay out and make a turnpike-road

First Massachusetts Turnpike: State Road in Warren

from Western bridge, near the Upper Mills, so called, in Western (now Warren) in the county of Worcester, to the county road, near the house lately called Scott's tavern, in Palmer, in the county of Hampshire.

Through travelers between Boston and New York, at that time, had their choice of three routes—one along the shore of Long Island Sound, the middle following more nearly a direct line, and the northern route through Worcester and Springfield. The last led through Palmer, and it was for the improvement of that through route, to hold its trade, and very likely with a view to financial profit, that the turnpike was protected. It was built according to Temple's *History of Palmer*, "through Palmer Old Centre, and kept on the northerly side of the river eastward; and was the leading thoroughfare for long travel between Boston, Worcester, Springfield, Hartford, New Haven, and New York, for many years. The toll gate was about two miles east of Palmer meeting house."

Thirty-one solid citizens were named in the act of incorporation, among whom are some of note. Levi Lincoln, at that time a member of the house of representative, from Worcester County, and later senator, congressman, attorney-general of the United States, lieutenant governor and acting governor of Massachusetts, whose son Levi attained the highest office in the state, was one. Another, Captain Levi Pease, seeking employment after his arduous duties in the Revolutionary Army, had started a line of stages between New York and Boston, over the northern route, in 1783. By many he is hailed as "The father of the turnpikes" and "The father of the stage coach," and there is no disposition here to dispute his claim to either title. Salem Town, of Charlton, was a prominent man and at the time of this incorporation was a member of the senate. He appears to have become a

First Massachusetts Turnpike: State Road in Wilbraham

turnpike authority later, for we find him often named as one of a committee to locate a new road. But the chief interest centers around the name of Thomas Dwight, who, four years later, wrote a letter to a friend on the subject of turnpikes which is almost a treatise. This letter is to be found among the papers of the Norfolk and Bristol Turnpike Corporation, now deposited with the Dedham Historical Society, and gives much interesting reading. From it we learn that the first section of the First Massachusetts Turnpike was built by Captain Bailey of Connecticut, who later built the turnpike from Hartford to New Haven, and that his contract price was three dollars per rod of length, yielding him $8640 for the nine miles of road which he built.

Mr. Dwight criticizes this price as too much by fifty per cent. An extension of the road to Wilbraham was allowed by the legislature in 1798, and four miles of this, including one half mile along the Chicopee River, where the mountain approached so close to the river as to necessitate a cut and a retaining wall ten feet in height, was contracted by one Blair of Western for two dollars per rod, or $640 per mile. Mr. Dwight thought that the contractor received too much profit out of that. He cautioned his friend to watch the contractors, as they would cheat, placing stumps and large stones in the fill instead of good road material, and he advises the retention of ten per cent of the contract price for two years while the behavior of the work is observed. The First Massachusetts Turnpike Corporation had made a mistake, he wrote, in having so many shares at a small price each, and he warned his friend, who was about to embark in such an enterprise, that the expectations of the promoters of the First had not been realized.

The road of the First Massachusetts was relocated in 1799, and made four rods wide instead of three as formerly. This appears to have been done in connection with the laying out of the extension to Wilbraham, which was allowed by the legislature of 1798, and a peculiar error is found in the county records at Springfield and Northampton, where appears the approval of the court of sessions of the relocation and layout and the decree of the court establishing the road as "a county road." That it was not so established is plainly shown by the legislative acts which followed. In 1813 a special act allowed the acquirement of real estate adjoining the road for the accommodation of its toll gatherers. In 1819 the corporation was released from its obligation to maintain its road east of the road to Northampton. How much longer the toll gatherers continued their work is not known, as the county records in Springfield, Northampton, and Worcester do not definitely record the public laying out of the old First turnpike.

In the next eighteen years ninety-seven corporations were chartered, one or more being ground out of the legislative mill in every year except 1798, with 1803 as the banner year, having sixteen for its record. Few new companies were organized after 1814, although a revival occurred in 1826, when six appeared. 1832, 1841, and 1868 saw the birth of the last three, none of which seems to have built a road. In all, one hundred and eighteen acts of incorporation were passed, with one authorizing a New Hampshire company to build in Massachusetts. Ten of these, however, were in the district which afterwards became the state of Maine. It was the early custom to designate each company like a regiment going to war, and we have the "First Massachusetts," "Second Massachusetts," "Third Massachusetts, and so on to the Sixteenth, although, as the compiler of the special acts quaintly observes, "there is a chasm in the course of numbers," there being no Seventh, and the "Williamstown Turnpike Corporation" coming in the place of the Fourth.

2. The Second Massachusetts Turnpike

A notable piece of construction was the road of the "Second Massachusetts," chartered March 8, 1797, to build "from the west line of Charlemont, in the county of Hampshire, to the west foot of Hoosuck Mountain in Adams, in the county of Berkshire." This road was the predecessor of the Hoosac Tunnel, following closely the same route. It followed up the valley of the Deerfield River on the southerly bank as far as Buckley Brook, near the present Hoosac Tunnel station. Then bearing southerly it described a semi-circular course up the east side of the mountain, and so on to North Adams. That the project was long in maturing is shown by the finding of a plan dated 1795 in the Massachusetts archives, on which the route of the proposed turnpike is shown. In 1804 the company was authorized to build a bridge over the Deerfield River at the easterly end of its turnpike. They must have been long in availing themselves of this privilege, for not until 1817 were they allowed to erect a gate on the bridge. An unobstructed bridge at the far end of the road must have been extensively and freely used, and it is not to be expected that the company waited long under such circumstances before applying for relief. An instance of how closely the corporation was held to the privileges contained in the act of incorporation is found in 1830, when, by special act, David White of Heath was authorized to call a meeting of the proprietors "for the purpose of choosing a clerk," and nothing else. Evidently the corporation had lost its clerk, by death or otherwise, and by no other person could the stockholders be called together; and only at a meeting called by a duly elected clerk could any business be transacted. That the receipts did not yield sufficient revenue can be seen from an act passed in 1817, in which the company is allowed to erect an additional gate, which meant one more collection of tolls, while the rates of toll were slightly increased also. In 1833 the corporation was dissolved and the road made free.

This route over Hoosac, or Florida, Mountain followed approximately the line of the old Mohawk Trail, over which those dusky warriors proceeded in 1664 on their terrifying raid, which resulted in the extermination of the Pocumtuck tribe, which lived in the Connecticut Valley. In 1914 the Massachusetts Highway Commission completed the construction of a state highway over nearly the same line, and the route, originally blazed in savage vengeance and hatred, has now become one of the most popular and beautiful roads of the country. At the highest point, where the road crosses the backbone of the old Bay State, and for two miles easterly from it, the Mohawk Trail, as the new state highway is called, is on the line of the old Second Massachusetts Turnpike.

The Second Massachusetts was a route for several of the stages from Boston to Albany, which continued on the Williamstown Turnpike to Williamstown, and then followed up the valley of the Green River and the West Branch to Hancock Center.

3. The Third Massachusetts Turnpike

The "Third Massachusetts," incorporated on the day after the "Second," built its road from the east side of Roberts Hill in Northampton to the eastwardly line of Pittsfield, and, under authority given the next year, across the town of Hancock, to the New York line. A break in the system is thus seen across Pittsfield, which town seems to have always been able to provide needed highways from its public funds. Turnpike travelers thus had free passage over what are now known as Unkamet and West streets in Pittsfield. In 1800, as we are told in Smith's *History of Pittsfield*, the company petitioned the legislature, stating that it had been able to pay no dividends on its expenditure of $30,000, and asked that it might collect larger tolls. It also made what seems an unreasonable request, that the towns should be required to break out the road after snowstorms, and that they should expend more money on the bridges. While the road was private property, the towns seem to have helped maintain the bridges. No act has been found granting these requests. All turnpike corporations were required, by their charters, to file with the secretary of state a statement of the cost of the road and, annually, a summary of their receipts and expenditures. The "Third" was the first to do so; no penalty being provided, most of the companies neglected the matter. From the returns of the "Third" we learn that its road cost $29,989.34. The length being roughly thirty-two miles, made the road cost about $940 a mile. From the returns filed between 1801 and 1814, we see that its net earnings averaged about $600 yearly, or about two per cent. The name of this corporation was changed, in 1814, to "The Worthington

Turnpike Corporation." On petition of the corporation, its road was made free in September, 1829.

4. The Williamstown Turnpike

The Williamstown Turnpike Corporation was the fourth to be incorporated in Massachusetts, and its road formed a continuation of that of the Second across Williamstown to the New York line. It seems to have been the original of the present Adams and Main streets and Petersburg Road in that town.

The cost was about $1000 a mile, and during the two years for which it deigned to file returns its profits were $490.21, or about two and one half per cent on the investment.

This turnpike connected at the New York line with the Eastern Turnpike of that state, but it does not seem that the combination invited much stage travel. The Boston to Albany stages came as far as Williamstown Center but turned southerly there, and ran the length of the town of Hancock before turning to the west again.

5. The Fifth Massachusetts Turnpike

"The Fifth Massachusetts Turnpike," authorized by an act passed March 3, 1799, was the most extensive and ambitious project sanctioned by the state. The mileage undertaken and the rough character of much of the country which it traversed, together with the scarcity of settlements along much of its length, show conclusively that its projectors were more intent upon other benefits to be derived than upon dividends from their investment. The turnpike was projected in Greenfield, which place had hitherto been accessible only by way of the Connecticut River, and the construction of the road

Fifth Massachusetts Turnpike: Cross lots to Montague City

opened a direct line to the eastern part of the state. The route was also designed to connect Northfield and southern New Hampshire with the same section, the whole being defined in the charter as

from Capt. Elisha Hunt's in Northfield through Warwick, Orange, Athol, Gerry, Templeton, and Gardner, to Westminster Meeting-house; from thence to Jonas Kendall's tavern in Leominster; and also from Calvin Munn's tavern in Greenfield, through Montague and up Miller's River, through unincorporated land, so as to intersect the road aforesaid in Athol.

A stage had been established between Boston and Northfield as far back as 1789, according to Temple and Sheldon's *History of Northfield*, which ran by way of Worcester, Holden, Barre, Petersham, Athol, Orange, and Warwick; and in 1790 its trips were extended to Bennington by way of Brattleboro.

The turnpike corporation was formally organized at a meeting held in the inn of Oliver Chapin in Orange, probably early in 1799, and sixteen hundred shares were issued with a par value of $100 each, as Frederick A. Currier told the Fitchburg Historical Society. Work must have been commenced at once and prosecuted with remarkable energy, for in June, 1800, the legislature authorized the company to open all of its road except about three quarters of a mile which passed close to the Westminster meeting-house and which apparently did not satisfy the corporation, as they had appealed to the general court for a change in that part of their location. The matter remained open for nearly a year when the company was required to locate its road "to the northward of said meeting-house, in the most convenient direction." At the November term of 1800, of the court of sessions of Hampshire County, the "layout according to survey by Ebenezer Hoyt from Greenfield to Athol and in Warwick" was approved. At about the same time the layout in Worcester County was approved through the towns of Athol, Gerry (now Phillipston), Templeton, Gardner, Westminster, Fitchburg, and Leominster.

Starting in Greenfield the road had its western terminus at the tavern of Calvin Munn, which occupied the site of the Mansion House, as Thompson states in his *History of Greenfield*, and followed what is now Highland Avenue and on by Highland Park and the Bear's den to Montague City bridge; thence passing south of Turners Falls to Millers Falls, where it crossed the Millers River and followed easterly on its northerly bank substantially on the line of the present state highway to Fitchburg, and thence to Leominster. The length from Greenfield to the Athol line is given by Hoyt's survey as twenty miles, sixty-eight rods, and six links, which with the added length of the branch to Northfield and the long section in Worcester County must have given the company a total mileage of nearly fifty-eight. The statement filed with the secretary of state gives the cost as $54,965.06, from which the average cost per mile would be about $950. The section running to Northfield appears to

Fifth Massachusetts Turnpike: State Highway in Montague

have been originally projected as the main line, but it clearly was destined to be a side issue, as the heavier traffic naturally followed the route along the Millers River, to Greenfield, on the way to central New York.

What we here call the Northfield branch left the main road in Athol, passing through Pinedale and Warwick, to Houghton's Corner, in Northfield, which was chosen for the terminus instead of Capt. Elisha Hunt's, as specified in the charter. This branch was relocated in 1815 so that it crossed Millers River just west of Athol and then followed up the west side of Tully River. The act authorizing this relocation also provided that the corporation might alter its road in any such places "as shall facilitate the travel by going round instead of over hills, without much increase of way," which indicates that the straight-line mania had somewhat clouded the issue with the original locators. Two other branches were authorized, one in February, 1803, from Athol to the New Hampshire line in the west part of Royalston, and the other, in June of the same year, from the corporation's road in Warwick to the line of Winchester, New Hampshire. No indication has been found that the first was ever built, but the Hampshire County records establish that the second was built, connecting with the road of the Sixth New Hampshire, and its construction approved within about three years.

An additional gate was allowed in 1811 and the rates of toll were increased, by which we judge that dividends were not forthcoming. In June, 1827, the corporation was allowed to build a new section, to replace a part of its old road, which extended down the "Gulf road" in Warwick, and in December of the same year a committee was appointed to estimate the value of land occupied by the new construction.

At the December, 1829, meeting of the county commissioners of Franklin County a petition was entered for the freeing of the Fifth Massachusetts within Franklin County, but no action seems to have followed, for in 1832 Ephraim Stone, Calvin Townsley, Lipha French, Benjamin Estabrook, and Joseph Young, directors of the corporation, renewed the petition, but this time asking that they might be relieved of the entire system of roads and the same thrown open to the public. The request being granted, the old turnpike became a part of the public road system of the respective counties in that same year, 1832.

At the time of the establishment of Franklin County and during the contest between various aspirants for the location of the county seat, Greenfield set forth its claims, stating, among other boasts, that the Fifth Massachusetts Turnpike had been promoted in that town and had cost $60,000. In all probability extensive repairs were required, which could not be financed from the earnings, and hence additional expenditures of capital were needed. The Millers River is a turbulent stream and no doubt made easy work of washing away long sections of the early roadbeds.

The corporation filed returns, as required by the charter, from 1798 to 1801, in 1818, and again from 1822 to 1827. In 1801 the receipts were nearly $1800 with expenses of $1046, leaving a net of about $754. In 1822, 1823, and 1824 the receipts averaged about $1030 and the expenses about $730, leaving an inconsiderable amount for dividends. Receipts increased and expenses were lessened in the next year, but apparently trouble was saved for the following year, for then the expense jumped to over $1600, and in 1827, the last year in which reports were made, there was a deficit of nearly $800. That dividends were paid, however, for a few years is stated by Frederick A. Currier in *Proceedings* of the Fitchburg Historical Society. In 1810 one of $.50 a share was declared; from 1811 to 1817, $.75; in 1818, $1.25; 1820, $.25; and in 1823, $.75. By the above, 1818 would seem to have been a most prosperous year; but the returns filed at the state house for that year show a net income of only about $600, little in such a showing to induce investment in similar projects for monetary gain.

The town of Ashburnham became mildly excited over the project of the Fifth Massachusetts, as it hoped thereby to be relieved from the impending cost of a new county road, Stearns' *History of Ashburnham* recites, and much negotiating with the corporation occurred. Finally an agreement was reached, by which the town contributed $1000, but the corporation reserved the right to build its road where it saw fit. As none of the road was ever built in Ashburnham, it would be interesting to know what became of that thousand dollars.

6. The Sixth Massachusetts Turnpike

Once more, before the close of the eighteenth century, the legislature incorporated a turnpike corporation, this time the Sixth Massachusetts, on June 22, 1799. It was proposed by this company to build a road "from the east line of Amherst, on the county road, near William Breton's house, through said towns '(given in preamble: Pelham, Greenwich, Hardwick, New-Braintree, Oakham, Rutland, Holden, and Worcester)' to the great road in Shrewsbury aforesaid," the great road in Shrewsbury being the road from Boston to New York. Records in Worcester and Northampton show that the turnpike was completed in 1800. Jonas Reed was the proprietor's clerk, or as would be said now, clerk of the corporation, and he, in later years, published a history of the town of Rutland, from which is extracted first hand information regarding this turnpike. It is learned that the road was forty-three miles and one hundred and twelve rods in length; that it was built in one summer, which the records show was that of 1800; and that the cost was about $33,000, or at the rate of about $760 a mile. At a town meeting, Rutland voted its approval of the project and voiced its wish to have the turnpike built through the town, and appropriated $1000 to help the cause along. The appropriation was later rescinded, whereupon a number of individuals associated themselves and contracted to build the road through Rutland for $1.70 a rod, taking their pay in stock of the company at $25 per share. The work was sublet, Moses White undertaking the construction of five hundred and nineteen rods of the west end at the rate of $2.39 a rod, while the remaining seventeen hundred and fifty rods was divided into seven sections, each of which was let at a price of $1.41 per rod. The average price per rod is thus seen to be $1.63, which gave the first contractors a profit of a little less than $.07 on each rod, but since they took their pay in stock, it is not supposed that any of them grew rich from it. Information as to the location of gates on any of the roads is generally vague, but the one on this road in Holden stood a little west of the center, according to Estes' *History of Holden*, to which position the legislature allowed it to be moved by an act passed June 17, 1820. In the same act the corporation was allowed to discontinue such of its road as lay in the towns of Pelham and Greenwich, and was discharged from all liability for maintaining the same. In 1829 the remainder of the Sixth turnpike was laid out as a county road and became free.

As already stated, no corporation bearing the name of Seventh was ever incorporated. Had it been the Thirteenth which was omitted, one could easily conjure a reason therefor, but nothing is known to explain the failure to recognize the number seven.

7. The Eighth Massachusetts Turnpike

The Eighth, Ninth, and Tenth Massachusetts Turnpike corporations were the legislative grist for the year 1800. The Eighth, incorporated on the twenty-fourth of February, had an elaborately worded route, but which, on account of reference to temporary local objects, has little meaning to-day. But it is plain that the authorized line commenced on the southerly bank of the Westfield River where the same crossed the line between the towns of Westfield and Russell, and followed thence up the Westfield River and the West Branch of the same to some point in Chester. From there it was allowed to take over an existing road, locally known as the "Government road," to Becket Village, and thence by another existing road from Becket to the Pittsfield line.

No evidence has been found that the section over the "Government road" was ever utilized by the turnpike corporation; in fact, the Berkshire records show that the company was allowed, in 1802, to abandon a section of its layout in Becket, but it did improve and operate the road from Becket to the Pittsfield line. There must have been serious construction difficulties in rendering the "Government road" suitable for a turnpike to induce the company to give up that section. That there was business enough to make it remunerative is clearly shown by the fact that, in the year following the abandonment by the Eighth, another corporation was formed, which built a turnpike connecting the same terminals and closely paralleling the "Government road"; and by the many later efforts to improve this same route, of which more on subsequent pages.

The Eighth, as constructed, followed up the Westfield River, as already described, to a junction with the Becket Turnpike in the southwest corner of the town of Chester. Then, from a point in the south central part of the town of Becket, it ran northerly across that town northwesterly across Washington, and across the southwesterly corner of Dalton to the Pittsfield line. The portion of the road from Russell's westerly boundary to where the Becket Turnpike later took up the burden was built in time to receive the approval of the Hampshire court of sessions at its August term in 1801, but it was not until March of 1805 that a committee was appointed to inspect and approve the part built over an old highway from Becket to the Pittsfield line.

In 1819 the corporation was allowed to abandon the Becket-Pittsfield section, and at the same time they were required to make an alteration in the road between the foot of Becket Mountain and the easterly end of the Becket Turnpike. That this was needed for the public convenience is evident from the fact that two years were allowed, in which two thousand dollars should be spent on such alteration, penalty for failure being reduction of tolls at one gate by one half. In 1838 the company obtained permission to improve its grades by cutting out a section on Dickinson's Hill and substituting a length of road in a better location. The balance of the Eighth Massachusetts was thrown open to the public in April, 1844.

Four miles beyond Westfield the west-bound traveler on the Boston and Albany line crosses the boundary line between the towns of Russell and Montgomery, where the latter town draws down to a point at the river. On the opposite bank may be seen the place where the turnpike began, and the old road itself may be seen, now on one side of the train and then on the other, at various spots all the way to Chester, although many sections of it must have been effaced during the railroad construction. Opposite Woronoco station a tollgate formerly stood, and the corner of the roads, which can be seen from the train, is where the Hampden and Berkshire Turnpike branched off from the Eighth Massachusetts.

Above Woronoco, formerly known as Fairfield, the river swings in a wide semicircle with a steep hill rising abruptly from its southerly bank, and carrying the old road shelved in its side. Along this section the ambitious western extension of the Springfield street-railway system is laid.

8. The Ninth Massachusetts Turnpike

It has been noticed, no doubt, that so far all the projects were in the interests of the western part of the state, although the Sixth had its terminus as far east as Worcester. But now comes a turnpike partly in Norfolk County, and affecting Boston, inasmuch as it sought the improvement of the through route to Hartford from that city.

The Ninth Massachusetts Turnpike Corporation, chartered February 25,

Ninth Massachusetts Turnpike: Westerly part of Bellingham

Ninth Massachusetts Turnpike: In Uxbridge

1800, built its road "from the end of the turnpike road in Thompson, in the State of Connecticut, where it adjoins the line of this commonwealth in the Town of Douglass, in the County of Worcester, to the east line of the Town of Bellingham in the County of Norfolk."

The length was about twenty-two miles and the cost was certified to have been $13,222.83, or about $600 a mile.

That this project had been brewing in the minds of local men for some time appears from the town records of Mendon, from which we learn that a committee was appointed, in August, 1796, to go to Ashford, Connecticut, to meet the commissioners of that state, who had been appointed to survey and lay out a road from Hartford. Philip Ammidon was one of this committee, and later was the first named among the incorporators of the Ninth; and since to him was addressed the long letter from Thomas Dwight, to which reference was had in writing of the First Massachusetts, it seems that the investors in the Ninth had ample warning of the failure of the First to yield revenue. It will be recalled that Mr. Dwight expressed the opinion that two dollars a rod was too much to pay for a road, and it is interesting to note that the recipient of the advice obtained an average of about one dollar and eighty-eight cents a rod on his road.

In 1780, when Milford was set off from Mendon, an old road was designated as the boundary, Ballou's *History of Milford* tells us, and the two towns were burdened with equal shares of its maintenance. Such has ever been an annoyance to towns so burdened, and it must have been welcome to each town when the Ninth Massachusetts offered to include that section of road in its turnpike. The same boundary now exists between the towns of Hopedale and Mendon, another survivor of the turnpike days. The old road is known to-day as Hartford Street, in Bellingham; Westcott's Road, in Mendon; and apparently Northeast and Southwest Main streets, in Douglas.

Returns of financial matters were made in 1802 to 1819 and from 1824 to 1827, during which years the average net earnings of the road were $121.20 per year, or nine tenths of one per cent, on the cost of the turnpike. Returns were omitted from 1820 to 1823, both inclusive, but a suggestion that those years were no fatter than the ones for which reports were made is found in an act passed in 1823, by which an additional gate was allowed to be erected in the westerly part of Mendon.

The turnpike became a county road in Douglas in 1831, and the portion in Norfolk County, or in the town of Bellingham, was laid out by the county commissioners in 1833, while alterations were decreed on portions in the other towns. At a town meeting held June 17, 1831, we find in Metcalf's *Annals of Mendon*, it was voted to oppose the discontinuance of the Ninth Massachusetts as a toll road, and a committee was chosen to conduct such opposition, but that vote was rescinded at a meeting in November of the same year. The records of Worcester County, of which Mendon and Uxbridge are a part, give no date for the final freeing of the road in those towns.

The Ninth Massachusetts was a link in an important line of turnpikes, which extended from Boston to Hartford over the "Middle Road," by which the distance was one hundred and six miles, according to the *Old Farmers' Almanac*. On this route was located landlord Taft's tavern in Uxbridge, the service in which so pleased President Washington, when he stopped there on his tour in 1789, that he afterwards sent presents to the host's two daughters, accompanied by a most graceful letter.

9. The Tenth Massachusetts Turnpike

The Tenth Massachusetts Turnpike Corporation, created by an act passed June 16, 1800, was generally known as the Farmington River Company, on account of its road following the bank of that stream for so large a part of its course. It clearly was designed to form a link in a turnpike system connecting Hartford with Albany, as the Massachusetts portion did not pass through any important centers except Lenox courthouse. In fact, the road was locally known also as the Hartford and Albany turnpike, by which name it is mentioned in a *History of the County of Berkshire*, published in 1829. The road commenced at the termination of a Connecticut turnpike, on the state boundary line where the Farmington River crossed the same, and followed up the valley of that river, now in Sandisfield, then in Tolland, through Otis and Becket, to the east side of Greenwater Pond; thence through Lee, Lenox, Richmond, and Hancock, to the New York line. Southerly from Becket the road seems to be locally known as the "Old Turnpike" to-day, while the portion in Lenox appears to be called Walker Street and Cliftwood Street, and Richmond and Hancock folks know it as Lebanon Road. It passed through that portion of Lee called "Cape Street."

The length of turnpike was about thirty-six miles and the cost of construction was about $1340 per mile.

By 1814 concessions were made, provided that persons under certain conditions should pass free, and the same act provided that anyone falsely claiming exemption on account of those conditions should be liable to the corporation, in an action of debt, for the sum of ten dollars. In 1819 the corporation was allowed to discontinue all of its road westerly of the Stockbridge road in Lee, about one third of its system, and increased rates of toll were granted on the balance. In 1840 and in 1842 acts were passed authorizing changes in the location of the road, the two totaling only about four hundred rods, which seems small business for a legislature.

By 1854 the turnpike had become so badly out of repair that various suits had been commenced for the annulment of the charter, and the legislature of that year took drastic steps toward forcing proper maintenance by the company. Even the franchise itself was made liable to attachment in suits for damages sustained by fault in the road. The county commissioners were empowered to throw open the gates, that all might pass free, whenever they deemed the road to be out of repair; and they were further empowered to lay out the road as a public highway, at their discretion, paying to the corporation the amount awarded by three referees. The Berkshire records show that the road was laid out as a public highway on petition of William Taylor, in September, 1855. Nothing is known about the financial part of the corporation's affairs as no returns were ever filed at the state house.

10. The Third New Hampshire Turnpike

Four acts were passed in the year 1801, the first on June 18, allowing the proprietors of the Third New Hampshire turnpike road to extend their road into Massachusetts "from the line of the State of New Hampshire, on the north side of the Town of Townsend, communicating with a turnpike road laid out in that state by said corporation, to the county road in said town near Goss' Bridge, so called, a distance of about four miles."

The Third New Hampshire was chartered in that state on December 27, 1799, to build from Bellows Falls, through Keene, toward Boston, and its road appears to have entered Massachusetts in the northwest corner of Townsend, close to Walker Brook, and run thence directly to Townsend Center. After it was built, as Cutter tells in his *History of Jaffrey, New Hampshire*, it became common practice among the inhabitants of the region traversed to carry products to Boston in their own teams after snow fell, and it was not unusual to see twenty to forty sleds or sleighs journeying over the turnpike together. Dearborn and Emerson established a line of stages between Boston and Walpole, New Hampshire, in 1803, passing over the Third New Hampshire, through Jaffrey and Keene.

In 1824 the New Hampshire legislature authorized the corporation to surrender its charter and make its road free, and in 1826 Massachusetts followed suit.

So far all applications for charters have been marked by sincerity of purpose and further ability to carry out the intention, but many of the charters granted in the later years were never utilized. Some of them are readily detected, while others are hidden in the mists of long ago. One of the former class is the Eleventh Massachusetts, which was chartered June 19, 1801, to build from the Connecticut line through Granville to Blandford meeting-house, and thence to a connection with the Eighth Massachusetts in Becket. A plan has been found showing the route proposed between Blandford and the state line, but roads appear to-day over but a part of such route. The records of Hampshire court of sessions show that a location of the road was made in 1801 and a change in the location in 1802, but nothing further. That the road was never built is plainly shown by the act passed in 1809, incorporating the Granville Turnpike Corporation and granting it the route laid out by the Eleventh Massachusetts.

11. The Twelfth Massachusetts Turnpike

But better luck attended the promoters of the Twelfth Massachusetts Turnpike Corporation, which received its franchise on the same date as the Eleventh. The road of this company was to be built from the Connecticut line in the southeasterly part of Sheffield, northwesterly across that town and across Egremont to the easterly end of the Hudson Turnpike, the road of a New York corporation. In 1803 the location was made by a committee of the Berkshire Court of sessions, and authority was given for a branch of this turnpike at its southeasterly end, under which a road was built, about two miles long, to another point on the Connecticut line. Another branch was built, without any authorization as far as now appears, leaving the main road at a point in the easterly part of Egremont and running northerly across the southwesterly corner of Alford to the New York line, on the way to Albany.

The Twelfth evidently had trouble with "shunpikes," or feared it would have, for we find it enacted into law in 1806 that no landowner should allow a road to be maintained on his land, parallel to the turnpike, within forty rods of any gate. Penalties were also provided for any person who injured the road, fifty to one hundred dollars being the amount to be inflicted, and other penalties for evasions of toll were specified.

The Twelfth seems to have been locally known as the Litchfield Turnpike, probably because its Connecticut connection, the Greenwoods Turnpike, traversed Litchfield County. The route described in the charter is unique inasmuch as it is located almost entirely by reference to the dwelling houses of various men, and in only one case gives the town in which a house is to be found.

This road, with its Connecticut connections, the Greenwoods and Talcott Mountain turnpikes and its extension in New York, formed for over half a century, the great highway between Hartford and Albany and was a heavily traveled route.

By the branch authorized in 1803 connection was later made with the Warren Turnpike in Connecticut, over which access was had to the lower Housatonic Valley.

The cost of construction was reported as $12,771.18. The length being twenty miles makes the unit cost about $640 a mile. In 1857 the company petitioned the county to take the road and it became free.

June 19, 1801, the ominously named Thirteenth Massachusetts Turnpike Corporation was formed, to build "from the line of the state of Connecticut, near Holmes' Mill, by the meeting-house in the middle parish in Granville, to the northwesterly part of the Town of Loudon, in the County of Berkshire."

Apparently the blight of the unlucky number could not be overcome, for no further record has been found either in state or county records, and we are obliged to include this turnpike among those probably never built. Loudon, by the way, became Otis in 1810.

12. The Salem Turnpike

A cursory glance at the map will suffice to show the difficulties which beset land travelers essaying to journey between Boston and Salem in the early days. The many broad creeks meandering back into the country and the many swamps, still to be seen, made the trip one of wider detour and extra mileage. The passage by sea, passing outside of Marblehead, Nahant, and Winthrop, must have been exasperatingly long, and no doubt travelers by either route begrudged the time consumed in passing from place to place, only thirteen miles apart. Tradition has it that the first party of Salem people who journeyed to Boston by land were four days on the way, and publicly gave thanks for their safe return. Spasmodic efforts to maintain a stage between those places commenced as early as 1766, but nothing regular or satisfactory was accomplished.

But having "got along" for nearly two hundred years with such poor accommodations was no argument for the Salem people that they should continue thus handicapped, and on March 6, 1802, we find the Salem Turnpike and Chelsea Bridge Corporation formed to build a road beginning near Buffum's Corner, so-called in Salem, thence to be continued through the Salem Great Pastures, so-called; thence by the southeasterly side of Farrington's Hill, so-called, in Lynn, over Breed's Island, in Lynn Marshes, and by the southeast side of Cheever's Hill, so-called, in Chelsea, to a place on the Chelsea side of Mystic River, between Winnesimmit Ferryways and Dr. Aaron Dexter's gate, and over said river to a place on the Charlestown side thereof, north of, and near to, the Navy Yard; and thence to said Charles River Bridge in Charlestown.

And the company was further empowered to build "bridges over the rivers and waters between Buffum's Corner and Charles River," a most necessary provision, in view of the nature of the country to be traversed.

By an act passed February 26, 1803, the route of the company was shortened and it was allowed to build only to "Main Street, in Charlestown," or in other words, to City Square. The road, as built in conformity with the above description, formed what are now known as Highland Avenue, in Salem; Western Avenue, in Lynn; Broadway, in Saugus, Revere, and Chelsea; Chelsea Street, in Charlestown; and included Chelsea Bridge, over the Mystic River.

We read in Lewis' *History of Lynn*:

On Thursday the 23rd of September (1803) the Salem Turnpike was opened and began to receive toll. The Lynn Hotel was built this year. The original number of shares in this turnpike were 1200, and the original cost was $189,000. This road will become the property of the Commonwealth when the proprietors shall have received the whole cost with 12% interest; and the bridge over Mystic River, when 70 years shall be accomplished. This turnpike, for nearly four miles, passes over a tract of salt marsh which is frequently covered by the tide. When it was first projected many persons esteemed it impracticable to build a good road on such a foundation. One person testified that he had run a pole down to the depth of 25 feet. Yet this turnpike proves to be one of the most excellent roads in America.

The length of the road, exclusive of the bridge over Mystic River, was twelve and one half miles; and the cost was officially given as $182,063.21, or about $14,600 a mile.

June 1, 1813, was the day on which this turnpike did the greatest day's business in its history. This was the day of the famous sea fight between the *Chesapeake* and *Shannon* off Salem Bay, and one hundred and twenty stages passed over the turnpike that day filled with passengers eager to witness the combat from the commanding hilltops of Salem.

Besides the sections through swamps, described above, there were other sections even more difficult to build. There seemed to be no medium; it was either soft marsh or the hardest of hard rock, and it seems incredible that the promoters should have dreamed of ever earning dividends on so expensive a proposition. But nearly five per cent net was averaged down to 1820, and five and seven eighths per cent was the average for the six years preceding the opening of the Eastern Railroad. After that competition began, the earnings fell at once nearly one half and steadily dropped from that date

Salem Turnpike: Broadway, Revere

until 1868. On June 5 of that year the legislature declared the turnpike a public highway. . . .

In 1825 the corporation was authorized to convey such land to the United States as might be necessary to make the Navy Yard boundaries straight, and to buy enough other land "to compensate it." In 1831 the discontinuance of the turnpike between Charlestown Square and the northwest corner of the Navy Yard was allowed. The town was to accept the road within four months, have it well paved as far as Caswell's Corner and the rest of the distance put in good repair, in return for which the corporation was to pay the town $1000.

Salem Turnpike: Across the marshes

Salem Turnpike: Floating Bridge

And thereafter the corporation was to be allowed to maintain a guide board in Charlestown Square directing travelers to its turnpike.

June 5, 1868, the legislature declared the turnpike and the bridges a public highway. The Lynn and Boston Street Railway Company, chartered April 6, 1859, had been allowed to lay its tracks along the turnpike, and the act provided for the appointment of commissioners who were to determine what amount the street-railway company should pay toward the maintenance of the new highway. By the same act the county commissioners of Essex were required to make public six toll bridges over the Merrimac River and one between Beverly and Salem.

For its entire length to-day the Salem Turnpike is a busy and important thoroughfare, being the principal street of the cities of Chelsea and Revere and passing through the manufacturing district of West Lynn.

In the northwesterly corner of Lynn is still to be seen the famous "Floating Bridge," a unique and unprecedented piece of construction. Collins Pond, seventeen acres in area, lay across the route selected for the road, and being of great depth with a soft, peaty bottom offered serious obstacles to any known form of bridge construction. So a new method was evolved by which a long raft was built, making a continuous floating structure across the pond five hundred and eleven feet long and twenty-eight feet wide.

The bridge was built in three sections on the shore of the pond and floated into place. First a course of logs hewn on the upper sides was placed. Then a course of timbers one foot square was laid at right angles upon it, the operation being repeated until there were five such layers, when a top course of plank was laid, making the whole bridge about five and one half feet deep.

Salem Turnpike: Near the Lynn-Salem line

The timbers were fastened together with dowels, which allowed an undulating movement as loads passed along the surface, and provided flexibility between the fixed ends on the banks and the portion affected by the variations of water level in the pond.

Construction of this bridge delayed the completion of the turnpike about a year, the bridge being built in 1804 at a reported cost of $55,469. Turnpike operation, however, did not wait its completion, a detour being provided around the pond and over what is now Waitt Avenue. Of late years renewal of the planking has been necessary about every three years, and the usual custom has been to add it to the worn timbers already in place until the bridge

Salem Turnpike: Through Salem

Salem Turnpike: Northerly end, Boston Street, Salem

is now said to be over fifteen feet thick.

A large drove of cattle once attempted to cross the bridge stopping on the way to drink. Many of them gathering on one side and thrusting their heads under the railing caused the bridge to list, and the railing, catching their horns, held the heads under water until they were drowned.

In later years the construction of a high-speed electric railroad called for another bridge across this pond, but the invention of the pile-driver made the second effort less picturesque. A double-track pile trestle is now to be found close beside the "Floating Bridge."

The portion over the Lynn marshes still traverses a waste region, although the roadbed has been brought to a scientific excellence and firmness. Breed's Island, mentioned in the act of incorporation, is still in evidence, the hard ground being noticeable at the angle in the road about halfway across the marsh.

According to Tracy's *History of Essex County* one tollgate was located on this island, a point of great advantage in preventing shunpiking. Another gate stood on Chelsea Bridge, while a third was located in Salem Great Pastures about two miles from Salem. Tracy says that the Salem gate collected $5300 in the year 1805. That was about forty-three per cent of the total receipts of the road for that year and more than double the total expenses. As Broadway in Chelsea, the turnpike felt the full force of the disastrous conflagration which swept that city in April, 1808, burning across the main avenue and destroying several blocks on each side.

Salemites of years ago used to tell gleefully of one of their fellow citizens who, returning late one night in a snowstorm along the turnpike, was suddenly confronted by a burly figure which with extended arm seemed vigorously to demand "your money or your life." Mindful of the proverb which defines the better part of valor, the traveler hastily tossed his watch and purse to the dimly seen figure and retreated. Next morning with reinforcements he returned to the scene of his discomfiture only to experience bitter mortification when his valuable property was found in the horse trough at the foot of the old-fashioned pump, which still held its ground with handle horizontal.

13. The Norfolk and Bristol Turnpike

The *Columbian Centinel* of January 8, 1800, made the following announcement:

NEW YORK AND PROVIDENCE MAIL STAGES

Leave Major Hatches, Royal Exchange Coffee House, in State Street, every morning at eight o'clock, arrive at Providence at six the same day; leave Providence at four o'clock for New York, Tuesdays, Thursdays, and Saturdays. Stage book kept at the bar for the entrance of the names. Expresses forwarded to any part of the continent at the shortest notice, on reasonable terms: horses kept ready for that purpose only. All favors gratefully acknowledged by the Public's most humble servant

STEPHEN FULLER, JR.

Ten hours from Boston to Providence, and the rest of a week to reach New York, was the time required at the opening of the nineteenth century, so no wonder the spirit of progress presently manifested itself. Hence we find the following petition presented at the 1802 session of the Massachusetts general court:

COMMONWEALTH OF MASSACHUSETTS

To the Honorable the Senate and House of Representatives in General Court assembled:

The subscribers humbly shew

That it is expedient that the public roads should be made smooth and easy for travellers and for the conveyance of goods and commodities as well as produce. That the road between Boston and Providence is much used and of great public accommodation; but it is in a very bad state and they conceive is only to be made good by a Turnpike, that being the cheapest, and most equitable, and just mode of making the needed improvement. Wherefore they pray that they, with others, may be incorporated as a Turnpike Company to improve the road from the line of the State of Rhode Island at Pawtucket Bridge or falls to the Court House in Dedham, and that due authority may be given to straiten the road.

And as in duty bound, will ever pray

EPHRAIM STARKWEATHER and thirty-two others.

The incorporators comprised men of prominence in their respective towns from Boston to Pawtucket, and it is interesting to note that several of them were in controversy with the corporation two years later over the amount to be paid for land taken.

In answer to the petition the legislature duly granted an act of incorporation on the eighth of March, 1802, and authorized the building of a road by the Norfolk and Bristol Turnpike Corporation

from the Court House in Dedham, in the county of Norfolk, to the North parish meetinghouse in Attleborough in the county of Bristol, and from thence to Pawtucket Bridge, so-called, and for keeping the same in repair. 'The said turnpike to begin at the Court House in Dedham aforesaid, and thence to run as near a strait line from the said Court House in Dedham to the said Pawtucket Bridge, as a Committee appointed by the General Court, shall, with due regard to the nature of the ground, direct; and which Committee is hereby authorized to locate the same road accordingly . . .

On the following day the committee provided in the act above was appointed: Salem Town, Esq., from the senate and Messrs. Kendall and Rice of Hingham from the house. Of Salem Town we have already heard as an incorporator of the First Massachusetts. He was a man of note, and at this time was serving in the senate for the second time after having declined advancement to the council. He had been a quartermaster in the revolutionary army, according to Daniels' *History of Oxford*, and later was the second major general of the Massachusetts militia. He served seven years in the house and eight in the senate, being first elected to the latter body as a successor to Moses Gill, who was advanced to a lieutenant governor in 1704. In 1802 and 1803 he served as a member of the governor's council. Besides his connection with the First Massachusetts and with the Norfolk and Bristol he later appeared either as an incorporator, or on the committee for laying out, of several other turnpike corporations.

The first meeting of the corporation was held March 30, 1802, at the

Norfolk and Bristol Turnpike: Northerly terminus, Washington and Bartlett streets, Boston

Norfolk and Bristol Turnpike: Between Norwood and East Walpole

house of Joseph Holmes in Attleboro. Colonel Israel Hatch was moderator and Fisher Ames was elected president. The number of shares was fixed at eight hundred, of a par value of fifty dollars each. The number of shares was afterwards increased and assessments amounting to two hundred dollars per share were laid, but only nine hundred and sixty-four shares were thus paid in, and that number constituted the capital stock of the company throughout.

Colonel Israel Hatch was a native of Attleboro, and at the outbreak of the Revolution was a stage driver over the post road between Boston and Providence. He saw service in the Revolution, but attained the rank of colonel in the militia of later days. In 1780 he bought the old Garrison House in Attleboro, and kept a public house there until his death in 1837. But he appears to have divided his time between the Attleboro house, which he called "Steamboat Hotel," and various taverns in Boston, of which he was at one time and another the proprietor. . . .

The stand in Attleboro which Colonel Hatch purchased was the oldest tavern stand in Bristol County, as July 5, 1670, John Woodcock was licensed " to keep an ordinary at the ten mile river (so-called) which is in the way from Rehoboth to the Bay. . . ." Madam Knight stopped there for dinner on the second day of her journey, and has left a most unappetizing account of her meal.

Fisher Ames was Dedham's most brilliant son. Graduating from Harvard in 1774, he became a lawyer in his native town, and was sent as a delegate to assist in framing the Federal Constitution. For the first eight years of the country's existence he served in Congress, and upon the retirement of

Washington was chosen to deliver the address in behalf of that body. While the turnpike was building, in 1804, he was elected president of Harvard College, but was obliged on account of ill health to decline.

Construction of the turnpike was commenced promptly and it was opened for traffic in 1806. February 10, 1803, an additional act was passed by the legislature, by which an extension was allowed from the courthouse in Dedham "to the southerly side of the pavement near to the Brick School House in said Town of Roxbury." Under the two acts the road was built from the present corner of Washington and Bartlett streets, in the Roxbury section of Boston, straight through Forest Hills to Dedham, the only notable break in the straight line coming at a point a little north of Germantown, where the road curved to avoid a large rock, which has lately been removed by the state highway commission. Reaching Dedham at at the old Phoenix House, the turnpike made almost a square bend to the right and followed the present High Street to the old courthouse, which occupied the site of the present one. From thence to Pawtucket Bridge the road ran so straight that we can imagine the few bends were due to inaccuracies in the old-fashioned survey-ors' compasses, except at one point, at High Rock in Wrentham. There we find good reason for the crook in the road, for the hill would have been impassable if the line had been carried straight over it.

Although as we have seen, the promoters of this road had the benefit of the advice of Thomas Dwight that two dollars a rod was too high a price to pay for construction of turnpikes, the directors actually contracted with Colonel Hatch for the construction of three and three quarters miles of the road at *seven* dollars a rod. The original contract may still be seen in the rooms of the Dedham Historical Society. It is in the form of a bond, Colonel Hatch being holden and standing firmly bound for a certain sum, the conditions being that he is to construct the road from Hatch's Corner to the Allen Road, twenty-four feet wide and crowned twelve inches. The specifi-cations required him

to form a smooth regular surface covered in every part with coarse hard cementing gravel not less than six inches thick for seven feet in width and three inches at the sides of a true slope, the whole cleared of stones within one foot of the surface, with trenches on each side of sufficient depth to carry off the water and sluices where necessary and where they are not made by the said corporation of sufficient sizes, made and covered with good stone and projecting two feet on each side of the travelled part of said road.

And the contract further provides for the building of three bridges for which the timber was to be furnished by the company. The section which Colonel Hatch built under this contract extended from what is now the corner of Washington Street and the road to Plainville, at the upper end of North Attleboro Village where Hatch's "Steamboat Hotel" stood, to the corner of Washington Street and Allen Avenue, at the top of the highest hill between North Attleboro and Pawtucket. At two points on this section are still to be seen interesting instances of the difference between turnpike construction and that of earlier days. The Old Post Road passed through what is to-day North Attleboro Village, coming down over the top of the high hill by the water tower, where it is now known as Elmwood Street, and passing in a long radius curve to the west of the location of the present Baptist meeting-house. The turnpike, coming down the hill into North Attleboro on the line of the present Washington Street, cut across the Old Post Road and continuing the straight line made a chord across the curve above mentioned, after which turnpike and post road were blended into one for a few miles. Again, about one mile below North Attleboro where the trolley cars leave Washington Street to pass through the village of South Attleboro is a place where the Old Post Road was badly crooked, but the turnpike still held to the straight line, and the two roads are to-day in their old positions, like a bow and cord. Entering Dedham from Boston, Washington Street the, turnpike, and East Street the Old Post Road, emphasize the same lesson.

Once and once only did this corporation deign to file a return of its doings, as required by its charter. In that the total cost of the road is stated to have been $225,000, which makes the cost per mile about $6440. This figure was undoubtedly inflated, as we have already seen that the total capital was only $192,800; and taking the latter figure as the cost of the road would give a cost per mile of about $5500, which is less than forty per cent of the pro-rata cost of the Salem Turnpike. The report of Secretary Gallatin states that this road was covered with a stratum of gravel or pounded stone, which accords with the specifications in the Hatch contract and accounts for the great

Norfolk and Bristol Turnpike: Courthouse in Dedham

excess of cost over the previous turnpikes, which were simply dirt roads. . . .

Thirteen miles of this turnpike was built by Oziel Wilkinson, probably the five miles connecting the end of Colonel Hatch's contract with, Pawtucket Falls, and another eight miles in Wrentham and Foxboro; and it is instructive as to the state of manufacturing at that time to note that he was obliged to fit up a shop of his own in Pawtucket, in which he manufactured the shovels to be used by his workmen.

Although the road was opened for traffic in 1806, it was not until November 6, 1809, that sufficient surplus had accumulated to justify a dividend. Then the sum of $1205 was distributed, about five eighths of one percent. The corporation by-laws required semi-annual dividends, and they were declared fitfully after that. . . .

The section between Boston and Dedham paid so much better than all the rest, for "Hartford Stage" may be noted as a source of income. The Hartford and Dedham Turnpike, which by its connections with the Norfolk and Bristol at one end and with the Ninth Massachusetts at the other, formed the best through line to Hartford, connected with the Norfolk and Bristol at the courthouse in Dedham, and all its Boston business passed thence over the latter company's road.

In 1805, while the expectation of dividends may have been still vivid, the corporation sought and obtained an extension of its franchise rights from its authorized terminus at the corner of Washington and Bartlett streets to Pleasant Street in Boston. But such a piece of work, involving the building of a bridge or causeway over a mile long across tidal flats, proved too great an undertaking, and the turnpike continued throughout to deliver its travelers to the public road in Roxbury.

Norfolk and Bristol Turnpike: Section of which Walpole town meeting disapproved

Norfolk and Bristol Turnpike: An almost forgotten path through the woods

The old turnpike is in existence throughout its length to-day as a public road, except for the few places where changes have been made in connection with railroad crossings. Commencing at its end at the corner of Washington and Bartlett streets, for about two miles it may be traced under the gloom and reverberations of the elevated structure to Forest Hills, where the first tollgate was encountered by the old-time travelers. For many years the railroad station at Forest Hills was known as "Toll Gate Station"; and "Toll Gate Cemetery," "Toll Gate Way," and "Toll Gate Inn," still chronicle the location of the old gate. In the grade-crossing abolitions of 1895 the present bend in the street was formed to afford a better passage under the tracks. About the time of the Centennial celebration in 1876 a concerted movement resulted in having the old turnpike named Washington Street in all the Massachusetts towns through which it passed; hence as Washington Street we look for it and follow the same to Dedham, the latter part of the way, over a broad boulevard constructed by the state highway commission. Here, however, a slip occurred, and for the next mile Washington Street is not the old turnpike at all. The old-time travelers on reaching Dedham Square found the Phoenix House on the corner at the right, where it stood until burned in 1880. Turning around this corner the turnpike followed the present High Street to the courthouse, and thence over Court Street to its junction with Washington Street. Then to the Rhode Island boundary Washington Street is the old turnpike. Glance at the map of this section of Massachusetts and you will have no trouble in picking out the old road. The straightness of its course makes it stand out as if emphasized by heavier lines. From Dedham to East Walpole it is an important road with twenty-minute trolley service and heavy teaming; thence to South Walpole it is a much-used country road;

but between South Walpole and North Attleboro it is an almost forgotten path through the woods. Below North Attleboro it is a state highway, which in summer gives off its surface in an almost continuous cloud of dust from passing automobiles. Entering Pawtucket we find the road called Broadway, now in Rhode Island. Prior to 1860 the easterly shore of the Seekonk River was the boundary between the states, and the turnpike was built in Massachusetts as far as the easterly end of the bridge in the center of Pawtucket, where it connected with the Providence and Pawtucket Turnpike, the road of a Rhode Island corporation, later owned by the state.

Except for the section between Norwood and North Attleboro the turnpike was laid out along the line of the previously existing road, which led through the centers of Walpole, Wrentham, and Plainville. But there the straight-line mania was allowed to warp better judgment, and from Norwood for fifteen miles it was laid out as straight as it could be made through what must then have been a wilderness, and over hills that called for the greatest allowance in grades. Lewis tells us in his *History of Walpole* that that town, in town meeting, voted to oppose the granting of the charter for this turnpike, and he wonders at the opposition to progress. Rather it would seem that the hardheaded old settlers knew of the proposed route through the wild outskirts of their town, and were far-sighted enough to see that it would not succeed. For the old road refused to be put out of business by the new turnpike, and, having the advantage of easier grades with little additional distance and also the travel and traffic of the intermediate towns, it proved a formidable competitor of the turnpike. In the comparison of business by districts, shown on the chart already mentioned, the comparatively small business done on the Foxboro and Attleboro sections is probably largely due to such competition. According to Lewis' account, John Needham ran the stage route from Boston to Providence through North Walpole and the Plain

Norfolk and Bristol Turnpike: Mendon Road, South Attleboro, site of Tollgate

in close rivalry with the stage line which passed through East Walpole. Now that section of the turnpike is an almost forgotten path through the woods for much of its length, but the old road, located by earlier theories along lines of least resistance, is still a much-traveled highway and the principal road between Boston and Providence. President Monroe, on his tour of New England in 1817, passed over the turnpike from Pawtucket Bridge to Hatch's Tavern, where he stopped for refreshments. His journey was resumed through Wrentham and Walpole over the old road.

There were thrilling scenes on the old turnpike in the years preceding the advent of the railroads, when the demands on the meager transportation facilities were taxing them to their utmost and loudly calling for further and improved methods. With sometimes sixteen stages a day over the road, it is not hard to imagine the bustle attendant upon their passing, the hurry and excitement where the hungry travelers alighted for their meals and horses were changed, and the keen excitement of a race when stages of rival lines met the temptation. And there is a touch of romantic interest in the old freight wagons which plodded their way so slowly that taverns were provided for them every few miles. The telegraph had its predecessor in those days, too, for they had their way of handling important messages. President Jackson's message was carried from Providence to Boston in two hours and forty-five minutes on one occasion. Wrapped around a whip handle it was thrown on to the Providence wharf as the New York steamer neared its landing. Instantly seizing it a waiting rider dashed away with the message at full speed, which he maintained until he overtook another who was jogging along easily, waiting for him to catch up. In this manner the message was passed from one to another, so that the utmost speed of a horse was constantly being employed.

One often wonders if tollhouses, situated often in remote and lonely districts, were not subject to robbery, and lest we too rashly conclude that they were immune on account of the high moral character of a century ago, let us read the following affidavit which is to be seen among the Norfolk and Bristol Corporation's papers.

Mass^ts.   Norfolk   ss Dedham March 27th, 1806.

Personally appears Cyrus Knowlton of Roxbury in the County of Norfolk, keeper of the toll gate on the Turnpike Road from Boston to Dedham in said Roxbury and upon oath complains and declares that between twelve and one o'clock yesterday morning being in bed and asleep in the Toll house of the lower Gate at Roxbury aforesaid I was awakened with the noise of several People whom I heard talking but did not first distinguish what was said then they took hold of the door and attempted to open it—I said halloo—upon which they told me to be still and open the door—or let them in—I asked them what they wanted—They said to come in—I asked who they were—They said none of my business (or to that effect) let us in—I told them they should not come in, but they might pass the Gate and pulled out the bolt—They then demanded my money—I told them I had none—they insisted I had—They then told me to hand them the two watches, (hanging up in the Toll house which they could see by the lamp which stood in the window) I told them I would not—Thereupon they stove in the window—and one attempting to get in and having about half his body within the Toll house aforesaid—I struck with a sword at the half body so within as hard as I could the lamp being put out and no fire or light remaining upon which he fell back as I thought, then I saw a hand holding a pistol within said Toll house and snaped the pistol at which hand I again struck with my sword, but suppose I struck the pistol as I afterwards found my sword battered—Thereupon they all seemed to be moved off except one who threatened my life if I made any noise. I stood still awhile and then thought I saw somebody attempting to come at the window and struck him but did not suppose I hit him—After waiting awhile I spoke but nobody answered—Then I hallooed and exclaimed Murder—Then I heard the report of a pistol, as I supposed, against the door of said Toll house against which I was standing—and found one bill had lodged in the door—& another ball passed thro' the door and lodged in the board siding opposite the door—Then a person without said Toll house said "I have got another loaded (or ready, I can not recollect which) and if you attempt to come out or make a noise before day I will blow your brains out"— I stood still untill a team came up to the Toll house and found no person remaining —The Teamster went and alarmed the neighbors then I went with him and others and traced the blood on the snowy ground towards Boston about thirty rods—which others say they traced a mile off quite thick—and further saith not.

CYRUS KNOWLTON.

Some famous hotels were located along the Norfolk and Bristol and drew their trade from its travelers. First at the northerly end was found the old Norfolk House, still standing in Eliot Square, Boston, not on but "contiguous to the Providence Road," as its old-time circulars announced. In Dedham accommodations were to be had at the Phoenix House, already mentioned, which was burned in 1880, and the Norfolk House, which is now a private residence and stands just back of the courthouse. This house, erected in 1803 in the early turnpike enthusiasm, continued to receive travelers hospitably until about 1866, and like many others of its class breathes traditions of presidents and great generals who have been sheltered by its roof. It is a three-and-a-half-story brick structure of colonial design, with a large ell in the rear, in which is a large dance hall with spring floor and suspended orchestra balcony. Standing beneath several ancient elms, it presents a singularly attractive view and forms a delightful link between the past and present.

Next, in Norwood, came the tavern which gave the nickname to that section for many years. Until about 1914 this tavern remained on its original site on Washington Street in the center of the village, but lately, in a rush of civic improvement, it has been relegated to a less conspicuous position. In olden times a large hook had its place in front of the tavern, and riders approaching would easily toss their reins over the hook, thus losing no time in putting themselves in position to have their thirst quenched. As "The Hook" that section of Norwood was therefore known.

Famous throughout the country were the two taverns in South Walpole, and many have sung the praises of the dinners served there. Situated on opposite sides of the road, almost exactly halfway between the terminal cities, they naturally had almost a monopoly of the noonday dinner business, and their rivalry grew so keen that a friendly compromise became necessary. Tradition tells us that by such agreement all stages pulled up at the tavern on the right-hand side of the road, thus giving the Boston-bound business to one and that in the opposite direction to the other. Each of these old taverns stands to-day, but woefully fallen from their once high estate. In one you will reverently be shown the room in which President Washington once slept; but since there was no tavern there until the turnpike was built, and since there was no turnpike there until seven years after the death of Washington, you may reserve your decision. Many an old-timer treasured sweet memories of the entertainment at Polly's Tavern, which enjoyed a wide popularity.

Down in Foxboro, near the Wrentham line, the old turnpike intersected the ancient "Cape Road," which led from Wrentham and points beyond through Foxboro Village, and on to Plymouth and Cape Cod. The crossing occurred at the summit of a high hill known since early days as "Shackstand Hill"; and this location, on two important lines of travel, logically determined the site of the old Shackstand Tavern which, under the famous management of "Pennyroyal" Cobb, flourished through the turnpike days. About a mile southwest the turnpike curved slightly at the summit of "Turner Hill," and the traveler was thrilled by the sight of the long, straight stretch of road, dipping into the valley and then rising over successive hills, until it finally disappeared over the horizon to follow an easy down grade into Attleboro

Norfolk and Bristol Turnpike: Scene in Wrentham

North Parish, now the thriving town of North Attleboro. But one traveler, back in the early days before railroads had simplified the transportation problem, felt no thrills over the inspiring scene, for he was driving a jaded team hauling a heavy load over the soft road and through the mud of early spring. Ephraim Jewett held the contract to haul from Providence to Boston a newly coined issue of silver dollars, packed in kegs, consigned from the United States Mint to various banks in Boston, and he had struggled with his duty and urged his weary horses, for many miles until late in the evening when tired horse flesh could do no more, and the valuable cargo came to a stop on the steep grade of "Turner Hill," oozy and deep with mud from the spring thaw. Despite the desperate efforts of the driver, who thus found himself stalled at night in a lonely part of the road, the horses could not advance another inch, and finally, as he told it himself, Ephraim "got mad," and leaving his trust where it stood betook himself and the horses to the "comfort for man and beast" offered by the Shackstand Tavern. No worry oppressed his sleep, and he arose the next morning sufficiently refreshed to extricate his wagon and resume his journey, with the cargo undiminished by thieving hands.

Only a little over five miles back on the road from the scene of his discomfiture Jewett had passed Colonel Hatch's "Steamboat Hotel," of which mention has already been made. A little farther toward Providence, on the site of the modern Emerson House, on the corner of Washington Street and Commonwealth Avenue in North Attleboro, stood the old "Union House," built by Richard Robinson, and famous far and near for its dances.

Still standing on the State Highway, as the turnpike is now called in that section, is the old Barrows Tavern in South Attleboro, another link to the turnpike past. Here Milton Barrows, the first postmaster in the south part of the town, sorted and passed out mail.

One tollgate stood in what is now Forest Hills Square, where the railroad later made a grade crossing, and the second was located "near the old road Westward of Mill creek," probably near the corner of the present East Street. These were half-gates, at which one half the authorized tolls were collected—an arrangement which was authorized by the legislature by an act passed in 1804. Another gate stood at the crossing of the Neponset River, below South Walpole, according to Lewis' *History of Walpole*, and Timothy Gay divided his attention between his gristmill and the tollgate. In 1825 James Boyden was performing those duties. Another gate stood at the corner of the Mendon Road in South Attleboro.

The Boston *Traveller* of October 2, 1833, printed an account of a journey just completed on which the wanderer left New York by steamboat at five

Norfolk and Bristol Turnpike: Barrow's Tavern, South Attleboro

o'clock in the afternoon, landing in Providence at eleven the next forenoon. The journey to Boston was continued by stage over the turnpike in a coach of the Citizens' Line which, "without any dangerous attempt at racing," arrived in that city soon after five that afternoon. So rapid was the stagecoach travel considered that the editor of the Providence *Gazette* suggested that anybody desiring to move faster should send to Kentucky for a streak of lightning. He had just been "rattled over the road" in four hours and fifty minutes, which was probably about the record attained by stages.

The fare from Boston to Providence previous to the turnpike opening had been one dollar. The Massachusetts act incorporating the Citizens' Coach

Norfolk and Bristol Turnpike: The two taverns in South Walpole

Company, in 1829, limited the fare to two dollars and a half in spite of the interstate nature of the business; but nevertheless it is said that three dollars was the rate in 1832.

At the May sitting of the court in 1821 a petition was presented for two public roads, one to lead from Dedham Common, the other from the courthouse, to unite on Dedham Island and then proceed to Spring Street in Roxbury. The turnpike corporation opposed the granting of this petition, and it was finally dismissed upon the corporation's agreeing to move its gate from its position on the west side of Mill Creek to some place on the east side of the creek. If that had been done, Dedham people would have been able to follow the turnpike until they had crossed the meadows of the Charles River, and then could have continued their journey over the old road without paying any toll; so we are hardly surprised to find further along that the corporation did not carry out its agreement, and further petitions appeared until the matter was finally dropped about September, 1824. . . .

Following the opening of the Boston and Providence Railroad in June, 1835, the dividends dropped to about one half of one per cent with frequent omissions altogether, and in 1843 the corporation petitioned the legislature to allow it to relinquish all of its franchise between Dedham and Pawtucket Bridge, stating that an agreement had been made with the Norfolk county commissioners by which the road from Dedham to the northerly line of Foxboro was to be laid out as a county road, but they further wished to be relieved of the section in Foxboro, Attleboro, and Seekonk. One hundred and forty-six Attleboro citizens' signatures may be seen in the state archives attached to a protest filed against the corporation's request. Said they: "The undersigned had much rather pay the legal tolls on said road, when kept in good order by the proprietors, than receive it as it now is as a gift."

Nevertheless the legislature granted the petition, and the road was relinquished, within those limits, under authority of an act approved March 23, 1843. The portion in Norfolk County promptly became a public highway, but not until 1855 did Attleboro add its portion of the turnpike to its town roads.

The petition of 1843 further recited that the portion of the road between Dedham and Roxbury still yielded a small income, and desired that the corporation might be allowed to retain its rights over that. That being granted, the company continued to operate that portion with steadily diminishing dividends until, in 1857, the county commissioners laid it out as a public road.

14. The Quincy Turnpike

Like the famous chapter on Snakes in Iceland, we might open this section by saying that there never was any "Quincy Turnpike." But there was a road which was known by that name, although miscalled, and it was built in connection with the Neponset Bridge between Dorchester and Quincy.

As early as 1635 the need of crossing the Neponset River near its mouth seemed great enough to demand a ferry, and the right to conduct such a business was granted to John Holland in that year. That ferry crossed from Preston's Point in Dorchester to Billings' Rocks in Quincy, and in 1802, on March 11, the Neponset Bridge Corporation was formed to build a bridge between the same points. But Holland's ferry did not pay and was soon given up. In 1638 another ferry was established farther up stream, which was known as the "Penny Ferry" on account of that coin being charged for a single passage. Ten years later we find that the ferry had disappeared, and "Mr. Joh Glour" was then given a franchise for a period of seven years. The need of better means of crossing was so great that Quincy voted in a town meeting in 1802 to choose two agents to assist the promoters of the Neponset Bridge Corporation in their efforts to secure the franchise.

Serious difficulties were found in building the bridge at the location specified in 1802, so the next legislature was appealed to for an amendment, which was granted, allowing the bridge to be erected at "Horse Hummock" instead of at Preston's Point. The first charter contained the right to build a road from the bridge to the Quincy meeting-house but provided for no tolls upon it. In the amendment the same road was allowed with another on the Boston side running to "Dorchester Lower Road." Dorchester and Quincy people were to have the free use of their respective roads. The corporation was to maintain the road in Dorchester, but Quincy was to share the expense of the road on its side.

Hancock Street to-day follows the lines laid out by the bridge corporation from its road to Quincy meeting-house. It was over two and a half miles long, but no gate was erected upon it nor tolls collected, so it was not a turnpike but a feeder for the bridge. But on some maps and in many papers the road is spoken of as the "Quincy Turnpike," as has also been found the case with the road on the Dorchester end.

As with turnpikes, returns of business done were required from toll bridges, and the Neponset Bridge made its statements with reasonable frequency. From 1810 to 1841 returns were made without a break and intermittently after that. These . . . seem to emphasize the fact that a toll bridge was not in the same class as a turnpike in the matter of earnings. Between 1810 and 1841 the average of the net receipts was about fourteen per cent. The banner year was 1835, with a gross of $7464.72 and a net of about twenty and three fourths per cent. When returns were resumed in 1844 the Old Colony Railroad was in operation, crossing the river but a few hundred feet below the bridge, and naturally the tolls were much reduced by the competition.

May 26, 1857, an act was passed by the legislature under authority of which the County of Norfolk assumed the management of the Neponset Bridge and the Braintree and Weymouth Turnpike, with its bridge. Tolls continued to be collected under county control until September 13, 1863, when all became free. . . Early in 1864 the Norfolk county commissioners voted to sell the tollhouse at Neponset Bridge and it was soon after moved to another location, where it has served as a dwelling ever since.

The approach on the Dorchester end passed under control of the county at the same time as the bridge, and that seems to be the only public dedication which that street has had. It is now known as Neponset Avenue, and extends from 358 Adams Street to the Neponset Bridge.

The present Neponset Bridge was built in 1877, replacing the old toll bridge; and it, too, is soon to give way to a more enduring and ornamental structure built under the control of the Metropolitan Park Commission.

15. The Fourteenth Massachusetts Turnpike

The Fourteenth Massachusetts Turnpike Corporation was the next, being chartered March 11, 1802. The road of this company was to complete the system of turnpikes from Boston to the Hudson River, and it was to connect the Fifth Massachusetts with the Second, covering an intervening distance of about twenty-four miles. The description of the route contains two hundred and forty-four words, ten words for each mile, and is noteworthy for specifying that at each river intersection there must be a bridge. Hampshire County records show the location of the road, but only for a distance of about six and one eighth miles westerly from Greenfield. Damages were awarded the various landowners whose land was taken for the road to a total of $340.50, or about $56 per mile, for right of way.

Money was not easily obtained for this road, and the whole was evidently never completed. Greenfield men were the promoters, and apparently their efforts were exhausted when they had built to Shelburne, for we find an act passed in 1807, which allowed the company to operate that much of its road. In 1808 the time within which the road might be built was extended, but nothing further appears. When the road was thrown open to the public is not on the records. An inspiring ride is offered over the old road to-day. Starting from the Mansion House in Greenfield one follows westwardly over Main Street, dipping down to the crossing over Punch Brook. Then in a little less than three miles the old turnpike climbs seven hundred feet, by a devious course bristling with overhanging rocks and plunging deeply through ledge cuts. After much solicitation by the local people this road was at last built over as a state highway.

After the opening by the Massachusetts Highway Commission of the Mohawk Trail, which generally followed the route of the old Second Massachusetts Turnpike, a rush by enthusiastic motor tourists began, and the trip soon became one of the most popular in the state. As of old, the route from the east led over the line of the old Fourteenth Massachusetts, and those bound for the Mohawk Trail found themselves obliged to climb the steep grades over Shelburne Mountain after leaving Greenfield. As some of those grades ran as steep as eleven per cent and severely taxed the power of all makes of automobiles, much complaint of that route was heard, so that the commission's engineers began, in 1916, the survey for a new road which, by passing a longer distance on the northerly side, would reduce the grades to a maximum of six per cent.

16. The Camden Turnpike

The District of Maine was next to be favored, and we find the Camden Turnpike was incorporated June 23, 1802. This company was also known by the name of its chief promoter, Daniel Barrett, and by the name of Meguntikook Mountain. It was the first project that had the courage to make a survey before obtaining its charter, and the description of its route is worth reading.

Beginning at a birch tree, the boundary line between the plantation of Canaan and the town of Camden ; thence running south four degrees east, forty-four rods; south six degrees east, forty rods; south seventeen degrees east fifty-four rods; south twenty degrees cast, one hundred twenty-six rods; south thirty-two degrees east, fifty-four rods; to the southeasterly side of Smelt Brook, so called agreeably to the plan and survey of said road, being about one mile in length; and that the made way and path for travelling be in no place less than ten feet wide, and where the mountain and pond will admit, to be sixteen feet wide, with eleven places for turning out, at proper distances, as marked in the plan and survey of said road, for the accommodation of teams in passing over the said Megunticook Mountain.

One gate was allowed, which was located at the southerly end of the turnpike. No returns were ever filed by this company, so we have no authentic data of the cost nor of the business done, and were it not for Robinson's *History of Camden and Rockport* we probably should know nothing of the road. But that tells us that the road was built at a reported cost of five to six thousand dollars, and that from three to six years were occupied in the work. The cost, it will be noticed, was excessive for a dirt road, and was so great on account of the tremendous amount of grading required and the large amount of rock handled. The turnpike was designed to connect Camden Harbor with Lincolnville Center, supplanting the earlier road which led over Meguntikook Mountain, and which could not be traveled by any sort of vehicle, being even dangerous for a horse. It passed through narrow defiles, over lofty cliffs, and on the edges of precipices where a misstep would result

Camden Turnpike: Turnpike Drive and Meguntikook Lake, Camden, Maine

in horse and rider being hurled into rocky chasms hundreds of feet below. It was a section of road dreaded by all who had to travel it, but nevertheless a favorite place for those with leisure to gratify their love of nature. Such a road became intolerable as soon as business began to make any demands upon it, and Daniel Barrett boldly attacked the problem by cutting directly through between the base of the mountain and the lake. The photograph shown gives an excellent idea of Mr. Barrett's audacity. The lake here is close to the road on the left, and but for the shelter of the summer's leaves on the trees would occupy a large part of the picture. It is very likely that the water washed the very foot of the cliff shown, and that only the turnpike construction forced it away.

When one considers the lack of all sorts of conveniences for doing such work, even shovels being obtainable only in small numbers, the courage and energy of Daniel Barrett in undertaking a work of such magnitude must be held in reverence. The lake must have been deep where he desired to make his road, for we are told that it was necessary to detach large rocks from the steep mountain side and roll them into the lake, there to form a rough retaining wall, within which smaller rocks and stones and finally earth were placed to form the road. Every common expedient was used in thus detaching the rocks, undermining bowlders, and blasting granite. Large rocks were prepared for their trip to the lake by digging under the lower sides and substituting props from time to time. When enough earth had been taken away, it was necessary for someone to knock out the props, a decidedly risky piece of work.

The number of workmen varied from five to fifty, many of them being local residents who performed their labor in consideration of free passes over the toll road when opened, those who worked a specified length of time being entitled to pass free for life.

Camden at that time numbered but eight hundred and seventy-two residents, so we are not surprised to learn that Mr. Barrett did not receive legal interest on the money he expended. But he kept up the business until

Camden Turnpike: Turnpike Ledges, Camden, Maine

1834, when he sold out to various citizens in behalf of the towns for three hundred dollars.

Of the road to-day Robinson writes:

Words are inadequate to give an appropriate impression of its romantic scenery. It must be seen to be properly appreciated. Riding along this drive the traveller sees on one hand, the steep and rocky cliff rising to a height of nearly one thousand feet, with rocks and boulders of all sizes and descriptions lying at its base as if hurled there by the hand of Jove, and Maiden Cliff standing clear cut against the sky, while on the other hand lie the sparkling waters of Lake Meguntikook, gemmed with green capes and islets, with the western mountains rising from its opposite shores. Grandeur and loveliness combined make the Turnpike a unique spot in our scenery, which has been celebrated often in prose and verse.

17. The First Cumberland Turnpike

A corporation was created June 24, 1802, with a franchise to build a short road in Scarboro in the District of Maine.

Tourists between Saco and Portland by trolley or automobile, passing through the village of West Scarboro, or Dunstan's Corner as it is locally known, and within a very short distance after passing the soldiers' monument, going toward Portland, will observe a country road bearing off to the left. That was the old road, and the one straight ahead was the First Cumberland Turnpike, and the first buildings on the left of the corporation's road were the farm buildings and home of Horatio Southgate, the leading spirit in the turnpike three quarters of a century ago.

Just north of Old Orchard Beach is the narrow outlet of a broad area of marshland which extends inland for a distance of about three miles. The early road between Boston and Portland bore well inland to avoid this marshy tract, and at West Scarboro made a wide detour around it, passing over Scottows Hill, and traversing a length of over two and a half miles between points less than a mile and a half apart. Over that interval the turnpike was built, probably soon after the granting of the charter.

It was on a raw, rainy, January day that the writer stepped from a trolley car at Dunstan's Corner in his search for data on this old road. Having a tip that Mr. Noah Pillsbury of that village was once the collector of tolls, he sought him out and found him, although seventy-eight years old, performing the duties of rural mail carrier, and driving over his route of twenty-five miles every day. He gladly welcomed the searcher, made him welcome to all he had to impart, and proudly exhibited the treasurer's book of the corporation from 1834 to the end of business. . . . It shows, as do many of the others, the large increase in stage and wagon traffic, reaching a climax in the thirties, with a disastrous slump upon the advent of the railroads.

The tollhouse stood north of the Southgate house, within speaking distance, and the gate was a horizontal bar swinging in a quarter circle, and pivoted on top of a post. The cost of a new gate is given as $5.97 in the accounts for 1836. The rate of toll for a one-horse wagon was eight cents, but if the wagon had a top, it was regarded as an indication of the ability to pay more, and twelve cents was assessed accordingly. Stages were mulcted twenty-five cents for passage over this mile and a half, which so wrought upon the feelings of the owner of Paine's line of stages that he built, at his own expense, a road of several miles' length by which the turnpike could be avoided. As he never collected tolls on his new road, it is but just that his name should be perpetuated in "Paine Road."

The artillery of the anti-turnpike sentiment was turned on this corporation in 1834, when representations were made to the Maine legislature that the earnings of the road had been sufficient to repay the original investment with twelve-per-cent interest, and that, therefore, under the conditions imposed by the Massachusetts act of incorporation, the road should become free. By vote of both houses the attorney-general was instructed to institute proceedings to dissolve the corporation.

The attorney-general did a little investigating, however, before taking any drastic action, and called upon Horatio Southgate, the treasurer of the corporation and chairman of the standing committee, who exhibited the books to him and showed that the earnings had not realized the conditions alleged. The attorney-general's report to that effect was referred by the governor to a committee of the legislature which reported the same in March, 1835. Thereupon it was voted that proceedings should not be instituted. Ten days later the representations of sufficient earnings were renewed, and a resolution was adopted giving the governor authority to call for the corporation's books and to appoint one or more auditors to investigate them. No report has been found, and this seems to mark the end of the agitation.

In 1847 the proprietors of Vaughn's Bridge, between Portland and South Portland, finding that travel over the Paine Road was diverting business from their bridge, made a contract with the management of the First Cumberland Turnpike, whereby the collection of tolls was discontinued in consideration of a yearly payment by the bridge company of one hundred dollars. This arrangement lasted through the year 1851, after which the turnpike company endeavored by resuming the collections and making repairs to derive more revenue. But the day for such operations was past, and after struggling along for a few years, with no dividends, the road was sold to the county for two thousand dollars, to which the town of Scarboro added five hundred. The tollhouse was sold in 1860 for thirty-six dollars and moved to its present position, near the corner where the branch car line to Old Orchard turns off, where, with a second story tucked under the original roof, it now serves as a dwelling-house.

First Cumberland Turnpike: Southgate Farm, Scarboro, Maine

18. The Belchertown and Greenwich Turnpike

The first of the sixteen companies created in the enthusiasm of the year 1803 was the Belchertown and Greenwich Turnpike Corporation, which dates from February 7 of that year. It was to build its road from Belchertown, through Enfield, to the South Parish in Greenwich, and by an act passed in 1805 was allowed to extend to the North Parish in Greenwich.

It would seem that this company did not meet with success on its first attempt for a charter, for we learn from Parmenter's *History of Pelham* that that town voted, a year prior to the date of the act which incorporated the company, to have its representative in the general court oppose the granting of the franchise. It was then proposed to run the road perhaps well to the east and into the town of Hardwick; and Pelham, which then included part of the present town of Prescott and adjoined Greenwich, would have been left far to one side. But failure to secure the franchise in 1802 did not discourage the promoters and their renewed efforts in 1803 brought success, although it may be surmised that they compromised with Pelham by running a little nearer to the boundaries of that town. But the raising of money apparently was slow, for an extension of the time within which they might build was granted in 1807, as they had actually begun operations.

At the January term of court in 1807 a committee had been appointed to lay out the road and its report was presented a year later. The location, as found in the Hampshire records, is given by metes and bounds, by means of which we are able to trace the road to-day. It commenced at the corner of the roads southwest of Snow's Pond in Belchertown, and ran easterly and northeasterly through Enfield Village, thence northerly crossing the south end of Davis Pond to Greenwich Village, where it joined the Petersham and Monson Turnpike. That road, chartered in 1804, had already been built between the South and North Parishes in Greenwich, so the Belchertown and Greenwich did not avail itself of its right to build to the latter place. Curiously enough the locating committee reported the end of its layout as "the North Parish meeting-house," but the surveyor's description plainly shows that it stopped at the South Parish.

Returns were filed for 1808-15, by which we see that the net earnings for the best year amounted to three and one half per cent on the cost of the road. Construction cost was $4899.83, or about $633 a mile.

A petition filed in 1825 stated that the road had been abandoned by the corporation and was badly in need of repairs, but since it was a public necessity, prayer was made that the county should lay it out as a public highway. Such was accordingly done, with a total award of fifteen dollars for damages, which were granted to one individual, the company getting nothing.

19. The Fifteenth Massachusetts Turnpike

Again the regimental system of designating was resumed, and we next consider the Fifteenth Massachusetts Turnpike Corporation, the product of an act passed February 12, 1803. This company built about nineteen and a half miles at an expense of about $840 a mile. The road was what is now known as the "Sandy Brook Road" in the southwest part of Sandisfield, and it continued through New Marlboro at Hartsville, and over the top of Three Mile Hill in Great Barrington, to the southerly line of Stockbridge. Although the charter was granted in 1803 it appears that the road was not built for several years, for an extension of the time for construction was granted in 1807, giving until February, 1809, for that purpose. Returns of receipts and disbursements were made for the years 1810 and 1811, which probably indicates the time of completion of the road. Gross income for 1810 is given as $114.81, on an investment of $16,353, while 1811 shows equal receipts and payments of $193.23

It seems that the county laid out a public road which entered the turnpike about three quarters of a mile south of the Stockbridge line and followed it thence northerly, for an act was passed by the legislature in 1812 by which that portion of the turnpike was discontinued, although the gates were allowed to stand as they had been, with no reduction in rates of toll.

In 1829, on the twenty-ninth of September, as shown by the Berkshire County records, the Fifteenth Massachusetts asked that its road might become a part of the public system, and the request being granted the gates ceased their functions.

The *History of the County of Berkshire*, already mentioned, says that, although discontinued as a turnpike, this road was a county road of considerable importance.

20. The Wiscasset and Augusta Turnpike

February 22 was the date of the act which created the Wiscasset and Augusta Turnpike Corporation for the purpose of connecting those Maine towns, and its road was to run from the Wiscasset courthouse to the newly built Kennebec toll bridge in Augusta.

The records of the court of sessions of Lincoln County show that the promoters early got to work with a petition for a committee to lay out and locate the road, and presented the same at the May term of 1803. But not until January, 1807, was the committee appointed, and they duly reported a location from the Wiscasset courthouse to Bridges' Bridge in Dresden.

This turnpike formed a link in a series of such roads which extended from Brunswick to Augusta, and rendered feasible a journey from the latter town to Portland, Boston, and beyond.

21. The Medford Turnpike

The Medford Turnpike Corporation, dating from March 2, 1803, was, according to Brooks' *History of Medford*, occupied for three years in efforts to obtain its charter. The road of this company was laid out by the proper committee in 1803, and its construction approved by the court in September, 1804. Brooks tells us that it was never profitable, but considering the nearness to Boston with the large tributary region back of it, and the fact that the corporation strenuously resisted efforts to take away its toll privileges, continuing to operate its road for over sixty years, we may reasonably doubt this. Of course no turnpike was a gilt-edged security, but the Medford must have been one of the best and a moderate dividend payer. A public highway was opened over Winter Hill not long after the turnpike was opened, over which free passage could be had, but enough travelers still preferred to follow the toll road to make it worth keeping. Efforts by the town of Medford to throw the road open were successfully resisted in 1838, and not until 1866 was a step accomplished toward that end. In that year the legislature allowed the Middlesex county commissioners to make a public layout, put the road in proper repair, and assess the cost upon various towns and the county, provided the corporation consented and asked no damages. This was accordingly done, and in 1867 the road finally became free. The turnpike to-day is known as Mystic Avenue, and is the long straight street leading from the

Sullivan Square Terminal of the Boston Elevated Railway in Charlestown to Medford.

Realizing the possibilities of large business for the tavern keeper when the Medford Turnpike turned so much Boston travel through Medford, Andrew Blanchard built the Medford House the same year that the turnpike was finished. These buildings are still standing in Medford on Main Street, and offer the best illustration of the accommodations offered in the old stage days which the writer remembers to have seen. The old-fashioned tavern seems typical, and the large barn with its spacious yard and sheds still suggests the day when numerous stages and Conestoga wagons spent the nights within its limits.

The Mystic Marshes across which the Medford Turnpike made its way were dreary and lonesome in 1821, and late one afternoon in that year, as Major John Bray and his wife were driving along the turnpike in their one-horse chaise, they were held up and robbed by Michael Martin, who had achieved an extensive and unenviable reputation in that line of business, and who subsequently ended his career on the gallows at Lechmere Point.

22. The Braintree and Weymouth Turnpike

One of the important eastern roads now appears, the Braintree and Weymouth Turnpike Corporation being incorporated March 4, 1803, to build a road along the route now occupied by Quincy Avenue in Quincy and Braintree, Washington Street in Weymouth, and Whiting Street in Hingham, thus extending from Quincy Center to Queen Anne Corner on the boundary line between Hingham and Norwell, which was then a part of Scituate. This was on the main route between Boston, Plymouth, and Cape Cod towns. . . .

The road which this corporation built was about eight and one half miles in length, and its cost was reported to the secretary of state as $38,250, or about $4500 a mile. Returns of business done were filed for the years 1810 to 1821, and 1828 to 1849. . . . Unlike those of other companies, it shows the peak of business in the year 1845 and a sloughing-off of receipts sufficient to cause the practical abandonment of the road before the opening of the competing railroad.

In November, 1849, a complaint was entered by the turnpike company against the South Shore Railroad Company, which was the name first given to the railroad running from Braintree, through Hingham and Cohasset, to Plymouth. It set forth that the railroad company

have, since said turnpike road has been established constructed a railroad across said Turnpike road at Braintree in the County of Norfolk and have obstructed the free passage over said Turnpike, taken a portion of the same, diverted the travel therefrom, and otherwise greatly injured your petitioners' road and rendered it of no value.

At the hearing held at the hotel of Asa B. Wales in Weymouth testimony showing loss of toll by diverted travel and fear of collisions at the crossing was rejected as "legally inadmissible," but the turnpike company was allowed to prove loss of toll while the turnpike was obstructed during construction of the railroad. The commissioners awarded damages to the extent of three dollars to the turnpike corporation and assessed the costs upon the railroad.

Fifteen years after the incorporation and more than ten since the laying out of the road, some technical omission seems to have been found in the proceedings, and the legislature was appealed to for an act confirming the layout, which was granted February 20, 1818. At the same late date authority was obtained to finally settle the cost of the right of way, and one landowner who had persistently refused to accept the company's offers was obliged to close the account.

The Braintree and Weymouth evidently was not in favor with the legislature of 1850, for we find some harsh terms laid down. In case of a public layout of the whole or any part of the turnpike, if the corporation did not accept whatever might be awarded it, it should at once lose the privilege of collecting one half of its authorized tolls.

This company died in sections. In September, 1851, all that portion lying in Hingham was laid out as a public road by the commissioners of Plymouth County, the corporation receiving two hundred and fifty dollars as compensation. Portions of the road in Norfolk County were laid out by the commissioners in Braintree, Weymouth, and Quincy in the same year; a further portion in Weymouth in 1852; and the "Queen Anne," which must have been the lower end of the same road, in 1854. But the corporation still retained a section of road in Weymouth and Braintree with the bridge over Weymouth Fore River, which it operated for a few years longer.

The Neponset Toll Bridge, crossing the Neponset River between Dorchester and Quincy, necessarily had to build sections of road at each end of the bridge in order to make it accessible, and the bridge, with its connecting roads, made practically a unit with the Braintree and Weymouth Turnpike in the route from Boston to Plymouth. Hence we find them treated together in the legislation of May 26, 1857. In the act of that date it was provided that the Norfolk county commissioners could, with the consent of the proprietors, lay out the Braintree and Weymouth Turnpike and the Neponset Bridge as common highways, but they were not to assess any betterment charges upon the towns. Instead, the collection of tolls was to be continued under the direction of the commissioners, deficiencies to be met by the county, and surplus to accumulate until it amounted to a fund sufficient to yield interest to amount of cost of maintenance. This act took effect upon being ratified at a Quincy town meeting, and it seems strange that, with the number of turnpike companies that had recently gone out of business and the generally poor nature of such investments, the state legislators and a majority of Quincy citizens as well should have thought the plan advisable. But there were many toll bridges in New England at that time, and the Neponset Bridge was a pretty good paying property, so it is probable that the turnpike end was but a minor consideration, and that the main object in view was the removal of the two bridges from private ownership that they might ultimately become free to all travelers.

The accounts of the commissioners at Dedham show that the turnpike and its bridge was operated at a net loss of $1766.37, from March 14,1859, to July 1, 1862; but the revenue from the Neponset Bridge was sufficient to show a gain on the whole account, which amounted to $7224.72 on the first of the year 1863. An act was then passed providing that the operation should continue until the surplus had reached the sum of $15,000, when roads and bridges should become free and the fund be divided between the various towns in which the properties lay. Bristol county commissioners were to divide the fund, as the Norfolk officials were the trustees.

During the first nine months of 1863 the increase in the fund was $2564.70, and on September 13, 1863, the bridges and the turnpike became free, although only $9789.42 of the required $15,000 had been laid aside from tolls.

The Quincy Railroad Company was incorporated February 15, 1861, to operate a line of horse cars from Quincy to Dorchester, passing over the Neponset Bridge, for which privilege it was to pay toll either periodically or in gross. As the road commenced operations about the time the bridge became free, it seems obvious that the railroad company supplied the deficiency and brought the fund up to the prescribed $15,000.

The Braintree and Weymouth Turnpike Corporation was favored with long service by James H. Foster, who was its treasurer during the entire period of thirty-nine years for which returns were made.

23. The Chester Turnpike

The name of Chester was given to two turnpike corporations, the first being created by the act of March 5, 1803, to build a road from the West Parish in Partridgefield, through Middlefield and Chester, to Parley Cook's in Chester. Probably on no other turnpike are so many changes of name and township allegiance to be noted. The West Parish of Partridgefield became a part of the new town of Hinsdale in 1804; Partridgefield itself became Peru in 1806; while it appears that Parley Cook's farm was transferred from Chester into Norwich in 1853, and found itself a part of Huntington in 1855. In three counties was the road located: in Berkshire in 1804, and in Hampden and Hampshire in 1805, as is seen upon the records of each.

The road apparently commenced on the southwest side of Great Moose Hill, which is now in the southwesterly part of Huntington near the West Branch of the Westfield River, and followed over what is now known as the "Cook Road," to Chester Center, over the Chester Hill Road and South Street to Middlefield Center, and thence by North Street up the valley of Factory Brook across the southwest corner of Peru, and into Hinsdale over Southeast Street.

Nothing has been found to indicate when the corporation ceased to maintain the road, but since the name of Chester was given to another company to build in a different section in 1822, we are justified in concluding that collection of tolls was discontinued a few years at least before that date.

24. The Cambridge and Concord Turnpike

The Cambridge and Concord Turnpike Corporation was chartered March 8, 1803, to provide facilities between those towns. This company suffered so severely from the straight-line mania that it is said they attempted to have their road laid out diagonally across Cambridge Common so as to preserve direct alignment, but fortunately they did not succeed. On March 5, 1805, an extension of the road was authorized "to the causeway of West Boston Bridge, in as straight a line as circumstances will admit," but it was not to be allowed to pass within ninety feet of Stoughton Hall, which was mentioned as "the new building of Harvard College."

At the May term of the Middlesex court of sessions in 1803 the corporation entered a petition for a committee to assess damages but not to locate the road—such a strange request that we are not surprised to find that it was withdrawn at the next term in November, and a petition for a locating committee substituted. The resulting committee seems to have established a record for expeditious work, for its warrant was not issued until August 17, and yet it reported the location, with awards for damages, at the next September term. According to the law a committee of the general court had gone over the route previous to the granting of the charter, and the committee of the court of sessions laid out the road along the same lines. Awards were made for land taken to the amount of $5258.50, but Andrew Craigie and John T. Apthorp, to whom nothing had been awarded, secured damages by jury award, which raised the total to $6509.73. If that is all that was paid for land damages the cost for that item was about $500 a mile, or about $62.50 an acre.

In the South Middlesex Registry of Deeds is found the record of the agreement by which the differences between the corporation and Mr. Ap-

Cambridge and Concord Turnpike: Easterly end, Kendall Square, Cambridge

thorp were adjusted. By that it is seen that the road had been built over Apthorp's land, on the northerly side of Fresh Pond, extending easterly about five eighths of a mile from the crossing of Alewife Brook. As the parties could not agree on a price, suit had been entered and judgment rendered against the company for $732.42 in damages and $16.86 for costs. In the agreement conveyance is made of the strip of land, fifty feet wide, occupied by the turnpike, and payment was made to the company by Apthorp of $300, in return for which the corporation bound itself not to make the road any wider and never to erect or maintain a tollgate at any place easterly of the easterly end of the land thus conveyed. It would seem that this was a doubtful

Cambridge and Concord Turnpike: Broadway, Cambridge

advantage to the corporation, for the most expensive part of its turnpike, that extending from Cambridge Common to West Boston Bridge and over which there must have been a heavy travel, was thus shut out from any toll collections. Mr. Apthorp was evidently too shrewd to accept any agreement that he should pass free of toll, with endless chances of disputes, and he took the surer means of securing exemption, when passing from his home in Cambridge to his farm at Fresh Pond, by shutting out all chance of a gate ever barring his way.

The directors of the corporation were Richard Richardson and Jeduthan Wellington of West Cambridge, Leonard Hoar of Lincoln, Peter Clark of Watertown, and James Jones of Concord.

The "lower part" was completed by September 3, 1805, and the rest of the way to Concord by December 1, 1806. An order issued by the court in February, 1807, declared the road open for business and allowed the erection of two gates which were not to be "closely located."

In those days Concord was the "shire town" of Middlesex and a place of considerable commercial importance, in addition to the prestige which follows court procedure, and with this town for one terminal and Cambridge and Boston for the other, this road of only about fifteen miles seems to have had special encouragement. No returns were ever filed, so we have no clue to the nature or amount of business done. Three blunders were committed through yielding to the straight-line obsession, two of which merely added to the amount of money invested, but the third of which caused loss of business every day of operation. Not to be swerved from its aim toward its objective in Concord, the corporation allowed itself to be obliged to build a scant two miles from the village of Lexington, without touching that center, and thereby lost a large amount of heavy teaming from New Hampshire towns, which could easily have been lured by the attractions of a good road. Over Wellington Hill in Belmont, and over another hill near the Concord and Lincoln line, the road was laid with such steep grades that the location had to be almost immediately abandoned for a better one around the foot. The map of the United States Geological Survey indicates that the road over Wellington Hill had an average grade of over six and one half per cent, while the maximum must have been fully twice as steep. That part of the location to-day is a residential section, although retarded by the steep slope, but the section over the Lincoln hill still recalls to the old residents memories of the juicy berries which grew uncrushed between the walls.

The good effects of broad tires were much appreciated a century ago, and many turnpike companies gave reduced rates to wagons so built. In March, 1804, an act forbade the Cambridge and Concord demanding more than half toll from "carts or waggons with wheel fellies six inches wide." No information is at hand as to how this law was interpreted, but it is not hard to imagine a predecessor of our present-day public-service officials demanding full toll because the "fellies" slightly exceeded six inches.

The extension to West Boston Bridge did not progress as rapidly as the originally proposed portion. A petition for a locating committee, entered in September, 1806, dragged along until December, 1810, when it was dismissed on account of neither party appearing, and in March, 1811, the corporation petitioned to be released from its obligation to build. No gate was to be allowed on that portion, which was to be over two miles in length, and the authorities of Harvard College had so interfered with the location that it was unsatisfactory to the company, which therefore did not wish to complete the extension. This petition was dismissed at the January term in 1812, so it is to be surmised that the corporation had to complete the road according to its franchise. This extension is the Cambridge Broadway of 1919.

In September, 1826, all papers in the court of sessions records relating to highways were turned over to the county commissioners, and consequently it was to the county commissioners that the company made application in September, 1828, to be released from its obligations and to have its road laid out as a public highway, which was done in May, 1829.

The turnpikes of Middlesex County were generally short lived, an indication of poor business, and a suggestion of the reason may be found in the fact that between 1808 and 1822 one hundred and fifteen public roads were established and only four turnpikes. With such energy directed toward public roads, it can readily be surmised that turnpikes found too much free competition to allow them to be profitable.

The *Memoirs* of the Concord Social Circle tell us that a triweekly stage

Cambridge and Concord Turnpike: Near Waltham Street, Lexington

ran between Concord and Boston during the years around 1817, and it is interesting to note that it did not follow the turnpike through the woods in a straight line, but went by way of Lexington usually, and one or two seasons by way of Bedford. Passengers and their baggage were called for in any part of the village of Concord and delivered at any desired point in old Boston except the South End, similar accommodations being rendered on trips in the opposite direction. Three hours was the running time for the trip in good weather, and sometimes five in bad.

The Cambridge and Concord Turnpike commenced at the westerly end of the West Boston Bridge in Cambridgeport, at what is now known as Kendall Square, its layout there being one hundred feet in width. From that point it followed the lines of the present Broadway to Cambridge Common, passing through Magoun Square, where the Middlesex Turnpike, now Hampshire Street, joined it. At the Common, had the corporation had its way, the center line of the road would have passed close to the soldiers' monument, and would have clipped a generous portion off from the northerly side of the grounds of Harvard College. But the legislature said they must not build within ninety feet of Harvard's new building, and the town erected a fence around its common, so the turnpike had to pass around.

From the Common in Cambridge to the line of the town of Lincoln the old turnpike is known as Concord Avenue. Through Lincoln it seems to lack any distinctive designation, but Concord, true to its rich historic associations, has named the road and so marked it by signboards "Cambridge Turnpike."

From the Common to Belmont the old road is now lined with residences, but at Belmont Depot one gets the impression of being in a park, so ornamental is the stone arch bridge carrying the Fitchburg Railroad overhead and the hedges lining the roadways around the station. At Belmont town hall Concord Avenue makes a square turn to the right, gradually rising, and then, by a sharp corner to the left, climbs bravely to the top of Wellington Hill. That is the turnpike as it existed after the builders came to their senses and laid out a road possible for horses to climb; but let us look for the original turnpike, the one of which such fanciful tales are told. F. H. Kendall tells us in the *New England Magazine* that baggage wagons went over that hill once but never attempted it again, and that one farmer who had a log team of two yoke of oxen, one pair being old and experienced, the other but partly broken, had an especially trying time coming down the steep hill, holding his load and keeping the green steers from bolting. And the oxen never could be coaxed to attempt the descent of the hill again.

Standing in front of the Belmont town hall and facing westerly one sees in front and bearing slightly to the left an unimposing street with the imposing name of Center Avenue. Following this avenue the houses are soon passed,

Cambridge and Concord Turnpike: A turnpike vista

and within five minutes the street has become but a crooked footpath through a jungle of thick bushes. Peering through the leaves on either side reveals the old stone walls which lined the turnpike at a distance of four rods apart. To the experienced eye the indications of the old road are plain until a square corner to the right is met, which is not consistent with turnpike procedure. But look carefully for the wall which has bordered the road on the south, and it will be seen continuing its former course and pushing straight ahead, while the modern footpath goes off to the north. That was where the old turnpike went, and traces of its former graded roadbed can be

Cambridge and Concord Turnpike: At the corner of the Lincoln road

noticed by sharp eyes. Follow the footpath and it will bring you out on Concord Avenue, the revised turnpike. Turn to the left and go as far as the first bend in the road and you will see where the new route departed from the old. From that bend on westward the original turnpike can be traveled for many miles. Elms are the distinguishing feature of the Cambridge and Concord Turnpike, and many fine specimens may be seen along its borders.

Just after crossing the Hobbs Brook Reservoir of the Cambridge water-works, at the first rise in the road may be seen another instance of the straight-line obsession. Instead of going the easy way on the macadam road, push straight ahead through the bushes and see again the testifying walls and note the graded surface on which you walk. Continue your straight line and you will enter the road again at the entrance to the Farrington Memorial, and the old turnpike will lie dead ahead of you. Two miles before you reach Concord the road will suddenly bear to the left, but "straight ahead" you will see an opening through which the sixty-two-wire line of the telephone company passes. Electricity cares nothing for grades, and conversations by telephone now constantly pass and repass over the hill that wore out the horses of a century ago. Where the old and the new come together again is also indicated by the lines of telephone wires which follow the turnpike thence to Concord.

The turnpike builders did not avail themselves of their privilege to build to Concord Common, but ended their road where it intersected the old Lexington Road, over which the British soldiers marched on that memorable April morning twenty-nine years before. Later, that corner became famous the world over, not from turnpike associations, but as the location of the home of the "Sage of Concord," Ralph Waldo Emerson.

25. The Newburyport Turnpike

On the same day as the Cambridge and Concord the Newburyport Turnpike Corporation was incorporated to build a road from the head of State Street in Newburyport to Chelsea Bridge "as nearly in a straight line as practicable," and "in a course south twenty-four degrees west, as nearly as possible." This seems to be the most positive straight-line requirement imposed upon any company. The road was built in very close compliance with the rule, for only for a short section through Lynnfield and Saugus was any substantial devia-tion from an air line made.

Petitions were entered for locations and awards of damages in the towns of Essex County in August, 1803, and the reports of committees were generally received by December of the same year. A similar petition was made in Middlesex County for location through Melrose and Malden in November, 1803. As one of the committee appointed died soon after, it became necessary

Newburyport Turnpike: View in Saugus. Mass.

to appoint a new committee, which was done in September, 1804, and this body reported finally two years later, with location and award of damages. The amount awarded for land in Middlesex County was $2306.58, part of which was taken from what is now Everett Square in the city of Everett.

The road was nearly completed in one year, as the following advertisement, found in the *Columbian Centinel* of January 2, 1805, and in the Salem *Gazette* of December 28, 1804, shows:

NEWBURYPORT TURNPIKE CORPORATION

The Directors of the Newburyport Turnpike Corporation, at their meeting on the 24th inst. Voted, that the following statement concerning the progress of the Turnpike-road be communicated through the medium of an advertisement, viz.

That there is already made twenty-five miles of the Turnpike-road; that bridges over six rivers are built; that, in some instances, hills have been reduced twenty-five feet; that two Houses for entertainment are erected, one of which is now open for the reception of travellers; and that it is their opinion that the whole route of twenty-six miles (from Newburyport to Malden Road) will be opened early in the spring.

Per order of the Directors
B. MARSTON WATSON
Clerk of the Corporation.

December 25, 1804.

And in the same advertisement the sixteenth assessment of twenty dollars on each share of stock is called.

It may be noticed that the directors in their communication refer to the Malden Road as if that was to be the southerly terminus of the turnpike, while the original charter gave them the right to build to Chelsea Bridge.

Evidently the terminus at Chelsea Bridge was not attractive to the projectors, and they halted the work at the junction with the Malden Road, which was in what is now the southerly part of Saugus, opposite Cliftondale, until they could secure a more desirable franchise. In March, 1805, this was granted them in an act which allowed them to build from Jenkins Corner, probably the junction with the Malden Road, to Malden Bridge instead of Chelsea Bridge. The Middlesex committee, which had reported on the first layout in 1805, had to go at it again, and its report locating to the Malden Bridge was filed in September, 1806, with land damages as already stated.

The Massachusetts Highway Commission, in its report for 1907, said of the location of this road:

In its building no change of direction was made, either to avoid hills or to accommodate the population to the right or left of a straight line.

The road from Andover Street to Newburyport is improperly laid out, the grades are excessive, the population along it is sparse, the villages on either side are provided with other roads better laid out, and there appears to be no reason why it should become a State road.

Certain citizens of Salem foresaw the disadvantage of sacrificing everything for a straight line, although some self-interest may be suspected in their viewpoint, for which read the following news item which appeared in the Salem *Gazette of* February 11, 1803.

TURNPIKE—Some gentlemen of Newburyport have it in contemplation to cary a road straight from that town to Boston, which will of course run to the northward of the seaports in this county, and have no connexion with the Salem turnpike. But it is expected that an actual measurement will discourage it by showing that the saving will not be more than a mile more than if brought strait to this town.

The route which this turnpike was designed to improve was one of the

Newburyport Turnpike: View in Saugus, Mass.

earliest stage routes of the country, and the early and constant travel over it surely gave promise of good business for the improved road. In 1761, on the twentieth of April, John Stavers started what has been claimed to be the first stage in America, which ran from Portsmouth to Boston. The vehicle was a two-horse curricle wide enough for three passengers, and it made the round trip once a week, leaving Portsmouth on Monday mornings, stopping over night at Ipswich and reaching Charlestown Ferry the following day. The return was made on Thursdays and Fridays, and the fare each way was 13s. 6d. Evidently this stage was not continued many years, for between 1770 and 1790 the mail was carried from Boston to Portsmouth once a week on horseback.

Jacob Hale and Sons established permanent facilities from Portsmouth south in 1794, when they established a four-horse stage line which continued to run until the railroad had absorbed all its patronage. By leaving Portsmouth at half-past two in the morning this line succeeded in getting through to Boston the same day, with breakfast at Newburyport and dinner at Ipswich. According to an advertisement in the Essex Journal and Merrimack *Packet* in May, 1774, Ezra Lunt ran a four-horse stagecoach on weekly trips between Boston and Newburyport, but it is doubted if he continued very long.

Currier in his *History of Newburyport* tells us that the first meeting of the Newburyport Turnpike Corporation was held in Boston April 14, 1803, William Tudor being elected president and Enoch Sawyer treasurer. The work was commenced on the twenty-third of August of the same year, as we learn from the Salem *Register* of the twenty-ninth of that month, which said:

Newburyport Turnpike: A bend in Lynnfield

Newburyport Turnpike: Through Topsfield

New Turnpike

NEWBURYPORT, August 24.

The workmen on the direct Turnpike from this town to Boston commenced the important undertaking yesterday. It is to run from the head of State Street, Newburyport, in as straight a line as possible. The inhabitants of New England have long gained attention for their enterprising and public spirit, and the present undertaking may be well said to justify this claim.

There were nine hundred and ninety-five shares in the capital stock according to Coffin's *History of Newbury*, and they were paid in the form of twenty-dollar assessments, so that they cost nearly $420 each, or a total of $417,000.

The work started with a cut ten feet deep at the head of State Street, the material excavated being used for filling across the treacherous "Pine Swamp." A hotel was built by the corporation at Topsfield and another at Lynnfield, which indicated expectations of heavy travel and intention to take care of it in every detail. The hotel at Topsfield provided for travelers for thirty years, after which in 1834 it was moved intact to Phillips Beach in Swampscott. This may have been the house on the beach long known as the "Martin House," which was torn down years ago. A witness of the moving, then a boy of ten years, tells an interesting story of the operation as the occupants remained, the women calmly continuing their home work on shoes, as was the custom then. The big chimneys were cut off at the floor level and supported on special beams inserted under them. The Lynnfield hotel evidently expected patronage from the sporting fraternity, as provision was made for horse-racing by making a mile of the adjacent turnpike of double width, we learn from Tracy's *History of Essex County*.

No returns are found from this company among the Massachusetts archives, so we must be content with Coffin's statement of the capital and Currier's record that a small dividend was paid each year. In general there must have been a great disappointment, for the heavy grades prevented the road from being much used by private travelers, most of whom preferred the old route through Rowley, Ipswich, and Salem. The stage-coach companies, however, usually shared the delusion of the preference for the straightest line, and we commonly find them adhering to the turnpikes. It was so in this case, and the Eastern Stage Company, as the syndicate formed in 1818, which anticipated the Boston and Maine Railroad, was called, paid annually in commuted tolls from $800 to $1000.

As was the case with so many of the others, this turnpike received its mortal thrust from railroad competition. In 1840 the Eastern Railroad was completed to Newburyport, and the turnpike in that town and in Newbury lasted but seven years longer. The portion in Rowley, Ipswich, Topsfield, Danvers, and Peabody became free in April, 1849, and in Lynnfield and Saugus in the same month of 1852, in which year the Middlesex section also became a public road, and the entire Newburyport Turnpike was free from toll. . . .

The brains of the state were occupied with other problems for the next three months, and not until June 22, 1803, was another turnpike launched. On that day the Becket, Boston and Haverhill, and Essex Turnpike corporations were created.

26. The Becket Turnpike

The Becket filled in a gap which was left in the construction of the Eighth Massachusetts. When that road was built it had the authority to locate over a section of old road in Becket known as the "Government Road," but either on account of local opposition or other reasons the court of sessions of Berkshire County released the company from that part of its franchise. In other cases the legislature only seems to have exercised such power, and a company once having accepted the franchise to build over a certain route was held strictly to its duty therein. For instance, see the case of the Cambridge and Concord, previously recited, in which the company sought release from its obligation to build an extension to West Boston Bridge, but was refused.

The reason for the neglect by the Eighth to improve its opportunity to build over the "Government Road" is hard to conjecture, unless it was on account of construction difficulties. Apparently the "Government Road" passed on the north of Center Pond and uncomfortably close to Becket

Mountain, and the cost of such a route looked too great. The Eighth did build, however, over a portion of that location and for a short distance into Becket, and the Becket corporation undertook to complete its line westward over a more practicable section of country.

The charter of the Becket contained none of the straight-line requirements, and the road looks on the map as if it had been laid out with some conception of grade resistances. The length cannot be determined reliably, but apparently it was about seven miles. The cost was reported as $4228.88, and it seems safe to say that the average cost was about $600 a mile. The road connected the Eighth Massachusetts, from a point in the southeasterly part of Becket near Walker Brook, with the Tenth Massachusetts near the village of West Becket.

Berkshire County records show that this road was located by a committee of the court in 1804, and that in 1832, upon petition of the company, it became free.

By an act passed in 1819 permission to move the gate was given, but a restriction was laid that only one quarter toll could be collected from inhabitants of Otis and Becket. The Chester Turnpike, incorporated in 1822, seems to have taken over a section of the Eighth and to have improved on the Becket by paralleling it for a distance of eighty rods on the easterly end. By act of June 18, 1825, that eighty rods of the Becket was discontinued and the parallel section of the Eighth was annexed to the road of the Becket corporation. As an instance showing how remote those old roads were from our modern improvements, it may be noticed that this last-named act was passed on the same day that Governor Levi Lincoln approved the act which established the Boston Fire Department.

The Becket corporation followed the precedent set by the English bishops, and, unrestricted by any requirements regarding number of stockholders, constituted itself a corporation sole. The report giving the cost of the road is signed by Joseph Goodwin, "only proprietor of said road," and Eliada Kingsley, "sole proprietor of the Becket turnpike," in 1819 was allowed by the legislature, to move his gate. And in 1832 the same Eliada Kingsley, in his "sole" capacity, asked that the road might become free.

The Boston and Haverhill was intended to run south three degrees west "as nearly as possible" from Haverhill Bridge to Malden Bridge, but no evidence has been found that anything was ever done beyond securing the charter.

27. The Essex Turnpike

The Essex Turnpike was projected from the New Hampshire line across the Merrimac at Andover Bridge, now the city of Lawrence, and thence to Captain Felton's store in Danvers, on the way to Salem, the county seat. It was also to run south thirteen degrees east from Andover Bridge to the line of Middlesex County in Reading. The Andover and Medford, which was chartered two years later, did not avail itself of its permission to build to some point in Andover, but stopped at the Essex County line where it joined the road of the Essex corporation. The two corporations were allowed, by act passed in 1807, to maintain one tollgate jointly at the county line, the rates of toll and the division between the companies to be established by the commissioners who were to view the roads.

From the New Hampshire line to that of Middlesex County was located by the committee early in 1806, the branch line to Salem being laid out two years later. Construction was slow, the act of 1807 giving powers to the commissioners whose verdict allowed the road to commence business, and another act, passed in 1809, extending the time within which construction must be completed. But the roads were finally completed at a cost of $67,905.25, or about $2425 a mile, and opened for travel. Lawrence's Broadway and the continuation of it to the New Hampshire boundary is the perpetuation of the Essex Turnpike, as is Main Street, through Andover Center to the Reading line. The Salem branch of the turnpike may be followed from Lawrence over Winthrop Avenue, across the town of North Andover, over North Main Street to Middleton and South Main Street to the Danvers line; thence over Andover Street until one reaches Peabody Center, which was probably the location of Captain Felton's store, that part of Danvers having been set off as South Danvers in 1855, and the name changed to Peabody in 1868.

The original charter required that the traveled part of the roadway should be thirty-two feet wide, but that was modified to twenty-four feet in 1806.

This turnpike formed a link in a much-traveled route between Boston and points in New Hampshire and Vermont. By its connection at the state line with the Londonderry Turnpike direct communication was had with Concord, and over the Litchfield and Second New Hampshire turnpikes with Claremont and the Vermont territory beyond. Southerly, Boston was reached over the connecting Andover and Medford Turnpike, which extended to the market place in Medford, whence the journey was continued over the Medford Turnpike, which landed the traveler at Sullivan Square in Charlestown, after which reliable public roads could be found. Of the Second New Hampshire, Cochrane writes in his *History of Antrim* that, opened in 1800, for twenty-five years it carried an enormous traffic in farm products and

Essex Turnpike: Broadway, Lawrence

timber to Boston, with return loadings of store goods and rum. This historian, too, has his criticism of the custom of tackling the hills head on, and he speaks of the severe competition by free roads in more favorable locations.

The Salem road became a free highway in December, 1829, while the portion from the New Hampshire line to the connection with the Andover and Medford collected its tolls until December, 1835. No returns of business done were ever filed by the Essex corporation, which is to be regretted, as figures relating to the commerce with southern Vermont and New Hampshire at that time would be interesting.

Essex Turnpike: Methuen Center

Essex Turnpike: Through Middleton

A portion of the Salem branch of this turnpike has been utilized in late years by the Massachusetts Highway Commission, which has constructed a considerable length of concrete roadbed, divided into several experimental sections of different compositions. Each of these sections is designated by a board set by the side of the road, on which can be read the proportions of the concrete mixture in the adjacent section with a statement of its reinforcements.

The Andover Bridge in Lawrence to which this turnpike was directed, and which furnished the means of crossing the Merrimac River, dates back several years ahead of the turnpike, the charter having been granted March 19, 1793, for a term of seventy years. This term was made perpetual in 1799, but the bridge was ultimately made free in July, 1868, in accordance with chapter 309 of the acts of that year.

At Methuen Center the turnpike rose abruptly over a steep, although not very high, hill which is now more in use by automobiles than it has been for many years past by horse-drawn vehicles. The public authorities laid out another road, forming a letter "S" on the turnpike, which avoids the hills and has no steep grades.

The two roads are known locally as the one "over the hill" and the one "around the hill."

28. The Wiscasset and Woolwich Turnpike

The needs of the District of Maine were given attention on the twenty-third of June, 1803, when the Wiscasset and Woolwich Turnpike Corporation was chartered to build from Wiscasset to Day's Ferry, which crossed the Kennebec to Bath. This ferry had probably been operated for several years prior to 1762 by Samuel Harnden, but in that year he received a license "to keep and run a ferry," which was renewed to his son Brigadier in 1769. Since 1788 the ferry had been called Day's Ferry, according to Reed's *History of Bath*.

The road was laid out and its location reported at the May term of the court of sessions, 1805. Reverend Henry O. Thayer, who presided in Woolwich for twenty-five years, writes: "The old Wiscasset road, earlier than the turnpike, went from the ferry to Nequasset Mills, or Church, and then east by present lower and main road to Wiscasset, and that road was formerly called 'The King's Highway.'" The new town laid a road over the same course in 1760-61, discontinuing a portion of the old road. In the discontinued part is a sharp turn where General Henry Knox had an overturn of his carriage, 'from which the spot was formerly known as "Knox's Corner."

This turnpike, in connection with the one from Brunswick to Bath formed later, and the Wiscasset and Augusta already noted, formed a continuous route of about forty-five miles, and put Augusta in closer communication with Portland and points beyond.

In 1837 a steam ferry-boat was installed at Day's Ferry, but the day of the railroad had not then arrived, and for many years the stages crossed and recrossed, assisted by the same force that was soon to accomplish their downfall.

29. The North Branch Turnpike

The North Branch Turnpike Corporation, under authority granted it on the twenty-third of June, 1803, built seventeen and a quarter miles of road at a cost of $25,740.46, or about $1500 a mile, according to official records. This road was located by a committee of the Worcester court of sessions in 1805 through Fitchburg, Westminster, Ashburnham, and Winchendon, and extended, according to a contributor to the Fitchburg Historical Society, from the New Hampshire line between Fitzwilliam and Winchendon, through Ashburnham, through Scrabble Hollow in Westminster, to the Fifth Massachusetts Turnpike near Osborne's Mills in West Fitchburg. The present-day maps show a road from West Fitchburg to Ashburnham in as straight a line as the rugged topography of that region will allow, which from Ashburnham runs directly along the route of the Cheshire Branch of the Fitchburg Division of the Boston and Maine Railroad to Winchendon, and then straight as a string to the Fitzwilliam line. Indications are strong that this is the old turnpike, but positive evidence has not yet been uncovered. Once before we noted the yearning which Ashburnham had for turnpikes, so we are not surprised to learn that that town contributed five hundred dollars toward the building of the road.

The North Branch Turnpike served travelers between Bellows Falls and Keene, and Boston. Across the state line the Ashuelot Turnpike continued the route toward Bellows Falls, while the Branch Road and Bridge Corporation's turnpike gave access to Keene.

The North Branch was opened for free use in 1829.

The year 1804 saw the birth of eleven corporations, the first being the Warwick and Irwin's Gore. This was designed as a feeder for the Fifth Massachusetts from southwestern New Hampshire, but apparently it never got beyond the formative period.

30. The New Bedford and Bridgewater Turnpike

The New Bedford and Bridgewater Turnpike Corporation, created February 29, deserved success from the devout nature of its route, which required it to pass as near as practicable to six churches. It never was intended to reach as far as New Bedford, and its southerly terminus was defined as the post office near the Great Ponds in Middleboro. Thence it extended in a remarkably straight line, even for a turnpike, through the villages of Titicut, Bridgewater, East Bridgewater, Whitman, Abington, North Abington, and South Weymouth, to a junction with the Braintree and Weymouth Turnpike in Weymouth, at the corner now designated as Main and Washington streets. The length was about twenty-five and one half miles and the cost of construction was reported as $49,662.50, or about $1950 a mile. Although this road suffered from the adherence to the straight-line theory, its chief fault appears to have been in not having improved connections with New Bedford, but in turning its travelers off at a distance of thirteen miles from that center to follow their way over tortuous country roads. It also seems that it would have been better if the road had turned from Bridgewater to Middleboro and run thence to New Bedford. That route has always been the favorite, and is to-day the principal one between Bridgewater and New Bedford. Excessive grades were not caused by the straight line, and the centers along the way were properly served, except in the case of Middleboro.

So it seems in this case that the road failed because there was not enough business in its territory. No returns of business done were ever filed.

No record of the location was found in Norfolk County, but in Plymouth a petition for a committee was made in April, 1805. In August, 1806, the committee reported the location of the road four rods wide with no description of the route, but with a measurement and valuation of each lot of land taken. Weston's *History of Middleboro* says that the road was three years in building and was never a pecuniary success. Over it passed one stage each way per day between Boston and New Bedford, and seven freight wagons

New Bedford and Bridgewater Turnpike: Old bridge over Taunton River

each week. One tollgate stood at the southerly end, where the Lakeville town house now stands, another was in the "Haskins Neighborhood," while a third was near Solomon Eaton's tavern, a well-known house at that time.

Another excellent tavern was kept by Mrs. Goodwin in Titicut Village near the Baptist Church. The old church which had heard the rumbling of many stages past its door gave way about twenty years ago to a modern edifice, and the old-fashioned shut-in pews were replaced by modern oak benches. And the services on Sundays now are disturbed by the roar of trolley cars.

New Bedford and Bridgewater Turnpike: North from Taunton River crossing

The appropriate name of "Turnpike" is given to the little station on the Taunton to Middleboro line of the New York, New Haven, and Hartford Railroad where the track crosses the old turnpike. To-day the road is known as Main Street in Weymouth, and as Bedford Street throughout the rest of its length.

Norfolk County records show a public layout of the portion in Weymouth in the year 1830, and the Plymouth County records that the part between Bridgewater and the Weymouth line was freed in December, 1829, upon petition of the corporation. The section from the Great Ponds, or Lakeville Town House, to Titicut was thrown open in January, 1845; the next two and a third miles northerly became public in August, 1847, the balance of the road from that section to Bridgewater having been laid out in January, 1844.

31. The Petersham and Monson Turnpike

The Petersham and Monson Turnpike Corporation was created also on February 29, 1804, and authorized to build a road from the Fifth Massachusetts Turnpike in Athol to a connection with a Connecticut turnpike in the town of Stafford. Twice were acts secured extending the time within which construction might be completed, the last running to June, 1809. No records of the location of this road were found in a search of the records in three counties, but that it was built is well established. It extended from the village of Athol at a point on the Fifth Massachusetts almost due south into Petersham, crossing the west end of that town and the northwest corner of Dana, then southerly close to the west line of Dana, and entering Greenwich near Greenwich Village, at which point it crossed the Sixth Massachusetts. From Greenwich Village, or North Parish, it ran to Greenwich South Parish, where it joined the Belchertown and Greenwich Turnpike; thence across Enfield and through the westerly part of Ware, following Beaver Brook valley and passing on the west side of Beaver Lake, through Palmer Center and Tennyville, after which the road followed the route afterwards chosen by the New London Northern Railroad through the town of Monson to the Connecticut line.

We learn from Temple's *History of Palmer* that the turnpike was promoted by men in Norwich, Connecticut, who thought to rival Hartford by paralleling the water route by the Connecticut River. The road was almost exclusively a freight road, very few stages using it, and it carried a heavy traffic for many years, but not enough to make it a profitable investment.

The town of Ware voted in 1806 to expend two hundred dollars on road construction along the line of the turnpike, the resulting road to be given to the corporation if it completed the whole project, as Chase recites in his *History of Ware*.

The length of road was about forty-one miles and the cost of building $14,317.17, or about $350 a mile. Temple is authority for the date of the road becoming free, which he states as 1819, which gives the turnpike a life of only ten years. This turnpike did not die from railroad competition, as the New London, Willimantic, and Palmer Railroad, the predecessor of the New London Northern, was not built until thirty years later.

32. The Union Turnpike

March 2, 1804, the Union Turnpike Corporation was formed and authorized to build:

from where the Cambridge and Concord Turnpike Road terminates in Concord, in the most convenient and direct route, to the place where the Fifth Massachusetts Turnpike Road terminates in Leominster.

This turnpike was intended to form a link in a system of such roads, which was a predecessor of the Fitchburg Railroad. Thus, it is readily seen, the Hoosac Tunnel line was anticipated by the route over the Cambridge and Concord, Union, Fifth Massachusetts, Fourteenth Massachusetts, Second Massachusetts, and Williamstown turnpikes.

Petitions for location were duly entered with the Worcester and Middlesex courts in 1805, and the layout was made in Worcester in that year. But not until September, 1806, was the layout reported from the county line to Main Street in Concord. It does not appear that the Cambridge and Concord or the Union ever built as far as Concord Common, although allowed to do so by their charters. At the September, 1808, term of the Middlesex court the company reported that its road was completed and asked for a committee to view and accept it. That the road was accepted is evident from the fact that the company filed returns of business done in 1809.

The turnpike started at the corner of Main and Elm streets in Concord and followed the lines of the present Elm Street along the northerly wall of the reformatory, and then directly to West Acton, straight across Boxboro to the westerly side of that town, where it curved slightly to the northwest. It ran northwesterly across Harvard, where the road long since disappeared, and, crossing the northerly part of Lancaster, to Leominster Village, where it connected with the Fifth Massachusetts. The length was about twenty-two miles, and the cost was $35,483.71, or about $1600 a mile. Returns filed of business done from 1809 to 1814, inclusive, showed an excess of expenditures over receipts of $9660.35, which causes wonder that operations were continued for sixteen years more.

By an act of the legislature passed in 1809 the corporation was allowed to incorporate "the present travelled county road" in Leominster into its turnpike, and in 1810 the time limit was extended to March 2, 1812. By this

Union Turnpike: Easterly end, Elm Street, Concord

it is seen that the portion in Worcester County was not built as early as that in Middlesex.

Promptly upon the opening of the turnpike the following petition was entered with the Middlesex court, which is here introduced as showing the manners of a century ago.

Petition of Ephraim Wood and others, "shewing that whereas a Turnpike-road known by the name of the Union Turnpike is laid out and made and now travelled upon through the westerly part of Concord in said County on and near the county road where it was heretofore travelled and has rendered a part of said County road useless and unoccupied as to any public travel to wit from the dwelling house of Ephraim Wood, Esq. on westerly to where said Turnpike-road comes into said County

Union Turnpike: Bridge over Sudbury River

road near where the late General James Colburn deceased lived, it being one hundred rods and praying that the section of the County road above described and thus rendered useless may be discontinued."

In March, 1810, the road was discontinued as requested, and the records show that the committee to whom the matter was referred recommended such discontinuance upon the *understanding* that no gate should be erected to take toll from those who might have used the discontinued part. There is no evidence that the corporation had a different understanding of the matter later.

The proprietors were released in 1819 from their liability to maintain the easterly end of their road, apparently that portion between the reformatory and Concord.

The legislators of 1804 seem to have had a fear of monopolies, for they inserted a provision in the charter of this company that no one stockholder should cast more than ten votes regardless of how many shares he owned. In 1826 this provision was repealed.

The original location of the turnpike passed through the village of Harvard and then bore due west for about a mile and a half, bringing it a short distance south of the summit of Prospect Hill. Then it deflected slightly to the north and, descending abruptly, went straight across the valley of the Nashua River, climbing the steep banks on the westerly side through deep cuts, and then on in the same direction through the town of Lancaster. Tollgates were usually erected on or near the bridges, for the reason that opportunities for going around them did not so conveniently exist, and it is probable that the Union had its gate in the vicinity of the bridge over the Nashua River.

Willard's *History of Lancaster*, published in 1826, says that a serious freshet on the Nashua in 1818 damaged all the bridges over that stream and carried away most of them. The turnpike bridge went downstream with the others, and the corporation, with expenses exceeding its receipts, as we have already seen, found itself unable to meet the expense of a new one. A county bridge less than a mile up-stream. from the turnpike was soon rebuilt, and toward it the corporation cast covetous eyes.

January 31, 1820, an act was passed by which the corporation was authorized to alter their road by leaving its original route, near Benjamin Willard's in Lancaster, thence running in the most direct and suitable course to where the county road leading to Harvard, crosses the Nashua River, thence in or near the course of said county road so as to reunite with said turnpike near Jonas Bateman's in Harvard.

The section of the original turnpike which was thus cut out measured about two and a half miles, and extended from the corner of the roads a mile west of Harvard Village to the corner of the roads at the old Lancaster

Union Turnpike: A shady section

almshouse. Of this section only about a half mile exists to-day as a public road. Now one following the course of the old turnpike comes to an abrupt stop on the brink of Prospect Hill, where a magnificent view is had of the broad valley of the Nashua, and where the Lancaster Road meets the turnpike at right angles. Thus it was with a party of investigators in the early fall of 1916, when the author, with two sympathetic companions, sought to trace the road abandoned ninety-six years before.

At first no sign was seen of a continuation straight ahead ever having existed, but gradually the eye picked out a growth of trees running across the valley, which was strongly suggestive of the parallel rows of elms which we

Union Turnpike: A rough cart-path inclosed by stone walls

Union Turnpike: Old Lancaster almshouse

had seen on either side of the road for so many miles. Passing through the farm gate opposite the end of the road which we had been following, we noticed a rough cart path inclosed by stone walls leading straight ahead down the hill. Following this we found unmistakable indications of an old road, the stone walls on either side and the comparatively even grade on which we walked mutely testifying to that effect. At the railroad we found where the old road had passed on a high ridge, through which the railroad builders had ruthlessly dug a deep cut for their track. At the easterly end of this ridge was observed an old cellar close to the turnpike remnants, and it required little

Union Turnpike: Site of turnpike bridge over Nashua River, 1812-18

Union Turnpike: At the corner of the Shirley road

imagination to picture that as once having been covered by the tollhouse, with the gate close by. Beyond the railroad the ground was low and swampy, and as far as we penetrated we saw the remains of the banks and causeways over which the old stages had passed.

Passing around through the village of Still River and crossing the Nashua where the turnpike crossed after the act of 1820, we renewed our search on the westerly bank of the river, in the town of Lancaster, and on the crest of the bank which rises from the river bottom we soon found a cut so deep that it plainly was never made by a landowner for his private use. Following this clue we found a continuous grade which brought us to the bank of the Nashua, where, although all signs of a bridge have long since disappeared, the graded banks of the roadway leading to it on both sides could be distinctly traced.

Having climbed the grades up the bank of the Nashua we easily followed the embankment of the old road across the slightly rising ground until at the summit a wall-like ledge of rock crossed the line at an abrupt height of five or six feet. Through this ledge the early public-utility constructors had blasted a cut for their road with perpendicular walls, in which the old drill marks are still plainly visible.

Farther west, at the corner where stands the large farmhouse formerly used to shelter the poor of Lancaster, the path of the turnpike is so smooth and plain that, with the trees removed from its limits, one could safely drive over it. At the old poor farm the spirit of the turnpike again asserted itself, and from there to Leominster it is still in existence as a public road, except where modern engineering has made deviations.

The old residents know this abandoned section as the old turnpike, and several of whom we inquired, verified our conclusions regarding the origin of the traces through the woods and swamps.

The road became free in Worcester County in 1829, but in Middlesex that formality was delayed until 1830, as the corporation neglected for two terms of the commissioners' meetings to obey the orders relative to advertising a hearing.

33. The Taunton and New Bedford Turnpike

The Taunton and New Bedford Turnpike Corporation, created by act of March 3, 1804, planned to build from Taunton Green to the head of Acushnet River, on the way to New Bedford. The road was to pass through the towns of Berkley and Freetown and the village of Assonet. No records have been found, and personal knowledge of the country allows the assertion that there are no roads there which can be imagined as ever having been turnpikes except a short piece in Taunton. A straight street stretches from the Green to Weir Village, which is known as Weir Street, locally pronounced "Ware." A map was found in the Bristol County Registry of Deeds, dated in 1806, on which Weir Street was marked "Turnpike from Greene to Weir." The length of that street is a little less than a mile, so it was not much of a turnpike, if it was ever so operated. In 1808 the time limit was extended to 1812.

34. The Blue Hill Turnpike

On the seventh of March, 1804, the Blue Hill Turnpike Corporation received its charter to build

from Randolph meeting-house, in the county of Norfolk, through Scotch Woods, or the Blue Hills, so called, in the most direct and convenient route, to Joseph Babcock's, in Milton.

But the location described did not satisfy the proprietors, so they secured the passage of another act, in June, 1805, allowing them,

instead of laying out and making the same from an apple tree in the land of Ezra Coates in said Milton, to the house of Joseph Babcock, to lay out and make the said turnpike-road from said apple tree, to, or near to, the guide post in Milton at Swift's Corner, so called, near to the house of John Swift in Milton.

The apple tree in question has not been identified but the location of the road is well established. The legislature, in 1830, required all towns to file with the secretary of state a map of their territory, and the one filed by Milton shows the Blue Hill Turnpike plainly. It extended nearly due south from Milton Lower Mills until it reached the Quincy line; crossing the west end of that town it curved slightly, and then bore about south-southeast to Randolph Center. It is known to-day as Randolph Avenue in Milton, and as

Blue Hill Turnpike: Northerly end in Milton

North Main Street in Randolph. The layout was partly made in 1804, and the balance in 1805.

Two returns were made of the cost of construction, for what reason is not apparent, the total being $78,302.68. The length being about eight miles gives a per-mile cost of about $9800. This is a pretty high figure, and the work must have been heavy. On this question we quote from Teele's *History of Milton*, which says:

Like most of the turnpike enterprises of that period the road had limited uses for travelling. Its location was principally through wild land or woodlands, with a succession of heavy grades, long steep hills and narrow viaducts, requiring frequent

Blue Hill Turnpike: Where a causeway once spanned the valley

Blue Hill Turnpike: At the corner with Reedsdale Road

and expensive repairs.

Returns of business done were filed from 1816 to 1849 inclusive, and show net income averaging between one and two per cent, with a maximum of about two and a half per cent in 1834.

In 1815 the company was allowed to hold real estate not exceeding ten thousand dollars in value, and a penalty was laid upon any persons who turned off the road at gates to avoid payment of tolls. By the last it is evident that the Blue Hill had to compete with a "shunpike." Evidently at first there had been but one gate erected near the halfway point, and much of the travel used only one end of the road without passing the gate at all, for we find an act in 1807, allowing the corporation to erect two half-gates instead of the one whole one, provided neither was put up where an old road had been taken.

The Norfolk county commissioners laid the turnpike out as a public highway in 1848. By its connection, or close to a connection, with the Dorchester Turnpike at Milton Lower Mills, this road gave through communication between Boston and Randolph, the travel of which was absorbed by the railroad which passes through Brockton.

35. The Hartford and Dedham Turnpike

The next was planned for through travel rather than local, as the Hartford and Dedham Turnpike Corporation, chartered March 9, 1804, was designed to close the gap left by a Connecticut corporation, the Ninth Massachusetts, and the Norfolk and Bristol, in a through line between Hartford and Boston. The road was located over the present High Street from Dedham Center to

Hartford and Dedham Turnpike: High Street, Dedham

Westwood Center, thence through Westwood and Dover over Hartford Street, through Medfield by Cedar Hill and Main streets, over the Main Street of Millis and Medway to the northeast corner of Bellingham, where it joined the road of the Ninth Massachusetts. The centers of Dedham, Westwood, Medfield, Millis, and West Medway are located upon the line of the old turnpike.

The town records of Medway show that in 1803 the town was asked to give its suffrage to a turnpike, but declined. The *History of Medway*, published by the town, states that the petition for legislation establishing the Hartford

Hartford and Dedham Turnpike: Looking east from the Charles River crossing

Hartford and Dedham Turnpike: Through Medway

and Dedham was signed by sixty-nine citizens, and was opposed by others who sought to build a road between the same terminals, but through Franklin, North Wrentham, and Walpole. Although unsuccessful in their opposition, these parties succeeded the next year in securing a charter for their route in the name of the Winsocket Turnpike Corporation.

The road was about sixteen and a half miles long, and cost about $1940 a mile, or $32,029.50 all told. Returns were filed for the years 1808 to 1812, both inclusive, during which time the net earnings averaged one half of one per cent per annum.

Medfield saw good prospects in the proposed turnpike, for that town in 1803 voted seventy to eight, for endorsement of the project says Tilden's *History of Medfield*, which also informs us that the stock sold for a few years at fifty dollars, but quickly declined to ten dollars, and was soon worthless.

In 1830 the portion in Dedham, Dover, Medfield, and Medway became free, and in 1838 the balance was thrown open. Medfield was assessed thirty dollars, and Medway one hundred and sixty dollars, as their respective portions of the damage to be paid the corporation for its road.

One tollgate stood where the railroad now crosses the old road at Millis, another barred the way at the corner of Main and Bridge streets in Medfield. The last was located under authority of an act passed April 12, 1836, but it would seem that the gate had been established there for some time previous to that date, for the act further relieves the corporation from any liability on account of its being illegally placed.

An increase of twenty-five per cent in the rates of toll on one-horse vehicles was granted in 1813, which might have served as a warning to the electric railway company which secured a franchise over the same road three quarters of a century after the abolition of tolls. That company, unable to exist on five-cent fares, sought to assess six instead, and when threatened with legal process to restrain it therefrom gave up running its cars until the increase was allowed it.

The Connecticut corporation which provided the road to complete the system from the westerly end of the Ninth Massachusetts to Hartford was the Boston Turnpike Company. This public utility was incorporated by the Connecticut legislature in October, 1797, with a capital of 4800 pounds, and a franchise to build a road "from Hartford through the towns of East Hartford, Bolton, Coventry, Mansfield, Ashford, Pomfret, and Thompson, to the Massachusetts line," a distance of approximately forty-eight miles. In the usual language of the early acts, it was authorized "to erect and establish four turnpikes on said road," one of which was to be "at or near the notch of the mountain in Bolton," where the trains between Willimantic and Hartford pass through a cut of solid rock with perpendicular walls seventy feet high.

In May, 1798, the company was released from its obligation to build between Bolton and the Connecticut River, but in 1812 it secured a renewal of the privilege, and connected with the Hartford and Tolland Turnpike in East Hartford, over which and the East Hartford Ferry travelers from Boston reached Connecticut's capital.

36. The Dorchester Turnpike

In 1805 the South Cove District of Boston and the Commonwealth Flats in South Boston were under water, and the present Fort Point Channel was a portion of so broad an expanse of the harbor that that restricted name had

Hartford and Dedham Turnpike: Hartford Street, Westwood

not been applied to it. The northerly point of South Boston, known as Nook Point, barely reached north of Fourth Street, hence the first bridge connection from Boston to South Boston was on the line of the present Dover Street.

March 6, 1804, the Proprietors of the Boston South Bridge were incorporated for the purpose of building a bridge from Front Street, now Harrison Avenue in Boston to Foundry Street in South Boston. The bridge was opened for public travel October 1, 1805, and was operated as a toll bridge for twenty-seven years, being sold to the City of Boston April 19, 1832. By vote of the city council it was named Dover Street Bridge in 1857. Approach to the South Boston end was had over the road now known as West Fourth Street.

While the bridge was under construction a proposition for a turnpike to lead from it was brought forth, and in consequence the Dorchester Turnpike Corporation was created by act of the legislature March 4, 1805, with a franchise to build a road from "the bridge over Neponset River, commonly called Milton Bridge, to Nook Point, so called, in Boston." The northerly part of South Boston had been annexed to Boston in 1804, hence the charter of 1805 speaks of Nook Point as in Boston.

Under the authority thus given, the Dorchester Turnpike was laid out and built from the bridge at Milton Lower Mills to Fourth Street in two straight stretches, passing through Ashmont, Harrison Square, Savin Hill, Washington Village, and South Boston. At Milton Lower Mills, except for a short intervening distance, it connected with the Blue Hill Turnpike. As Dorchester Avenue the Dorchester Turnpike is known to-day for its entire length.

In Orcutt's *Good Old Dorchester* we read that the road cost more than was anticipated, which obliged the corporation to charge higher tolls, thus making the road unpopular, many preferring to go without toll by way of Roxbury. The charging of higher tolls is open to doubt, as we have seen that rates of toll were fixed in the act of incorporation and could be changed only by subsequent legislation, and no act authorizing higher rates has been observed. But beyond a doubt the road cost more than expected.

The cost of this road was $43,686.20, or a pro rata of about $8740 for a length of about five miles. Returns were filed intermittently at first, but continuously after 1825. These . . . show the Dorchester to have been one of the best paying of the turnpikes. Receipts began to climb in 1826 and reached their peak in 1838, in which year the gross earnings were fourteen per cent and the net about nine. In the last years before the railroads the earnings were heavy, but dropped at once upon the opening of the Old Colony Railroad in November, 1844. In 1852 the corporation was the loser in a lawsuit for damages on account of an accident on its turnpike, and was assessed the sum of $2215.06 in consequence. In its return for that year that item was rendered separately, with a pitiful cry of injustice and claim that the accident was through no fault of the corporation.

The maps of to-day would give one the impression that the turnpike continued straight to the present bridge over Fort Point Channel, but as already seen it ended at the road leading to the Dover Street Bridge. The Federal Street Bridge, which is the one over Fort Point Channel, was built in 1827 and 1828 by the Boston Free Bridge Corporation and deeded to the city of Boston September 26, 1828. Included in the bridge layout was the portion of what is now Dorchester Avenue between the end of the bridge and West First Street. From the end of the Dorchester Turnpike to the approach to the bridge at West First Street a street was built near the close of the year 1828, which was named Turnpike Street. This was done by the municipal authorities of Boston, and that street was never a part of the turnpike.

The Dorchester Turnpike was laid out as a public way April 22, 1854, Orcutt says, by public subscription, and was then named Dorchester Avenue, which name had been given to Turnpike Street about a month earlier. In 1856 the name was changed to Federal Street, but "Dorchester Avenue" was restored in 1870. The entire length of the Dorchester Turnpike is now included within the limits of the city of Boston, while if built one year earlier it would then have laid wholly in the town of Dorchester. Dorchester Neck, as South Boston was formerly called, was annexed to Boston on March 4, 1804, Washington Village being added in 1855, and the balance of Dorchester becoming a part of Boston in 1870.

By its connection with the Blue Hill and the latter's connection with the Taunton and South Boston, the Dorchester Turnpike offered a direct and improved road all the way from Boston to Taunton, which in those days was foremost in the production of brick and iron as well as a shipping port of prominence. So it is easy to imagine a heavy traffic over the turnpikes named, in which we are confirmed by a historian of one of the towns along the Taunton and South Boston.

Only two years after the corporation relinquished its control over the Dorchester Turnpike, horse cars appeared on the new public street, and a portion of the taxpayers, who now maintained the road, continued to pay toll for riding upon it.

37. The Bath or Governor King's Turnpike

Maine claims our attention again, for we find the Bath Bridge and Turnpike Corporation formed March 15, 1805, to build a road in a straight line from Bowdoin College in Brunswick to Bath, with a bridge over New Meadows River. This corporation, which was principally owned by Governor William

King, promptly built its road of about eight miles at a cost, including the bridge, of $16,840.20. As the bridge was the chief obstacle to a free highway, it is probable that a large part of the cost was due to such construction, so a

Bath Bridge and Turnpike: Bowdoin Pines, Brunswick, Maine

pro-rata cost per mile would be misleading. We gather from Wheeler's *History of Brunswick* that

This turnpike was well made, and the roadbed was hard and smooth. It went through the woods nearly all the way east of Cook's Corner. The bridge over the New Meadows River was a few rods south of where the Maine Central Railroad now crosses, and the gate and toll house were at the west end of the bridge.

According to Lemont's *Historical Dates of Bath*, there was another turn-pike between Bath and Brunswick, crossing the New Meadows River at Brown's Ferry. Wheeler disputes this, however, saying:

there is no evidence that another turnpike was built in Brunswick. The bridge at Brown's Ferry was built previous to that of Governor King, and only the abutments and piers remained in 1808. It is more probable that what Lemont calls the second turnpike was a "shunpike" as it is well known that, to avoid paying toll, travellers from Brunswick left the turnpike at Cook's Corner and crossed the river at Brown's Ferry. It was owing to this fact that Governor King established a gate on the turnpike west of Cook's Corner. That expedient proved of no avail however, as travellers thereafter drove across the plains to Cook's Corner, and then down to Brown's Ferry, thus avoiding both toll gates.

This turnpike followed the lines of the present Bath Street in Brunswick, and Center Street in Bath, the westerly terminus being on High Street on the north side of the courthouse. Connecting by means of Day's Ferry across the Kennebec with the Wiscasset and Woolwich Turnpike, which in turn connected with the Wiscasset and Augusta, it opened improved communication between Portland and the town which was to be the capital of the new state.

An act defining the general powers and duties of turnpike corporations was passed March 16, 1805. Hitherto each act of incorporation had been a dreary repetition of those before, each petty detail of powers and liabilities being set forth at length. But after this act every company incorporated was to have such powers and be liable for specified things under a general law. No more charters were to be granted until the route desired had been viewed at the expense of the petitioners, by a committee of the legislature, of which view public notice was to be given. The charter was granted, the road to be laid out by a committee consisting of five disinterested freeholders, residents of the county in which the road was to be built. All future roads were to be twenty-four feet wide, in the improved portion, and four rods altogether. Rates of toll were fixed for all comers, leaving the adjustment of earnings to be regulated by the location of the gates. Permission was given to commute tolls. One half rates only could be collected on' wagons having "fellies" six inches or more in width. Treble toll could be demanded of vehicles which damaged the road, and on the other hand the corporation was liable for from two to ten dollars in damages for delaying travelers or demanding excess toll. The liability of the corporation for defects in its road was clearly stated. A gate could be moved by permission of the court of common pleas; three disinterested freeholders being appointed a committee to give a hearing, relocate the gate, and report to the court. If the road was out of repair, upon complaint a justice of the court of common pleas could order the gates to be opened if after ten days' notice the repairs had not been made. When any road was made free, all land owned by the corporation reverted to the former owners, even if the same had been purchased in fee. A new feature was introduced in section eleven, which provided that the legislature might dissolve any corporation thereafter established "after the expiration of twenty years, or sooner if it shall appear to their satisfaction that the income of said road shall have compensated," etc. And any charter was to be void if the road was not completed within five years. This appears to be the earliest general corporation law. . . .

38. The Brush Hill Turnpike

The Brush Hill Turnpike Corporation, also of the sixteenth of March, built its road

between Davenports Corner, so-called, near the west end of Blue Hill in Milton, in the county of Norfolk, and near the four mile stone in Roxbury, near the dwelling-house of Ebenezer Seaver Esq. as follows: Beginning at said Davenports Corner, by the most favorable route, to the Upper Bridge, so-called, near Boies' Mills, from thence, by the most favorable route, at or near the said four mile stone.

It will be noticed that the usual straight-line requirement is left out of this franchise, and yet the resultant turnpike stands out prominently on the map on account of the rigidity of its alignment.

An interesting paper on "Milestones in and near Boston" was read before the Brookline Historical Society by Charles F. Read, from which we obtain information regarding the "four mile stone" mentioned as the end of the turnpike franchise.

In stage-coach days nearly all the important routes were marked with milestones, and at the opening of the turnpike era Massachusetts was liberally supplied with them. The work was commenced in 1707 by judge Samuel Sewall, whose diary is familiar to all students of Boston's early days, and by him were set the first two milestones, measuring the distance along Newbury Street, as Washington Street was then called, from the "Boston town house." From a point beyond the second and not far enough for the third, five roads radiated, and the work for a few miles along each of these was continued by Paul Dudley, afterwards chief justice of Massachusetts Bay, in 1734 and 1735.

The "Upper Road" to Quincy followed practically the present lines of Warren and Washington streets through Roxbury and Dorchester to Milton Lower Mills, and thence over Adams Street through East Milton. The "four mile stone" mentioned in the charter of the Brush Hill Turnpike was on this road, and is still standing on Warren Street opposite number 473, and between Harrishof and Wyoming streets. It is marked

B 4
1735
PD

At the inception of the Brush Hill Turnpike Bugbee's Tavern stood near this milepost, the first resting place on the tiresome journey to Quincy.

The turnpike was located, according to Norfolk County records, in 1805, but the corporation did not improve its franchise as far as the "four mile stone," ending its road at the square now known as Grove Hall, nearly a half mile from the stone. The broad boulevard, called Blue Hill Avenue, extending from Grove Hall past Franklin Park to Mattapan, and the beautiful road through Milton to the westerly foot of Great Blue Hill is the legacy left us by the Brush Hill Turnpike.

Teele's *History of Milton* tells us of a town meeting at which it was voted that we do highly disapprove of a turnpike being made from the road at the west end of the Blew Hills to the upper bridge, as petitioned by Samuel Leonard and others.

But high disapproval did not prevail and the road was completed by 1809. No returns of cost or business done were ever made by this corporation. Apparently the free list, as originally made up, had overlooked military and spiritual preparedness, for in 1810 an act was passed applying to this road, providing that the corporation should not collect toll "from anyone on military duty, on religious duty, coming to or from any grist mill, or on the common or ordinary business of family concerns, or from anyone who had not been out of town with a loaded team or carriage."

An interesting comparison with later days may be drawn from a legislature's assuming that every toll gatherer would be able to tell the nature of

Brush Hill Turnpike: Brush Hill Avenue, Milton, 1903

Brush Hill Turnpike: Blue Hill Avenue, Boston

his customer's business and how far he had been or was going. To those of us who have spent much time in certain of New England's rural regions, that assumption may not seem so very unreasonable, after all.

It is hard at the present time to see what prospects of financial success this road ever had. It was not projected as a through route to any large place. Beyond Mattapan, which was but nothing then, the route led through and ended in unbroken woods. Canton, for whose business the road must have looked, lay five miles beyond the authorized southern terminus. True the turnpike was built in the route of the "Old Bay Road," which was the earliest line of travel between Boston and Taunton, and it may have been expected that travelers would follow the old lines, thankfully accepting as much turnpike improvement as was given them. Another turnpike, the Stoughton, was authorized a year later, which commenced two miles south of the southerly end of the Brush Hill and ran thence to a junction with the Taunton and South Boston, in Easton, thus opening a through route, except for the two miles noted, from Boston to Taunton. But evidently the combination was not a paying one.

In 1857 the Brush Hill corporation was allowed to surrender its road in Milton without receiving compensation for the same being made a free highway. That it was not a road of much public value is evident from the fact that the town of Milton neglected to lay it out until prompted by the legislature, which set February 26, 1860, as the limit within which the road could be publicly laid out without compensation to the corporation. A portion in Milton and Dorchester had been laid out by the county commissioners in December, 1849, and in October, 1856, the corporation relinquished its rights on the northerly end as far as Grove Hall, and the commissioners accepted that part of the road for the county, naming it Grove Hall Avenue, by which name it was known until 1870.

The custom of placing milestones was revived after turnpikes had opened new lanes, and the Brush Hill received attention from John McLean. He was the Boston merchant who bequeathed one hundred thousand dollars to the Massachusetts General Hospital, and for whom the McLean Asylum was named; and just before his death, in 1823, he commenced the erection of milestones to mark the distance along the Brush Hill Turnpike. The work not being completed when he died, was continued by his business partner, Isaac Davenport. The measurements commence with Dudley's "four mile stone," the first stone being set where Harvard Street now intersects the old road and marked

BOSTON
5 MIILES
J. MCLEAN
1823.

The McLean stones are uniform, except for the figure indicating the distance, and may be seen to-day along the road, the last, the ten mile, being safely set in the stone wall of a private estate not far from the boundary line between Milton and Canton.

At the Upper Mills stood an old bridge, built by the towns of Dorchester and Milton in 1733. Far out in the wilderness as it was, the towns gladly allowed the Brush Hill Turnpike to assume its maintenance. At the northerly end the corporation was allowed to incorporate into its toll road about three thousand feet of the old Canterbury Street, but elsewhere the turnpike broke its way through unopened districts.

39. The Andover and Medford Turnpike

The Andover and Medford Turnpike Corporation was incorporated in the following June, on the fifteenth, with authority to build from a point in Andover to the Medford market place, but, as already noted in connection with the Essex Turnpike, it improved its franchise only as far as the line between Reading and Stoneham, leaving the portion in Essex County to be built by the Essex corporation.

The cost of this road was $48,920.95, or a pro rata of about $8150 for a length of about six miles. Returns were filed for only two years, 1807 and 1808, the showing for those years being an algebraic sum of minus $250.

The location was duly made by a committee of disinterested Middlesex freeholders, who reported to the court in September, 1806, and the road evidently was promptly built. Three miles was saved in the hauling of ship timber and country produce from New Hampshire points, the road forming a link in the through and direct route to Concord and other New Hampshire towns, as well as to the southwestern part of Vermont. But according to Brooks in his *History of Medford* the receipts did not compensate for the outlay. Brooks' further statements regarding the efforts of the corporation to give away its road in 1830 appear to be at variance with the records in East Cambridge, which show quite a contest over taking the franchise away.

A petition entered by various citizens for the freeing of the road in May, 1833, met with sufficient opposition to cause it to drop out of sight, and not until January, 1836, did the road become free of toll. Then the county commissioners declared the road public, and the corporation was allowed until the eighteenth of that month to remove its gates and other personal property. Three thousand dollars was the amount which was allowed the corporation as damages for the loss of its privileges, from which the company appealed, making petition for a jury to decide that question. Upon the refusal of the commissioners to entertain the appeal the supreme court was asked to intervene with a mandamus, but that also was refused. The commissioners, thus sustained, dismissed the whole matter in May, 1837, and the Andover and Medford Turnpike passed into history.

By the act passed on February 27, 1807, this company and the Essex were allowed to maintain one gate together where their roads joined at the county line.

A beautiful ride is offered to-day over the old turnpike, traversing, as it does, the heart of the Middlesex Fells Reservation of the Metropolitan Park System and following close to the west shore of Spot Pond, as it was required

Andover and Medford Turnpike: At the first milestone, Medford

Andover and Medford Turnpike: Along the borders of Spot Pond

to do, away back in 1805. Forest Street in Medford and Main Street in Stoneham are to be followed if one desires to trace the old Andover and Medford Turnpike.

40. The Middlesex Turnpike

The Middlesex Turnpike Corporation, chartered on the same day, appears to have been the most aggressive and the most antagonized of any of the companies. For over four years the battle raged over the location of the road, the diversion to private control of long-established public highways, and the erection of gates where all had been wont to pass without hindrance for

Andover and Medford Turnpike: Through the Middlesex Fells

generations—the contest being carried from the county courts to the halls of legislation when necessary to override or change the existing laws. Only in the local histories of Arlington is any mention of this controversy to be found, while one impressive memorial history of a town, in which much of the trouble originated and where intense public feeling must have been aroused, makes no mention at all of the controversy or building of the road, the sole reference to the subject being the statement that of three great highways crossing the town the Middlesex Turnpike was one.

The route specified in the charter began at Tyngsboro meeting-house and ran to Chelmsford, thence to Billerica, and thence to a point in Bedford described as "a stake in land of Abel Wyman, about twelve miles and one hundred and twenty rods from Boston." At the point thus precisely and definitely located the road was to divide, one line running to Medford Village by way of Symmes' Corner, and the other passing directly to "the rocks, so called, in Cambridge," thence over "the old road " to a point between the houses of Stephen Goddard and Walter Frost, probably near the center of the present Arlington, from which place the route was to run directly to a connection with the Cambridge and Concord near the westerly end of the West Boston Bridge.

"The Rocks" mentioned in the prescribed route were situated on the present-day Massachusetts Avenue about a half mile toward Boston from Arlington Heights, where a tablet suitably inscribed may be seen by all who pass recording the location. The stake, so accurately located, might have "tossed up" to see if it would place itself in Bedford or Billerica, so close to the extreme northeast corner of Bedford did it come. It plainly was placed

Middlesex Turnpike: Hampshire Street and Broadway, Cambridge

Middlesex Turnpike: Massachusetts Avenue and Lowell Street, Arlington Heights

on a mathematically straight line between Tyngsboro and Medford, which evidently was intended to be the main line of the turnpike, while the portion through Cambridge was but a side issue. But the latter was the part which was built, the section between Bedford and Medford never getting beyond an application for a layout.

A little common sense may be discerned in the foregoing description of the route, as it will be observed that the road was to pass through the centers of Chelmsford and Billerica, but that did not last long for, on June 23, 1806, the corporation secured an amendment to its charter allowing it to locate its road *straight* from the famous stake to "Buisket Bridge in Tyngsbury," thus

Middlesex Turnpike: Through Lexington

leaving Billerica one mile to the east and Chelmsford about three quarters of a mile to the west. The total saving in distance by this cut off could not have been over a mile, and it is of record that the bulk of the expected traffic refused to desert its old route, the drivers from New Hampshire towns preferring to put up at the taverns they had known so long. Had the road to Medford been built the result might not have been so disappointing, but the Cambridge route asked them to journey through regions hitherto unknown, and they declined.

Not until February, 1807, did the corporation file its petition for a committee to lay out the route and assess the damages to landowners, and then the fun began. For nearly two years the committee labored on its task, and it is easy to imagine the pressure brought to bear upon it to influence the location. The route finally decided upon by the committee followed the bank of the Merrimac River from Tyngsboro to about the line between that town and Chelmsford, thence it ran straight, crossing Nuttings Pond in the middle to a point in the northeast corner of Bedford, almost in Billerica. From that point it ran southerly across the western edge of Burlington until it intersected an old road near the house of Joseph Harrington in the northeast part of Lexington, and followed that old road to "the rocks." Then it followed an old county road along the north bank of Mill Brook to Stephen Goddard's house, about in Arlington Center now. From that point the route ran as straight as could reasonably be expected to the Cambridge and Concord Turnpike at West Boston Bridge. According to Parker's *History of Arlington*, construction along the north bank of Mill Brook would have destroyed every mill in that vicinity, which fact naturally aroused intense opposition, which

Middlesex Turnpike: Through Lexington

Middlesex Turnpike: Near the Lexington-Burlington line

was supported by similar feelings in Lexington over the appropriation of a part of their old town road.

So all these interested parties were on hand in December, 1809, when the report of the locating committee was received by the court, and so strenuously did they fight the proposed location that the report was rejected *in toto*, and the matter again referred to the same committee for further action. Immediately upon the rejection of the report various Lexington citizens entered a petition for a layout of a county road from Joseph Harrington's house to "the rocks" over their existing town road. Apparently there had been for many years a town road leading from "the rocks" across the easterly corner of Lexington into the western edge of Woburn, and thence to Woburn Center, and it was over a part of this road that the corporation desired to build its turnpike. Following the rejection of the report including such part in the turnpike, the effort was made to further embarrass the movements of the corporation by giving that piece of road the prestige of a county layout. A committee was at once appointed to view the route and report.

We are told in Cutter's *History of Arlington* that a special town meeting followed, at which a committee was chosen to effect a *reconciliation* between the corporation and the landowners, and to try to locate the turnpike where it would do the most good and the least damage.

The corporation, unable to obtain what it wanted from the county court, went higher and appealed to the sovereign people themselves, as represented at the state house. Mindful of its own interests, the town of West Cambridge, by which name Arlington was known until 1867, instructed its representative to endeavor to have the turnpike located "at the foot of the rocks and at no other place." The resultant act, passed March 6, 1810, seems to have been a compromise. West Cambridge secured the location at "the foot of the rocks," but the corporation scored by having the town obliged to improve "the great road" from the "foot of the rocks" to what is now Arlington Center, and contribute it for the turnpike; and further, the town was to pay all damages caused by abandoning the portion of the original route for which the "great road" was substituted. To Lexington it was granted that the turnpike should be located from Harrington's to the "foot of the rocks" at the "great road." This "great road" was the one over which the British troops marched in the early morning hours of the memorable nineteenth of April, and it was at Arlington Center, then known as Menotomy, that a plucky force of old men, beyond the years of active service, waylaid and captured a train of supplies on its way to relieve the harassed soldiers of the king later in the same day.

Spurred by the legislative action, the Middlesex court of sessions reconsidered its rejection of the report made in December, 1809, and in March, 1810, accepted the same except the portion between Joseph Harrington's and "the rocks" in the old road. The effort to forestall the turnpike by making a county road over that section was still alive, and during the same month the committee reported in favor of such proceeding, and another committee was appointed to proceed to lay it out. In June that committee reported, the road was accepted, and hurry-up orders were issued to the towns of Lexington and West Cambridge to build the road and close all accounts within ninety days.

In September, 1810, the corporation made petition for approval of the portion of its road that had been completed, and to have the location of its gates determined. The ninety days within which West Cambridge and Lexington were to build the new county road from Harrington's to "the rocks" having expired without the building of the road, the turnpike corpo-

Middlesex Turnpike: At Turnpike Station, Billerica

Middlesex Turnpike: Old abutments at the crossing of the Concord River

ration now renewed its application for the court's approval of its layout over that section, but in December, 1810, the court dismissed the application.

At the same term, December, 1810, the corporation entered a new petition. West Cambridge had not completed the "great road" and paid the damages as required by the legislative act of the sixth of the previous March, and the turnpike company demanded that it be allowed to go ahead and build the road itself. But it appeared that West Cambridge had completed the road, or much of it at least, but that the road was a county road, and hence beyond the power of the town to convey to the company. So appeal was again had to the legislature, and on February 28, 1811, the state cut the Gordian Knot, by decreeing that the road should be taken from the county and given to the turnpike corporation. Therefore the company withdrew its petition to build that section itself.

The injustice of the foregoing is plainly to be seen and suggests a powerful lobbying force in behalf of the corporation. Because the town objected to having the larger part of its mill interests destroyed and prevented the turnpike from so locating as to accomplish that result, the legislature loaded it with the expense of building a mile and a half of improved road, took away from it its long-established free highway, and obliged it to pay the costs which the corporation had prematurely incurred before it had legal right to do so. Considering the power which towns and counties had to lay out free roads which would divert travel from the turnpikes, and the need which the turnpikes ever felt of the good will of their communities, it causes wonder that the Middlesex Turnpike Corporation should ever have pursued such high-handed methods. The cash payment by the town for damages on account of the abandoned location was $516.49, according to Parker.

Definite progress appeared in the report made to the court in June, 1811. The road, twenty-six miles in length, was almost completed and four gates had been erected, and the court was asked to give its final approval so that the road might legally be operated. One of the gates was located in Lexington five rods south of the house of Reuben Reed, who owned land adjoining that of Joseph Harrington on the south side. This gate was on the section over which Lexington had made such a determined fight, and it appears that the corporation had finally succeeded in getting its franchise over that portion. But the fight was not over yet, for Lexington citizens entered their protest, declaring that the road had not been built as required by law, and demanding that the gate should not stand in its location,

which place is part of an ancient highway over which they and all the citizens of the Commonwealth have from time immemorial had a right to pass and repass free of toll or any toll whatever. And on which they conceive by law no toll gate can rightfully be erected.

This report was recommitted.

By this diversion from public to private ownership of the road in Lexington and the "great road" in West Cambridge, a large number of people living in Lexington and towns beyond, with a few in Woburn, were cut off from free travel over their natural routes to the Boston markets and obliged to travel over the same roads but to pay toll therefor. Their grievance being placed before the legislature, and the manifest injustice shown, an act was secured on June 21, 1811, whereby it was provided that all the inhabitants of Lexington and five of Woburn, "their families and future occupants," should pass free of toll over such portions of the turnpike. The towns beyond Lexington had their choice of other routes and were not included in the benefits of this act.

Matters being thus adjusted the road received its legal sanction and proceeded to do business. By the act of March 6, 1810, authority had been given to extend the turnpike from Tyngsboro meeting-house to the New Hampshire boundary, where it connected with the road of the Amherst Turnpike Corporation, a New Hampshire company operating a road from the Massachusetts line to a junction with the Second New Hampshire in Amherst. The Second New Hampshire, incorporated in 1799, had built its road from Amherst to the "lottery bridge" in Claremont, and thus improved connections were had all the way from Boston to the lower Connecticut Valley towns of Vermont and New Hampshire.

The Middlesex Turnpike was destined to be of less use a century after it was built than at its completion, and much of it to-day is discontinued. To follow the old road at the present time one would start in Cambridge at

Middlesex Turnpike: Encroachments in Billerica

Mechanic Square and pass over Hampshire Street and its continuation as Beacon Street.

At the corner of Beacon and Washington streets a tollgate formerly stood, and it was over this Washington Street that the Continental troops passed on their way to fortify Bunker Hill after prayer for their success had been made by the president of Harvard College.

The line of Beacon Street is continued in Somerville Avenue and Massachusetts Avenue through North Cambridge to Arlington, where the successor of the old turnpike passes by the Soldiers' Monument and the venerable Cooper's Tavern, and continues as the main street of Arlington to the "Foot

Middlesex Turnpike: Old tollhouse, Chelmsford

of the Rocks" near Arlington Heights.

At the "Foot of the Rocks" the old turnpike left the "Great Road," and as Lowell Street and Westminster Street it is perpetuated to-day. A nice macadamized road, with an easy, inviting down grade, it often lures motorists from the better road only to heartlessly abandon them some miles away in a sandy grass-grown path. For a few miles the road is smooth and well kept, but about the time that Lexington's jurisdiction is left grass appears in the middle of the track and the bushes crowd closer to the sides of the vehicle. This condition prevails through the town of Burlington, but in Billerica the old road assumes an air of more importance.

Nuttings Pond is crossed on a causeway which divides it almost equally, and that part of the road presents a busy appearance in the summer, especially on Sundays. An extensive colony of camps and bungalows has grown up around the pond, and the old turnpike is their only avenue. Over it the campers reach the little station, appropriately named "Turnpike," at the crossing of the Billerica Branch of the Boston and Maine Railroad.

A quarter of a mile farther and the road comes to an abrupt end, a fence barring the way, and for the next mile the old turnpike has reverted to private interests, except for the easement which the telephone company has improved in the erection of its line of poles. By those poles and the path followed by the line patrolmen the line of the turnpike can still be picked out. In the mile thus abandoned occurs the crossing of the Concord River, and the abutments and approaches of the old bridge are still to be plainly seen. Approaching the old bridge on an August Sunday in 1917, the author, following the exact line of the old Middlesex Turnpike, walked through a field of newly cut hay, climbed a wall, passed through a cornfield, then crept through a wire fence, and traversed a pasture in which many cows were peacefully grazing.

For the next four miles to Chelmsford the road is still open for travel, but apparently little used. At one of the Billerica crossroads the turnpike formerly passed between a large farmhouse and its commodious barn, but the present proprietor has seen fit to place two hen-houses directly in the line of the road, and such travelers as use the road to-day must wind in and out to avoid the encroachments.

Manning's Tavern still stands on the turnpike at the point nearest to Chelmsford Center, and opposite it may be seen a little house which formerly sheltered the toll gatherer and his family. Beyond the tollhouse the road again disappears and for over two miles can hardly be traced at all. No help is had here from the telephone company, for its poles have left us, bearing oft to the right on the way to Lowell. Usually a road abandoned many years is easily

Middlesex Turnpike: Manning's Tavern, Chelmsford

detected, but this section of discontinued highway is the most completely obliterated that the author has ever seen.

From North Chelmsford to the New Hampshire line, along the west bank of the Merrimac River, the turnpike has again assumed importance as one of the Lowell to Nashua boulevards.

English's *History of Bedford* says that the turnpike enjoyed a measure of success for a while, but professional teamsters were slow to abandon the familiar routes and discard the hospitality of the long-established taverns of Bedford. No costs or returns were filed by this corporation, so nothing of its financial affairs is known.

Middlesex Turnpike: Through Tyngsboro

In 1823 a county road was opened between Chelmsford and Bedford, which at once diverted a great deal of travel from the turnpike, even the stagecoaches forsaking it for the new road. That road paralleled the turnpike but a mile distant from it, and later was the cause of the complete abandonment of the portion of the turnpike between Chelmsford and North Chelmsford.

When the turnpike was built Lowell was not even thought of, the system of locks and canals having originally been built for navigation facilities and not devoted to the production of power until 1821 , but the road was convenient to the new city when it came and should have received a generous share of its travel. But until the day of railroads the Middlesex Canal served the mills of Lowell, and the business was not great enough to divide between turnpike and canal.

The portion of the road over which so much controversy had been, had in Lexington became a part of the public system in 1840 and at about the same time portions of the road in Chelmsford and Tyngsboro, interfering with the location of the Nashua and Lowell Railroad, were sold to that company. March 13, 1841, upon its own petition the corporation was dissolved by the legislature, and the balance of its road discontinued. But the county commissioners a year later revived the roads thus abandoned and laid them out as county highways. In 1846 the Nashua and Lowell Railroad Company was relieved from obligation to maintain its portion of the road, and that became free in some places and was discontinued in others. . . .

41. The Worcester and Fitzwilliam Turnpike

A charter was granted to the Worcester and Fitzwilliam Turnpike Corporation June 15, 1805, to build a road from Worcester, through Holden, Hubbardston, Templeton, to the line of Fitzwilliam, New Hampshire. This project lagged, and five years later the company was granted additional time for building, but the route was cut down so that it only extended from the Fitzwilliam line to Baldwin's Mills in Templeton, now known as Baldwinsville. Another extension was granted, so that they ultimately had until June 15, 1815, to complete the road. Construction was finally completed between the last-named points at a cost of $4300,or a cost per mile of about $500. The location of the road through Winchendon is shown on the 1830 map of that town at the state house. Worcester County records show the public layout through Royalston, Winchendon, and Templeton in 1834.

42. The Ashby Turnpike

Another spoke in the wheel-like system of turnpikes which radiated from Boston was the road of the Ashby Turnpike Corporation, the charter for which was granted also on the eleventh of February, 1806. This road started at the line between Ashburnham, Massachusetts, and New Ipswich, New Hampshire, and crossed the northeast corner of Ashburnham into Ashby, crossing that town easterly about in the middle and passing through Ashby Center and West Townsend to Townsend Plain, where it joined the road of the Third New Hampshire at the end thereof. Townsend must have been fortunate in its roads in its eastern part, for both the Third New Hampshire and the Ashby seem to have been satisfied to terminate their roads at Townsend Center, leaving their patrons to continue their journeys over the county road. At the westerly end the Ashby seems to have been pointing toward Keene, New Hampshire, but no turnpike franchise has been found in that state which would complete the connection.

Petitions for locating committees were made in Worcester and Middlesex counties in September, 1806, and in February, 1807, the layout was reported and approved. The land damages in Middlesex were divided among twenty owners and totaled $1475, which was about $155 a mile. The road was completed in the summer of 1810 and approval was asked in September of that year. Formal acceptance was had in December, and the corporation was allowed to transact business, the tollgate being located in Ashby, "near the old county road, and a little to the northward of the house of Jonas Hodgman."

The toll gatherer continued to discharge his duties for twenty-three years, until the turnpike became free in 1833.

43. The Worcester and Stafford Turnpike

Direct through communication between Worcester and Hartford was provided by the Worcester and Stafford Turnpike in Massachusetts, connecting at the state line with the Stafford Pool Turnpike, which went as far as the courthouse in Tolland, and thence over the Hartford and Tolland Turnpike, which led from the state house in Hartford to the courthouse in Tolland. The Massachusetts corporation received its charter February 15, 1806, but, like other enterprises at that time, found the financing a slow process. The road followed the straight-line principle in its original layout, and we find it was located over such a steep hill in Sturbridge that, before building the road, the company saw fit to petition the legislature for permission to so change the route as to pass around the objectionable hill. This was granted them in June, 1809.

In 1810 the road was completed and accepted by the officials of Worcester County, and by the court of sessions of Hampshire County in behalf of the towns in Hampden County. Some delay occurred in consequence of the death of one of the committee whose duty it was to view and approve the road, objection being raised to the legality of proceedings by the rest of the committee without him; but the matter was cleared by legislative action March 6, 1810, which confirmed the doings of the diminished committee, filled the vacancy, and allowed the work to be completed.

The road commenced at a point on "the post road in the town of Worcester," about a quarter of a mile beyond the westerly end of the present Main Street, and led through Leicester, about a quarter of a mile from the Auburn line, to Rochdale; thence to Charlton City, where a gate was placed;

Worcester and Stafford Turnpike: Looking back to Worcester

Worcester and Stafford Turnpike: Scene in Leicester

thence across the central part of Sturbridge, and diagonally across Holland to the boundary line between that town and South Brimfield, which it followed for about a mile., Then it made a short cut across the southeast corner of South Brimfield, and in about five eighths of a mile reached the Connecticut line. South Brimfield will not be found on the maps of to-day, as its name was changed to Wales in 1828.

No returns were ever made by this corporation and no items concerning it have been found in local histories, but that it was an important road serving a prosperous territory is plainly evident. Much of the travel over the "north-

Worcester and Stafford Turnpike: Its now grass-grown pathway

Worcester and Stafford Turnpike: Approaching Charlton

ern route" from Boston to New York must have been diverted from the line over the First Massachusetts to this of the Worcester and Stafford, as the new route was much more direct between Worcester and Hartford than by way of Springfield.

The turnpike was thrown open in Worcester County in 1834 and in Hampden County in October, 1835. It is known to-day in Leicester as Stafford Street, and in the other towns it seems to go by the name of "Old Turnpike." Portions were discontinued in Sturbridge in 1850 and in 1868, and in Charlton in 1851, but these appear to have been minor changes, some due, no doubt, to improvements in railroad crossings.

44. The Plum Island Turnpike

An informal organization was made in 1804 in Newburyport by certain gentlemen who had conceived the idea of developing a summer resort on Plum Island, in connection with which they proposed to build a turnpike between the two places. A committee, chosen to estimate the cost of such work, reported so favorably that an application was duly made for a charter, which was granted on the twenty-fourth of February, 1806, incorporating the Plum Island Turnpike and Bridge Corporation. This company was to be allowed to build its road from Rolf's Lane, now Ocean Avenue, to a point on Plum Island about one mile north of Sandy Beach. Following. a careful survey the road was built in the summer of 1806, and continued its existence as a chartered investment for a period of ninety-nine years, making it the long-est-lived turnpike in Massachusetts, and exceeded in longevity only by the Peru Turnpike in Vermont.

Plum Island Turnpike: Westerly end

Currier's *History of Newburyport* devotes quite a little space to this road, and we learn further from it that the company continued its operations in 1807 by building a hotel on the island, thus anticipating the policy put into effect a century later by the electric-car lines, which established places of amusement at the ends of their routes to induce additional riding.

No returns were filed by this company and its monetary affairs are wrapped in mystery. Its career was uneventful until 1839, when a severe storm washed away a portion of the road and badly damaged the bridge. About this time the United States authorities constructed a breakwater in connection with its improvements of Newburyport Harbor, in consequence of which, in the

Plum Island Turnpike: Across the marshes

winter of I 840, the ice was backed up against the bridge, carrying nearly all of it away. Consequently a petition for relief was made to Congress, which on June 4, 1842, passed the "Act for the relief of the Plum Island Bridge and Turnpike Company," giving the corporation eight thousand dollars in compensation.

For many years the corporation was practically extinct, but in 1884 the prospects seemed to justify further action, and business was resumed. In 1887 the property and rights were sold to a company which desired to operate a horse railway over the road, and that form of transportation continued until 1894, when the horses gave place to the buzzing trolley.

By legislative act of May, 1905, the county commissioners were required to lay out the Plum Island Turnpike as a county road, not over six thousand dollars to be paid the company as damages. Essex County records show the finish of the old road on July 22, 1905, one hundred and one years after the project was first agreed upon by the enterprising Newburyport gentlemen.

45. The Worcester Turnpike

Next, on March 7, 1806, came the Worcester Turnpike Corporation with a franchise to build "from Roxbury to Worcester."

In the early days of the Massachusetts Bay Colony there was but one road leading out of Boston—the original of Washington Street, over the Neck. As we learned in connection with Judge Sewall's milestones, at points between two and three miles from the old Boston Town House five roads radiated and led to various adjoining towns. One of these, the Cambridge Road, had from the earliest days been a traveled path, forming the eastern end of the old Connecticut Path; and part of this, comprising what is now

Worcester Turnpike: Where modern improvements left the Turnpike on the hill

Worcester Turnpike: Looking west to Newton Upper Falls

Roxbury and Tremont streets and Huntington Avenue to the Parkway near the Brookline boundary, was formally laid out as a public highway January 19, 1662. The portion lying beyond Muddy River had been publicly dedicated some five years earlier.

The portion of this "ancient Highway" between the present Dudley Street Station of the Boston Elevated Railway and Brookline Village was monopolized by the Worcester Turnpike Corporation when its road was located in 1808, and the long-established free highway became a part of the privately owned toll road. In a paper presented to the Brookline Historical Society, the reader told of the peregrinations of the locating committee, which started from the Boston end and stopped for rest and refreshment at the Punch Bowl Tavern in Brookline. So far they had followed the old road, apparently lacking the courage to locate a road in a new and untried place; but after their reception at the tavern fresh courage arose, and thenceforth they paid no attention to old roads, but laid their compass for the longest possible straight lines. So the turnpike left the "ancient highway" at what is now Brookline Village and blazed a new path through the woods straight to Mitchell's Tavern in Newton, then across the Charles River "near General Eliot's mills," now Newton Upper Falls, near the famous Echo Bridge of the Boston waterworks; thence across the town of Wellesley, which was a part of Needham then, to the "Neck of the Ponds," which was the narrow part of Lake Cochituate in Natick; thence through Framingham, Southboro, Westboro, and Shrewsbury to Shrewsbury Pond, later known as Lake Quinsigamond, and then "to the street in Worcester near the courthouse."

There were ancient milestones on the old road which was thus appropriated for turnpike purposes, two of which fell within the limits thus liable to toll. The first of these, the three-mile stone, has disappeared from its place on Roxbury Street, just beyond Eliot Square, but the four-mile stone may still be seen, directly opposite its original position, embedded in the wall surrounding the grounds of the House of the Good Shepherd, where it was set with the consent of the church authorities, at the solicitation of Mr. Irwin C. Cromack of the Boston Street Department. These were Paul Dudley stones, as attested by the initials "P D" on the one thus preserved. The turnpike itself was marked off in this manner in 1810, the measurements starting from the Boston boundary line. The first of the later ones may be observed near Roxbury Crossing, set in the wall in front of a schoolhouse. It is marked:

To Boston
Line 1 M
1810

Another stands in a location to which it was recently moved for preservation—at the corner of Boylston and Warren streets in Brookline.

Smith, in the preparation of his *History of Newton*, seems to have had access to first-hand information regarding this corporation, for he tells us that the first meeting of the stockholders was held in Concert Hall, on the corner of Court and Hanover streets in Boston, on October 30, 1806. The capital stock was divided into six hundred shares of a par value of two hundred and fifty dollars each, making an investment of $150,000 to build forty miles of road, which allowed about $3750 a mile. No further figures are available, for the company never filed any returns with the secretary of state, as it should have done. Smith also says that sixteen shares were taken by

Worcester Turnpike: Near Parker Street, Newton Center

Worcester Turnpike: Through Wellesley

Newton men, and that there were few dividends, none amounting to six per cent.

The fallacy of straight-line locations was thus observed by Lincoln in his *History of Worcester*:

On this plan [straight line] the turnpike to Boston, going out from the north end of the village, went through a considerable eminence by a deep cutting, passed a deep valley on a lofty embankment, ascended the steep slope of Millstone Hill, crossed Quinsigamond by a floating bridge, and climbed to some of the highest elevations of the country it traversed; when an inconsiderable circuit would have furnished a better and less costly route.

An act passed by the general court March 3, 1809, provided for changing the location of certain gates in order to check the custom of "shunpiking" and also to protect the public from paying full tolls when it used the turnpike for only a part of the journey. The preamble is a dissertation on the "shunpike," which is worth reproducing.

WHEREAS the said Worcester Turnpike Road, as the same is now located and made, makes such intersections of various old roads, over which the same crosses and passes, as to render it easy at all times for persons to travel on the same a greater part of the way, and by turning off on said old roads, near the several places assigned to receive toll, to avoid the payment of the same; and whereas there are several portions of said Turnpike Road, over which there would be a great travel, provided the said corporation were authorized to erect gates, subdividing the toll, established and by their act of incorporation, which would be a great saving and convenience to many people who wish to travel on certain portions of said turnpike if it could be done without paying a full toll. . . .

Worcester Turnpike: Near Cedar Street, Wellesley

Consequently the justices of the court of common pleas were authorized to make such changes in the gates, and signboards giving the subdivided rates were to be erected.

Many interesting taverns stood on the line of the Worcester Turnpike. The Punch Bowl Tavern, which stood on what is now the corner of Washington and Pearl streets in Brookline, was a famous place of resort for gay parties from the surrounding towns, and even from Boston, and it was much frequented by the British officers before the Revolution. Drake, in his *The Town of Roxbury,* thus describes it:

Worcester Turnpike: West of White's Corner

It was of a yellowish color, and had a seat running along the front under an overhanging projection of a part of the second story, where loungers congregated to discuss the news of the day. In front and near each end were large elm trees. Under the westerly one stood a pump. The ancient sign, suspended from a high red post, had for its design a huge bowl and ladle, overhung by a lemon tree laden with fruit, some of which having fallen to the ground, lay around the bowl. This sign, known throughout New England, gave its name to the tavern and village.

Originally it was a two-story, hipped-roof house, and many additions were made from time to time by the purchase of old houses in Boston and vicinity, moving them to the Punch Bowl and tacking them on to those previously assembled. Consequently the old house was a curious medley of rooms of all sorts and sizes, one of which was a large dancing hall. Opened as a public house prior to 1740, the Punch Bowl Tavern served the public for over one hundred years, being torn down in 1839. The Richards Tavern, built about 1770, faced Heath Street near where the turnpike crossed the Newton-Brookline boundary, and the turnpike was built directly behind it, so that became a turnpike tavern and was conducted as such until 1830.

The Mitchell Tavern stood on the turnpike in Newton Highlands on the present corner of Center Street. The Cook Tavern stood until the winter of 1915-16 on the corner where Eliot and Woodward streets come together at the turnpike, and upon its demolition yielded an interesting collection of old coins and pewter ware, when its inner spaces were revealed. Prior to the widening of the street and the building of the Boston and Worcester trolley line, it was a fine old house, with beautiful trees draping over it and surrounded by lilac hedges, as shown in the picture which we reproduce.

Another old tavern stood near the Charles River at the Upper Falls, and until the coming of the railway, about 1900, had before it a handsome sycamore in which was still planted the iron crane from which the sign of the tavern swung.

In Westboro rest and refreshment were to be had at Forbush's Tavern, which stood on the corner of the street now called Lyman. This house had long been built when the turnpike came, but it had the good fortune to be located directly on the line of the new road, so had no difficulty in adapting itself to the new conditions.

One tollgate was located in the rear of the Richards Tavern near the Brookline-Newton line, and another was in Newton Upper Falls, situated in a hollow between the two taverns which were about three quarters of a mile apart. A marsh and quicksand two hundred feet east of the gate obligated travelers to stay in the road, and prevented the much-practiced art of "shunpiking." The old tollhouse at this gate stood for many years on the bank above the street, where it was left by the grading incident to the trolley construction. Another tollgate stood in Needham, now Wellesley, just east of Blossom Street, according to Clark's *History of Needham*.

The operation of a toll road over the ancient highway in Roxbury could not have been remunerative, especially over the section between Wait's Mills, now called Roxbury Crossing, because twenty years ago a grade crossing of the railroad existed there, and the easterly end of the turnpike. There must have been a great deal of short-distance travel over parts of that section, paying no toll at all but wearing out the road which the corporation was bound to repair. In 1810 a turnpike charter was granted to the Boston Neck Turnpike Corporation, which it seems must have been sought in the interest of the Worcester Turnpike Corporation, as the construction of that road would have given the latter company a better connection with the road leading into Boston. But the corporation was held strictly to its obligations to maintain the ancient highway until the opening of the Punch Bowl Road of the Boston and Roxbury Mill Corporation. That road connected the Worcester Turnpike at the Punch Bowl Tavern with the westerly end of the road over the Mill Dam, and was opened for travel in 1821. By following this new route, over a mile was saved on the journey into Boston, and it can readily be seen that the operation of the ancient highway became still more a "labor of love," and we are not surprised that the corporation now made earnest efforts to be rid of the burden. But not until 1826 did it succeed when, on February 15, an act was passed relieving the corporation of all of the road east of what is now Brookline Village, providing that it paid two hundred and fifty dollars to the town of Roxbury to recompense that town for assuming

The Arch in Brookline

the road. The act declared that the easterly terminus of the turnpike should thenceforth be at "the arch in Brookline." The arch spanned the turnpike where it left the old road and entered upon the new location. Overhead the traveler westward bound read "Worcester 1810 40 Miles." Just why this arch should have been built at this point, or why it should have been built anywhere, is hard to determine. Its location marked the dividing line between the new road which the corporation built, and the ancient highway which it had appropriated, and it may be that the corporation, exasperated at the continual protests and faultfinding which always followed the passing of an old road into a turnpike, erected this arch to mark the beginning of the section on which it was morally as well as legally entitled to collect toll.

The "ancient highway" at once became the Washington Street of Roxbury. In 1868 the name of part was changed to Tremont Street; in 1874 another portion was named Roxbury Street; and in 1895 the end at the Brookline boundary was called Huntington Avenue.

Lake Quinsigamond, then called Long Pond, stretched its length about equally on each side of the air line which the turnpike surveyors felt obliged to follow and offered a serious engineering problem. The water was over five hundred feet wide at the desired crossing and from fifty to seventy feet in depth, and the early bridge builders, having no other material than wood, might have been excused for pronouncing the task impossible. But turnpike builders overcame all obstacles when a straight line was to be attained, and a floating bridge was designed. The first was a short-lived structure, lasting only a few years. It was made of two or three tiers of round timber laid lengthwise and then crosswise, and then overlaid with a course of hewn timber covered with plank and fastened to large abutments at the shores. The cost of this bridge was about nine thousand dollars, and it was soon found to be too weak for safety, and work was started on a much more ambitious structure.

Nine piers were sunk in the lake, on the line of the bridge, about thirty feet apart, the center one being sixty feet square and the others sixty by thirty. These piers were constructed separately in cob-house fashion. The first course was laid on the surface of the water above its ultimate resting place, and consisted of a mat of heavy timbers parallel to each other and covering a space the size of the pier. The second course was then laid crosswise on the first, each intersection being pinned by wooden treenails, and so on, the increasing weight causing the structure to sink gradually until the first course of timbers had found its resting place on the bottom of the lake, with several courses above the surface. It seems like a miracle that such construction remained perpendicular until the bottom was reached, but all the piers did so, and connections were made from one to the other by stringers covered with planking on which a heavy bed of gravel was placed.

Worcester Turnpike: Through the woods in Northboro

On account of the varying depth of mud on the bottom of the pond, the piers settled unequally and rapidly fell out of plumb. The buoyancy of the material caused such strains that many of the joints opened and timbers started from their fastenings. Efforts to remedy the trouble by piling on heavier loadings of gravel only hastened the end, and on the morning of September 19, 1817, while the workmen were at breakfast, the buoyant piers tipped and broke apart, the uncompleted bridge fell in all directions, and the surface of the lake was covered with the wreckage. That fifty-four thousand feet of lumber had been used and the cost ran as high as thirteen thousand dollars is learned from a history of Shrewsbury, published in 1826 by Andrew H. Ward.

In the spring of 1818 another floating bridge which had been built on the ice along the west shore was towed into place. This bridge cost about six thousand dollars and, in 1826, was still well answering the purpose.

Before the day of the railroad the old turnpike was ready to give up the struggle. Four and a half years before the opening of the Boston and Worcester Railroad, the corporation petitioned that its road between Kimball's Tavern in Needham and the Punch Bowl Tavern in Brookline might be taken off its hands; and a year later in January, 1833, Middlesex County complied with the request as far as its jurisdiction extended. Norfolk County also made the road free, except a portion in Needham adjacent to Newton Upper Falls.

The corporation was dissolved by the legislature March 10, 1841, and all of its road not previously thrown open was discontinued. Permission was given to Worcester and Shrewsbury, if they took over the bridge crossing

Lake Quinsigamond, to collect tolls thereon under supervision of the county commissioners, but whether they did or not has not been ascertained.

Thus were left considerable sections of the old road which had no standing whatever, being discontinued as highways. The inhabitants of Framingham, in January, 1843, petitioned the county commissioners for a public dedication of the portion of the turnpike in their town, and in September of that year the westerly seven hundred and two rods of the Framingham portion became a county road. The Natick section had been so treated the year before and the short section remaining at Newton Upper Falls received the same degree in 1843 and 1844. Worcester County took a hand in 1845 and laid out the road from Worcester to Lake Quinsigamond.

The old Worcester Turnpike is known to-day as Boylston Street in Brookline and Newton; as Worcester Street in Wellesley and Natick; as Eastern Avenue in Framingham; as Belmont Street in Westboro and Worcester; while Southboro and Shrewsbury seem to know it by the name of Old Turnpike. For much of its length it is followed by the cars of the Boston and Worcester Street Railway.

The passion for straight lines led this road apart from the previously beaten paths and it passed through no centers except that of Framingham. The prevailing impression at that time regarding turnpikes is echoed in the diary, kept by the author's grandmother during a journey which she took in 1829, the return being made over this road from Worcester to Boston. She wrote: "We rode principally on the turnpike and did not see many villages."

46. The Housatonic River Turnpike

Another project for connecting Hartford with the Hudson Valley was launched when the Housatonic River Turnpike Corporation was incorporated March 7, 1806. The road of this corporation connected with the road of a New York company, which led to Albany, at the state boundary near the northwest corner of West Stockbridge, and ran through West Stockbridge and Stockbridge to Stockbridge Center, whence it followed up the valley of the Housatonic River to the present East Lee Village, where it joined the road of the Tenth Massachusetts Corporation.

The directors promptly entered petition with the Berkshire county court for a location for their road and a committee was at once appointed, but progress was slow. In 1808 the land question was submitted to a jury, and a year later the awards were made. In 1809, after an alteration in the layout, the road was completed, accepted, and the location of the gates determined.

The cost of the turnpike was given to the secretary of state as $16,647, which gives a proportion per mile of about $1260. A return was made in the year 1818, only, which showed a net loss of $71.29. That the receipts were not satisfactory to the investors is plain from the fact that in 1815 an act was secured from the legislature, allowing the collection of full tolls instead of fractional at the gate in Lee. That proving unsatisfactory, a general revision of gates and tolls was made by the act passed the next year. Two half-gates in West Stockbridge were moved so as to permit the erection of an additional half-gate in that town, which was to be "east of the road leading from Great Barrington to the village of West Stockbridge." A new scale of collections at the Lee gate was given at length in the act, by which the former status of a half-gate was restored, although the allowed tolls became about twenty-five per cent higher than commonly authorized.

The *History of the County of Berkshire*, to which we have often referred, speaks of this turnpike as, by means of its connections, opening intercourse with Springfield, and states that it is a road "of great and increasing travel."

Legislative permission was given in 1808 for a revision of the location, but it was expressly stated that no change was to be made at either end of the layout already made. Nevertheless the committee appointed for that purpose did make a change in the western end, at the New York line, and the court approved the same, and a compliant legislature, the next year, accepted the action and confirmed it.

E. Kingsley entered a petition in 1837, in consequence of which the gates were ordered to be opened, probably until certain repairs had been made on the road. An act passed February 19, 1841, allowed the Berkshire county commissioners to throw open the western end of the road, but apparently they were not particularly keen to do this as no record of such action has been found, a suggestion which gains support when we read that in September, 1842, the commissioners dismissed a petition made by the corporation to have its road discontinued. In July, 1851, the company renewed its effort to get rid of its road, but evidently without success, for we find another petition for a public layout made in July, 1853. As we do not find the road on the records again we conclude that the last is the date on which the road finally became free.

The indications are that the old road was the original Albany Street and Stockbridge Street in West Stockbridge, but no name seems to follow it over the rest of its meanderings.

A road having the precipitous Stockbridge and Deonkook Mountains across its path could not expect to adhere to the straight-line principle, and it is refreshing to find this turnpike winding in and out with some regard to resulting grades.

47. The Alford and Egremont Turnpike

The Alford and Egremont Turnpike Corporation, March 13, 1806, was organized to build a road leading from the Twelfth Massachusetts Turnpike at South Egremont Village, northwesterly across the towns of Egremont and Alford to a connection with the New York corporation's Hillsdale and Chatham Turnpike at the state line, passing through the villages of Egremont Plain and North Egremont.

By a condition in its charter the company was required to divide with the Twelfth Massachusetts all tolls collected in the town of Alford, the Twelfth to have one fifth. This condition is hard to understand as the new road was to open a territory in which the Twelfth had not operated, the nearest point in which was fully three and a half miles from any point on the road of the Twelfth, and, at this distance it looks like the price paid by the new venture to remove opposition by the old. But the onerous condition was cleverly evaded before the opening of the road by securing an innocent appearing act from the legislature, which allowed the erection of the gate in Egremont instead of in Alford, in consequence of which there were no tolls collected in the town of Alford.

Between 1806 and 1810 the company was busy with its legal preliminaries, and by 1812 the road was in full operation, when certain roads in the two towns, made unnecessary by the building of the turnpike, were discontinued.

The length of the road was about six miles, and the cost was returned as $8218.66, or about $1370 per mile. Returns were made of the operations for the first two years, showing net profits of $93 and $139 respectively.

Three quarters of a mile of the road was relocated in 1824, the act providing therefor giving the exact route by a surveyor's description.

A bridge on this road was the cause of much concern to the patrons about 1839, and failing to convince the corporation of the possibility of accident they appealed to the county commissioners. That body decreed that, unless the bridge was put in safe condition by August 8, 1839, the tollgate should be thrown open and no tolls collected, which action proved sufficient, for the record shows that the bridge was repaired. The last record of this corporation is dated January, 1842, when one Forbes made petition to have the gate opened. This, we presume, indicates the date at which the road became free.

Tourists desiring to follow this road should proceed directly from South Egremont to Egremont Plain and then follow the road up the bank of the Green River to the New York line.

48. The Lancaster and Bolton Turnpike

The road built by the Lancaster and Bolton Turnpike Corporation, under its charter granted March 13, 1806, was a small affair, but it seems to have filled a gap between two systems of good free roads. The location is noticeable because it extended from Jacob Fisher's in Lancaster to Jacob Fisher's in Bolton, and from the east end of Main Street in Lancaster to the west end of Main Street in Bolton. The road is known to-day as the "Seven Bridge Road," suggestive of the "straight line" disregarded for watercourses as well as hills.

The Worcester County records show the location of this turnpike in 1806 "from Leominster road in Lancaster, through Bolton, to the County line," but the maps filed by the towns in 1830 show only about two and a half miles of turnpike between the limits as first stated, connecting at the easterly end with the ancient "Great Road " to Boston. According to a paper in the *Proceedings* of the Fitchburg Historical Society the better grades on this road diverted a great deal of travel from the Union Turnpike. There seems to be good reason to believe that this was so, and it offers damaging evidence against the "straight line" obsession which was fatal to so many turnpikes. Over the Union and the Cambridge and Concord, turnpike improvements were offered all the way to Boston, but adherence to the "straight line" carried them over so many hills that the old free roads through Stow, Sudbury, and Waltham were preferred. The principal lines of mail stages between Boston and Albany, through northwestern Massachusetts, followed this route over the Lancaster and Bolton Turnpike until they were superseded by the railroad trains.

Construction cost amounted to $6291.90, or about $2520 a mile, a figure which suggests that the Worcester record of the layout as extending to the county line may be right after all. In that case the cost per mile would be reduced to about $900. But, as stated, the 1830 maps limit the road to two and a half miles, and no record has been found discontinuing any part of the turnpike prior to that date.

The commissioners of Worcester County made the Lancaster and Bolton Turnpike a public road in 1847.

49. The Wrentham and Walpole Turnpike

After 1751, at which time a new road was laid out by the town officials of Attleboro and Wrentham, connecting the old Boston Post Road, at a point near the upper end of the present North Attleboro Village, with the old Woonsocket Road near Wampum Station on the Wrentham Branch of the New Haven Road, the main road from Boston to Providence passed through the centers of Norwood, Walpole, Wrentham, and North Attleboro, along the lines of the present-day state highway. The Norfolk and Bristol Turnpike sought to divert travel from this route by building a road in a straight line from Norwood to North Attleboro, but the grades were steep, and the country unproductive, and travelers still held to the old lines. A seven-mile section of the old route led through wild woods and cedar swamps between Walpole and $IWalpole, Mass.Wrentham, and it is easy to imagine that the road was poor and soft. On March 12, 1806, the Wrentham and Walpole Turnpike Corporation was incorporated for the purpose of improving this part of the route.

The general-law provision that five disinterested freeholders of the county should locate the road was brushed aside by the legislature two days later, when an act was passed providing that Eliphalet Loud, Elijah Crane, and Benjamin Randall should be the committee for that purpose. The location was made and damages were awarded and reported to the court in 1807. But some time elapsed without further action, and we find the company before the legislature of 1811 asking for an extension of the time for completing the road. It was allowed until March 14, 1812. Little seems to be known about the road. An old resident, one of the family which gave the name to Pondville, was once asked if that road was ever a toll road. After a brief hesitation he replied, "Yes, but it didn't last long." Norfolk County records show that it was laid out as a public highway in 1830.

Anyone desiring to trace the old turnpike to-day should simply go from Wrentham to Walpole. There is but one road, and it cannot be missed, except in the edge of Walpole Center, where alterations due to grade-crossing abolitions have badly warped the original layout.

50. The Stoughton Turnpike

The act incorporating the Stoughton Turnpike Corporation June 23, 1806, is noteworthy for being the first one in which the judgment of the persons investing the money is mentioned as a factor to determine the location of the road. This company was to build from a point in the "Old Bay Road" in Canton, about two miles beyond the westerly end of the Brush Hill Turnpike, to a point on the Taunton and South Boston Turnpike in the town of Easton. It may be noted that the Taunton and South Boston, mentioned in this act, was incorporated a day later, and had no actual existence at the time, much less was there any such road.

December 13, 1806, the five disinterested freeholders of Bristol County were appointed to locate the road, and in September, 1808, they reported, the section in Norfolk County being located at the same time. But work did not advance at once, and the company secured an extension of its time to June, 1813.

Northerly end, Stoughton Turnpike

Stoughton Turnpike: Near the Stoughton-Easton line

This turnpike is now the state highway known as Turnpike Street in Canton, and Washington Street in Stoughton and Easton. In its active days it offered a through route from Taunton to Roxbury, except for the two miles intervening between its northerly end and the end of the Brush Hill. At the southerly end, as stated, it connected with the Taunton and South Boston, which entered Taunton, and, by the construction of a later turnpike, through turnpike travel to Providence was provided.

Such a franchise as that of the Stoughton Turnpike would be almost impossible to obtain at this time. It closely paralleled a direct route, half of which was already built or under construction, with the other half seeking

Stoughton Turnpike: South Easton

incorporation and ready to proceed. It depended upon another company for entrance into Taunton and, by its connection, would take away one half of that company's through business. Evidently the principle of protecting investments in public utilities was not then established.

The Stoughton Turnpike Corporation was dissolved by act of the legislature in March, 1839, and its road was laid out as a county highway in 1840, except a portion in Stoughton, which was so laid out in 1856.

51. The Taunton and South Boston Turnpike

The Taunton and South Boston Turnpike Corporation was created by act of June 24, 1806, with the right to build a road

from Taunton Green, so called. . . . nearly on a straight line to the crossway over the Great Cedar Swamp, so called, and from thence over said crossway near to the house of Joshua Gilmore in Easton, and from thence through the towns of Bridgewater and Stoughton, the most direct and convenient route to the Blue Hill Turnpike.

Petitions entered late in 1806 resulted in the location of the road and in awards of damages during the year 1807. The report of the committee to locate the road and assess damages within the county of Bristol is found in full on the records in Taunton, and gives some interesting data on a subject generally indefinite.

The length of the road in that county was 9.11 miles, of which 3.08 miles, or 33.8 per cent, was built on land which the owners freely gave to the corporation. Twenty-three per cent of the right of way was obtained by purchase at an agreed price, details of which are not given; while, with the owners of 43.2 per cent of the needed land, no agreement could be reached, and the corporation was obliged to condemn the land and have the price fixed by the committee. That was done on twenty-nine parcels covering a length of twelve hundred and fifty-eight rods, on which the committee appraised the damage at a total of $2009. The corporation through a director, Samuel Fales, appealed from two of the awards and succeeded in obtaining a total reduction of twenty-five dollars. Thus, from the figures actually available, we see that the right of way in Bristol County cost about $505 a mile, or at the rate of about $63 an acre.

Two hundred and seventy-five rods of the way was through the Great Cedar Swamp, which occupies portions of Bridgewater, West Bridgewater, Easton, Raynham, and Taunton, swinging in a big semicircle northerly and westerly from Nippenicket Pond in Bridgewater to Scadding Pond in Taunton. The cedar swamps of southeastern Massachusetts plainly were not designed for road building. The straight, slender cedars grow so thickly that only the fittest survive, and the ones that die are so tightly wedged in the living mass that they cannot fall, but continue to stand, ghostlike, greatly increasing the difficulty of cutting a way through. One may walk at one

Taunton and South Boston Turnpike: Park Street, Stoughton

moment on firm soil and then suddenly step through a hole so deep that the length of his leg does not locate the bottom. Soundings have determined the hard bottom in several of these swamps to be anywhere from six inches to thirty feet below the surface, with water almost always within the depression made by a footstep. The surface is composed of a network of large roots, generally so thickly woven that the soil is held between them, but always liable to yield through a larger hole when a careless foot marks its center. Through such an inferno the builders of the Taunton and South Boston Turnpike had the courage to make .86 mile of their road. And it was the

Taunton and South Boston Turnpike: Crossing the cedar swamp

Taunton and South Boston Turnpike: Pearl Street, Brockton

obstacle presented by this cedar swamp to the building of earlier roads which gave the opportunity for a turnpike to be built where public funds could not be applied.

Enough has already been said concerning the through route from Taunton to Boston offered by this road and its connections, the Blue Hill and the Dorchester. The junction with the Blue Hill was made in the northerly part of the town of Randolph at what is now the corner of North Main and High streets. Thence this turnpike followed the roads now known as High Street in Randolph, Turnpike Street in Stoughton, Pearl Street in Brockton, Turn-

Taunton and South Boston Turnpike: Old tollhouse in Raynham

pike Street in Easton, and Broadway in Raynham and Taunton.

A tollhouse long stood in Raynham, near the Taunton line, where it stood so many years ago in an official capacity. Respected for its old associations it was allowed to remain, even through state highway improvement, and pushed its clapboards close to the macadamized portion until the road had been free for over sixty years.

Twenty-one and a half miles were built at a cost of $34,434.61, or about $1600 a mile. Returns were made to the state house from 1810 to 1849. . . . The showing is remarkably poor, the gross earnings never running as high as three per cent, while the expenses were generally close to them and often in excess.

An act passed in 1817 shows that this road suffered, too, from "shunpikers," for a penalty is there laid for all practicing such evasions.

Kingman's *History of North Bridgewater* (Brockton) testifies that at one time there was a heavy travel over this road, both of freight and passengers.

April 1, 1813, Joshua Gilmore, agent for the corporation, made appeal to the court. The selectmen of Easton had laid out a new road, taking some of the corporation's land, refusing any compensation therefor. The records show that a jury summoned by Abiezer Dean, coroner, found for the corporation in the sum of $23.17 and costs.

The Taunton and South Boston Turnpike became a public road throughout its length in 1851.

52. The Hingham and Quincy Turnpike

Prior to the construction of the road of the Hingham and Quincy Bridge and Turnpike Corporation with its bridges, travelers between those towns were obliged to go around the heads of Weymouth Fore and Back rivers, over Paine's Hill and through Braintree, finding themselves at the end of the trip only about half as far from the starting point as the distance they had covered. The corporation which was to remedy this difficulty was created by act of March 5, 1808, after a most spirited opposition from representatives of the shipping interests and from residents of the section which expected to be left on one side if the new road was built. Most conspicuous in the opposition was Minot Thayer, who has been mentioned as "one of the most permanent and active members of the legislature," and under whose leadership his home town of Braintree made a strong protest. It is difficult, at this time, to understand the fear caused by the proposition to erect bridges across the rivers named, especially when it is borne in mind that they were to be equipped as drawbridges. But it seems to have been generally accepted that such bridges would constitute a public nuisance, and even the people living on the land joined in the objections. Such strength in the hostile forces could

not be altogether overcome, and before the passage of the act of incorporation the petitioners had to consent to three conditions:

1. Payment to all vessels which passed the draw.

2. After 25 years and within 27 years the bridges might be removed as common
nuisances.

3. No land to be taken until payment was made or tendered.

The third condition was but a just one and is practically what is now
required of railroads under the general law. The second may have seemed
harsh, as it contemplated the summary removal of the bridges at the end of
twenty-five years, but the natural developments within that time made this
condition a dead letter. But the first condition was a real burden and was
most unjustly borne by the company for twenty years.

The section of the act of incorporation which prescribed this onerous
condition required that the bridge at Fore River should have "a suitable
drawer" not less than thirty-four feet wide, and the Back River Bridge, one
not less than twenty-four feet. The payments were to be made to the master
of each loaded vessel

of more than fifteen tons burthen that shall pass through said Drawers respectively,
for the purpose of unloading her cargo, three cents a ton for each and every ton, said
vessel shall measure.

It may well be queried, even by residents of the neighborhood of these
bridges, what navigable streams of such great importance the Fore and Back
rivers could be. A glance at the map will hardly explain the matter, for there
one will see but two crooked salt-water creeks penetrating hardly two miles
inland, and the reader must bear in mind that the turnpike was yet in its
infancy and that the early colonial dependence upon water transportation
had not yet been displaced. To the inhabitants of the town of Weymouth and
of the adjoining parts of Braintree and Hingham these water routes must
have seemed indispensable for the transport of their products to the markets
of Boston. A suggestion of the extent of the commerce on these rivers is
found in the returns made by the corporation. It appears from the payments
which were made that 14,308 tons passed the two bridges in 1818; 18,006
tons in 1819; while, in 1824, 11,612 tons sailed Fore River and 2408 tons
were warped through the draw of the Back River Bridge.

In 1909 the United States Navy Department acquired the land along the
easterly shore of Back River for a naval supply base, not anticipating serious
disadvantages from the presence of a drawbridge below. But navigation had
so fallen away from the old river that an antiquated form of draw was then
in use which, it was said, only yielded to the combined strength of eight men,
so the old bridge and its draw soon gave way to one more satisfactory to the
navy's demands.

Fore River Bridge has long had a modern opening, through which pass many vessels bearing supplies and raw materials for the great shipbuilding yards to which the river has lent its name, while it opens from time to time to let out a recently launched "mistress of the seas" or an unromantic "molasses tanker."

But the corporation found that its troubles were not over with the securing of its franchise. It has been noted that of the ten turnpike corporations incorporated next preceding this one not one did any construction, and most of the companies seeking to build at this time were obliged to apply to the legislature for an extension of their time. The Hingham and Quincy felt the hard times with the others and was a long time in raising the necessary money, but enough had been secured by February 3, 1812, to justify holding the first meeting and developing the general plans, and the first ground was broken in Weymouth on June 3 of that year.

At an early meeting of the board of directors it was voted to hire a superintendent, who should be paid seven shillings six pence a day. He was "to superintend the men and to work on the road to the best of his ability." Authority was given him to hire six men at a dollar a day, and seventeen more at twenty-two dollars a month. They voted to buy a scraper and a yoke of oxen and get ready to tear things generally. A local builder contracted to erect the tollhouse at the Back River Bridge for five hundred dollars.

Several committees were appointed to solicit subscriptions to the stock of the corporation, and one committee was intrusted with the single duty of so presenting the advantages of the enterprise to Reverend Henry Coleman of Hingham as to induce him to give his aid and influence to the undertaking.

Five miles of road, with two bridges of great magnitude for those days, were completed by November 19, 1812, on which day the courts of Norfolk and Plymouth formally accepted the road and allowed it to open for business. The cost was returned as twenty-four thousand dollars, but, on account of the two bridges, cannot be proportioned by miles.

On the opening day Mrs. John Adams, wife of the second president of the United States, wrote:

At twelve o'clock called for cousin Smith, by previous engagement, to accompany me to the bridge at Quincy Point being the first day of passing it. The day was pleasant; the scenery delightful. Passed both bridges and entered Hingham. Returned before three o'clock.

Much more might have been expressed on the subject of making a complete journey between twelve and three which previously had required the greater part of a day.

The next issue of the *Columbian Centinel*, November 21, 1812, announced:

The Hingham and Quincy Turnpike Road which shortens the distance between the two towns nearly one half—presenting the finest of views, and the most delightful ride in the vicinity of Boston, is now open for the accommodation of the public.

Through the first winter the Plymouth mail stage was allowed free passage over the new turnpike, but, April 1, 1813, that came under toll requirements also.

The bugbear of the drawbridge did not materialize, but the fear died hard, and it was not until 1832 that it disappeared entirely. By that time the benefits of the road and bridges and the rights of travelers by land had become so well established that the legislature on March 12, 1832, repealed the unjust provision, and relieved the corporation from further payments to masters of vessels. The company had made frequent efforts in previous years to obtain relief from this condition, and we learn from Nash's *History of Weymouth* that that town, in meeting on April 21, 1820, voted to appoint a committee to oppose the petition which had been made for that purpose.

In the fifty years of the turnpike's operation but two accidents occurred, the first in 1824, for which Benjamin S. Williams recovered one thousand dollars, and the second in 1844, when Reverend Thomas Whittemore was paid one hundred and fifty dollars.

A notable record of long service is shown by this company. The office of president was filled by Martin Fearing of Hingham for the forty-three years between 1820 and 1863; Lemuel Bracket of Quincy performed the duties of clerk for one year less from 1813 to 1855; and Thomas Cushing commenced his duties as toll gatherer November 20, 1818, only to relinquish them when the road and bridges became free July 4, 1864. Upon the dissolution of the corporation a gift of thirty dollars was voted to him.

Returns of business done were made by this company from 1824 to the end of its existence. . . . The receipts did not drop off as abruptly upon the advent of railroad competition as did those of other companies. But that the management feared such a result appears from an item of $84.08 for legislative expenses in 1845, "remonstrating against Railroad Petitions." A most noticeable drop may be seen in the expenses following the year 1833, when payments to masters of vessels ceased. The gross earnings of the Hingham and Quincy seem to have generally run from eight to twelve per cent of the cost of the road, with the expenditures far enough below in most years to yield a fair dividend. But it must be remembered that this was more of a bridge proposition than a turnpike, and bridges were usually more profitable.

The legislature of 1860 provided for the laying out of this turnpike and bridges as a public highway by the county commissioners, if the corporation consented; but evidently consent was not forthcoming, for we find more drastic action two years later. April 30, 1862, the great and general court peremptorily laid it out as, and decreed that it should become on the fourth day of the next July, a public highway, except that the selectmen of the three towns were to collect tolls on the two bridges for two years more. As all the gates maintained by the corporation were the ones on the two bridges, matters were not much improved until the two years had passed.

As the legislature did not provide any compensation for the taking away of the corporation's franchise and property, the supreme court, upon the company's appeal, appointed three commissioners who awarded damages to the amount of $ 17, 810.15. In the final distribution of this amount each stockholder received $106.75 for each share of stock, this being the only case, as far as is now known, in which the original investment was recovered.

In accordance with the above-mentioned act, the road and bridge passed into the control of the town officials July 4, 1862, and became free of all tolls July 4, 1864.

The last echo of the company's affairs was heard in 1870, when the legislature enacted that the governor should appoint commissioners to determine which towns, and in what proportion, should bear the expense of laying out the Hingham and Quincy turnpike and bridges.

To-day the turnpike serves the public along the same old routes but without recompense. As Beal Street it is known in Hingham; as Bridge Street in Weymouth; and as Washington Street in Quincy. . . .

53. The Hudson Turnpike

We have already seen that the road of the Housatonic River Company terminated at the northwest corner of the town of West Stockbridge, where it connected with a New York turnpike which continued the journey to Albany. There was another New York turnpike which came to its end at the West Stockbridge line, but a mile south of the junction made by the Housatonic River. This was the Hudson Turnpike, and it came from the town on the river of the same name, and at its terminus found itself with an intervening distance of about two and a half miles in West Stockbridge from an improved road or important center. So the Hudson Turnpike Corporation was chartered March 8, 1808, possibly by the owners of the New York company, to build "from the bridge at Thayer's Mills in West Stockbridge . . . . to the west line of this Commonwealth, in the same town . . . in the most convenient place to accommodate the public travel."

As the road thus contemplated was only about two and a half miles in length, it does not seem probable that a separate corporation was financed for the purpose of building it, and on account of the similarity of their names it seems justifiable to assume that the Massachusetts Hudson company and the New York company of the same designation were children of the same financial parents. But if so, difficulties must have been encountered in administering the affairs of the two companies jointly, for the Massachusetts Hudson Turnpike became practically a part of the Housatonic River, and was treated and considered as a branch of that road.

The Hudson Turnpike was located, built, and accepted in Berkshire County in 1808, and apparently was the road which to-day leads from West Stockbridge almost due west, passing south of Crane Pond to the New York line.

It was laid out as a public highway, in connection with the Housatonic River Turnpike, in 1853.

54. The Douglas, Sutton, and Oxford Turnpike

The last act passed in 1808 incorporated the Douglas, Sutton, and Oxford Turnpike Corporation June 10. This company spent $6256.26 in the construction of about eleven miles of road, or at the rate of about $570 per mile. By its charter it was authorized to commence its road at Douglas Center and run thence through the extreme southwesterly corner of Sutton, and into Oxford as far as the county road near where the Central Turnpike was later built; but the committee appointed by the Worcester court saw fit to amend the act of the legislature and proceeded to locate the road from a point on the Rhode Island line, where the Providence and Douglas Turnpike of Rhode Island terminated. From that point the road ran straight, in continuation of the line of the Providence and Douglas, for about five miles to Douglas Center; thence over the line of the present Northwest Main Street, winding around the easterly shore of Whiting's Pond in Douglas, and through Sutton, and into Oxford, as already explained.

Douglas, Sutton, and Oxford Turnpike: Southeast Main Street, Douglas

Douglas, Sutton, and Oxford Turnpike: At the Rhode Island line

Only once did this company file a return, and that, in 1812, gave only the gross receipts, which were $186.47—about three per cent on the cost of the road.

Daniels, in his *History of Oxford*, mentions this road, but only to state that it was finished in 1810, and thrown open to the public in 1834, which latter date is also found on the Worcester County records.

55. The Great Barrington and Alford Turnpike

The Great Barrington and Alford Turnpike Corporation was incorporated in 1811 on June 25. This company apparently built its road from the county road at the northerly end of the Fifteenth Massachusetts Turnpike, in Great Barrington, to the New York line, circling around the easterly and southerly side of Monument Mountain, and running westerly by Jacob Van Deusen's house, and south of Long Pond, and far enough into Alford to enable it to turn a corner in that town; thence southwesterly across the town of Egremont, passing through North Egremont Village and south of Prospect Lake, and heading, at its westerly terminus, for the village of Hudson on the Hudson River in the state of New York.

The road described was about nine and a half miles in length, and cost, according to the return at the state house, $8798.71, or about $925 a mile. The location was made and the road built in 1812, according to the Berkshire records, and an old road was discontinued as a public highway on account of the turnpike having absorbed it.

Returns of business done were filed for one year only, 1815, in which year the net earnings were $169.41, or a trifle less than two per cent on the cost of the road.

A portion of the turnpike in Great Barrington was made free on petition of the corporation, April 26, 1831, the balance becoming a part of the public road system in 1846. Apparently the corporation was not the moving party at the latter date, for the records show that it made petition for a jury to estimate the compensation to be awarded it for the loss of its privileges. The petition was refused and the Great Barrington and Alford passed into public management.

56. The Mill Dam

Although not a turnpike corporation, the Boston and Roxbury Mill Corporation, chartered June 14, 1814, had authority to do a turnpike business on the mill dam which it was to construct, and it did operate one of the most important toll roads for many years.

This corporation was organized primarily for the purpose of impounding the tidal waters in the basin known as the Back Bay, which lay on the westerly side of the original Boston peninsular, and by drawing off the same during low-water periods, to derive power for manufacturing purposes. To accomplish this the corporation was authorized to build a dam from the present corner of Beacon and Charles streets, in Boston, to the upland in Brookline at Sewalls' Point, with two other dams tending to turn the water through the sluices provided in the main dam. This latter was to be not less than forty-two feet wide on the top, and was to be provided with locks sufficient in size to pass rafts of logs and lumber containing not over ten thousand feet. The capitalization of the corporation was not to be over two million dollars.

The turnpike provision was found in section three of the act of incorporation, which read:

Be it further enacted, That the said Corporation shall have power to make and finish the dam, in this Act first mentioned and connect the different parts thereof by bridges and causeways, so as to render the same a good and substantial road, suitable for the passing of men, loaded teams, carts, and carriages of all kinds, and shall open a road not more than eighty feet and not less than forty-two feet wide, from some point of said Dam, where it crosses the marshes in Brookline, to the end of the Worcester Turnpike, near the Punch Bowl Tavern, so called, in said Brookline, which road shall be made in a straight line, as nearly as can be done with convenience; and when the road on said Dam shall be finished, railed at the sides, and furnished with lamps to the satisfaction of the Selectmen of Boston, the said Corporation may receive toll for passing over the same, at the same rate which is now granted to the Proprietors of the West Boston Bridge.

A provision that no tolls should be collected until two of the dams were completed was amended two years later, when it was enacted that toll might be collected whenever either of the dams was finished sufficiently to yield a power equal to that required to turn twenty pair of common millstones, one half of which power was to be actually in use.

"Boston's Growth," a pamphlet published by the State Street Trust Company, tells us that work was commenced on the main dam in June, 1814, but Winship's *Historical Brighton* gives the date as 1818. The dam was built along the line of the present Beacon Street from the corner of Charles Street to the junction with what is now known as Brookline Avenue and Commonwealth Avenue; and Brookline Avenue was built by the Mill Corporation from the end of its dam at Sewalls' Point to the Punch Bowl Tavern, on the Worcester Turnpike, as required in its charter. According to "Boston's Growth," the construction of this mill dam furnishes the first record of the importation of Irish laborers. The required stone was obtained from the quarries on the adjacent Parker Hill, and the completion was made the occasion of a civic celebration comprising a parade and a reception by the town fathers.

The importance of the turnpike provided by this improvement can be readily appreciated by reference to the map. Previously the only access to Boston by land had been over the Dorchester Turnpike and the bridge in South Boston; over the Neck, along the present Washington Street; and over the West Boston Bridge which connected the metropolis with Cambridge. Hence the large territory occupied by Waltham, Newton, and the country behind them had been obliged to make the wide detour either through Cambridge or Roxbury, while over the new Mill Dam Road its inhabitants could make a direct trip to the center of Boston. Naturally, as the operation of a toll road was but an incidental item in the larger scheme, and since the length of the road was so slight, the allowed tolls were not to be like those on more extended turnpikes. We have seen that tolls at the same rate as allowed on West Boston Bridge were to be collected, so let us look at the charter of that corporation. The proprietors of the West Boston Bridge were incorporated March 6, 1792, for the purpose of building a bridge between Cambridge and Boston, on the site of the present monumental Cambridge Bridge. Three hundred pounds a year, later reduced to two hundred, was to be paid to Harvard College for assistance of needy students. Tolls were to be collected as follows:

Each foot passenger or one person passing, 2/3 of a penny.

Single horse cart, sled, or sleigh, 4 pence.

One person and horse, 2 pence, 2/3 of a penny.

Each wheelbarrow, hand cart, and every other vehicle capable of carrying like weight, 1-1/3 penny.

Each single horse and chaise, chair, or sulkey, 8 pence.

Coaches, chariots, phaetons, and curricles, 1 shilling.

All other wheeled carriages or sleds drawn by more than one horse, 6 pence.

Sleighs drawn by more than one beast, 6 pence.

Neat horses or cattle exclusive of those rode or in carriages or teams, 1-1/3 penny each.

Swine and sheep, 4 pence per dozen and proportionally.

The dam was completed, and the road opened for travel July 2, 1821, and at once became a most important avenue into Boston. It was considered one of the grandest constructions in the world. The sides of the dam were built of solid stone for eight thousand feet in length, from three to eight feet in thickness and twelve to seventeen feet high, while the width between the walls varied from fifty to one hundred feet. The material was the local pudding stone of Roxbury and granite from Weymouth. Over a mile was saved for the travelers over the Worcester Turnpike by turning off at the Punch Bowl Tavern and taking the Mill Corporation's road to the Mill Dam, and thence into Boston, which was undoubtedly the cause of the Worcester company's being willing in 1826 to pay the town of Roxbury two hundred and fifty dollars in consideration of being released from obligation to maintain its road easterly of the point of diversion. This Punch Bowl Tavern was an ancient hostelry and stood in Brookline for many years, between the present Brookline Avenue and Pearl Street on Washington Street. Another turnpike was soon projected, which led from the westerly end of the Mill Dam to Watertown, an improvement rendered practicable only by the opening of the Mill Dam.

A new corporation was created in 1824, the Boston Water Power Company, which took over all the holdings of the Mill Corporation south of the dam in 1832; the dam, road, and all holdings on the north side remaining with the original company. As an enterprise for the development of power, these projects were not phenomenally successful, but the subsequent filling of the Back Bay and the proceeds from sales of land made the investment most lucrative.

June 9, 1854, the corporation made an indenture with the Commonwealth of Massachusetts by which it was agreed, among many other matters, that the corporation should convey to the Commonwealth the land covered by the Mill Dam "to be forever kept open as a public highway," but the agreement was not carried out for several years. In 1856 it was enacted that the Mill Corporation might continue to collect tolls on the Mill Dam at the same rate as allowed on the West Boston Bridge, which rate had been reënacted and expressed in American currency. In 1861 the commissioners of public lands were authorized to arrange with the corporation about continuing the collection of tolls, which was to be done until the road was laid out as a public highway by the county officials. This occurred on December 7, 1868, when the Boston Board of Aldermen accepted the road as a public highway.

Under the management of the Mill Corporation the Mill Dam Road had been known as Western Avenue until 1865. Since that time it has borne the name of Beacon Street.

The Mill Corporation followed the usual custom in locating its toll-house and gate and placed the same on the bridge over the main channel. Its site is now occupied by the parkway called Charlesgate.

In 1824 various parties, acting in the interests of the Mill Corporation, secured a charter for a turnpike to connect the westerly end of the Mill Dam with Watertown. This road, which will be treated more at length in its turn, caused a panic in the minds of the proprietors of the West Boston Bridge who foresaw a serious diversion of traffic from their bridge, and they sought to offset the advantage thus gained over them by building a turnpike of their own. This latter turnpike, being built purely as a feeder for the bridge, made no claims of being a public necessity, which later gave rise to some unique legal questions.

The history of the larger operations of the Mill Corporation and of the Boston Water Power Company is especially interesting to the student of Boston's development. The ebb and flow of the tidal waters in the ponded area soon gave rise to serious and unhealthy conditions, and many were the efforts to adjust between the public good and the corporate rights. It was finally settled that the entire area was to be filled with clean gravel, while satisfactory sewers were to be laid, and the resulting land was to be divided between the state and the two corporations. The filling was done between the years 1857 and 1894, the gravel being hauled in over the Boston and Providence and the Boston and Albany railroads, and distributed over spur tracks laid in all directions over the area. A large excavated pit can still be seen near Dedham Road Station of the Boston and Providence Railroad, which supplied much of the gravel.

57. The Barre Turnpike

By the year 1820 the Massachusetts public had generally understood that turnpike investments were very unsatisfactory, and only nineteen companies were incorporated after that date, ten of which completed their roads. Of these the Barre Turnpike Corporation was the first, being chartered February 5, 1822, to build a turnpike from Barre Common through Hubbardston and $IPrinceton, Mass.Princeton.

This company filed no returns of its business, but on a plan of its turnpike which was filed at the state house, the cost is given as $10,000, and the length eleven miles, or about $910 a mile. The road of this company was laid out by the authorities of Worcester County in 1823, "from Barre meeting-house, through Hubbardston, to Edward Goodenow's, in Princeton," which apparently brought it within two miles of Princeton Center, and on the "Depot Road." The distance by the old route had been seventeen miles, so the turnpike reduced the journey over one third.

At the opening of the year 1824 the turnpike had not been completed, for on January 28 of that year an act was passed allowing the erection of one gate in Princeton upon completion of the road. But construction soon followed, and in 1826 the corporation again appeared at the state house, this time with a complaint regarding working conditions. It seems that the turnpike cut a straight line across the big letter "S" of the old road, and travelers were content to cut off the first half circle, following the turnpike where no gate opposed them, and then taking the longer route, which kept out of sight of the toll gatherer. So another act was secured changing the first gate to a half-gate and allowing the erection of another half-gate on the westerly portion of the road.

In 1832 the Barre Turnpike was laid out as a public highway.

58. The Chester Turnpike

We have seen that in the construction of the Eighth Massachusetts and the Becket turnpikes considerable difficulty was found in selecting a satisfactory location. As finally built the two roads made a physical connection, but apparently that part of the road was poor and unsatisfactory, for on February 14, 1822, the Chester Turnpike Corporation was chartered for the purpose of making a better road than the existing turnpikes afforded, between Walton's Bridge in Chester to some indefinite point on the Becket Turnpike. The need of such improvement must have been urgent, for three years earlier the persons who later were incorporated as the Chester Turnpike Corporation had associated themselves and had built a section of the road now proposed for a turnpike, and had had the same accepted by the court of common pleas as a public road. In 1822 they asked that they might be allowed to build farther along the same line and have their former effort and the new one combined in the Chester Turnpike. Their prayer being granted the road was at once built, and the Eighth Massachusetts was relieved from the maintenance of the now useless part of its road westerly of Walton's Bridge.

This turnpike apparently extended from near the present Chester post-office to the Becket line, and about an equal distance into the town of Becket. By an act passed in 1825 eighty rods was taken from its west end and annexed to the Becket Turnpike.

The Chester Turnpike was made free in Berkshire County in September, 1842, and in Hampden County in June, 1843.

59. The Watertown Turnpike

Until the opening of the road over the Mill Dam there was no entrance to Boston between Washington Street, on the Neck, and West Boston Bridge, but the Mill Dam Road opened a direct route to and from a large number of towns, the Boston-bound travel from which entered in Watertown Square, and which had previously followed as best it could over the existing public roads to the West Boston Bridge. An attractive opportunity for another turnpike was thus offered, to connect Watertown Square with the Mill Dam Road, yielding revenue for itself and adding to the earnings of the Mill Corporation's road.

So the Watertown Turnpike Corporation was created February 7, 1824. While the persons incorporated are not the same as those forming the Mill Corporation, it was common knowledge, as brought out in legislative hearings in later years, that the two corporations were practically one. The turnpike was to cross the Charles River close to the United States Arsenal, and the right to build a bridge was conditional upon "the consent of the proper authorities of the United States, and not otherwise."

The road was laid out by a joint committee of the senate and house May 1, 1824, the report being filed with the Middlesex court by which it was approved in the same month. One tollgate was allowed at which the same rate of tolls was to be collected as had been allowed at the Bellingham gate of the Ninth Massachusetts, rather a lazy way of legislating. No returns were ever filed by this company and nothing has been found to give an idea of the

Watertown Turnpike: Commonwealth Avenue, Boston

business done. But the location was a good one, with populous towns to be served and no serious difficulties to impede construction or operation. Besides which the Brighton Abattoir was directly on this road, and with the heavy business in native cattle, which was carried on years ago, must have added materially to a revenue which was well fed from other sources.

Being a subsidiary of the Mill Corporation, the road of this company was included in the negotiations with the state over the Back Bay conditions, and it was provided for, as was the Mill Dam Road, in the act passed April 11, 1861. Provision was made therein that tolls were to be collected until such time as the local authorities should accept the road as a public highway. This was done by the town of Brighton November 19, 1868, when the road became free.

The Watertown Turnpike was known as Brighton Avenue under the Mill Corporation's management, and was named Avenue Street by the town of Brighton in 1840, although it was not a town road. Similarly it was named Beacon Street in 1846, and again changed to North Beacon Street in 1860. To-day, commencing at the end of the old $IMill DamMill Dam, the road is known as Commonwealth Avenue, then Brighton Avenue, and then North Beacon Street through the Brighton section of Boston and through Watertown.

It is a busy and much-used thoroughfare and makes a striking contrast with most of the other turnpikes, whose projectors did not so accurately foresee the tendencies of transportation.

Watertown Turnpike: Old bridge over Charles River

Central Turnpike: Passing Wellesley's Quadrangle

60. The Central Turnpike

It is hard to understand how in 1824, when turnpikes had generally fallen into disrepute as investments, a comprehensive scheme for connecting Boston and Hartford could have been exploited. But such was done, and the Central Turnpike Corporation was incorporated on the twelfth of June in that year to build from a point on the Worcester Turnpike in Needham through Natick, Framingham, Hopkinton, Upton, Northbridge, Sutton, Oxford, and Dudley to the Connecticut line in the town of Thompson. The Center Turnpike Company was incorporated in Connecticut in May, 1826, to build from the Tolland courthouse through Willington, Ashford, Union,

Central Turnpike: Turnpike, trolley, and railroad

and, Woodstock to the Massachusetts line in Dudley, where it connected with the road of the Central Turnpike Corporation. From Tolland to Hartford the turnpike had been in existence for a quarter of a century.

Thus was opened another improved route from Boston to Hartford over which passed the "Boston and Hartford Telegraph line" of stagecoaches in alternate direction daily, except Sundays. One tollgate stood in Wellesley on the north side of the road opposite Morse's Pond and about six hundred feet from the Natick line.

The road was laid out in Middlesex County in January, 1826, and in Worcester County at about the same time, but the construction did not progress rapidly, for we find that it was not quite finished when the time limit approached. June 11, 1829, the legislature granted the corporation a further time of four months in which to finish the road, and an act passed March 5, 1830, plainly shows that it was completed, as it speaks of the road "as now made and traveled."

The map filed in 1830 by the town of Needham shows that the Central Turnpike commenced near the present center of Wellesley, and not on the Worcester Turnpike. The act of 1830, just mentioned, recites that the layout committee had made some slight changes in the location, which were approved, and this was doubtless one of them. Starting, then, to-day from the Square in Wellesley, the old turnpike would be followed westerly over Central Street along the northerly side of the grounds of Wellesley College, over East and West Central streets in Natick, Waverley Street in Framingham, Union Avenue in Ashland, Main Street in Hopkinton, Oxford, and Sutton, and Sutton Road in Webster.

This is one of the shortest-lived roads that we have noted. As stated, it was opened about 1830, and in January, 1836, upon petition of the corporation itself, was laid out as a public highway throughout its length in Middlesex County. The portion in Northbridge, Upton, and Sutton was made free in the same year; that in Dudley in 1838; while the last tolls were collected in Douglas and Webster in 1839, which put a period on the Central's operations.

No financial returns are available, but from the above it is evident that the road was a failure.

The Connecticut connection continued operations until 1853.

61. Turnpike from Cambridge to Watertown

We have already seen how the persons composing the Boston and Roxbury Mill Corporation, upon the completion of their Mill Dam with its road, built another road by which the travel which centered in Watertown Square was invited to use the Mill Dam for its entrance into Boston. Previously all persons thus inclined had found their only practicable route through Cam-

Cambridge to Watertown Turnpike: Western Avenue, near the Harvard Stadium

bridge and over the West Boston Bridge, which connected Cambridgeport with Boston's West End. The revenue from the bridge tolls, although quite remunerative, was evidently not sufficiently so that the proprietors could view the loss of this Watertown travel with unconcern. So in order to retain as much of that business as possible the bridge proprietors sought and obtained a charter to build a turnpike of their own, which should lead, not from the Mill Dam, but from their own bridge to Watertown Square. The route was first surveyed by William Taylor, and his plan, dated May 6, 1824, now in the possession of the Bostonian Society, shows the route "from the

Cambridge to Watertown Turnpike: Bridge between Cambridge and Brighton

pump in Watertown to Cambridge, on the way to the pump in Dock Square." We have seen roads laid out by churches, by taverns, and by dwelling-houses, but this is the first instance of a road being built between pumps. The charter for this road was granted June 12, 1824, and allowed it to be built through the towns of Cambridge, Brighton, and Watertown, with two bridges over the navigable waters of the Charles River. As the Watertown Turnpike skirted the Arsenal grounds on the southerly side so this turnpike did on the north, and the two rapidly converged as they approached their goal in Watertown Square. Plainly there was no crying need of this road from the public's point of view. The Mill Dam Road and its subsidiary were giving ample service, and the old public roads of Cambridge were still available. It was simply and plainly a feeder for the West Boston Bridge, hence certain provisions in the charter, which have not been observed in those of earlier companies, were inserted. These were that the towns of Watertown, Cambridge, and Brighton should never "be compelled to support any part of said road or bridges without their own consent." Of this much was to be heard thirty-five years later. A further provision was that the road could only be laid through land "bounding on the old road or square in Watertown," with the consent of the owners. If the new turnpike had been a public necessity it would have been empowered to take the land.

The road was promptly built but, although allowed to collect the same tolls as were granted to the Watertown Turnpike, no gate was ever erected, and the owners never availed themselves of the privilege. In this we see a parallel with the case of the First Cumberland Turnpike, which was leased by the owners of Vaughn's Bridge so that they might make it free of toll and a better feeder for the bridge. The road thus built was four and one tenth miles in length, of which 3918 feet in Brighton was laid over an old county road. To-day the road is known as Western Avenue in Cambridge and Brighton, and as Arsenal Street in Watertown. It commenced in Cambridge, on Main Street, 2647 feet westerly of the intersection with the causeway of the West Boston Bridge, so that except for that half mile, the proprietors of the West Boston Bridge built and maintained a continuous highway from Boston to Watertown.

As already stated, the proprietors of the West Boston Bridge were incorporated March 6, 1792, and their bridge was opened for traffic November 23, 1793. In 1846 long-continued agitation, looking to the abolition of tolls on the Boston to Cambridge bridges, culminated in the incorporation of the Hancock Free Bridge Corporation, which was organized for the purpose of purchasing the bridges and continuing to operate them as toll bridges until the purchase price was repaid. Then a fund was to be accumulated sufficient to provide for the maintenance, after which the bridges were to become public property. The Hancock Free Bridge Corporation, on July 1, 1846, purchased the franchises and property of the proprietors of the West Boston Bridge for seventy-five thousand dollars, the deed expressly including the turnpike to Watertown. In 1852 the turnpike had fallen into such a bad condition that an indictment was secured against the Hancock Free Bridge Corporation, its owners. In answer to this the corporation denied the ownership and claimed that the deed from the proprietors of the West Boston Bridge conveyed only the bridge structure extending from shore to shore, but the supreme court, in 1854, decided that the corporation did own the turnpike and was bound to keep it in repair. Apparently the corporation found means to evade its responsibilities even after that, for we find a competent witness testifying before a legislative hearing in 1859, that over ten thousand dollars would be required to put into proper condition the portion of the turnpike within the limits of Watertown. But before that the effort had been made to get rid of the road.

May 30, 1857, the Hancock Free Bridge Corporation secured an act of the legislature by which it was allowed, whenever it had the funds, to pay one hundred thousand dollars to the city of Cambridge, which, in return, was to assume full responsibility for the West Boston Bridge and the one between Cambridge and Brighton, taking them, with the Cambridge section of the turnpike, off the corporation's hands. By the same act it was provided that the corporation was to tender fifty-five hundred dollars to the town of Watertown, and sixty-five hundred dollars to the town of Brighton. Only that a tender of money was to be made was specified; the act did not provide anything to be done by the towns in consideration. But whether the towns accepted the money or refused it, the Hancock Free Bridge Corporation was to have what it desired; it was to be released from liability to maintain the turnpike.

Satisfactory arrangements were promptly made with Cambridge, and that part of the turnpike became a public road, for which the city was responsible; but Watertown and Brighton viewed the proposition askance. July 1, 1857, a Watertown town meeting voted to refuse the money which had been tendered it by the corporation in accordance with the act. Brighton, however, showed a little more shrewdness. There was nothing in the act imposing any obligation on the town if it accepted the money, and if it refused, the corporation got rid of the road just the same. So the astute Brighton citizens voted to accept the money, but specifically declared in the receipt which was given therefor that they did not accept the road and stood upon their rights as specified in the original charter, which provided that the towns should "never be compelled to support any part of said road or bridges without their own consent."

So the turnpike became "Nobody's Road" in the sense of anybody being responsible for its maintenance, but the land over which it was built still belonged to the Hancock Free Bridge Corporation in fee. Many persons had bought land and built houses along the road, and such a condition could not last long, so, in 1858, James T. Austin and others petitioned the county commissioners for a layout as a county road. This was resisted by both Watertown and Brighton, and legal questions were raised regarding the authority of the commissioners to make a layout under the circumstances, especially as the road crossed navigable waters and provision had to be made for the care and operation of two drawbridges. Consequently the same petitioners next appealed to the legislature for a bill which would confer the desired authority upon somebody. The committee on roads and bridges, to whom the petition was referred, made a lengthy report, giving the history of the bridges and turnpike from the beginning. While conceding that the turnpike was not at first a public necessity, the committee logically concluded that it had become so by its long use and the establishing of homes upon its sides. The resulting bill, passed April 4, 1859, removed all technicalities and allowed the turnpike to become a county highway.

An interesting side light is thrown upon legislative proceedings by the charter of the Watertown Turnpike Corporation and the one for the West Boston Bridge proprietors' road. The general law required that the location of turnpikes should be made by disinterested freeholders appointed by the court, but the legislature in each of these cases took that privilege away and conferred it upon a committee of its own body. These were rich companies, and the returns of many of the turnpike corporations give an item for "entertainment of locating committee."

62. The Gore Turnpike

A road which would probably be classed by the Interstate Commerce Commission as a "spur to an industry " was that of the Gore Turnpike Corporation, chartered February 16, 1825. This road was evidently built as a means of access to Samuel Slater's cotton factory, near the shore of Lake Chaubunagungamaug, in Oxford, South Gore, now a part of the town of Webster. No details of its business were ever made public.

The Worcester County freeholders made the layout for the turnpike in 1825 from Douglas meeting-house to Samuel Slater's in Oxford, over what is now Webster Street in Douglas, and Douglas Road in Webster. Operation as a turnpike continued for sixteen years, the Worcester county commissioners laying it out as a county highway in 1841. The road was about five and a quarter miles long.

63. The Pontoosac Turnpike

Judging by the turnpike efforts throughout the first quarter of the nineteenth century, the need of a road between Springfield and Pittsfield must have been great. The Eighth Massachusetts first made the attempt, coming to grief, as we have seen, on the construction difficulties through the town of Becket. The Becket undertook to remedy the defect, but its road, covering the portion omitted in the building of the Eighth, offered too roundabout a route. The Chester, following in 1803, erred as much on the northerly side, and its road also was too far from the direct line. The Dalton and Middlefield sought to attack the problem boldly, but its promoters lacked the courage to carry the project through. The trouble was in the exceedingly rough and hilly nature of the country in that part of the Berkshires, which made construction very expensive and maintenance difficult and costly, and for many years no feasible route was known.

Smith's *History of Pittsfield* tells us that, about 1818, it was discovered that a good route could be followed through the "Pass of the Westfield," along Westfield River to North Becket, and thence over Washington Mountain to Pittsfield, but people generally refused to believe it. Certain "judicious and cautious citizens" of Pittsfield, Southwick, and Springfield, however, satisfied themselves on that subject, and on February 15, 1826, obtained a charter for the Pontoosac Turnpike Corporation, although, as Smith says, "with few exceptions, turnpike stocks were then notoriously worthless."

The route which this corporation was allowed started from the southeast corner of Pittsfield and ran through the towns of Hinsdale, Middlefield, Washington, and Chester, following all the way through Middlefield on the northerly bank of the Westfield River and keeping close to the same river in Chester, until it reached the "road leading from Albany to Westfield, at a point near the tavern house of Colonel Henry." This tavern is shown on Baldwin's map of the survey for the railroad from Boston to Albany, made in 1827 and 1828, and was located at the mouth of Walker Brook, on the westerly bank of the Westfield River. By this we see that the southerly terminus of the Pontoosac Turnpike was to be directly across the river from where the Chester Station of the Boston and Albany Railroad is now.

That the incorporators of the Pontoosac were actuated by other motives than hopes of financial profit is plainly to be seen. For nearly four years they postponed construction, hoping that the counties would undertake the work, but Hampshire, of which Middlefield was a part, bitterly opposed the plan, as it feared resultant diversion of trade to Springfield. So the incorporators prepared to build the road themselves in 1829, first getting an amendment to their charter by which specified points were omitted, and they were allowed to build from Pittsfield to the conjunction of the Westfield River and Mill Brook by any route they chose.

The quaint *History of the County of Berkshire*, to which we have frequently referred, was written about this time and has this to say of the Pontoosac:

As it is to pass from the easterly part of Pittsfield through the low parts of those towns and around the hills, the ascents will in no place, it is said, exceed 5°, although it crosses the eastern range of hills. This road will greatly facilitate the communication between the middle part of the county and the middle part of the Commonwealth through Springfield. A part of this road is located along the line of the proposed rail road.

At this time the state was intensely interested in the matter of railroad construction, by means of which it was hoped to offset the advantage given to New York by the Erie Canal, which had been completed about four years and was turning the increasing western trade to that city. Surveys had been made for roads from Boston, to Providence and to Albany, but many people still maintained that such methods of transportation were wild and impracticable. Of that class must have been the promoters of the Pontoosac Turnpike, for they located and built their road for nearly ten miles along the Westfield River, where they must frequently have seen the stakes set by the railroad surveyors two years or less before. Had they not felt sure the railroad was a wild dream they would hardly have dared to build their turnpike at all, much less to set it where the later construction of the more up-to-date road would obliterate much of their work.

The route was surveyed early in the life of the charter, but not until 1829 was construction begun, and the road was completed about October, 1830. Hampden County seems to have been the interested section, with Berkshire indifferent, and Hampshire openly hostile. On this account the incorporators again petitioned the legislature and secured the passage of an act whereby the Hampden county commissioners were authorized to "examine, accept, and establish the turnpike road" in their own and in two other counties. Consequently we fail to find any record of the establishing of this road in Pittsfield or Northampton; and do find in Springfield a record of the acceptance of the road from Colonel Henry's to Pittsfield, which carried it through three counties. This acceptance was made in December, 1830, after the road was completed, and no record has yet been found of its location in accordance with the law. It seems fair to assume that the promoters did not abandon the idea of having the counties assume the expense of building the road and take it as a public highway until they were well along toward its completion. Then, in order to get back some of their outlay, they concluded to operate it as a turnpike, and having neglected to comply with the preliminary formalities for turnpikes, secured the act above recited to properly establish them.

The Western Railroad Company was chartered by the Massachusetts legislature on March 15, 1833, to build what later became the section of the Boston and Albany between Worcester and the state line. By the first of January, 1837, its surveys had been completed and much of the road was under contract. The location had been made through the "Pass of the Westfield," conflicting with the Pontoosac Turnpike in many places, and in 1839 alterations were made in the toll road to allow the railroad to be built.

No records are known to exist of the money affairs of the Pontoosac, but it does not seem possible that it ever could have begun to pay. After nine years the railroad came, and practically paralleled it, as well as connecting the same terminal points, so its life must have been short. Nothing has been found to show when it became free. In 1842 a petition was entered in Berkshire for the discontinuance of the turnpike and the laying out of the same as a county road, but it was dismissed. The section of road through the "Pass of the Westfield" has now disappeared from the map, only short stubs of roads showing at either end where corners were formerly made with other roads.

Travelers through the Berkshires over the Boston and Albany line follow close to the old road's path for many miles. Passing through the bowl in which lies the village of Chester, the old Pontoosac can be seen on the opposite side of the little river, and running northerly from Cheater's main street, where it formerly terminated. A sandy country road now, it keeps along close to the railroad until the narrow semicircular valley prohibits the existence of two distinct routes of transportation. At the boundary line between Chester and Middlefield, where the steep slopes of Gobble Mountain run straight into the river, suggesting unfathomable depths, the old road ceases to exist, but traces may be seen, now on one side and again on the other, all the way to North Becket.

64. The Taunton and Providence Turnpike

The next charter granted was for a short road between two thriving towns, the Taunton and Providence Turnpike Corporation being incorporated on the . . . third of March [1826], and authorized to build

from Taunton Green, in Taunton, in the county of Bristol, in the most convenient and suitable direction to Seekonk River, in said county, so as to connect the said town of Taunton and the town of Providence, in the state of Rhode Island, by the most convenient and practicable route.

Operations began promptly, as the corporation entered petition for a locating committee at the April term of the court of sessions. The committee was appointed and performed its duties during the summer, the surveying being done by "Squire" George Walker, who lived at West on the line of the proposed road. A full report was rendered to the court at the September term in 1826, giving a complete surveyor's description of the route and an award of land damages. The location was 11.52 miles in length, terminating at "the northerly side of a well " which stood on the easterly side of Watchemocket Square, in what is now East Providence, Rhode Island. The award for land damages amounted to $7604.92, or about $662 a mile.

The authorized route as fixed by the act of incorporation extended from Taunton Green to the Seekonk River, but the locating committee commenced their labors at a distance from the Green of one hundred and thirty-five rods, starting from the "northerly side of the road leading from the Green to the Paper Mill," and they ended at the well before mentioned, "which is about twenty-five rods southeasterly from the easterly end of India Bridge at Seekonk River."

A year later, at the September term of 1827, the corporation made a new petition, reciting that the location did not commence at the Green, as required by the charter, and that they were afraid of illegality on that account. Hence would the court call back the committee and have them complete their work? This was done and the committee's report, filed in May, 1828, shows a location for the turnpike from the easterly end of its first location to Taunton Green, where it ended at "the southeasterly corner of the bar room of George B. Atwood." Then with a bar room at one end and a well at the other, the corporation seems to have rested content.

When it is noticed that the original location did not go as far westerly as the charter required, and that, consequently, if illegal at the Taunton end it was equally so at the Seekonk River, one may reasonably doubt if fears of illegality were really at the source of the movement. Taunton was an old town and doubtless closely built around the Green. The second location covered

Taunton and Providence Turnpike: Winthrop Square, Taunton

a length of one hundred and thirty-five rods and the land awards amounted to $1437, or at the rate of about $3400 a mile, and it seems much more probable that fear of this expense caused the promoters to have the location of that part delayed until they could raise some more money.

The road is conspicuous on the map to-day on account of its direct alignment. It must have been a much-needed road, and it is strange that it was so late in being built. It is now a state highway and is occupied in part by a high-speed interurban electric-car line which could not find a more direct route. Since 1826 the boundary between Massachusetts and Rhode Island has been shifted easterly from the Seekonk River, so that, although the turnpike was entirely in Massachusetts at first, about two miles of what was its westerly end are now in Rhode Island, in the town of East Providence.

At the meeting of the county commissioners in June, 1846, a petition was presented signed by Charles F. Davenport, of Davenport and Mason's express, and others asking for a public layout of the Taunton and Providence Turnpike from Taunton Green to the Rev. Alvan Cobb's meeting-house, which was in Westville, about seven hundred feet from the crossing of the Three Mile River. The records show that the road was laid out as asked, and, in December of the same year, a section in Seekonk became free also; and in December, 1849, the portion between Palmer's River, in Rehoboth, and Three Mile River, in Taunton, was thrown open. The records show that the corporation did not appear to offer objection to the proceedings in 1846, so it is possible that the road had been abandoned and that tolls had ceased to be collected prior to that date.

In East Providence the turnpike is called Taunton Avenue, and Winthrop Street, in Taunton.

65. The Hampden and Berkshire Turnpike

The fourth turnpike act of the third of March, 1826, incorporated the Hampden and Berkshire Turnpike Corporation, with the right to build a road from a point in Russell, through Blandford Center, to the westerly end of the Becket Turnpike in Becket. This road was plainly projected as an improvement on the route between Springfield and Albany, over the Eighth Massachusetts and the Becket turnpikes, and the Hampden and Berkshire was commonly referred to as the turnpike between those cities.

A location was promptly secured, and it was approved at the September term of the Hampden court of sessions, at which time the change in the law went into effect, whereby the approval of road locations became a duty of the county commissioners. The turnpike was laid out and built from a point on the Eighth Massachusetts on the westerly bank of the Westfield River, about opposite where the Fairfield Station of the Boston and Albany Railroad

now stands, and followed up the valley of Potash Brook to Blandford Center.
Thence it continued to North Blandford, and from there over what is now
called the Lee and Westfield Road, through the northeastern part of Otis,
into Becket, to a junction with the Becket Turnpike, about a mile and a
quarter southeast of West Becket Village. A saving of about five miles and a
half was made by this route over that previously followed, which was ample
reason for its adoption by the stages. Figures of cost and earnings of this road
would be especially interesting, but none are to be found.

In one of the few books essaying to treat of turnpikes, *The Taverns and
Turnpikes of Blandford* by Sumner Gilbert Wood, we naturally find much of
interest concerning this road. From it we quote:

This turnpike shortly revolutionized the traffic of the country hereabout. Two of
the four daily stages which had run for years by the Boston and Albany road, were
transferred to this turnpike, while an immense and incessant traffic of business and
pleasure developed and continued until, gradually, the railroad (which followed the
lines of the Eighth Massachusetts and Pontoosac) brought quiet and solitude again.
What commotion this new line of travel stirred within the town itself by way of
adjustment to new conditions is dimly echoed in the county records. A network of
crooked roads had pervaded the Gore; now there was a thoroughfare. The old post
road itself was in large part side-tracked by the new turnpike. The selectmen of the
town petitioned the court in this year 1829, to discontinue some of these roads, or
sections thereof, a thing which was shortly accomplished. . . .

There was one toll gate on this 'pike within the limits of the town, about a mile
below the village. Later there was another, succeeding the first one, a little lower
down. That house is still standing, familiarly known as "the gate house," at the
junction of the old mountain road and the newer one under review.

An aged Blandford resident said:

As compared with the modern country road, the turnpikes were rough and miry,
"all chomped up." You couldn't look out of the window, hardly, but you would see a
team. Team after team of lime, drawn by four horses each, passed along from the
Berkshire limekilns. Great droves of cattle, sheep, and hogs were driven to the
Brighton market. Stages here, as everywhere throughout the country, were often
getting stalled in the mire, when passengers had to get out and the men, with the
help of the neighbors, would help the tired and overburdened horses lift the vehicle
up and on to more solid ground.

Many are the stories of the old taverns, but the book mentioned gives us
a unique method by which one landlord eked out an additional income. His
specialty, it seems, was to entertain swine and their drivers, and his barn was
ingeniously fitted for that purpose. A dropping trapdoor in the floor, operated
from a distant viewpoint, would open at the psychological moment, and a
good fat porker would be added to the landlord's herd below.

The length of the Hampden and Berkshire was about sixteen and a half
miles, and according to the book quoted, it was opened for business in 1829.

It is interesting to note in this connection that the Becket Turnpike went out of existence at its own request three years later.

In 1832 the Hampden and Berkshire was allowed to change the location of its road by running around two hills in the town of Russell instead of continuing over them in a straight line. It is indeed strange that a road built as late as 1826 should have been subject to the old delusion of going straight over all obstacles.

The record of the public layout of this turnpike is doubtless to be found in Springfield, if one knows how to find it, but we will rely upon the statement of Mr. Enos W. Boise, an old resident and town clerk of Blandford, who advises us that it became free in 1852 or 1853. He clearly recalls that in 1851 a spirited pair of horses owned by his father *ran away on the turnpike* and smashed the gate.

This was the last turnpike charter granted in Massachusetts, under authority of which a road was built. Six more acts of incorporation were passed but none bore fruit. Another road was built in connection with a toll bridge.

66. The Granite Turnpike

The granite quarries of Quincy first came prominently before the country when it was decided to construct the Bunker Hill Monument from their product. They were four miles from tidewater and the only means of transporting the blocks of stone was over the roads of that period, of which but a few miles tributary to the quarries were turnpikes. To reach Boston required a roundabout journey either by way of the Neponset Bridge or by way of Milton Lower Mills, and there was no satisfactory way of reaching Charlestown, where the monument was to be built. Hence a railway was conceived by which the stones were carried down hill to the tidewater of the Neponset River at Gulliver's Creek, where they were loaded on to barges which were floated around to the dock in Charlestown. This served very well as long as the stones were wanted at points accessible by water, but an early demand arose for building stone to be used in the new parts of Boston; and a more direct route was needed.

April 13, 1837, the proprietors of the Granite Bridge were incorporated for the purpose of building a road from the old county road at or near the store of I. Babcock, Jr., in Milton and running thence north ten and three quarters degrees west, about two hundred and seventy-two rods; north nineteen degrees west, about fifty-six rods; north twenty-five and one half degrees west, about one hundred and twenty-eight rods to the Neponset River, "and to locate, build, and construct a bridge across said river in continuation of said last-mentioned line of said road to Dorchester"; and

Granite Bridge and Granite Railway, Milton: Granite Bridge of 1914

thence to continue the road north eight and three quarters degrees west, about one hundred and eight rods to the "lower road" in Dorchester on or near the land of Rev. Ephraim Randall. A draw not less than thirty-one feet wide was to be located by commissioners appointed for that purpose, and wharves or piers seventy-five feet long were to be built on each side to assist vessels in passing through the opening. The total cost of bridge and road was not to be in excess of fifteen thousand dollars and the management was not allowed to incur annual expenses of over fifteen hundred dollars.

Plotting the description of the route of the road plainly shows that it began in the center of East Milton Village adjacent to the crossing of the Granite Railway by Adams Street, the old county road and the old colonial road to Plymouth. Thence it marked out the lines of the present-day Granite Avenue across the marshes and river to Adams Street in Dorchester, the "lower road."

This "lower road " was an ancient institution at that date, having been an alternate route by which the bridge over the Neponset at Milton Lower Mills was reached from Boston, the other road passing through Grove Hall and following the Washington Street of to-day. The "lower road " commenced at the corner of Washington and Eustis streets near the boundary at that date between Boston and Roxbury, and followed over what are now known as Eustis, Mall, Dearborn, Dudley, Stoughton, Pleasant, Bowdoin, Adams, and Washington streets to Milton Lower Mills. At its beginning is found one of the oldest cemeteries in New England, interments having begun there in 1633 and continued until 1854. At that point, also, was the first barricade erected by the Americans to prevent the British troops from making a sortie during the siege of Boston.

Granite Bridge and Granite Railway, Milton: Road across the marshes

As the road built by the bridge company commenced almost on the location of the Granite Railway and was only a few hundred feet away from it at the railway's terminus, it may not be amiss to consider here the cars and track which became so familiar to the turnpike workmen. When the bridge and turnpike were built the Granite Railway had been in operation about eleven years and the railroads from Boston to Providence, Worcester, and Lowell about two years.

The track of the Granite Railway was originally composed of stone crossties bedded in the ground at intervals of eight feet with wooden rails faced with a bar of iron on which the wheels ran. By 1837 the wooden rails

Granite Bridge and Granite Railway, Milton: Old granite rails on the railway pier

had been replaced with stringers of granite hammered smooth on the upper face and having similar bars of iron pinned to their tops. It was officially stated that the maintenance costs on this form of track had not amounted to ten dollars a year, and the track continued in use until 1871, when it was sold to the Old Colony Railroad Company and replaced by a modern railroad construction. The first car had wheels six and a half feet in diameter with the load carried on a platform running just clear of the rails and hung from the axles by chains. The capacity was about six tons.

In 1846 the Granite Railway Company was authorized to extend its road, crossing the Neponset River not over five hundred feet below the Granite toll bridge and uniting with the newly chartered Dorchester and Milton Branch Railroad in Dorchester. It was also given authority to sell its road to the Old Colony Railroad Company, a privilege which was renewed in 1848 but which was not utilized until 1871. Then the Old Colony introduced a curve in the track at the foot of the hill on the edge of the marshes and carried the track easterly along the southerly bank of the river to a junction with its main line at Atlantic. The section running out over the marsh and the pier at Gulliver's Creek were thus left out of the reckoning, but the pier is still to be plainly traced, and on it can be seen to-day about two hundred feet of the old granite rails still in the place where they carried the cars of stone. The iron plates which received the tread of the wheels are gone but rust clearly shows where they were, and the pins which held them are yet in place.

It would seem that the drivers of teams which passed over the Granite Bridge were not satisfied with the capacity of the railway car, for the company was obliged to ask the passage of an act in 1845 by which the owner of a load of over seven tons was made liable for any damage done to the bridge.

With Yankee shrewdness the company reported the bridge and road as costing fifteen thousand dollars, all that the law allowed, which does not seem to have been an unreasonable figure. There was considerable difficult construction of the road across the soft marsh and the bridge abutments must have been costly to build. The corporation made returns of business from 1840 to 1854, but complete for only eleven years. For those years the net earnings were about three hundred and seventeen dollars on an average, or two and eleven hundredths per cent. The gross receipts ran from five hundred and fifty to fifteen hundred dollars, but generally around seven or eight hundred. In one year only, 1852, was a loss reported when the business ran behind to the amount of three hundred and sixty-three dollars.

May 4, 1865, the Norfolk county commissioners were authorized to lay out the bridge and road as a public highway. The property had fallen into a bad condition and the commissioners were required to put the same into proper repair, after which the towns of Dorchester and Milton were to assume the maintenance. The commissioners, under that authority, laid out the road and bridge September 8, 1865.

The present bridge was in part built under the provisions of an act passed June 13, 1913, by which a commission was provided for the purpose of constructing a new bridge with suitable approaches, substantially replacing the old bridge. Seventy thousand dollars was to be advanced by the Commonwealth to be repaid later by Suffolk and Norfolk counties, Milton, and Quincy. The control is now vested in the mayor of Boston and the chairman of the selectmen of Milton.

The Turnpikes of Maine

Upon the severance of Maine from Massachusetts in 1820, the turnpike inheritance consisted of five roads: The First Cumberland Turnpike, in Scarboro; the Bath Bridge and Turnpike, from Brunswick to Bath; the Wiscasset and Woolwich; the Wiscasset and Augusta; and the Camden turnpikes. Each of these has been treated in its order in the Massachusetts section.

Evidently anticipating considerable business in forming corporations for that purpose, the new state adopted a comprehensive code of general laws closely following the Massachusetts practice, in which the procedure in such cases was fully outlined. The only radical departure from Massachusetts custom was in delegating to the county commissioners instead of to a committee appointed by the court the duty of laying out the line of the road. But the labor of preparing these laws was wasted, for only one company was formed by the Maine legislature and that company failed to carry out its plans. . . .

The following turnpikes are reported by Wood to have been chartered but never operated as toll roads:

1801	Eleventh Massachusetts	Connecticut line, Granville to Blandford
	Thirteenth Massachusetts	Connecticut line, Granville to Loudon (Otis)
1802	First Maine	Prospect to Augusta, Maine
1803	Sixteenth Massachusetts	Hampshire and Berkshire Counties
	Ipswich	Beverly to Newburyport
	Maine	New Hampshire line through Portland to Augusta, Maine
	Boston and Haverhill	Haverhill Bridge to Malden Bridge
1804	Warwick and Irwin's Gore	Warwick vicinity
	Springfield and Longmeadow	Between the towns named

	Salem and Chelmsford	Between the towns named
	Wiscasset and Dresden	Between the towns named
	Sheffield and Tyringham	Between the towns named
1805	Tyringham and Lee	Tyringham (Monterey) to Sheffield
	Winsocket	Connecticut state line to Dedham
	Blandford and Russell	Between the towns named
	Fryeburg, Baldwin, and Portland	Between the towns named
	Williamsburg and Windsor	Williamsburg to Cheshire
	Ossapee	Saco, Maine, to Sandwich, New Hampshire
1806	Norton	Warren, Rhode Island, to Canton
	Second Brush Hill	Roxbury to Boston
1807	Lancaster	Fitchburg to Sudbury
	Stockbridge	Through that town
	Sheffield and Great Barrington	Sheffield to West Stockbridge
	Mashapog	Norton to Milton
	Westford and Lexington	Between the towns named
	Bethlehem and Tyringham	Bethlehem (later part of Otis) to Tyringham
	Alford and West Stockbridge	Hillside, New York, to Stockbridge
	Dalton and Middlefield	Between the towns named
	Sturbridge and Western	Sturbridge to Western (now Warren)
1808	Nashua	Concord to Ashburnham
	Dartmouth and New Bedford	Between the towns named
	Middleboro and New Bedford	Between the towns named
	Brookfield and Charlton	Between the towns named
	Providence and Northampton	Rhode Island line to Northampton
1809	Groton and Pepperell	Westford to New Hampshire line in Pepperell
	Granville	Granville to Becket
1810	Boston Neck	Boston to Roxbury
	Worcester and Sutton	Between the towns named
	Woburn and Dracut Bridge	Woburn to New Hampshire line in Dracut
1811	Tyringham and Sandisfield	Lee to Sandisfield
1812	Worcester and Leicester	Between the towns named
1813	Taunton and Dighton	Taunton to Warren, Rhode Island
1814	Granville and Tolland	West Springfield (now Agawam) to Sandisfield
	Wrentham and Attleboro	Wrentham to Cumberland, Rhode Island

1818	West Stockbridge and Alford	Between the towns named
1820	Wilbraham	Through that town
1825	Tolland and Otis	Granville to Blandford
	Sterling	Through that town?
1826	Wilkinsonville	Westboro to Sutton
	Pawtucket and Taunton	Seekonk to Taunton
	Norfolk and Middlesex	Holliston to Brookline
1827	Hoosac Mountain	Charlemont to Adams
1829	Providence and Bristol	Between the towns named
1832	Hoosac Rail or McAdamized Road	Williamstown to Cheshire
1841	Clam River	Sandisfield to Tyringham
1868	Chelsea Beach and Saugus Bridge	North Chelsea (now Revere) to Saugus
1863	Milford and Princeton (Maine)	Greenfield to Princeton, Maine

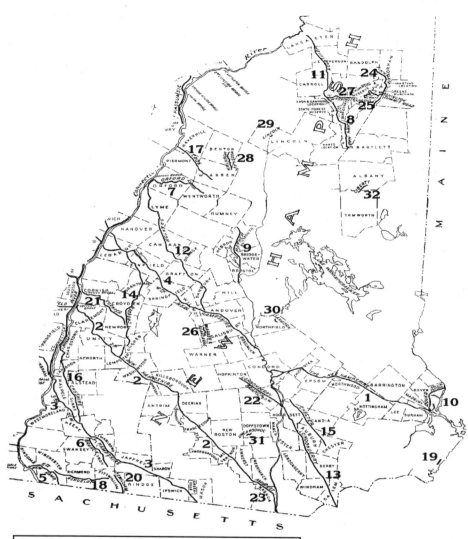

1. New Hampshire Turnpike	17. Coos
2. Second New Hampshire	18. Ashuelot
3. Third New Hampshire	19. Hampton Causeway
4. Fourth New Hampshire	20. Fitzwilliam
5. Sixth New Hampshire	21. Cornish
6. Branch	22. Londonderry Branch
7. Orford	23. Amherst
8. Tenth New Hampshire	24. Pinkham
9. Mayhew	25. Mt. Washington Summit Road
10. Dover	26. Warner and Kearsarge
11. Jefferson	27. Mt. Washington
12. Grafton	28. Moosilauke Mountain
13. Londonderry	29. Lincoln
14. Croyden	30. Sanborn
15. Chester	31. Uncanoonuc Road
16. Cheshire	32. Liberty Road

TURNPIKES
OF
NEW HAMPSHIRE

SCALE - MILES

The Turnpikes of New Hampshire

THREE days behind Massachusetts, New Hampshire set the turnpike movement going on the fourteenth day of June, 1796, when the "Proprietors of New Hampshire Turnpike Road" were incorporated. It would seem that the promoters of this road did not anticipate the eighty-one other corporations which were to follow them when they chose a name with so little to distinguish it and so little suggestive of the road's location. But the movement grew, two more being incorporated in the same century, while forty-seven appeared on the statute books during the first ten years of the nineteenth. In this state the agitation for turnpikes continued long after it had been looked on as a thing of the dim past in the others. Seven acts of incorporation were passed in the sixties, seven in the seventies, three in the eighties, and one in 1893, nearly all of which were exploited in the interests of summer tourist travel.

As in Massachusetts, the custom in New Hampshire generally called for the location and building of entirely new roads, although there were cases in which old roads were utilized. But in the matter of tolls the Granite State followed the lead of Pennsylvania and adopted a system which has stood the test of time, it being on a mileage basis. Under this system the gates and tollhouses could be erected at any suitable points, and the rates for collection scaled according to the distance to the adjoining gates. The rates of toll granted to the first company were as follows:

	Per mile. Cents.
Every ten sheep or hogs	1
Every ten cattle	2
Every horse and his rider, or led horse	1
Every sulkey, chair, or chaise, with one horse and two wheels	1½
Every chariot, coach, stage, waggon, phaeton, or chaise with two horses and four wheels	3
Either of the carriages last mentioned with four horses	3
Every other carriage of pleasure the like sum according to the number of wheels and horses drawing the same.	
Each cart or other carriage of burthen drawn by one beast	1
Each waggon, cart, or other carriage of burthen drawn by two beasts	1½

If by more than two, one cent for each additional yoke of oxen or horse.

Each sleigh drawn by one horse 1½

By two horses 2

Each sled drawn by one horse. 1

Each sled drawn by two horses or yoke of oxen 1¼

If by more than two horses or a yoke of oxen one cent for each pair of
horses or yoke of oxen.

One might wonder after inspection of the above how a toll gatherer would compute the lawful toll on a flock of turkeys such as were often driven over the roads in the old days, but the schedule seems to be very complete otherwise, and it is a source of surprise to learn that there was an omission which gave rise to much trouble. The vehicle which was not classified was the "sleigh of burthen." Consultation of the dictionary leaves us with the feeling that between sleds and sleighs of various horse power the "sleigh of burthen" would hardly have found a vacancy on the above list, but such vacancy was found. It would seem that "sleigh of burthen" must have been a local name for what we now call a "pung," and that it was considered neither a sled on low solid runners, nor a sleigh for pleasure riding.

Whereas impositions on the publick have taken place in consequence of the omission of the words "sleigh of burthen," after the word "sled " in several acts passed for the purpose aforesaid; for remedy whereof—

Be it enacted by, the senate and house of representatives in general court convened, That from and after the passing this act, every sleigh of burthen shall pay no more toll than is charged on a sled drawn by the same number of beasts, although the words "sleigh of burthen" are not inserted in said act or acts,

after the passage of which on June 17, 1806, we hope there was no more trouble.

The straight-line requirement does not appear in any of the New Hampshire charters, due no doubt to the rugged topography which forbade such a layout. From first to last the authority to build and maintain a road was expressed as follows:

And be it further enacted, that the said Corporation are empowered to survey, lay out, make and keep in repair, a Turnpike-road or highway of four rods wide in such rout or track as, in the best of their judgment and skill, will combine shortness of distance with the most practicable ground from . . . . to . . . .

Combining shortness of distance with the most practicable ground is certainly an acceptable definition of a modern scientific location. . . .

Special acts were passed in nearly every emergency in New Hampshire, only four general acts being found. Three of these appear in the Revised Statutes of 1830, but they had disappeared in 1842. One was the act just quoted; another, passed in 1806, allowed the proprietors of turnpike roads and toll bridges to reduce their tolls whenever they wished and as much as they wished, a most inestimable privilege; the third provided that alterations in a road might be made upon application to the court of common pleas, and upon its order. In the revision of 1857 a new law appeared providing that the franchise of any corporation entitled to collect toll might be seized on execution and sold at auction. Bids were made in units of time, the successful bidder being the one offering the shortest time, and being entitled to collect tolls during the period named in his bid, in return for which he paid the judgment. Except for these few laws each corporation was controlled by special acts passed in reference to it.

1. The New Hampshire Turnpike

As already stated the first company was entitled the Proprietors of New Hampshire Turnpike Road. The petition for incorporation set forth that communication between the seacoast and the interior parts of the state might be made much more easy, convenient, and less expensive than hitherto by a direct road from Concord to the Piscataqua Bridge; but that "the expensiveness" of such an undertaking would render it difficult of accomplishment "otherwise than by an incorporated company" to be "indemnified by a toll for the sums that should be expended" by it.

This company's road was promptly completed, covering a distance of thirty-six miles and passing through the towns of Durham, Lee, Barrington, Nottingham, Northwood, Epsom, Chichester, Pembroke, and Concord. Its eastern terminus was at the Piscataqua Bridge, which connected Durham and Newington over a half mile of water, and was considered in those days a marvel of bridge building. The western end was at the "Federal Bridge" over the Merrimac in Concord, and the road there is now known as Portsmouth Street. In 1803 an additional act was passed which allowed the building of a

The New Hampshire Turnpike: East from Federal Bridge

The New Hampshire Turnpike: Across the plains

branch turnpike leaving the main road on the "Dark Plains," about two and a half miles from the "Federal Bridge," and running southwesterly to the Concord Bridge.

No tolls were to be collected on any mile until six hundred dollars had been expended thereon or a proportionate sum upon several miles covered by one gate. Miss Thompson, in *Landmarks in Ancient Dover*, says that proposals for construction were invited in Portsmouth October 3, 1800, and that March 19. 1803, public notice was given that the required sums had been expended and that the company would avail itself of the privilege of collecting tolls on and after April 1 of that year. Miss Thompson states the cost of construction as having been nine hundred dollars a mile.

As rates of toll were by the mile the company was at liberty to erect as many gates as it saw fit, and it appears that there were three within the limits of the town of Durham. The first was near Johnson's Creek; the second a little below Durham Corner; and the third at Mast Road crossing. A short distance farther and within the town of Lee another gate was found at the Oyster River Bridge. By an act passed June 14, 1824, the corporation was allowed to sell its road to the various towns through which it passed. Concord's history tells us that that town voted in the same year to purchase its portion of the road if the price was not over five hundred dollars, and from a communication to the New Hampshire *Gazette* of October 26, 1824, we learn that Portsmouth had appropriated a sum not in excess of four thousand dollars for the same purpose. Wadleigh's *Notable Events in the History of Dover* gives January 28, 1825, as the date on which the road became free to all. . . .

The New Hampshire Turnpike: Down hill to the Merrimac

Visitors to Concord see many neat granite stones marking spots of historical interest; and if one will go to the cast end of the Pennecook Street Bridge over the Merrimac he will find there such a marker. From it he will learn that there is the site of the first ferry which was established by Captain Ebenezer Eastman in 1727, and that Tucker's Ferry was in operation there in 1785, the Federal Bridge appearing in 1798. Another note should be cut on that stone as it also marks the westerly terminus of the First New Hampshire Turnpike in 1799 or about that year.

Passing over the bridge and taking the first road to the right brings one to Portsmouth Street, the old turnpike as it was first built. This route made the terminus on the Merrimac nearly two miles north of the business center of

The New Hampshire Turnpike: Approaching Concord Bridge

Concord, and the turnpike proprietors must have only waited the completion of the Concord Bridge to secure a better entrance to Concord. As stated, this was done in consequence of an act of 1803, a new road being cut from a point on the Dark Plains straight to the Concord Bridge. That road now enters Concord as Bridge Street and leads the traveler to Main Street nearly opposite the state house. It is a state highway, but Portsmouth Street is a neglected sandy track through the woods.

Both the Federal and Concord bridges were authorized by acts of incorporation passed in 1795, the Federal being opened in 1798 and the Concord a few years later.

2. The Second New Hampshire Turnpike

The Second New Hampshire Turnpike Corporation was created in 1799 and lasted until 1837, when its charter was repealed. Its route was "from lottery bridge in Claremont to the plain in Amherst, near the Court House." The matter of this turnpike was considered at an Antrim town meeting November 18, 1799, and a vote of "no objection " was passed. Cochrane wrote in his *History of Antrim* that the road was built across the eastern edge of that town in 1800 and for twenty-five years carried an enormous traffic of farm products and timber to Boston, the teams returning with loads of rum and store goods. The gates were about eight miles apart, there being two in Francestown and one at Hillsboro Upper Village. Although not obliged to do so by its charter this company fell into the prevailing error and made its road too straight, for Cochrane tells us that free roads in better locations cut deeply into its

Second New Hampshire Turnpike: Lottery Bridge, Claremont, N.H.

earnings.

3. The Third New Hampshire Turnpike

The Proprietors of the Third Turnpike Road in New Hampshire were incorporated December 27, 1799, to build "from Bellows Falls in Walpole, on the Connecticut River, through Keene, toward Boston, to the Massachusetts line," and in 1808 were allowed to build a short branch in the town of Marlboro. Cutter tells in his *History of Jaffrey* that when the turnpike became available it soon became the common practice for most people to carry their products to Boston in their own teams, after snow fell, and it was not uncommon to see from twenty to forty traveling together.

The corporation was organized in February, 1800, at a meeting held in Major William Todd's tavern in Keene, and construction was started the same year we learn from Griffin's *History of Keene*. The turnpike did not enter the center of Keene, that is Central Square, but curving to the west passed around it. In 1808, at the solicitation of Keene's selectmen, a revision of the line was made in that village and the present straight lines of Court Street became the new turnpike limits.

In December, 1803, Dearborn Emerson started a line of stages over this road, running between Boston and Bellows Falls. Under earlier conditions it had cost six dollars to be carried from Keene to Boston, but Mr. Emerson's enterprise reduced the fare to four-fifty.

June 18, 1801, this corporation obtained from the Massachusetts legislature an act granting it the right to extend its road about four miles into that state. By 1821 the business had become so poor that the owners had

Third New Hampshire Turnpike: Court Street, Keene, N.H.

practically abandoned the road, and we find the town of Keene voting in that year to keep the old turnpike in repair. Two years later the town laid it out as a public highway.

In 1824 the corporation was allowed to surrender its charter and turn its road over to the municipalities, which it had already done apparently. July 4, 1837, the legislature repealed the act of incorporation.

The location of this road at Bellows Falls was determined by the fact that a bridge across the Connecticut, the first one erected over that river, was already in place. Another turnpike company was incorporated in Vermont six weeks before the act creating the Third New Hampshire, which continued the line of travel from the bridge at Bellows Falls well along toward Rutland. That company was the Green Mountain, and in connection with it in the Vermont section some notes on the Bellows Falls Bridge are given.

The Third New Hampshire Turnpike was the predecessor of the Cheshire Railroad, now the Cheshire Branch of the Fitchburg Division of the Boston and Maine Railroad. But while the turnpike had dared to cross the foot of Monadnock's steep sides, the railroad engineers used better judgment and bore their road well to the south.

4. The Fourth New Hampshire Turnpike

The Fourth New Hampshire Turnpike Corporation was formed in 1800 with authority to build from "the east bank of the Connecticut River in Lebanon, nearly opposite the mouth of White River, to the west bank of the Merrimac River in Salisbury or Boscawen; and a branch running to it southeasterly from White River Falls Bridge in Hanover." Boscawen was selected for the easterly terminus and the road began there at the bridge from Fisherville, according to Coffin's *History of Boscawen and Webster*, which also notes that turnpikes were built in response to the increasing demands of travelers, due to the rapid advance of civilization northward to northern New Hampshire and Vermont.

Directly opposite to the Massachusetts custom, the incorporators of New Hampshire companies were allowed to lay out their roads in accordance with their own judgment, a much more equitable method and which, subject to approval by a public-service commission, now prevails generally in provisions for railroad locations. In this connection it is interesting to note a statement in an article on this corporation in the Granite *Monthly* for March, 1881, that this road was located by a committee selected entirely from men outside of New Hampshire. McClintock says the estimated cost was six hundred dollars a mile, but the road actually cost $61,157, or over $1200 a mile.

Eastman's *History of Andover* recites that completion of the road was delayed by the competition between the south and center villages of Salisbury, which was finally compromised by building through both. The Andover section was built by Captain Stephen Harriman of Vermont, who gathered quite a remarkable contractor's outfit. A light frame house was built on trucks for the accommodation of himself and family, which was moved as the work progressed by eight yoke of oxen. The twenty men who composed his force were accommodated in tents, and two daughters of the boss prepared their meals by means of a large iron-hooped brick oven built on a solid platform on wheels. The road was completed and opened in the fall of 1804, and the toll gatherers installed, being sworn to the faithful discharge of their duties and giving sureties for five hundred dollars each.

As in the country served by the Third New Hampshire, the custom soon prevailed in the section of the Fourth of making annual fall trips to Boston for the disposal of products. On many a pleasant winter, evening the Common, east of Moulton's Tavern in Andover, might have been seen covered with parked sleighs and sleds of many varieties, from the huge van drawn by eight horses to the little one-horse pung filled with the butter, cheese, poultry, etc., of the New Hampshire or Vermont farmer seeking a market "down below."

In 1833 changes in the road were allowed in Lebanon and Enfield, and in 1840 the road became free, Andover paying five hundred and sixty-six dollars for the privilege of owning the portion in that town. Eastman says that travel thereupon increased and continued in a steady stream for about seven years, or until the Northern Railroad was opened between Concord and White River junction. A line of freight wagons was run by Balch, each team composed of eight well-groomed white horses, one seat being occupied by a stalwart negro, a striking figure and unusual in those days. Heavy pieces of single freight were taken by four. or six-horse teams; while the miscellaneous travel was carried in three-horse or "spike" teams; two-horse or "pod" teams; and one-horse teams or pungs in winter.

The Fourth New Hampshire was the predecessor of the Southern Division of the Boston and Maine from Concord to White River Junction, but took a much more direct course. Travelers by rail to-day may observe the old turnpike close beside the track between Andover and Potter Place stations and again in Lebanon, but elsewhere the two are far apart.

The Fifth New Hampshire Turnpike Corporation hoped to build about forty miles of road from Piscataqua Bridge to Meredith Bridge, connecting Portsmouth with Lake Winnepesaukee. A five years' extension of time was secured in 1810 but nothing further has been found.

5. The Sixth New Hampshire Turnpike

The Sixth New Hampshire Turnpike Corporation, chartered in 1802, appears to have been primarily a toll-bridge corporation, although it had authority to build about ten miles of turnpike through Hinsdale and Winchester to connect with the branch of the Fifth Massachusetts which was built to the state line prior to 1806. The New Hampshire corporation had authority to build a toll bridge across the Connecticut River in Hinsdale and completed the same in 1804. The bridge was almost immediately destroyed and was rebuilt in 1805, this time standing until 1807, when it was seriously damaged by a freshet. To enable the company to finance the repairs the legislature of 1807 gave sanction to a lottery by which eight thousand dollars might be raised. The name of the corporation was changed in 1852 to Hinsdale Bridge Corporation, which justifies the supposition that the turnpike had been previously abandoned.

6. The Branch Turnpike

The Branch Road and Bridge Corporation was granted its charter in the same year to build from the north line of Fitzwilliam to a road between Keene and Swanzey. This seems to have been a part of a scheme of which the Worcester and Fitzwilliam was to form the Massachusetts section, but the New Hampshire people had better luck, for the *History of Keene* tells us that construction was commenced in 1803 and carried through.

A bridge that would stay in place had never been built across the little river at the foot of Keene's main street, so town and turnpike united, the town contributing four hundred dollars, and built the first "permanent" bridge in that location.

Another corporation was later formed which built a section of the same route extending about halfway across the town of Fitzwilliam, leaving the balance to be traveled over the public road.

From Keene to the Massachusetts line these two turnpikes followed closely along the route later adopted by the engineers of the Cheshire Railroad, and while the Third New Hampshire anticipated that line in its general plan the Branch and the Fitzwilliam were its predecessors in their limited locality.

7. The Orford Turnpike

The Orford Turnpike Corporation followed in 1803 with a franchise to build from Orford Bridge on the Connecticut River, through Orford and Wentworth to Aiken's Bridge on the Baker's River. The power to take land was not granted in the original act of incorporation, and two years later they were back asking that that omission might be remedied. The request was granted and we may suppose that they then proceeded to build. No records nor references to this road have been found, except one act of the legislature which speaks of the Orford Turnpike as an existing road.

8. The Tenth New Hampshire Turnpike

The Tenth New Hampshire Turnpike Corporation, chartered in 1803, was the means of bringing all the north country into communication with the seaports and of stimulating settlement and development to a greater extent than any other New England road.

Following the Revolutionary War settlements began to creep up the valley of the Connecticut, and by 1785 a considerable number of people had made their homes as far north as Lancaster, New Hampshire. But their zeal had exceeded their prudence and once settled there they found themselves practically isolated, the only means of communication with the older parts of the country being by way of the Connecticut River which, for all reasonable purposes, was passable only in winter when frozen over. Much trapping was done, the accumulated skins being sent down the river when the traveling became good. It is related that Emmons Stockwell, a leading pioneer of Lancaster, on such a trip lost his horse and a valuable load of furs and almost his life by breaking through the ice. As late as 1791 the legislature was accustomed to refuse a seat to the representative from Coos County on account of lack of evidence of his election, due to the difficulties of communication. Southeasterly to southwesterly, except through the Connecticut Valley, the mighty towering ranges of the White Mountains seemed to shut off all possibility of northern Coos obtaining any direct route to the southern part of the state. The Crawford Notch had been discovered in 1771 by Timothy Nash, one of the pioneers of Lancaster, who had trailed a moose up one of the ravines, and he had noted the existence of an old Indian trail, but no thought was given for many years to the chance that a route might be

Tenth New Hampshire Turnpike: Through the Crawford Notch

found in that direction. Gradually, however, a rough pioneer road was developed, which was very difficult to keep in repair, and in 1803 the corporation was formed to improve the same as a turnpike.

The description of the route, as contained in the act of incorporation, read "from the uper line in Bartlett through the Notch in the white hills, containing twenty miles." In such brief words was expressed the location of a road which for scenic grandeur has few equals in the world. Grinding down through the bottom of that gigantic cleft in the mountains, with the peaks towering thousands of feet almost directly overhead and often hidden from view by the clouds, the builders of this road must have felt a reverential awe, as if in the immediate presence of Divinity itself. The scene is thrilling enough to-day when viewed from passing railroad train or automobile; even more so when seen, as by the writer, from on foot; but who can conceive the feelings of one who looked upon those mountain sides a century ago when in their primeval glory, and who was unprepared by painting or written description for the scene which burst upon him. Through such grandeur the Tenth New Hampshire thrust its road, which immediately became an avenue of great importance, and over which a heavy stream of traffic flowed for many years.

The *History of Coos County* says of this road:

This furnished an avenue to the seaports and became one of the best paying roads in all northern New Hampshire. Until the advent of the railroad, this was the great outlet of Coos County, and the thoroughfare over which its merchandise came from Portland. In winter often, lines of teams from Coos, over half a mile in length, might be seen going down with tough Canadian horses harnessed to pungs or sleighs, loaded with pot or pearl ash, butter, cheese, pork, lard, and peltry, returning with well assorted loads of merchandise.

In the heart of the Notch between the stupendous mountain sides the Willey family made their home beside the turnpike, and were widely known for several years among those traveling the road. One June morning in 1826 the father of the family witnessed one of the landslides which have left such deep scars on the slopes, and after that the family felt less secure in their home beneath the overhanging mountains. So when the furious storm of August 27 in the same year burst upon them their fears became more acute, and when above the roar of the storm they heard the grinding and crashing of another slide on its way down the mountain, a panic seized the entire family and they rushed forth from the shelter of the house directly into the path of the landslide, by which they were crushed. When traffic was resumed the first to pass found the Willey House standing as of old but without occupants. Various household articles were scattered around, as they had been dropped in the moment of flight,and the family Bible lay open on the table. For many days the fate of the family was unknown, but their bodies were finally uncovered by the work of repairing the road.

Tenth New Hampshire Turnpike: Scene in Crawford Notch

The Tenth New Hampshire was a part of a comprehensive turnpike scheme which planned to connect Portland with Lake Champlain. We have already noted the incorporation of a company to build a turnpike through the Maine towns of Fryeburg, Baldwin, and Standish on the way to Portland, and that the road did not appear in consequence of such incorporation. Such a turnpike would have been another link in the scheme. The Littleton Turnpike, incorporated later, was to connect the Tenth with the Connecticut River at Upper Waterford; and from there to Lake Champlain the Northern Turnpike of Vermont was to complete the route. But the Littleton did not materialize, and the Northern succeeded in building only about eight miles of its road from St. Johnsbury to Danville. So the great turnpike scheme failed of consummation, but the public roads over the greater part of the route were sufficiently good to encourage the continuance of the heavy traffic demanded by the trade of Coos County and northern Vermont.

Certain doings of the corporation were confirmed by the legislature by an act passed in 1853, from which it appears that the turnpike continued its collections for a full half-century and only ceased, like many of its Massachusetts contemporaries, when obliged to do so by the competing railroad.

In turnpike days the travelers were stern and sober men intent upon the hard problems of wresting a living from the pioneer soil, or those engaged in the weary and arduous task of teaming the necessary freight over the hundred miles of dusty roads. Seldom we can imagine did women or children pass over the turnpike, and but few sounds of merriment might be heard. To those who did pass, luxury was unknown, and the journey was made with the jolting and discomfort of "dead-ex" wagons.

How different to-day is the personnel of travel. Almost entirely is it made up of light-hearted summer tourists, the gay dresses and laughing voices of the fair sex predominating, as they whirl by in luxurious automobile or view the wonderful scenery from the specially fitted observation car on the railroad.

Along the primitive road through the Notch, which is said to have been built as early as 1785, a number of small taverns for the entertainment of travelers, including the Willey House, were built at an early date. But with the advent of the turnpike in 1803 the first real hotel in the White Mountain region appeared, it being erected near the site of the present Fabyan House. This was an ambitious structure of two stories and its opening marked an era in the development of transportation to the north country.

The storm of 1826, to which allusion has already been made, was almost a vital blow to the turnpike, many miles of the road being washed away and all but two of its many bridges emigrating toward the ocean. Tradition tells us that the business men of Portland, appreciative of the great good done to that town by the Tenth New Hampshire, made a liberal contribution of cash toward the reconstruction of the road.

The Portland and Ogdensburg Railroad, realizing the old turnpike ambition of connecting Portland with northern Vermont, completed its track through the Crawford Notch and commenced running its trains in 1876, which is as near the date of the freeing of the Tenth New Hampshire Turnpike as we have been able to determine. Most of the authorities consulted agree that the road became free about the time that the railroad was opened.

9. The Mayhew Turnpike

The Mayhew Turnpike Corporation, created in 1803, built a road sixteen miles in length from the southerly part of Bristol to the westerly edge of Plymouth near the Rumney line. The charter did not confer the right to take land by condemnation, which delayed the beginning of the work. In 1805 that omission was remedied and the road was promptly built, being completed that same year. The turnpike ran through the central part of Bristol, skirted the eastern shore of New Found Lake, and crossed the eastern part of Hebron and the western part of Plymouth to a junction with the old "Cohos Road," which ran from Plymouth to Haverhill.

We get some information regarding this road from Musgrove's *History of Bristol*, which tells us that the southerly termination of it was at the "Peaslee Graveyard south of Smith's River." One tollgate was on North Main Street and was attended for many years by the Rev. Walter Sleeper and his wife. Mrs. Sleeper must have been a woman of spirit, for it is related that one day after a storm a traveler, complaining that the road had not been broken out, refused to pay his toll, upon which she refused to open the gate. Finally he threw a silver dollar at her feet in the snow. Returning from the house with the change in small pieces she made delivery to him as she had received the dollar. A deed found in the registry of deeds in Woodsville establishes the location of this tollhouse. The land was conveyed to the corporation by Moses Sleeper and is described as a part of "lot 22 in the 3rd division," which lot lay across the outlet of New Found Lake about two thirds of the distance down to the confluence with the Pemigewasset River. It was then in Bridgewater, but is now a part of Bristol, and in 1816 the corporation was allowed to buy not over three acres near the tollgate, probably that the toll gatherer might have a garden.

At the November term of court in 1839 a petition was entered for a public layout over this turnpike, and in September, 1840, the road was made free, the corporation being awarded sixteen hundred dollars' compensation.

Mayhew Turnpike: Webster Tavern, Bridgewater, N.H.

Mayhew Turnpike: Webster Tavern, Bridgewater, N.H.

It is unlikely that this turnpike enjoyed a monopoly. Its object was to make a short cut across a long curve made by the road which followed the bank of the Pemigewasset through Bridgewater and Plymouth. The westerly part of Bridgewater through which the Mayhew passed is rough and hilly, and the turnpike had many steep ascents which made it a weak competitor with the easy grades of the "River Road." The latter was an ancient thoroughfare, being the southerly continuation of the old "Cohos Road," connecting that route with Concord and through that place with the Massachusetts region.

As early as 1760 a house was erected on the "River Road," near the banks of the Pemigewasset in eastern Bridgewater, which soon after was in use as a tavern. That the travel over the old road was not to any great extent diverted by the opening of the turnpike seems evident from the fact that another and larger house was erected within a hundred yards of the first one in 1806, the year after the completion of the Mayhew, to meet the increasing demands for hospitality. Under the able management of the Webster family these taverns thrived until the railroads finally diverted the travel which the turnpike could not entice away.

The Webster taverns still stand with barns of unusual capacity for keeping horses and wagons near by. Within, the old houses possess a wealth of articles of days gone by. The old four-post bedsteads are still in use, and light is often supplied by means of the old-fashioned dipped tallow candles. In the dining room an old-time brick fireplace has in recent years been uncovered from the board and wall paper which was thought preferable by an older generation and offers a most attractive picture to the fortunate guest. In and around it are grouped the various utensils by which the luxury of a century ago was produced; the tongs, shovel, and andirons for producing warmth and the warming pan by which that warmth would accompany the guest to bed. On the left may be seen the old Dutch oven, and in front of the coals stands the tin baker in which the direct and reflected rays from the fire produce heat enough to bake. To the right is the old tavern office and bar, the old bracketed desk seen through the open door, while the facilities for serving drinks are indicated by the halved door with a shelf on the lower portion.

10. The Dover Turnpike

The proprietors of the Dover Turnpike Road were incorporated also in 1803 and opened a road from Dover through Somersworth to Salmon Falls on the way to South Berwick, Maine, on May 17, 1805. We learn from Wadleigh's *Notable Events in the History of Dover* that the road became free February 7, 1840.

This road was promoted in connection with the Maine Turnpike Association, which proposed to continue the work to the Kennebec River at Augusta, but as we have already seen, the Maine corporation failed to carry out its plans.

11. The Jefferson Turnpike

The Jefferson Turnpike Corporation, formed by an act of 1804, connected the northerly end of the Tenth New Hampshire with the village of Lancaster. The public roads must have been good enough for the travel over them, for this road seems to have had little encouragement and did not last long. In 1810 an act was passed extending the limit within which the road must be completed to 1816. But it was finally built, and in true turnpike fashion, if we are to believe the *History of Coos County*, which tells us that "up Israel's River it was as straight as a line, was well drained, and worked twenty-two feet wide." According to the *History of Lancaster*, the Jefferson was abandoned by its proprietors soon after the floods of 1826.

12. The Grafton Turnpike

The Grafton Turnpike Corporation was formed by an act of 1804 for the purpose of building a road from Orford Bridge to the Fourth New Hampshire Turnpike in Andover. As was the case with other corporations formed about this time, the right to take land was not at first conferred, and it was necessary to appeal to the legislature of 1805 before the company could make headway in securing its right-of way. We read in Wallace's *History of Canaan* that the stock was peddled out in small lots among the residents of the district to be served, and that a long hard job was made of it. In 1807 the promoters were still soliciting subscriptions. Of the capital stock of three hundred shares, one hundred and seventeen were taken by residents of Canaan, which town must have felt a vital interest in the success of the road, for at a town meeting in 1807 it was voted to turn all available resources into cash with which to invest in Grafton Turnpike stock. Fifteen shares were consequently bought, which were sold four years later at a depreciation of one third.

A meeting was finally held on July 4, 1807, at the inn of Moses Dole, at which a contract was made with Thaddeus Lathrop and John Currier to build one hundred and thirty rods of the road for two hundred dollars payable in stock. The road was to be made thirty feet wide generally, but only twenty-four on causeways, and the surface was to have a crown of twenty-four inches. But as the expiration of the time approached in 1808, it was seen that the work could not be completed within the time allowed, so an extension was secured for another three years.

The road was finally completed, terminating on the Fourth New Hampshire at West Andover or Potter Place, as the railroad station is called, having passed through Grafton, Danbury, and South Danbury, "about as the main road is now travelled," says Eastman in his *History of Andover*.

Wallace says the road was made free in 1827. The charter of the corporation was repealed by the legislature January 3, 1829.

13. The Londonderry Turnpike

The road of the Londonderry Turnpike Corporation, also incorporated in 1804, ran as straight as it could be laid out from Butters Corner in Concord to the state line near Andover Bridge, where it connected with the Essex Turnpike of Massachusetts, and formed with that about as direct a line between Concord and Boston as one could reasonably wish. An additional act was secured in 1805 by which the erection of a toll bridge was allowed at "Islehookset Falls," where the turnpike crossed the Merrimac River.

The *History of Concord* says that this road was opened about 1806, having its northerly terminus at the corner of West and Main streets, where a stone stood for many years marked with the inscription "Boston 63 miles." Passing southerly the road skirted the river through Bow, although forming a chord across a long bend of the Merrimac, and passed diagonally across the town of Hooksett. In Auburn it passed between the Massabesic lakes and over Mount Misery and Rattlesnake Hill, leaving the future city of Manchester four miles to the west, thence through Derry Center and across the northerly end of Canobie Lake to the Essex Turnpike at the Massachusetts line. This turnpike pointed straight for the top of the hill over which the Essex climbed

Londonderry Turnpike: Butters Corner, Concord

in Methuen. Consequently we find that its last mile has given way to a detour which provides more distance for the rise.

In 1807 the corporation was authorized to buy land for tollhouses and buildings for public entertainment, provided not over two thousand dollars was spent for land.

14. The Croyden Turnpike

The Croyden Turnpike Corporation, chartered in 1804, built its road from the point in Lebanon where the branch of the Fourth New Hampshire intersected the main road of that company, southerly through Lebanon, Enfield, Grantham, Croyden, and Newport to the Second New Hampshire

Londonderry Turnpike: In Concord

Londonderry Turnpike: At the state line

in Lempster. This company also had to return to the legislature in 1805 to obtain the power to take land.

15. The Chester Turnpike

The seventh company created by the legislature of 1804 was the Chester Turnpike Corporation which began in a small way, entirely within the town of Chester, its route being defined as "from the highway leading to Pembroke, about a mile above Chester East meetinghouse, unto Chester line, on a direction to Pembroke street." But courage grew rapidly, and at the December session they secured an amendment by which they could build all the way to Pembroke Street.

In 1806 the corporation was authorized to buy land adjacent to the turnpike on which to erect houses for entertainment and accommodation of the public, provided it did not spend over six thousand dollars.

The charter of this company was repealed in 1838.

16. The Cheshire Turnpike

Another 1804 creation was the Cheshire Turnpike Corporation. This company built from the Connecticut River to Charlestown meeting house, thence through Charlestown, Langdon, Alstead, and Surrey to the court-house in Keene, where its road joined the Third New Hampshire Turnpike.

We learn from Saunderson's *History of Charlestown* that this road was built about the time that the First Cheshire Bridge was completed. That bridge was also authorized by an act of 1804. From Saunderson we get the impression that the road was not popular, for he tells us that the gates were often stolen—a crude way of expressing resentment which has not been noticed in connection with more than one other road.

The Cheshire Turnpike became free in 1841, but the Cheshire Bridge is still collecting its tolls in this year 1919.

17. The Coos Turnpike

The Coos Turnpike Corporation was formed in 1805, and its road extended "from Haverhill Corner, through Haverhill, Piermont, and Warren, to Baker's River, near Merrill's Mills, in Warren." The preliminaries advanced slowly as we have noticed in most of the northern projects. The region was new and poor, while the country at large was far from affluent, and the fact that any such public improvements were undertaken with such poor chances of financial success testifies to the sturdy spirit of the northern pioneers.

The route was surveyed in 1806 by Captain Benjamin P. Baldwin, and on December 3 of that year twenty-four landowners along the surveyed line executed a deed to the turnpike corporation, making conveyance of whatever land was needed for the building of the road. As no consideration was asked, the land being given freely, we must add a tribute to the public spirit of those farmer settlers.

Although Coos County had been given an outlet through the Crawford Notch over the Tenth New Hampshire, the old route down the Connecticut Valley still held its place on account of the ties which bound the Coos settlers to the lower valley towns from which many of them had come, and they all hailed with enthusiasm the coming of the Coos Turnpike.

Bettinger's *History of Haverhill* states that the road was completed in 1808 and was for more than a generation the great thoroughfare in northern New Hampshire, and made Haverhill during these years the most important and lively town north of Concord.

This turnpike was the predecessor in the section which it covered of the Concord and Montreal Railroad, later the White Mountain Division of the Boston and Maine, and it continued its operations well down toward the date of the railroad opening.

One day the passengers on a south-bound train passing through Warren noticed an old man who was eagerly gazing from the window as he rapidly went by the lower end of the old Coos Turnpike. At last as he passed a dilapidated old building he leaned back in his seat with the satisfied air of one who has found what he sought. On the conductor's sympathetic advances he told his story. When a boy in St. Johnsbury he had been hired as a helper in driving a flock of five hundred turkeys from that town to Lowell, and the tumble-down old rookery which he had recognized had been one of the comfortable taverns at which he had stopped on the way. The drive became a notable procession, and word of its coming was carried in advance by the more rapid travelers who passed it, so that whole villages would be on the watch for its arrival. As the birds became accustomed to the manner of progressing, more ceremony developed, and soon our youthful custodian found that he could lead the way with the flock following him. A gobbler of especial dignity soon assumed a position beside the leader, and thus the procession advanced at the rate of about twenty-three miles a day until its destination was reached without the loss of a single bird.

18. The Ashuelot Turnpike

In 1807 the Ashuelot Turnpike Corporation was created and made its road from "the turnpike in Winchester to Fitzwilliam Village towards Boston." Nothing has been found concerning this road except one legislative act which proves that the turnpike was built. In that act, passed in 1826, it was provided that unless the road was properly repaired before October 3 of that year the charter would stand repealed.

19. The Hampton Causeway

Taylors River, with long reaches of salt marsh on either side, separates Hampton from Hampton Falls, and in early days there was no way of journeying from one place to the other without a devious trip around the upper end of the marshes. This condition had become so onerous by 1807 that it was the subject of consideration at a Hampton town meeting in that year, when a committee was chosen to devise means of financing a road across the soft ground. The best this committee could do was to obtain from the legislature an act authorizing the town of Hampton to make extensive improvements in a certain causeway which seems to have existed over part of the route, to build a bridge over the river and to collect tolls on the same, which act was passed in the same year, 1807. But the town was not prepared to expend so much money and much dissatisfaction was expressed resulting in inaction.

In 1808 the Hampton Causeway Turnpike Corporation was formed to build a turnpike from Sanborns Hill in Hampton Falls to a point in Hampton, bridging the river, and widening, raising, and repairing the existing causeway. Davis' *History of Hampton* says that the town of Hampton subscribed for ten shares of the stock of the new company, and in 1810, in consideration of every inhabitant of Hampton being allowed to pass free of toll, agreed to gravel the turnpike annually "from the northerly end to the middle bridge on the causeway, over the sluiceway." The road thus sanctioned and built was about two and a quarter miles in length, mostly on the old causeway already noted, and was a safe and easy road to travel, but travelers from outside of Hampton chafed under the imposition of tolls. Some distance above a small bridge was built which was known as the "Shunpike Bridge," and although involving a longer trip, it diverted much travel from the legitimate road.

In 1821 the court of sessions laid out the road which passed over the "Shunpike Bridge" as a county road in spite of the opposition offered by Hampton. The contest was continued through 1822, in September of which year the town voted to incur more expense in fighting the new road "and to defend the turnpike." Although laid out by the court, the building of the new road was finally prevented.

Various citizens of Portsmouth and Newburyport petitioned the legislature for an investigation to determine if the Hampton Causeway Turnpike Corporation had not violated the provisions of its charter so that its turnpike had become forfeited. Although the asked-for investigation was ordered, it does not appear to have had any results adverse to the corporation.

Negotiations between the town and the corporation were carried on in 1825, in consequence of which legislative permission was secured and the road was sold; Hampton paying three thousand dollars, and Hampton Falls two thousand dollars. The road thus became free on April 12, 1826.

This turnpike and its bridge crossed the Taylors River about three miles up-stream from the upper waters of Hampton Harbor. To follow it to-day one should leave Hampton on the road passing by the old Whittier Tavern and journey out over the marshes. The turnpike must not be confused with the lengthy Hampton River Bridge on which tolls are still collected in this year 1919. That bridge was built by a corporation organized under the New Hampshire general laws December 5, 1900. It crosses Hampton Harbor, so called, a bay formed by the Blackwater River and the Hampton River. It is 4619 feet in length, by some said to be the longest wooden bridge in the world, and is located between Seabrook and Hampton, passing through a portion of Hampton Falls. It is owned by the Granite State Land Company of Haverhill, Massachusetts.

20. The Fitzwilliam Turnpike

The Fitzwilliam Turnpike Corporation was chartered in 1808 to build from Fitzwilliam Village to the Worcester Turnpike at the Massachusetts line. The road of this corporation connected, not with the Worcester Turnpike which led from Boston to Worcester, but with the Worcester and Fitzwilliam Turnpike, whose proprietors at the time of this incorporation were having a great deal of trouble in financing their road. As finally built the Massachusetts road reached from the state line only to Baldwins Mills, a distance of about eight and a half miles, falling short of reaching Worcester by about twenty-eight miles.

21. The Cornish Turnpike

The Cornish Turnpike Corporation, created in 1808, connected the Croyden Turnpike in Newport with Cornish Bridge, over the Connecticut, between Cornish and Windsor, Vermont.

The Cornish Bridge was built in 1796 at a cost of $17,099.27, we find by reference to Child's *History of Cornish*. Much of the traffic over the bridge must have followed the turnpike, so we may note that the bridge passed over a heavy traffic in sheep and cattle between 1824 and 1840, and that a full thousand sheep crossed September 30, 1833.

In 1829 the attorney-general of New Hampshire was instructed by the legislature to ascertain what corporate rights the Cornish Turnpike Corporation possessed. This probably indicates that the road had become unprofitable and had been allowed to fall into bad condition and possibly indicates the end of the turnpike. The thousand sheep passing on that September day would have paid toll of only a dollar a mile, so we can see that that business did not pay for the consequent repairs.

22. The Londonderry Branch Turnpike

The road of the Londonderry Branch Turnpike Corporation left the Londonderry Turnpike at the northerly end of the bridge at "Isle of Hookset Falls" and ran through the town of Bow to Hopkinton Center. This corporation was formed by act of 1812, and in 1816 secured an extension of one year on its time limit.

23. The Amherst Turnpike

The Amherst Turnpike Corporation, although created in 1812, did not complete its road for several years, obtaining a four years' extension of time in 1815. But it was finally successful and its road formed a continuation of the Middlesex Turnpike of Massachusetts, connecting with that road at the line of Tyngsboro on the westerly bank of the Merrimac River.

Continuous turnpike roads were thus offered from the West Boston Bridge in Cambridge to Claremont, New Hampshire, over the Second New Hampshire and to Hanover, New Hampshire, over the Croyden.

24. The Pinkham Turnpike

In 1824 a grant of public land was made by the state of New Hampshire to Daniel Pinkham upon condition that he should make a road running through such grant. This tract of land occupied the valley of the headwaters of the Ellis and Peabody rivers, extending practically from Glen Ellis Falls to the Glen House, and its remote situation offered so little assistance in road building that the grantee was obliged to appeal to the legislature for an extension of the time within which he was to complete such a road. In 1834 a corporation was formed under the name of the "Proprietors of the Pinkham Turnpike Road" to build "through Pinkham Grant to the Pinkham road in Randolph," thirteen miles. Apparently the conditions had not much improved since Pinkham's day, for the corporation four years later applied for and secured an extension of its time for one year expiring December 1, 1839. In 1840 a legislative act allowed alterations in the established rates of toll, from which it would appear that the road was built and operated as a turnpike. Whether so or not a road has existed for many decades along the route laid out for the toll road, and half a century ago it was a stage route of some importance. For its whole length the turnpike location is a state road to-day, part of it being in the New Hampshire "East Side Road" which leads from Portsmouth to Errol and thence to Colebrook. Two and a half miles northerly from the Glen House the old road, now known as the "Dollycops Road," bears off to the west and passing between the Presidential Range and the steep slopes of Pine Mountain follows across the southwesterly corner of Gorham, across Moose River to the main road in Randolph.

The Dollycops were an amiable old couple who lived in a house the cellar of which is yet to be seen near the bridge over the Peabody River. Local tradition has it that the husband and wife, although occupying the same house, did not speak to each other for twenty years.

Persistent inquiry in Gorham and Berlin has failed to discover anyone who ever heard of a toll road through the Pinkham Notch, and one descendant of Daniel Pinkham is positive that none ever existed. But why was an act passed regarding the rates of toll which could be collected on the road if the franchise had expired the year before and the road had not been opened? Reader, the case is left for your judgment.

But whether turnpike or not the old road offers not the least beautiful among the many noted White Mountain rides, yielding as it does from near the Glen House an unsurpassed view of the Great Gulf and the Presidential Range. Farther south a surpassing scene is revealed of Huntington and Tuckerman's ravines and the Alpine Garden, the sharp slopes and the mountain outlines rising in startling profile. About a mile west from the lower end of the turnpike franchise a less-known feature is found. Poised in apparent insecurity on a steep slope an enormous boulder seems about to roll down the hillside at the slightest touch. And for miles the Ellis and Peabody rivers show their charms at every turn.

25. The Mount Washington Summit Road

After the opening of the Tenth New Hampshire Turnpike a few venturesome travelers visited the White Mountains, but it was not until 1819 that any encouragement was offered for the making of a path by which the summit of Mount Washington could be reached. In that year Ethan Crawford cut a path for that purpose over which he could guide the few tourists who had the hardihood to make such an ascent, and in 1821 he opened another path along the line afterwards utilized by the mountain-climbing railroad. Both of these paths led up from the Crawford Notch, access to which was only to be had by means of the Tenth New Hampshire Turnpike, and it appears that early paths were soon after developed by which the summit might be reached from the eastern side; from the valley of the Androscoggin River.

The Davis Trail recently reopened by the Appalachian Mountain Club was first cut out about 1846 to accommodate travelers coming over the turnpike, but owing to its excessive length and steep grades did not prove successful.

In a short while the easterly routes became much more popular and the larger part of the travelers found their way to Mount Washington by way of Gorham. The Alpine House in Gorham, for many years before the advent of the Atlantic and St. Lawrence Railroad, now the Grand Trunk, was known as the Gate of the Mountains and enjoyed a large proportion of the patronage of the White Mountain travelers. When about 1850 the railroad approached Gorham, mountain travel that way increased, and in 1852, when the road was completed to that town, Gorham began to enjoy almost a monopoly of the mountainclimbing class of tourists.

At that time the means of access to the summit from the Gorham side consisted of a path leading up through Tuckerman's Ravine. Over this path and those from the Crawford side so many made the ascent that the construction of a modest hotel on the summit was completed in 1851. Encouraged by the increased rush of travelers over the new railroad the Glen House appeared in 1852, and soon after the proprietor of that hostelry cut out a bridle path to the summit over which he maintained a lucrative business with saddle horses for several years. But soon the turnpike idea invaded the solitudes.

In 1853 the Mount Washington Road Company was incorporated with turnpike privileges to build "from Peabody River valley, over the top of Mount Washington, to a point between the Notch and Cherry Mountain."

From Kilbourne's *Chronicles of the White Mountains* we learn that the corporation was organized in the same year at a meeting held in Gorham, and that the route was surveyed in 1854.

Commissioners were duly appointed to lay out the road and assess the damages for land taken. They reported that 248½ rods lay through the land of J. M. Thompson, the proprietor of the Glen House, for which they assessed damages to the amount of thirty-five hundred dollars. To John Bellows for land taken for ninety-seven rods of road they awarded one dollar, and for the 2280½ rods through Sargent's Purchase and other owners unknown, noth-

Mount Washington Summit Road: First arrivals at the Summit

ing. But it appeared that the commissioners were influenced in their award to Thompson by the fact that he was in the business of letting saddle horses for the trip to the summit over his bridle path and that the thirty-five hundred

Mount Washington Summit Road: Glen House about 1867

dollars was not payment for the land taken but was awarded to him as the conjectured damage which his business would sustain from the competition of the turnpike. From this award the corporation appealed, contending that the commissioners had not the power to assess conjectural damages of a collateral nature. Thompson came back at them with a sweeping set of declarations. He averred that the granting of a charter for a road for purely pleasure purposes was unconstitutional and such action by the legislature void; that if constitutional the charter was defective on account of no provision being in it by which the state could take the road or terminate the corporate existence; and that the power to take land was illegal because the charter did not specify that an appeal could be had to a jury if a landowner was dissatisfied with the commissioners' award.

To all of these assertions the supreme court in January, 1857, gave a denial, fully maintaining the legality of the company's formation. On the company's appeal from the award of damages it was decided that the commissioners had erred and that they had no authority to assess damages for any other purpose than to pay for land. So a new hearing on that question was ordered.

Construction commenced in 1855 and was pushed with so much energy that within two years the road was completed for half its length. Then financial difficulties stopped the work, and in 1858 the corporation was obliged to ask an extension of its time. The legislature allowed it until August 1, 1861, to complete the road; but the difficulties into which the company had fallen were too great for that remedy, and the Mount Washington Road Company gave up its existence. In 1859 the Mount Washington Summit Road Company was created and allowed a route worded the same as that of the earlier company, and that company took over the completed portion of the road and built the rest, giving access to the summit by carriages in August,

Mount Washington Summit Road: Huntington's Ravine, Mount Washington

Mount Washington Summit Road: Tuckerman's Ravine, seen from Pinkham Road

1861. Under the franchise of 1859 the carriage road up Mount Washington is still in operation, and for passing over it, tolls are still collected.

A writer in *Harpers' Monthly* for August, 1877, said of this road:

For the first four miles it winds among a dense growth of forest trees, and then passes through a ravine, and over the eastern side of the mountain. The grade is easy and the roadbed excellent. Each turn discloses some new prospect—a wide valley faintly green, with a brook or a river flashing through it; a deep dell, with a swaying sea of foliage; an overhanging cliff that seems to render impossible any further ascent; or a wonderful array of peaks.

The dense growth of forest trees noted in 1877 has disappeared by reason of successive lumbering operations, but a substantial growth of timber is in its place to-day, and still the first four miles of the journey is made through

Mount Washington Summit Road: Tollhouse at the Foot of the Mountain

its shadows. Approaching the halfway point the limit of vegetation is noticed, and for a half mile or so the road seems to be the dividing line, the growth on the lower side being noticeably heavier. Emerging from the timber at the Ledge near the Half Way House, the road continues in the same northerly direction for about a half mile, then doubles on itself and starts on its long climb up the crest of Chandler Ridge. As soon as the obstruction of the trees is removed a succession of magnificent views is opened to the eye of the northern peaks of the White Mountain Range, Jefferson, Adams, and Madison, and of the Great Gulf, which lies between them and Mount Washington. Nearing the summit the road skirts the edge of a sharp declivity, overlooking the Alpine Garden and Huntington Ravine.

In its length of eight miles the road makes the ascent from an elevation of 1543 feet above sea level to the altitude of 6293 feet, the highest point in New England. The average grade is thus seen to be 594 feet to the mile, while the maximum grade is said to be at the rate of 880 feet.

The memory of John P. Rich, one of the unlucky contractors under the first company and superintendent of construction for the second, is perpetuated by a memorial tablet set by the road near the base of the mountain. Others to whom credit for this bold enterprise and achievement is due are David O. Macomber of Middletown, Connecticut, the projector of the scheme and first president of the corporation, and C. H. V. Cavis, to whose engineering skill are due the practical grades by which the summit is reached.

On account of the deep cliffs often almost under the passenger's elbow and the possibility of a frightful accident, great care has always been exercised by the management in the selection of its drivers, and only extra strong and steady horses with specially built vehicles are used. Consequently but one accident in which a passenger was killed lies to the charge of the company. In the summer of 1880 a wagon carrying nine people down the mountain upset at a sharp turn in the road about a mile below the Half Way House, throwing the passengers on to the rocks, killing one, and injuring all the others.

26. The Warner and Kearsarge Turnpike

The Kearsarge Summit Road Company was incorporated in 1864, authority being given it to build from Kearsarge Village to the top of the mountain named. But the franchise was allowed to expire and was revived by legislative act in 1873. In 1877 a time extension of ten years was granted, which seems sufficient to prove that nothing was ever done under that charter. Especially are we inclined to think so because little need would seem to exist for two roads up that one mountain, and another company did build such a road.

In 1866 the Warner and Kearsarge Road Company was formed to construct a road to the summit from either Warner or Salisbury and that company carried out its plan. But not immediately, for we find that it had to apply for a revival of its expired rights in 1872, at which time the town of Warner was allowed to subscribe for shares of its capital stock to an amount not exceeding two thousand dollars. That the road had been completed by 1875 appears from an act passed in that year, which allowed the corporation to acquire land on the top of the mountain on the line of its road. Permission was given in the same act to sell land to the United States for the purposes of a signal station. On the ninth of March, 1893, the charter of the company was revived and given a new life of ten years, authority then being given to build a branch connecting the toll road with the highway at Smith's Corner. February 10, 1903, a further addition of ten years of life to the charter was enacted, since which time nothing has been found on the records. Since the expiration of the last period of grace the corporation has lapsed, and its road, while not assumed by the town of Warner, is free from toll.

27. The Mount Washington Turnpike

A successful venture was that of the Mount Washington Turnpike Company, which was chartered in 1867 and allowed a route extending from the Fabyan House to the foot of Mount Washington. After many years of persistent effort, in spite of ridicule and discouragements, Sylvester March had at last succeeded in interesting capital in his plan to build a railroad up Mount Washington, construction having been commenced on that undertaking in May, 1866. The form of cars and locomotive to be used on the new road, being adapted to the steep grades to be encountered, naturally was not suitable for operation on level ground and the mountain-climbing railroad necessarily made its terminus at the foot of the mountain. That was several miles from the nearest road, which was the Tenth New Hampshire Turnpike, while the nearest railroad station was at Littleton, twenty-five miles away. So the turnpike was conceived as a means of transporting to the site of the new railroad the various supplies necessary for its construction and equipment, and later to derive profit from the tolls collected from tourists on their way to the mountain. The view here reproduced from an old stereoscopic photograph shows the base of Mount Washington and the terminus of the railroad. This point then was the easterly objective of the Mount Washington Turnpike, and the photograph, taken about 1867, shows the nature of the region through which the road was built.

The profitable life of this turnpike was destined to be short, for summer travel to the White Mountains was growing very popular and it was unlikely that the railroads would long leave such a lucrative field unoccupied. As already stated, the Boston, Concord, and Montreal Railroad was completed as far as Littleton when the turnpike was projected, and it lost no time in pushing nearer. But times were hard and the construction proceeded by piecemeal. Between 1873 and 1876 the rails crept ahead a little at a time, until Fabyans was reached, after which the remaining five miles to the base was rushed, the whole length being opened for passengers July 6, 1876.

But the turnpike still held on, and its rates-of-toll sign at the Fabyans end was long a familiar object to tourists with its unique spacing. Many will recall the heading:

RATES OF TOLL ON THE MT. WAS

HINGTON TURNPIKE

The railroad must have felt the competition of the old-fashioned competitor, for early in 1882 a small block, three eighths of the total of the capital stock, was bought by the directors of the Boston, Concord, and Montreal Railroad, and later purchases resulted in the acquisition of it all.

In 1885 authority was secured from the legislature to extend the Mount Washington Turnpike, called in the act the "White Mountain Turnpike," to a junction with the Mount Washington Summit Road, but the plan was never carried out.

But even railroad managers could not make turnpike success and they were glad to get rid of the road. May 13, 1903, the turnpike was deeded to the state of New Hampshire.

28. The Moosilauke Mountain Turnpike

The turnpike from Warren to the summit of Moosilauke Mountain is another which is still collecting tolls in this year of grace 1919. That road was built

Mount Washington Turnpike: Easterly end, 1867

under authority of a franchise granted in 1870 to the Moosilauke Mountain Road Company, but like many others seems to have had difficulty in its financing. In 1872 the legislature granted the town of Warren the privilege of contributing not over eight hundred dollars toward the construction of the road, which must have overcome the troubles, for the road was built about that time. Kilbourne, *Chronicles of the White Mountains*, says that the Tip Top House on Moosilauke was much enlarged in 1872 in consequence of the greatly increased travel over the new road.

Leaving Warren Village and following the North Woodstock road along the bank of Baker's River for about three miles, one comes to a corner. The road turning sharply to the left and crossing the river will lead you to Breezy Point where the turnpike begins. Just beyond the Moosilauke Inn the tollgate is located and, having parted with the toll, you may proceed up the mountain. The road is straight for a mountain climber and its steep grades suggest that a better route might have been found by circling more. The length is a little over four miles, but the wonderful views from the summit are well worth the effort. Standing apart from other eminences Moosilauke offers a far wider range of view than other White Mountain peaks.

In 1881 the Moosilauke Mountain Road Company obtained additional franchises to build three "bridle paths or carriage roads " from various points to the summit of the mountain, but it does not appear that any work was done in consequence.

29. The Lincoln Turnpike

Visitors to Franconia always seek the Flume as one of the wonders never to be missed, and to reach that interesting spot they pass over and pay toll on another turnpike. The Lincoln Turnpike Company was created by an act of the legislature of 1871, by which it obtained the right to build its road "from the Flume House in Lincoln, on the main road, to near the Flume."

Tourists may have a delightful ride from the Profile House down the Pemigewasset valley, passing Profile Lake, The Old Man of the Mountain, The Basin, The Pool, and after five miles have been counted off find themselves at a picturesque opening in the stone wall through which automobiles are forbidden to pass. This is the gateway and place of collection for the Lincoln Turnpike, but barring automobiles seems inconsistent with the public-utility nature of the road.

At first the turnpike follows closely beside the main road but soon curves away from it, and then falls abruptly to the romantic covered bridge over the Pemigewasset River. A succession of steep ascents then brings the traveler to a looped end of the road by the rustic souvenir store. Thence to the Flume the climb must be made on foot.

In the first year of its existence the Lincoln Turnpike saw the destruction by fire of the old Flume House, the one named in its charter, but within another year saw the successor arise from a site close by, where it in turn was burned in 1917. The Flume House of 1919 is but a small building, merely a lunch room.

30. The Sanborn Turnpike

The Sanborn Turnpike Company was incorporated in 1872 with a franchise confined to the town of Northfield.

For many years a private road had existed across the Glidden Meadow in that town, but opinions as to its public necessity varied. Those believing such a road to be demanded by the mass of the people were unable to convince the selectmen who refused to give it a public layout. From the controversy which ensued the turnpike franchise evolved, the view of the landowners apparently being that, if the town would not accept and assume the road, those using it should pay for the privilege.

Although the road was kept in good condition and is in use as a public road to-day the privilege of collecting tolls was never utilized, and no gate was ever erected across the road.

31. The Uncanoonuc Road

A charter was granted in 1877 forming the Uncanoonuc Road Company and giving it a franchise to build from the mountain road on the southerly side of Uncanoonuc Mountain in Goffstown to the summit of that mountain.

The Pierce farm was on the southwesterly side of Uncanoonuc and the homestead set back a short distance from the mountain road. From these farm buildings the turnpike started, and by a precipitous winding course reached the summit altitude of thirteen hundred and twenty-one feet. The Pierce family acted as toll gatherers, and the gate was at the beginning of the toll road, convenient to their house. The road was promptly built and was operated for several years. Mr. Flanders, the fire warden on the summit, recalls that one Sunday soon after the opening he counted forty teams which had made the ascent.

Uncanoonuc Mountain is reached from Manchester by trolley and mountain railway in forty minutes and is the highest point in that vicinity. The ride to its base is particularly attractive, and the novel ride up the steep slope on the incline railway affords a most enjoyable, experience.

The Uncanoonuc Incline Railway and Development Company was incorporated in 1903. Its road climbs the mountain side at an average grade of thirty-five per cent. On the summit of the mountain a hotel has been erected, on which is the fire look-out tower of the New Hampshire Forestry Service.

In the old days another tower stood on slightly higher ground, a little north of the present tower. It was forty feet high and braced, we can believe, against any possible hurricane, for it is said that the spread of its posts was sufficient to allow the building of a dance hall within them at the bottom.

From the top of the present tower, just over the tops of the encircling trees nearly due west, can be seen three groups of farm buildings. The one to the left and closest to the line of tree tops is the Pierce farm and marks where the old turnpike began. The other end is close by but hidden in the trees.

Down to 1917 the road had been allowed to shift for itself, and it had become little better than a brook bed where the running waters had gullied it out, but in the spring of that year it was temporarily patched to enable an artesian-well contractor to get his outfit hauled to the summit.

32. The Liberty Road

After another four years a new turnpike charter appears, this time for access to the summit of Chocorua Mountain in the town of Albany. In the year 1887 James Liberty and his neighbors united to make a road up the south side of the mountain, the first from that direction, and in 1889 Mr. Liberty sought and obtained a charter for himself and those who might associate themselves with him under the name of the Chocorua Mountain Road. Authority was granted to maintain a "bridle path and carriage road from near the dwelling house of Charles Durell in said Tamworth (where said road is now located and constructed) to the line between the towns of said Tamworth and Albany, thence to the top of Chocorua Mountain in said town of Albany." This was the last turnpike charter granted in New England by virtue of which a turnpike was built or operated.

The road of this company offers the easiest of the seven routes by which Chocorua may be ascended. It leaves the highway in the north-central part of Tamworth, at the Durell Farm, and near the "Nat Berry Bridge." The first third of the distance is a carriage road at the termination of which the toll is collected. Thence to the Peak House it is a bridle path.

For nearly thirty years the Half Way House stood at the end of the carriage road, housing both the toll gatherer and his victims. But in a violent gale which swept the mountain in September, 1915, the building was lifted bodily and blown into the valley several hundred feet below.

The last turnpike charter granted in New England was enacted by the New Hampshire legislature March 22, 1893, when the Mount Prospect Turnpike and Hotel Company was incorporated. The plan of this company was to build a crossroad in Lancaster, connecting the Whitefield and the Jefferson roads; another road leading to the summit of Mount Prospect; and to erect a hotel on that eminence. Nothing was ever done under this charter.

Mount Prospect is now owned by United States Senator John W. Weeks and its summit is crowned by his summer residence. The road up the mountain is the private venture of Mr. Weeks.

The following turnpikes are reported by Wood to have been chartered but never operated as toll roads

1802	Seventh New Hampshire	Charlestown to Surrey
1803	Charlestown	Charlestown to Lempster
	Coventry	Warren to Haverhill
1804	Richmond	Royalston, Mass., to Swanzey
	Bath	Connecticut River near Lyman to Sandwich
	Union	Hillsboro to Concord
	Great Ossippe	Sandwich to Saco, Maine, via Effingham
	Littleton	Crawford Notch to Littleton
	Hillsborough	Andover to Massachusetts line toward Boston
	Chesterfield	Chesterfield to Warwick, Mass.
	Stoddard	Walpole to Amsokeag Falls on the Merrimac
	Sandwich	Sandwich to Dover Landing
	Sunapee	Sunapee Pond to Hillsboro
	Westmoreland	Walpole to Northfield, Mass.
1805	Piermont	Orford to Piermont
	Newport	Newport to Keene
	Monadnock	Milford to Marlboro Hills
	Hancock	Stoddard to Milford
1806	Pittsfield	Barnstead to Pittsfield
1807	Rindge	Northfield, Mass., to the Branch Turnpike
1808	Litchfield	Amherst to Metheun, Mass.
	Winnepiseogee	Gilmanton to Bridgewater
	Sanbornton	Pemigewasset Bridge to Sanbornton
	Northern Haverhill	Up the Ammonoosuc Valley to the Bath Turnpike
	New Chester and Danbury	Between the towns named
1809	Pemigewasset Middle Branch	Thornton to Lancaster
	Great Sunapee	Newport to Warner
1812	Andover	Salisbury to Andover
1815	Sunapee (second)	Fisherfield (Newbury) to Wendell
	Milford	Hollis to Mt. Vernon
1820	Pemigewasset	Peeling (Woodstock) to Franconia

	Upper Coos	Franconia to Bethlehem
1828	Franconia	Through that town
1837	Coos in New Hampshire	Dalton to Gorham
1838	Mount Washington	Northeast end of the Tenth New Hampshire Turnpike to Table Rock
1839	Coventry	Haverhill to Coventry (repealed 1840)
1852	White Mountains Plank Road	Littleton or Whitefield to the Notch
	Winnepiseogee and White Mountain	Tamworth to Tenth New Hampshire Turnpike
1866	Mount Hayes	Shelburne to summit of Mt. Hayes
	Mount Lafayette	Profile-Flume Highway to summit of Mt. Lafayette
1868	Waumbeck	Jefferson to Randolph
1870	Franconia and White Mountain Notches	Bethlehem to Franconia Notch
1873	Saco and Swift River	Bartlett to Albany
	Wilmot and Kearsarge	Wilmot to summit of Kearsarge Mt.
1881	Star King Mountain	Jefferson to Starr King Mt.
1885	Woodstock and Lincoln	North Woodstock to Lincoln

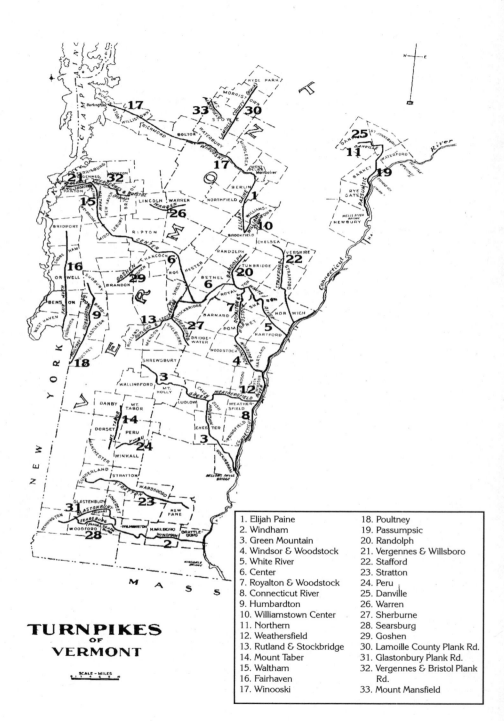

1. Elijah Paine
2. Windham
3. Green Mountain
4. Windsor & Woodstock
5. White River
6. Center
7. Royalton & Woodstock
8. Connecticut River
9. Humbardton
10. Williamstown Center
11. Northern
12. Weathersfield
13. Rutland & Stockbridge
14. Mount Taber
15. Waltham
16. Fairhaven
17. Winooski
18. Poultney
19. Passumpsic
20. Randolph
21. Vergennes & Willsboro
22. Stafford
23. Stratton
24. Peru
25. Danville
26. Warren
27. Sherburne
28. Searsburg
29. Goshen
30. Lamoille County Plank Rd.
31. Glastonbury Plank Rd.
32. Vergennes & Bristol Plank Rd.
33. Mount Mansfield

TURNPIKES
OF
VERMONT

SCALE - MILES

The Turnpikes of Vermont

ALTHOUGH a few colonists had established themselves at Fort Dummer, now Brattleboro, as early as 1724, very little settlement was made in Vermont until about 1760. Then a tide of immigration set in, and between that year and 1768 one hundred and thirty-eight townships were granted to colonists by Governor Benning Wentworth of New Hampshire. When the Revolutionary War was over many of its survivors sought homes in Vermont. The northern part of the state was much more popular than the southern, but access to that section was had only by means of a rough military road which had been built under order of General Washington in 1778. That road, known as the Bayley-Hazen Military Road, extended from what is now the village of Wells River in the town of Newbury, on the Connecticut River, northwesterly to a notch in the mountains in the town of Westfield, near the Canada line. But access to this road was only had over the old Cohos Road in New Hampshire, which led from the valley of the Pemigewasset River at Plymouth, up the valley of the Baker's River and to the Connecticut in the north part of the town of Haverhill, opposite Wells River, where the village of Woodsville is now found, and it is easily imagined that such dependence upon the older state was distasteful to the Vermonters whose long struggle for a separate government had so lately been successful.

There was much fertile land in the lower valley of the Connecticut and back from its banks, and facilities were needed for access to that region as well. So on the twenty-seventh of October, 1795, a resolve was passed by the Vermont legislature by which committees were appointed in the counties of Windham, Windsor, and Orange "to lay out a public highway from the south line of this state to the north line of the town of Newbury." The new highway was directed to be laid "as near the banks of the Connecticut River as may be eligible and convenient," and was to connect with the Bayley-Hazen Road, thus forming a main highway running the length of the state.

In February, 1797, similar action was taken looking to roads between Rutland and Salem, New York; Vergennes and Burlington; Burlington and the province line; and Salisbury to Onion River Bridge; and provision was made for additions to the Connecticut Post Road and for a road to Vergennes.

But the turnpike movement had been launched in Vermont three months before this last act, for in November, 1796, the First Vermont Turnpike

Corporation was chartered with power to build a road "from the east line of said Bennington to the cast bank of the Deerfield river, in said Wilmington, in such place or places as the said corporation shall choose for the same."

It seems that nothing was done under authority of this act of incorporation, for three years later the Windham Turnpike Corporation was created and granted the same route with the further privilege of extending to Brattleboro. But since the first charter in each state has been found to be a pretty accurate forerunner of the rest, a few notes will be given of the First Vermont. Although the regimental system was commenced, as we see, it was not continued and the First Vermont was the only one to be designated numerically.

Upon the corporation were conferred the same powers as were possessed by the selectmen of towns to take lands, lay out, and build a highway, and, when its road was approved by the county court of Windham, gates not exceeding two might be erected "in such manner as shall be necessary and convenient." The legislature might dissolve the corporation when its income had repaid the investment with twelve per cent. Five hundred dollars was to be spent within two years and the whole project completed within five. The usual requirement of a signboard appears, upon which the following rates of toll were to be given:

Coach, Phaëton, Chariot, or other four-wheeled vehicle, drawn by two horses	$0.75
If drawn by four horses	1.00
If drawn by more than four for each additional horse	.06
Cart, Waggon, Sled, or Sleigh drawn by two oxen or horses	.50
Each additional ox or horse	.06
Chaise, Chair, or other Carriage drawn by one horse	.37
Man and Horse	.25
Foot passenger	.04
Horses, oxen, and other neat cattle, not in teams each	.06
Sheep and swine, each	.01

Certain of the high rates contained in the foregoing schedule suggest that Vermont had cut a path of its own in the matter of levying tolls, and that it was the intention to prescribe the charges for the whole length of the road, such total to be divided by the number of gates at which toll was demanded. Although such a division of collections was not specified in the act of incorporation of the First Vermont, our supposition is confirmed by the charter of the Green Mountain which followed it. In that a table of toll rates is given, and then follows a paragraph which unmistakably sets forth that such tolls are to be collected at each gate only in the fraction which one gate bears to the entire number.

The preamble to the act creating the First Vermont is an exact copy (except for the towns named) of that found in the act of incorporation of the First Massachusetts.

Those passing to or from public worship were exempt from paying toll, as was anyone engaged in common labor on his own farm or in the "common and ordinary business of family concerns within the same town." A penalty of from one to ten dollars was provided for needlessly hindering travelers at the gates.

As in the other states, each Vermont corporation was created by a special act of the legislature, and very few general laws were passed for turnpike government. The *Revised Statutes of Vermont*, published in 1839, contained eleven sections of that nature, certain of which enacted in 1806 are especially interesting as providing governmental control of those public utilities, and being an early anticipation of the modern public-service commissions.

Each county court was required annually, in December, "to appoint three judicious freeholders to be inspectors of turnpike-roads in such county." Such appointees could not be stockholders in any turnpike corporation nor in any way connected with one, and upon being installed into office were required to make oath that they were free from that taint.

It was the duty of the inspectors, upon application by three freeholders, to inspect any turnpike within their jurisdiction of which complaint had been made. They were empowered to order repairs, and to enforce their orders by throwing open the gates for free passage by the public until such repairs were made. The corporations, however, were allowed the right of appeal to the court in cases of unreasonable orders.

Anyone who obstructed an inspector with the intention to prevent his allowing free passage by the public, pending the ordered repairs, or anyone who shut a gate after an inspector had ordered it to be left open, was liable to a fine of two hundred dollars.

If an inspector after his appointment became a stockholder in a turnpike corporation, his tenure of office automatically ceased.

Costs of the inspectors' proceedings were assessed on the party at fault. Accounts were rendered and it was the duty of the court to assess the costs and order their payment by the corporation or the applicants, issuing an execution at the end of thirty days.

The inspectors had authority to examine rates of toll, and could diminish the rate at any gate, if they raised it proportionally at another, giving due consideration to the distances between such gates.

In section eleven Vermont appears as the first to make provisions, whereby a town and a corporation having agreed might make the road free without a special act of the legislature. Therein it was provided that any corporation, "in its discretion," might sell a proportionate amount of its stock to any town through which its road passed. The town thereupon became the owner and operator of so much of the turnpike as lay within its limits, and was allowed to collect tolls thereon until its receipts had repaid the amount paid for the stock. November 19, 1839, a further act was passed, giving power to the supreme and county courts "to take any real estate, easement, or franchise of any turnpike or other corporation when, in their judgment, the public good requires a public highway." The taking, however, was to cover the entire franchise and could not be made on a portion of a road.

An old law which had been repealed in 1839 was revived in 1845, and by it the turnpike inspectors were empowered, upon application, to divide any turnpike into sections, placing a value on each division. Towns or individuals might then buy at the inspectors' prices one or more sections of the turnpike for the purpose of making it free. Such purchasers were allowed to continue the collection of tolls for a while under specified limitations.

The second Vermont act of incorporation formed the Green Mountain Turnpike Corporation on March 10, 1797, and gave it the right to build a road from the easterly boundary of Clarendon to the bridge over Black River in Ludlow. Evidently this route was not satisfactory to the promoters and they allowed their first charter to lapse, obtaining from the legislature on November 2, 1799, a new charter with a franchise covering a longer route. But meanwhile another proposition had received legislative sanction, and under the charter granted for that was built the first Vermont turnpike.

1. Elijah Paine's Turnpike

That charter was granted on October 28, 1799, and conferred on "Elijah Paine, his heirs, and assigns," the right to build and operate a turnpike road "from Experience Fisk's, in Brookfield, through Williamstown, Northfield, and Berlin, to the north side of Onion River."

As we are to meet frequent references to this Onion River, it may be well to mention here that the modern Winooski River once bore that name.

Although the first two corporations were granted rates of toll which were to be divided by the number of gates erected, that method was abandoned without being put to actual test, neither of the corporations carrying out its plan. Elijah Paine was granted the right to collect certain tolls at each of the three gates which he was authorized to erect.

The layout was to be sixty feet wide and the traveled path eighteen feet.

In granting lands to new settlers from the public domain it was the early custom to limit the acreage allowed to one person, but an additional area was generally granted sufficient to provide for the land required in the building of future roads. October 15, 1801, an act was passed providing that Elijah Paine need not pay any damages for building his turnpike through unimproved lands where such allowance had been made. A change in the location of the gates was also allowed in this act.

The construction of this turnpike was not the only contribution made by Elijah Paine toward the development of the state. Born in Connecticut, he graduated from Harvard in 1781, and in 1784 began the practice of law in Vermont, making his home in the edge of Williamstown near where he later built his road. He entered largely into agricultural enterprises, and while Northfield was yet a wilderness he expended forty thousand dollars in the establishment of a factory in that town for the manufacture of American cloth. At the time the turnpike charter was granted he was serving his adopted state as United States senator, and from 1801 to his death in 1842, he was judge of the United States court for the District of Vermont. The turnpike is often mentioned as "Governor Paine's turnpike," probably on account of his being succeeded in his business enterprises by his son Charles, who was governor of Vermont from 1841 to 1843. To Governor Paine was largely due the financing which allowed the construction of the Central Vermont Railroad, which must reflect credit on his public spirit, as his turnpike was thereby destroyed.

The Paine turnpike ran over the eastern spurs of the Green Mountains almost directly north for about twenty miles, and terminated on the north side of the Onion or Winooski River, in the center of Montpelier.

2. The Windham Turnpike

The next was the Windham Turnpike Company, created by the act of November 1, 1799. As previously stated this company took over the route which the First Vermont failed to improve from Bennington to Wilmington, with the addition of the further right from Wilmington to Brattleboro. Five tollgates were allowed, the first to be installed when seven miles of road had been completed. Ultimately the gates were to be located: one near the east line of Bennington; one in Readsboro; one near the Deerfield River in Wilmington; one in the west part of Marlboro; and one in the west part of Brattleboro. At the two eastern gates less toll was to be collected, for what reason is not apparent. The section of road in Brattleboro was to be built over an easier country, and it may have been considered that less expenditure was entitled to less returns, but such reasoning could not have been applied to the section to be built in Marlboro, for construction in that part involved steep grades and heavy work.

The turnpike climbed over a high divide in Wilmington, passing a short distance south of Ray Pond, to which has lately been given the more pretentious name of Lake Rayponda, and fell steeply into Wilmington Village. There it passed through the very center, being the road on which Child's Tavern fronts. The old Vermont House on the opposite side of the street from Child's could doubtless tell many a stage-coach story. West of Wilmington the old turnpike was the road now regularly traveled to Bennington, passing with many steep grades and circuitous windings through Searsburg and Woodford City.

The promoters of the Windham seem to have been able to secure what the Third Massachusetts tried in vain to get, as it is seen in their act of incorporation that the various towns along the road were to be obliged to keep the turnpike clear of snow.

The original charter provided that the corporation might build as far as the house of General John Steward in Brattleboro. But on October 27, 1800, another act was secured by which the location of the road was allowed to be changed and the easterly terminus fixed in Brattleboro, at the house of Rutherford Hayes, the grandfather of the nineteenth president of the United States.

The road was operated for about twelve years with an incomplete list of rates of toll, for after that lapse of time we find it enacted that a "waggon drawn by one horse " should pay a toll of twelve and one half cents. In 1815 the removal of the eastern gate was allowed, but no increased rates at the others in consequence. October 26, 1821, the corporation was allowed to give up all of its road cast of Wilmington, and in 1825 it was authorized to extend its road and change its gates wherever it saw fit. How long the western portion was operated has not been learned, but it apparently had been abandoned before 1828, as another company, the Searsburg, was chartered then to reclaim the road.

Over this turnpike journeyed the father of President Hayes about 1808 when, having received his "freedom suit" and attained his majority, he sought employment as a merchant's clerk in Wilmington, where he married and lived a few years before making his home in Ohio in 1817.

3. The Green Mountain Turnpike

The promoters of the Green Mountain Turnpike Company returned with a more attractive proposition and, on November 2, 1799, were granted a new charter to build "from the east line of Clarendon to the post road on Connecticut River, in Rockingham."

In this act of incorporation a bond in the sum of one thousand dollars was required to guarantee that the incorporators would complete their road within five years. Towns were allowed to subscribe to the capital stock, but no one town for more than one sixth of the total.

Bellows Fall Bridge: First Bridge over the Connecticut River, 1785

Under this franchise and the eight acts subsequently passed, the road was built from Clarendon to Bellows Falls following closely along the route afterwards taken by the Rutland Railroad. Hayes' *History of Rockingham* tells us that it was financed by the same interests which built the canal at Bellows Falls, and that the corporation operated the road for forty years.

It appears that there was considerable trouble in building the road, and it seems doubtful if it can be said that it ever was finally completed although it was operated for its entire length for many years. The matter of land damages gave much concern to the company and it secured the passage of an act in 1800, providing that roads near the turnpike, and rendered useless by its construction, should be discontinued by the selectmen, and the consequent reversion of the land to the original owners should be considered as an offset for land taken for the new road. Evidently their further efforts toward economical purchases of land were too successful, for a "great complaint about smallness of damages" resulted in the passage of an act in 1802, which gave the landowners a right of appeal. In 1817 the road was still under construction, and changes in the route for over a quarter of its length were then allowed. Under authority granted in 1818 the erection of a gate in Cavendish or Chester, with collection of half rates of toll, was made conditional upon the whole road being completed within four years from that date.

The road plainly was unsatisfactory, for in 1822 permission was secured to resurvey and alter the location in Mount Holly and Shrewsbury, the abandoned portions to be discontinued. But evidently nothing was done in consequence, for we find another act, passed in 1828, by which they might resurvey and make alterations for the whole length of the turnpike. Again they appeared before the legislature in 1831 and secured authority to make alterations on all of their road within Windsor County. A two years' limit on this last act was extended another year in 1832, after which we find no further legislation. So we must conclude that the extensive alterations were never carried out, much as they were desired. Had they been made, much more legislation would have been needed to provide for alteration of gates and disposition of the discontinued portions of the old turnpike.

The location of the eastern end of the Green Mountain Turnpike at Bellows Falls was due to the existence of a bridge over the Connecticut River there. The Bellows Falls Bridge was provided for by the New Hampshire legislature at its session in 1783, and was the first bridge built over the Connecticut. It was built in 1785 by Colonel Enoch Hale, and its construction is shown in the illustration photographed from an old painting in the Bellows Falls office of the local electric-light company. Considering the occasional turbulence of the Connecticut River it seems doubtful if such a structure could have lasted many years, but the present bridge is the next

Bellow's Falls Bridge: Tucker Toll Bridge and Railroad Bridge

one of which we have information, and that was erected in 1840. It is called the "Tucker Bridge," and is well shown in the illustration. It is of the type so familiar to travelers in northern New England, the Towne lattice truss, said to have been built by the mile and cut off in lengths to suit. Engineers will be interested to note the doubled web members over the pier, which can plainly be seen in the illustration. An interesting feature in all the old bridges is the manner in which the early builders provided for the strains, and here we see how the strains over the support of a continuous beam were countered. The "Tucker Bridge " was operated as a toll bridge until recent years and, since no legislative act authorizing its erection has been found subsequent to that of 1783, we must conclude that it was built and operated under the charter then granted.

The charter of the Green Mountain preceded that of the Third New Hampshire by about seven weeks. The New Hampshire road, as we have seen, led from Bellows Falls through Keene, and into the town of Ashby, Massachusetts, on the way to Boston. Thus it appears that the two turnpikes, with the Bellows Falls Bridge, were units of a grand scheme whereby the Lake Champlain country was to have an easy outlet for its produce, and an inlet for its supplies to and from Boston, a route in active operation to-day by railroads.

4. The Windsor and Woodstock Turnpike

November 5, 1799, the Windsor and Woodstock Turnpike Company was chartered to build "from the east parish in Windsor, to or near the Woodstock court house." The road was to be four rods wide and eighteen feet in the traveled portion. Evidently the incorporators expected to follow the old Connecticut post road for a portion of the way, for we find it enacted that no gate should be erected on any part of that road. This company was expressly allowed to commute tolls, or in others words, to keep book accounts with regular customers.

The East Parish in Windsor was situated on the bank of the Connecticut River at the Vermont end of the Cornish Bridge, which had been erected three years prior to the incorporation of this turnpike company. We have already noted that a heavy traffic in sheep and cattle passed over Cornish Bridge in its early years, and we are justified in assuming that much of it reached the bridge by means of this turnpike.

A change in the location of the gates was allowed by an act passed in 1802, and on October 26, 1820, the company was relieved of all obligation to maintain the road east of Lull Brook in Hartland.

5. The White River Turnpike

The White River Turnpike Company received its franchise on the first day of November, 1800, and built a road between twenty and twenty-one miles in length, extending from what is now White River Junction, up and along the north bank of the White River through the towns of Hartford, Sharon, and Royalton or, as the charter expressed it, "from the mouth of White River to the mouth of the second branch of said river."

Tucker's *History of Hartford* and Lovejoy's *History of Royalton* agree that the turnpike was in operation for fifty-two years. No bridges had to be maintained within the limits of Royalton, which eliminated one frequent cause of friction between town and corporation, and Lovejoy testifies to the continued harmonious relations in this case.

By 1852 the earnings had decreased so far that the owners of the road offered to sell to the three towns for ten dollars each, the turnpike to be given up as soon as one town had paid its ten. The reason is not far to seek. The Vermont Central Railroad, first chartered in 1835, in January, 1850, opened its line from Windsor to Burlington, and for twenty miles of its length was never more than five hundred feet away from the dust of the turnpike.

6. The Center Turnpike

The Center Turnpike Company, created November 4, 1800, was to provide turnpike facilities from Middlebury courthouse to Woodstock, with a branch turning off "at the most convenient place," and leading to the mouth of the second branch of the White River, at which point it would join the westerly end of the White River Turnpike. Three days later the Royalton and Woodstock was incorporated to build from Woodstock to Royalton, which it is easy to see paved the way for a controversy. In October, 1801, in consequence of the Center's proposing to "fall into" the Royalton and Woodstock location, an act was passed by which amicable relations were secured and the rights of the latter company protected. It is difficult to determine positively where the Center did build its road, but apparently it built a portion of the main line and the authorized branch, leaving out the part of the main location which would have taken it to Woodstock. As it was built, it formed an extension of the White River Turnpike, following up the river of that name to the headwaters of the west branch thereof in the town of Ripton, passing thence into the valley of the Middlebury River, which it followed to the Middlebury courthouse. That money was not easy in this case is evident from an extension of time which was granted, running to 1808.

In 1817 the company was relieved of obligation to maintain that part of its road which lay west of "Joshua Hyde's road in Middlebury," and in 1818 was released from its responsibility for all of the turnpike situated in Bethel and Royalton north of the White River. Nineteen years later, in 1837, the company again appeared in the halls of legislation and secured the passage of an act by which it was relieved of all of its road from the eastern end to where it left the White River, that part of the road being made a public highway. A new rate of tolls was granted, to be collected for a few years longer on the remaining portions of the turnpike. That must have been a very few miles in the towns of Ripton and Middlebury.

A very little at the eastern end of this turnpike fell within the territory afterwards occupied by the Vermont Central Railroad, but the toll road gave up its existence some years before railroad competition forced it to do so. A farther portion of the location later formed the route of the White River Valley Railroad.

7. The Royalton and Woodstock Turnpike

As already stated the Royalton and Woodstock Turnpike Company was incorporated November 7, 1800, to build "from Royalton meetinghouse to Woodstock court-house," and its road was built in spite of the effort of the promoters of the Center to improve their franchise, granted three days earlier.

Again we are indebted to Lovejoy, who tells us that the turnpike promotion was opposed by the inhabitants of the towns of Pomfret and Woodstock, and that to placate them much latitude was used in defining their domestic concerns, in the prosecution of which they were allowed to pass free over the road. This conciliation was continued until 1838, when David Bosworth, a local "man of the hour," was appointed toll gatherer and promptly drew the lines tighter. A merry war resulted, but it appears that the company, being within its legal rights, prevailed.

At the northerly end of the turnpike the company maintained a bridge over the White River, which, after twenty-five years' service, became unsafe. Owing to insufficient revenue the company felt unable to repair the bridge and sought to abandon it, seeking a new location by which it could use a bridge owned by the town. The usual opposition was encountered and as usual a compromise was made. The town of Royalton voted in 1830 that, if the company would properly maintain its road, the town would contribute twenty-five dollars annually toward the repairs of the bridge.

May 1, 1842, the road became free by action of the court under authority of the act of 1839.

8. The Connecticut River Turnpike

John Holbrook, Samuel Dickenson, and Lemuel Whiting were granted March 10, 1797, the exclusive right for eight years to run a stage from

Brattleboro "on the post road to Dartmouth College," because, as the act recited, "the said John, Samuel, and Lemuel have, at great expense and considerable loss, established a line of stages on said route." By this it appears that the post road contemplated in the act of 1795 had been constructed as far, at least, as Norwich, which lies on the Vermont shore of the Connecticut and opposite Hanover, the home town of Dartmouth College. Now comes evidence that the road had been poorly built, or if not so, that it was too heavy a burden for the towns to maintain, for we have a franchise granted to the Connecticut River Turnpike Company November 7, 1800, to cover the same territory as the post road, between Bellows Falls and the south line of Thetford, and probably occupying the post road itself. One would expect to find the afore-mentioned John, Samuel, and Lemuel interested in this turnpike over which their stages were to run for the remaining five years of their exclusive privilege, but apparently their "great expense and considerable loss" continued to follow them, for their names do not appear among the incorporators of the Connecticut River.

This charter specified the number of gates which the corporation might erect and prescribed the toll to be collected at each, but introduced a feature which is only found in Massachusetts by permission of a special act of the legislature. The corporation was allowed to erect as many additional gates as it deemed best, but to collect only fractional tolls at such extra barriers.

November 9, 1814, the corporation was relieved of all its road south of the road leading to Cheshire Bridge, but Hayes' *History of Rockingham* is our authority for saying that the rest of the turnpike continued to be so operated until about 1840.

9. The Hubbardton Turnpike

The trend of transportation in western Vermont to-day is southerly and westerly toward New York City, as evidenced by the records of the Rutland Railroad. While many of the early turnpikes seem to have catered to travel transversely with the Green Mountain range the Hubbardton Turnpike Company, chartered November 11, 1802, shows that at that date the drift toward New York had set in. That corporation desired to build a road from "Sudbury to the road leading from Rutland to Fairhaven, in the most suitable direction for Salem, New York."

The only portion of this route which is to-day occupied by any sort of a railroad is the section between Bomoseen and Castleton, which is served by a short branch of the Rutland street-railway system, but the farther portion of the journey which was made to Salem, New York, followed directly along the line later occupied by one of the divisions of the Delaware and Hudson. Doubtless a New York corporation furnished a road on the other side of the state line with which this road connected by means of the Poultney Turnpike, chartered in 1805 but it seems worthy of notice that this company, desiring to improve travel between Sudbury and Salem, asked for a franchise covering only about a quarter of the distance.

In 1808 the company petitioned the legislature, stating that the toll which it was obliged to collect had a tendency to lessen travel, and asking permission to reduce its rates. The act passed in consequence allowed such reductions, but provided that not over half was to be taken off. Imagine, if you can, the necessity of restricting the reduction of fares by a modern railroad.

Little has been found concerning the Hubbardton Turnpike, but enough to show that it continued in business until November, 1851, when its charter was repealed.

10. The Williamstown Center Turnpike

November 14, 1803, the act incorporating the Williamstown Center Turnpike Company was passed, providing for a road from "Experience Fisk's in Brookfield, northerly up the side of the branch of White River, through the notch of the mountains, to the road leading from Williamstown to Chelsea."

Twenty-five years after the completion of the road it was to become free and the property of the state, but the more liberal legislature of 1804 granted another fifteen years of corporate life.

Nothing was done for two years, and the date set in the original act for the first meeting, at which organization was to be effected, passed without that formality. But hope still lived and permission to hold the meeting on another day was secured in 1805.

This turnpike seems to have been known as "Ira Day's turnpike," and followed the "Gulf Route," according to Child's *Gazetteer* of Washington County. There are fanciful tales of the Boston and Montreal stages passing this way carrying the British Royal mail, guarded by a soldier of King George, but the course of the turnpike did not lend itself to direct stage travel in that direction, and the presence of a foreign soldier seems open to much doubt.

It is said that Cottrill and Day's stages followed this route.

11. The Northern Turnpike

An imposing array of names opened the act by which the Northern Turnpike Company of Vermont was incorporated February 6, 1804. Eighty-three individuals were therein constituted a corporation for the purpose of building a turnpike "from Lake Champlain to Connecticut River, through the counties of Franklin, Orleans, and Caledonia, and also a part of Essex, if judged best . . . in the most convenient direction for Portland, Maine."

It will be recalled that attention was directed, while considering the Tenth New Hampshire and the Littleton turnpikes, to the comprehensive scheme whereby Portland, Maine, was to be put in easy communication with Northern Vermont. Here we have the Vermont section of that scheme. The Northern of Vermont was to commence at the toll bridge at Upper Waterford and run across the state to some point, which we are unable to locate at this remote date, on the shores of Lake Champlain. Some difference of opinion was found among the old residents of Waterford as to whether the easterly terminus was to be at the bridge at Upper Waterford or at the one at Lower Waterford. The route of the turnpike was to include St. Johnsbury, and the present-day stage from that town to Upper Waterford finds its easiest route brings it to the Connecticut River some miles downstream from the site of the lower bridge. But turnpikes did not look for easy routes, while they did look for any influence which would lessen their land damages, and the presence of the name of Nathan Pike among the incorporators of the Northern strengthens the belief that the proposed route led to the upper bridge. Nathan Pike was the owner of a large farm running back from the Connecticut, on the Vermont side, and it was on to his land that travelers across the First Littleton toll bridge at Upper Waterford first stepped, and over his farm led the road by which the public highway was reached from the bridge. This Pike leased to the bridge company an acre of land for toll-house purposes, the consideration being that he and his heirs, with their families, should forever pass free of toll over the bridge. Ere a century had passed a multitude of Pikes, settled from Vermont to Louisiana with a liberal proportion living near the bridge, seemed to fall within the privileges of this rental. As the toll-house lot was owned by only two of the descendants, there seemed to be no way by which the extensive free list could be reduced until the company secured the passage of an act under which, in 1899, they took the tollhouse lot by condemnation proceedings and thereby became owners instead of lessees.

Further confirmation of the belief of a terminus at Upper Waterford is found in the fact that such a point is more nearly in a direct line with the general route, and that a detour by way of Lower Waterford would have required a similar return in order to reach the territory of the Littleton Turnpike.

But whichever bridge was aimed at by the turnpike, the road was never built east of St. Johnsbury, and the heavy traffic which followed the route for many years divided itself about equally between the two bridges, as is evidenced by the substantial taverns now standing in each village. We have already given some attention to the bridge at Upper Waterford, that of the First Littleton Bridge Corporation, and noted that it still serves its purpose.

The bridge lower down was built by the Second Littleton Bridge Corporation under authority of a charter granted by New Hampshire in 1820, and served the public until about 1890, when its westerly span went downstream on the crest of a jam of logs. The lumber company promptly bought up a majority of the stock and then decided not to rebuild. The easterly span remained in place for a few years longer and then followed its mate.

The promoters of the Northern may have given too much consideration to getting landowners among their incorporators and not enough to men of financial influence, for they seem to have had lots of trouble with their project. Apparently nothing at all was done for nearly two years, for we find the legislature speaking to them October 26, 1805, and providing a forfeiture of their rights unless the survey of the road was completed within nine months, ten miles built within two years, and twelve miles annually thereafter until the whole was done. In 1807 this was modified by an extension of one year, and a committee was appointed to make the layout. In 1809 a further extension was granted, and they were promised a gate when ten miles of road was finished. In 1811 it appears that seven miles of turnpike had been built reaching from Danville courthouse to St. Johnsbury Plain, and a special act allowed the erection of a gate in such section.

No more road was built by this corporation, a further extension of time granted in 1814 being insufficient for it, and the rights of the company expired. But that seven miles of road still remained, and in 1815 a new corporation, the Danville, was formed to take over and operate what little the Northern had succeeded in completing.

Although not strictly a turnpike tavern, the old house still standing in Upper Waterford Village is of interest in this connection, as it stood on the route of the Northern and furnished accommodations to those who had journeyed over what road the company did own. This old house, long kept by the Streeter family and still occupied by a granddaughter of the former innkeeper, is of great interest for its old associations with stage-coach travel and for its rare stock of old-fashioned furnishings. . . . The memories of many a mug of flip are set aside in the presence of the modern stove and lamp, and the public library, which is Waterford's share of that part of the Vermont educational system.

The tavern in Lower Waterford is a more imposing edifice, and from its larger proportions gives the impression that it must have profited from a larger circle of trade. Undoubtedly it did, for many of the teams crossing at the upper bridge followed down the river for the sake of the easier road leading to St. Johnsbury from the lower village.

12. The Weathersfield Turnpike

Another product of the sixth of February, 1804, was the Weathersfield Turnpike Company. Among the incorporators of this company we find the appropriate name of Henry Tolls.

The Weathersfield built from "Sumner's Ferry over Connecticut River, at the mouth of Sugar River," to a point in Cavendish on the Green Mountain Turnpike. The act of incorporation provided a committee of three to lay out the road so as to "best accommodate the public, and promote the general object and design of the corporation," which certainly was a happy form of defining the duty of the committee.

Apparently the legislature of 1805 was afraid that its predecessor had been too liberal with the Weathersfield, for we find an act passed in the latter year which gave a privilege of reducing the tolls to the future solons of 1840.

The company was dissolved by the legislature, at its own request, November 9, 1831.

13. The Rutland and Stockbridge Turnpike

November 9, 1804, the Rutland and Stockbridge Turnpike Company was formed and granted a franchise for fifty years. The road of this company was to lead from the main road, which ran north and south by the Rutland courthouse to the house of Zebidee Sprout in Pittsfield, and a committee was appointed by the original act to lay it out. But construction did not immediately follow, for in 1805 the company was required to complete three miles within two years, and a time limit of six years was placed on the whole route. That had the desired effect for the road was promptly commenced, and in one year more a franchise for an extension to connect with the Center Turnpike in Stockbridge was sought and secured. The company was the subject of legislative action again in 1813, 1828, and 1833, the last two acts allowing it to make alterations in its location.

November 7, 1805, was turnpike day in Montpelier, for on that day fourteen turnpike companies were incorporated, eight of them being combined in one act.

14. The Mount Taber Turnpike

The Mount Taber Turnpike Company constructed a road from a stone bridge on the East, or Creek Road in Danby, eleven miles through a part of Mount Tabor and Dorset, and ending in the easterly part of Manchester. This road continued in operation for over twenty years. In 1815 certain exemptions from toll were established, and on November 15, 1826, the corporation was allowed to surrender all of its road "south of Deming's saw-mill in Dorset," and the northerly end in Danby.

15. The Waltham Turnpike

The Waltham Turnpike Company built and operated its road from the end of the Center Turnpike in Middlebury to the courthouse in Vergennes. As in nearly all cases we see indications of difficulties in financing, and it was over three years before the road was completed. Major General Samuel Strong of Vergennes, an extensive landowner in that vicinity, was one of the incorporators of the company, and later acquired most of the stock according to Swift's *History of Middlebury*.

In 1808 the company sought permission to change its location so that it might pass over a new bridge which had been erected by the public authorities, thereby saving the expense of building one of its own. This was granted with the proviso that the company should return to its original location and build its own bridge thereon within twelve years. Alterations of the road were made in 1816.

In 1821 all of the road in Middlebury, except half of a bridge, and one mile in Weybridge adjacent to Middlebury, was surrendered to the public, and on October 30, 1828, the whole road was declared free, three acres of land with a tollhouse on it being all that was left to the corporation.

In the younger days of the generation which is now passing, this road was known as "The Old Plank Road," from which it appears that that form of construction was used in its later years, but since plank roads were of a much later date than 1828, it seems beyond question that the planking was done by the public authorities.

16. The Fairhaven Turnpike

The Fairhaven Turnpike Company had a road twenty-two miles in length and extending from the southerly line of Fairhaven, northerly through Fairhaven, Westhaven, Benson, Orwell, and Shoreham to the southerly line of Bridport, with a few miles additional, allowed to it by an act of 1808, which carried the road to the main road in Bridport. This road was aimed at the city of Vergennes, and apparently connected, at its southerly end, with a New York turnpike over which travelers could reach the lower Hudson River places.

In 1833 the charter was repealed, subject to the company's acceptance, and the road was made free with the several towns responsible for their respective portions, although the selectmen were allowed to discontinue the road if they deemed best.

17. The Winooski Turnpike

The Winooski Turnpike Company had a project for about thirty-six miles of turnpike, extending from Burlington courthouse up the valley of the Onion River to Montpelier, where it connected with the northerly end of Elijah Paine's turnpike. Two years later it appeared that the company had purchased the Onion River Bridge, a proceeding not specified in the charter, for which the legislature took speedy action, forbidding the company to collect any tolls thereon.

That the financial bed of the Winooski was no easier than that of many others is seen from the company's seeking in 1809, four years after incorporation, an extension of its time limit, and later in the same session, obtaining permission to erect a gate when eleven of its thirty-six miles had been completed. In 1811 the route was amended so as to begin at the college in Burlington, instead of at the courthouse; and in 1814 alterations in its main road were allowed. By this time the road appears to have been completed, but an extraordinary situation then developed.

From an act of 1815 we learn that the company's bills had not been paid, not even the damages for land taken, and the legislature ordered the committee to give hearings at once and make awards of damages, and if the company did not pay such awards within sixty days the gate between Montpelier and Waterbury was to be removed.

In 1851 the surrender of the portion of the road in Montpelier to that town was allowed if the town voted to accept. Apparently the town did not accept, for a final act, passed November 23, 1852, authorized the surrender of the whole road, regardless of the acceptance by the several towns, and made the turnpike free.

The Winooski was often called the Chittendon Turnpike on account of the connection with its affairs had by Governor Chittendon.

18. The Poultney Turnpike

The Poultney Turnpike Company was the one already mentioned as building a road extending from the southerly end of the Hubbardton Turnpike to the line of New York, but the building was a slow process. Five years after the date of the franchise an extension of time was granted, which was again extended in 1813. Exemptions from toll were specified by an act of 1816, from which we may infer that the road had been completed, and that the public had a tangible gate to kick at. The charter was repealed in 1834 and the responsibility for the road placed on the towns.

For a little short turnpike the Poultney made lots of trouble, seven acts of the legislature being passed in relation to it.

The last of the eight companies formed by the single act of November 7, 1805, was the Bennington Turnpike Company, which was to build from the Massachusetts line in Pownal to Bennington courthouse. The company has not again been found in legislation or in local history, and it is a question if the road was ever built.

Six more companies were formed on that same day but these were given the distinction of individual acts.

19. The Passumpsic Turnpike

The Passumpsic Turnpike Company was allowed to build "from near the mouth of Wells River in Newbury, through Ryegate, to the house of Deacon Twaddle in Barnet, to be laid as near the Connecticut River as may be convenient."

Under authority of this franchise, after several years, the company built its road not only to the house of Deacon Twaddle but nearly twice as far, reaching to St. Johnsbury. This was an active proposition, when it had survived the difficulties which beset all such enterprises at that time. The first step was a false one, for the meeting for organization was not held on the date specified in the charter, and the legislature of 1806 was called upon to legalize the proceedings of the belated gathering. For eleven years the money struggle went on, five acts being passed in that time to assist the corporation's efforts. Extensions of time were granted, privileges of gates conferred if they could only get a few miles built, and, in 1813 and 1816, permission was obtained to levy a tax on the stockholders for the purpose of raising money to pay the company's debts.

Wells tells us in his *History of Ryegate* that about a mile was built in Barnet

Passumpsic Turnpike: Wells River, Vt., in the turnpike days

Passumpsic Turnpike: Scene in Ryegate, Vt.

in 1807, and that, in 1808, the road was finished to the line between Barnet and Ryegate. After that the turnpike was extended a few miles at a time, until it reached Wells River Village, where it terminated at the upper end of the main street. It seems that the later money troubles, to meet which the right to lay a tax on the shares was granted, occurred in connection with the extension to St. Johnsbury for which no franchise has been found, and it is strange that no one seems to have observed that the company was seeking money privileges for an illegal purpose. When we recall how strictly the turnpike companies were held to the purposes of their charters, as in the case of the Winooski, when it had bought the Onion River Bridge, and of many

Passumpsic Turnpike: Over the mountain, Barnet, Vt.

Passumpsic Turnpike: Scene in Ryegate, Vt.

others, it is indeed remarkable that such an over-reaching of its privileges should have been overlooked. In 1830 a legislative resolution instructed the "state's attorney" to investigate the right by which this turnpike was being maintained in Newbury, Ryegate, Barnet, Waterford, and St. Johnsbury, and prosecute for any illegality, but no serious results followed.

Twenty-six thousand dollars is said to have been the first cost of the turnpike, with another seven thousand spent later for alterations covering seven miles. If these figures are authentic, the road being about twenty miles long, we have a figure of thirteen hundred dollars per mile for first cost, with a thousand dollars per mile for later alterations. These prices seem reasonable for a dirt road built under considerable difficulties. In many places it follows along the face of high hills, so steep as to require heavy grading, and often rock was encountered. A huge wooden plow was used in breaking up the soil preliminary to digging, which may still be seen preserved in the Fairbanks Museum of Natural Science in St. Johnsbury.

The tollgate on the lower section was first located on the Beattie Farm in the northerly part of Ryegate, later at a point a little below the Stevens Village toll bridge, and again in the upper end of McIndoe Village. At the latter place the gate was attended by James Monteith, who occupied his leisure between the passing of teams by knitting stockings.

The road seems to have aroused much hostility soon after 1820 and frequent efforts occurred to get it out of private control. In 1824 petition was entered with the supreme court, in consequence of which a committee was appointed to lay out a public road parallel to the turnpike, but the effort was too great for the towns involved, and the legislature of 1826 was sought for

Passumpsic Turnpike: Through McIndoe Village

relief, which was granted by setting aside the court's decree. The general law, under which towns were allowed to buy turnpike stock for the purpose of making the road free within their limits, seems to have had its inception with this road, for we find the town of Ryegate authorized by the legislature of 1828 to buy Passumpsic stock for such a purpose.

The town of Barnet tried another method of attack and built a mile of road adjoining the turnpike, but as soon as the road was finished the corporation took possession of it and incorporated it into its turnpike system. The town entered suit to retain its road, but after several appeals a final decision was handed down in favor of the company. It is to be regretted that

Passumpsic Turnpike: Old tavern at McIndoe

Passumpsic Turnpike: Above McIndoe Falls

more details of that case are not available, for from the facts at hand it is hard to see the justice of the outcome. Efforts in 1839 resulted more successfully, for then a committee was appointed for the purpose of laying out a public road which should parallel the turnpike and, therefore, put it out of business. This, of course, was resisted by the corporation, and more litigation ensued, but this time resulting adversely to the company, which was obliged to give up its road and accept the award of four thousand dollars which was given it. This form of persuasion consisted in giving authority to build a parallel road if the corporation refused to sell at what the authorities considered a reasonable figure.

A beautiful ride may be had to-day over the old Passumpsic Turnpike, yielding inspiring views of the upper Connecticut valley scenery. After leaving Wells River one must first pass through the winds and twists which have been put into the old alignment by the later railroad construction, but soon comes out into view of the river, which is seldom out of sight for the next several miles. After passing the busy paper mill at East Ryegate, a splendid view is had, from far down the river, of the Lyman toll bridge at McIndoe Falls. This quaint old structure, a covered wooden bridge built in 1834, makes a rare picture, framed on either side by the steep wooded banks of the river with a widened expanse of water for a foreground. Passing through the village of McIndoe Falls, one may see on the right the boarding house of the Connecticut Valley Lumber Company, formerly a turnpike tavern, but now, with the large ell added by the company, capable of 'housing many more people than of old. The Stevens Village toll bridge, a comparatively recent erection, built under a charter granted in 1846, is seen on the right after

Passumpsic Turnpike: Barnet, Vt.

passing over the next two miles of road, and then, after passing over a slight hill, the village of Barnet is seen. Originally the turnpike followed close to the river bank above Barnet, about on the line now followed by the railroad, but damage from high water caused its removal to a location high up on the hill before the railroad claimed its superior right to the location on the bank. Above Barnet, then, the old turnpike climbed, where now rises the public road, over the eminence most appropriately called "The Mountain" by the local travelers, and when it has returned to earth again it is in the valley of the Passumpsic and not in that of the Connecticut.

Passing through the little village of East Barnet, also known as Copenhagen, and as Inwood on the railroad time-tables, a hamlet famed for its production of croquet sets, the turnpike continues up the valley of the Passumpsic River, through the village of Passumpsic, and on to St. Johnsbury.

The territory served by this turnpike was occupied by the descendants of the thrifty Scotch settlers, for whom the county, Caledonia, was named, and they soon perceived that if the road was a good investment for the corporation it would be equally good for the general public, and they chafed under the imposition of tolls. Hence the corporation went out of business when the community became able to maintain free roads. That the road was a paying one is, evident from the resistance offered to the efforts to make it free, the company even testing, in the courts, the constitutionality of the act by which it was terminated. The Connecticut and Passumpsic Rivers Railroad was built in this section soon after 1850, so that did not hasten the end of the turnpike.

20. The Randolph Turnpike

The Randolph Turnpike Company's road extended from the westerly end of the White River Turnpike in Royalton ten miles up the Second Branch of the White River into the town of Randolph. Daniel Payne was the surveyor and he laid out the turnpike in the old road with one exception. Across the land of John Kimball he made a new location, and to the said John fell the distinction of being the only property owner in the length of ten miles, to whom was allowed any damages. To him it was allowed that he should receive sixty dollars, but if the section of old road thus cut out was discontinued, the land reverting to him, he was to receive only thirty-five dollars.

November 6, 1833, the corporation was dissolved, and on the eighteenth of the same month the corporation voted to accept the terms imposed by the legislature and stepped out.

Of the other four incorporated on that seventh of November we have gathered practically nothing, and there seems little reason for believing that any of them built a road.

21. The Vergennes and Willsboro Turnpike

On the fourth of November, 1808, a charter was issued to Major General Samuel Strong and others, residents of Vergennes and Ferrisburg, for the construction of a turnpike from the north end of the Waltham Turnpike, in Vergennes, to Hiern's Ferry, on Lake Champlain, in Ferrisburg. Major General Strong was a prominent and influential man in his community, and much of the land through which the building of the turnpike was contemplated belonged to him.

Financing the road was a slow proposition, as is evidenced by the fact that acts, extending the limits within which the road might be completed, were passed in 1810, 1812, and again in 1816. Local tradition tells that the turnpike was finally completed in 1820.

This is the road which now extends from the center of Vergennes about due west across the town of Panton, close to its northerly boundary, to the shore of Lake Champlain at Adams Ferry, which is the modem name for Hiern's.

Although originally projected through the town of Ferrisburg, no part of the road to-day is within that town, the section traversed by the turnpike having been transferred to Panton in 1847. Willsboro is a New York town bordering on Lake Champlain, but to-day it is far to the north of any service from Adams Ferry. An old map, however, shows. us that Willsboro in the day of the turnpike was a much larger town and included the land opposite Ferrisburg.

22. The Strafford Turnpike

The Strafford Turnpike Company was granted the right on November 11, 1808, to build from the Connecticut River Turnpike in Norwich, diagonally across the town of Strafford, to the courthouse in Chelsea. In 1813 the company made petition to the legislature for an extension of the time within which it should finish the road, stating in explanation that it had nearly finished the turnpike, but that heavy rains had done so much damage that completion within the required time would be impossible.

November 4, 1826, the corporation was allowed to surrender its charter and the road became free.

23. The Stratton Turnpike

The Stratton Turnpike Company, created by the act of November 10, 1808, at first proposed to build from the Stratton meeting-house to the foot of the Green Mountain in Sunderland, but later, in 1815, secured an extension of its rights by which it was allowed to build eastwardly through Wardsboro to Newfane at a point on the road from Brattleboro to Townshend, with an extension of the time limit on the original portion. By this it can be seen that the first proposition did not look attractive enough to those from whom the money was expected. Nor did the whole proposition for that matter, for we find extensions of time granted again in 1820 and in 1826. But the road was finally built, as can be attested by anyone familiar with the neglected and abandoned region through which it passed. For the entire town of Stratton, with large parts of the adjoining towns, is given up to the growth of timber, all the farms being sold and deserted and the region devoid of human presence.

Stratton Turnpike: Kelly Stand

Stratton Turnpike: Typical scene along the route

One sunny September morning, one hundred and five years after the incorporation of the Stratton Turnpike Company, the author found himself one of a jolly party whose automobile trip brought them to this old road at the snug little village of West Wardsboro, from which place the turnpike was followed to its former western terminus.

The first four miles was a stiff climb to the site of Stratton Village, with occasional glimpses of Stratton Mountain, 3860 feet high, and shaped like the back of a gigantic elephant, plowing its way toward the Massachusetts line. After leaving the outskirts of West Wardsboro, not a sign of human life was seen for the next twelve miles, although the roadside was marked at irregular intervals by former happy homes and secure shelters, now marred with gaping rents in the walls and falling roofs. Three entire villages are included in the list of desolation—Stratton, with its white-spired church; Grout's Mills, abandoned like the farms to let the timber grow; and West Jamaica, whose twenty houses and sawmill did not show even a cat to give life to the scene. Stratton Village yielded the two illustrations which are typical of the roadside adornments for mile after mile.

Three miles beyond Stratton we passed a guideboard which let us know that the trail up Stratton Mountain began there. Since our September ride a tower has been erected on the summit by the Stratton Mountain Club, in conjunction with the Vermont Forestry Bureau, and a most inspiring view is to be had from the added elevation above the tree tops, giving sights into the three adjoining states. Near here was also passed the field in which Daniel Webster is said to have delivered an address before an audience so large that one wonders where all could have come from. But the country has not always been so forsaken by man, and but a few years ago the little church at Stratton weekly housed a goodly sized congregation, and an attendance of a hundred at the social gatherings was not uncommon.

By noon we had covered twelve miles of the old turnpike and had reached "Kelley Stand," one of the old-time taverns, still doing some kind of hotel business in the midst of the desolation, which yielded us a dinner excellent beyond all our expectations. It seemed that "Kelley Stand " possessed some little reputation for its unique lonesomeness, which brought a profitable number of summer boarders from even as far away as New York City, and now that the frosty fall mornings had come, another class had arrived to keep the business alive. For the woods for miles around were alive with a busy throng who sought far and wide for the ferns which grew so abundantly, picking them in great armfuls, and carrying them to the roadside to be packed and shipped to the cities for the florists to use in decorating their boxes of flowers. To these workers the deserted houses and barns are a boon and, for a few weeks in each fall, they camp in such as have sufficient roof remaining to shed the rain. A large force were camped in some houses near "Kelley Stand," and the call for dinner brought them from all directions like hailstones in a summer storm.

Beyond Grout's Mills a long hill led up through the woods, and here, in the winter of 1821, occurred a most mournful tragedy, which was read in verse in many a school reader fifty years ago. A family of three, father, mother, and baby, encountered one of the severe winter storms and the two elders perished, but the baby was found the next morning, wrapped in its mother's shawl, and still alive.

Although the scenes along the old road are rather depressing with the striking suggestions of the rupture of old home associations, it is pleasant to think of the bustle of old-time stage travel, for this road pointed straight to Saratoga Springs, and the larger part of the fashionable visitors from Boston must have journeyed to the springs over the Stratton Turnpike.

24. The Peru Turnpike

The opening of the year 1916 saw but few turnpikes in operation in New England. A few were still doing business in New Hampshire but they were all of the summer-tourist variety, being those constructed up the sides of the high mountains for which that state is famed. The last one in New England of what might be called the commercial variety and, with the possible exception of the Plum Island in Massachusetts, the only one which ever collected tolls from automobiles, dates from November 9, 1814, when the Peru Turnpike Company was chartered and allowed to build its road from the "Lovel farm in Peru to the courthouse in Manchester."

Peru Turnpike

Chartered late in 1814, the road was commenced early in 1815 and completed the next year, it is told in the *History of Peru*, by Batchelder. This company must have had a peculiar brand of trouble over its land damages, for an act entitled "An Act for the relief of the Peru Turnpike Corporation" was passed in 1816, making the judges of the county court the committee on damages, with no appeal from their findings. Evidently the company could not secure anyone willing to act as such committee, or having done so, the selections failed to act.

This must have been the road mentioned in the *History of Rockingham*, as connecting the Green Mountain Turnpike in Chester with Manchester

Peru Turnpike

Peru Turnpike

courthouse, in which case we must note that authority as stating that this route became the most popular between Boston and Saratoga Springs. But it was a roundabout way to follow between those places, and it seems much more probable that such travel would have taken the Windham or the Stratton turnpikes, either of which lay in a much more direct line. But if not in line for Boston, the Peru Turnpike lay in the easiest pass through the Green Mountain range, and Boston tourists may have gone that way for more comfortable riding.

Batchelder further tells us that the road was built by General Peter Dudley, who also took care of it for twenty years; and that much teaming of merchandise and pleasure traveling was done over it until about 1850, when railroad competition reduced the amount seriously.

When the "Ideal Tour," from New York, through the Berkshires of Massachusetts to the White Mountains of New Hampshire, was laid out by the Automobile Association, the Peru Turnpike was found to be the most available and easy road by which the Green Mountains could be pierced and it was incorporated into the route. But the delay at the gate, and the imposition of toll at the rate of ten cents a mile so chafed the tourists that an agitation was soon started which was destined to seal the fate of the turnpike.

The Rutland (Vermont) *Herald* said of this road, in January, 1914,

By actual count there are 143 water bars on the six miles of road, mostly of the "comb" type, on which the low cars of recent years frequently become stalled. Many of the tourists after their first trip over the turnpike have carried from Manchester, short pieces of heavy plank with which to bridge the trenches in front of the water bars.

Aided by the protests of the automobile tourists, the local representatives succeeded in getting through the legislature of 1913 a bill designed to free the Peru Turnpike. By this act the state highway commissioner was authorized to purchase the road, or to assist the towns in which it lay to acquire the same by condemnation. Or failing to secure satisfactory terms from the corporation, the commissioner was to be allowed to use the pressure which we have seen applied to the Passumpsic, that is, he was to build a public road parallel to the, turnpike and leave the toll road to its own devices.

In September, 1913, the author had the experience of passing over this turnpike, and of paying toll of fifty cents at the gate, a photograph of which he made at the time. The trip over the road is sufficiently described by the photographs which are here reproduced.

None of the turnpike was ever built within the town of Manchester. It commenced at the line between that town and Winhall, near where the gate stood, and ran thence northeasterly across the corner of the latter town and into Peru, a length of about six miles. About a mile from the easterly end, the road to South Londonderry branches off, and nearly half the turnpike travel takes that road, making only five miles of turnpike used.

Very early in the year 1914 announcements of the immediate opening of the road appeared in various newspapers of New York and New England, but the realization was long in following. Encouraged by the support of the state, the towns of Winhall and Peru entered proceedings in the Bennington county court, for the taking of the road under the right of eminent domain. The commissioners appointed by the court duly held a hearing on the matter and made their report in the summer of 1916, fixing the price to be paid the corporation for the loss of its road with its franchise rights and all its real estate holdings at approximately twenty-two thousand dollars.

The report receiving the approval of the court, the turnpike finally became free in the early summer of 1917.

25. The Danville Turnpike

We have followed the struggles of the Northern Turnpike Company of Vermont, and noted that it succeeded in building only eight miles of its road. We now find an act, passed November 11, 1815, creating the Danville Turnpike Company, reciting that the rights of the Northern had expired, and giving the completed portion of its road to the new corporation. Thus the Danville is the only company which has been found which began its existence with a completed turnpike and a tollgate on it. This road connected the village of Danville with St. Johnsbury Plain, ending near the large scale factory of the Fairbanks Company.

By 1833 the company had fallen into bad financial condition, and on October 29 of that year an act was passed by which the corporation was to be dissolved, when it voted to accept the provisions of the act and paid a fine which had been imposed on it for failure to keep its road in proper condition.

26. The Warren Turnpike

The Warren Turnpike Company received its charter November 17, 1825. The route over which this company built its road extended from Sterling and Adams mills in Warren to the "east, north, and south road," passing through Lincoln. The length of the road was eight miles and it seems to have been promptly built, for the company was back at the next session of the legislature asking to have an omission in its rates of toll supplied. This was done by an act which specified that a "person and horse" should pay a toll of six cents.

Easterly from Warren the turnpike followed up the valley of Lincoln Brook to the town line, thence taking a direct line to its terminus in Lincoln.

27. The Sherburne Turnpike

November 6, 1826, the Sherburne Turnpike Company was formed to build a road over the route which the Woodstock and Rutland had tried to occupy in 1805. The year 1826 was more auspicious evidently, for the Sherburne was built from the "flat on the north side of the Queechy river in Bridgewater," up the river and over the hill, to a junction with the Rutland and Stockbridge in the northwesterly corner of the town of Sherburne. In 1829 an alteration in the rates of toll was provided by legislative act and the coveted privilege of reducing its tolls was bestowed on the company. Toll exemptions were reduced in 1835, and in 1847 it was enacted that certain exemptions on loads of goods should not apply to any loads bought outside of the town of Sherburne. These dates show that this turnpike lived to a voting age, but the date of its becoming free has not been found.

28. The Searsburg Turnpike

There does not seem to have been room for two companies in the territory granted to the Windham Turnpike Corporation, yet the Searsburg Turnpike Company was chartered October 28, 1828, to build from the east line of Searsburg to the east line of Bennington. Nor are there evidences on the map that two turnpikes ever were built, and the only explanation seems to be that the Windham Company had allowed its road to become impassable and had abandoned it, and that the new company was formed to recover the road and put it into a satisfactory state of repair. But that must have been a hard job, for they had to ask the legislature of 1831 for an extension of one year on their time limit, within which additional time the road was completed. That it was operated for at least thirty years is seen from the act of

November 2, 1860, in which the portion in Bennington and in the westerly part of Woodford was made free.

Apparently the Searsburg, at some period, was a plank road, for the company is named in an act of 1852 as the Searsburg Plank Road Company. A company to build a plank road connecting with the Searsburg Turnpike had been created in 1849, and in 1852 it was allowed to extend its road, section two of the act providing that the Searsburg Plank Road Company might construct and operate such road.

29. The Goshen Turnpike

A short piece of road to extend from "Blake's furnace in Brandon to Jones' sawmill in Goshen" was chartered October 31, 1834, to the Goshen Turnpike Company. A slight jolt was given this, company the next year by an act which required that the first meeting of the corporation should be held within a year. In 1838, 1840, and 1842, acts were secured extending the time within which the road must be completed, and we are justified in assuming that the turnpike was opened for business about the end of the year 1842.

October 26, 1852, after a scant ten years of life, the company obtained legislative authority to assign its stock to the towns involved, and to turn the road over to them whether they wished it or not.

The first charter for a plank, road in New England was granted November 7, 1849, to, the St. Albans and Richford Plank Road Company. This company proposed to build its road from St. Albans Bay to Richford and thence to the Canada line, but no reason has been found to believe it carried out its intentions.

30. The Lamoille County Plank Road

Two days later the Lamoille County Plank Road Company was granted a charter to build from Waterbury Street through Stowe and Morristown to Hyde Park, and the road of this company seems to have been the first plank road in New England, unless the Searsburg Turnpike had changed over before that date.

A peculiar privilege, noted in connection with several Vermont turnpikes, was granted to this company in 1858, when it was authorized "to survey its road." That this was not a preliminary to construction is seen by the act further providing penalties unless needed repairs were made. Probably the intention was to allow a relocation, but it seems worthy of note that such a simple piece of business was regarded as outside of the rights and privileges granted to turnpike companies, and only to be done after legislative permission had been secured.

The same act abundantly testifies that the business of a plank road had not been remunerative, and that the materials of construction were too short-lived for road purposes. In it the company was forbidden to collect tolls after fifteen days from the passage of the act, unless the road was repaired and kept "to the satisfaction of Hon. Thomas Gleed of Morristown, whose decision shall be final." It is refreshing to note that the honorable gentleman's name is spelled with an "l" and not with an "r," for the opportunities for graft thus conferred upon him were limited only by the gross earnings of the road.

31. The Glastonbury Plank Road

The Glastonbury Plank Road Company, created November 13, 1849, was the one which we have already noted as having been absorbed by the Searsburg Company. Its road was to extend from the Searsburg Turnpike, in Woodford, to the westerly line of the town of Somerset, passing diagonally across the town of Glastonbury. The prospect must have been discouraging, for two years later the company appealed to the legislature and secured an extension of four years on its time limit. It must have been soon after this that the management of the Searsburg became interested and built the road, for the act of October 26, 1852, shows that the Glastonbury had been finished, and that an extension was then allowed from its eastern terminus, through Somerset to the Searsburg Turnpike near Doane's Mills in Searsburg.

32. The Vergenes and Bristol Plank Road

The Vergennes and Bristol Plank Road Company received its franchise November 9, 1850, and, without asking any extensions of its time limit, built its turnpike between the places named. Nine years later the company was released from all obligation to keep its road planked but, instead, was allowed to "construct and repair their road with earth and gravel in the usual manner of constructing and repairing turnpike roads." This is interesting on account of the information regarding the life and durability of plank roads and the comparative expense of construction and maintenance. Here we have a plank road played out at the end of nine years, including the time spent in construction, and the proprietors convinced that the common dirt road is better and cheaper. That there was not travel enough over the road to pay for its upkeep is plainly to be seen, so we are left to conclude that decay was a prominent factor in its destruction.

But the receipts from tolls were not sufficient to pay for a common dirt road, and in 1861 the company was allowed to surrender its charter and its turnpike.

33. The Mount Mansfield Turnpike

Three attempts to climb Mount Mansfield are next noted. The Cambridge-Mount Mansfield Turnpike Road Company, created October 27, 1866, calls for comment on account of its location requirement being diametrically opposite the usual conception in the minds of 'turnpike promoters. It was to build

from the residence of Edward Hanley in Cambridge. . . . *on a zig-zag line* to the "Lake of the Clouds" so called, near that part of Mount Mansfield, known as the "Chin."

This company was to be allowed to locate its own gates and determine for itself its rates of toll, but even that privilege did not enable it to build. November 23, 1874, a duplicate of the charter was enacted, only this time the road was to commence at the residence of the "Widow *Charles* Gallup," and the stockholders were made liable for all debts in excess of one half the paid-in capital. The other attempt was made from the other side, "The Mount Mansfield Hotel Company at Stowe and such persons as may become stockholders" being incorporated as the Mount Mansfield Turnpike Company November 20, 1867.

This company, under its franchise to build from "near the Half Way House in Stowe to the Summit House, in such a line as the said stockholders may determine," constructed five miles of mountain climbing road up the valley of the west branch, and ending on the summit. This road forms a branch of the well-known "Smugglers' Notch Road" and is reached by turning to the northwest about a mile northerly from Stowe Center on the main road between Waterbury and Morristown. The Turnpike is now maintained, and tolls collected, by the management of the Summit House.

In this company, also, the directors and stockholders were liable for debts in excess of half the paid-in capital. The management was allowed to pick the location of its gates, but the rates of toll were to be fixed by the assistant judges of the county court.

The following turnpikes are reported by Wood to have been chartered but never operated as toll roads:

1803	Stamford	Readsboro, through Stamford to the Massachusetts line
1804	Caledonia	Newbury to Danville
1805	Boston & Montreal	Connecticut River in Orange County to Canadian border
	Dorset	Through town named
	Pawlet	Through town named
	Woodstock & Rutland	Bridgewater to Sherburne
	Mad River	Hancock to Moretown

	Mississiquoi	Through Highgate
	Sandbar	Through Colchester
1807	Manchester	Chester to Manchester
	Chelsea	Chelsea to Barre
1811	Orange & Corinth	Through Cornith to Connecticut River
1813	Middlebury	Sudbury to Middlebury
	Bridport	Bridport to Vergennes
	Burlington	Vergennes to Burlington
1814	Barre	End of Winooski to Williamstown
	Panton	East and west across Panton
	Memprhremagog	Lyndon Corner to Narrows of lake
1815	Burke	Canadian border (Holland) to Burke Hollow
	Mansfield	Cambridge to Stowe
	Benson	Massachusetts line to Fairhaven
	West River	Townshend to Winhall
	Putney	Through Putney and Brookline to Newfane
1818	Tinmouth	West end of Green Mountain Turnpike to Middleton
1822	Winhall	From Peru Turnpike into Winhall
1823	Jamaica	Jamaica to Winhall
1826	Ore-bed	Somerset to Glastonbury
	Ripton	From the Green Mountain in Ripton, to the Warren Turnpike
1833	Pownal McAdam	Southeasterly, across Pownal
	Readsboro	Woodford City to Whitingham
1835	Lincoln	Lincoln to Granville
	Huntington	Bristol to Huntington
1841	Willoughby Lake	Through Westmore
	Readsboro & Woodford	Through these towns
1842	Branch	Danby to Mount Tabor
1849	Montpelier & Lamoille Plank	Montpelier to Lamoille Valley
	Bellwater Plank	No information
1850	Shelburne & Hinesburg	Between those towns
	Williston	Williston to Burlington
	Williston & Jericho Plank	Between those towns
	Georgia & Johnson	Between those towns
	Hinesburg & Burlington	Between those towns
	Danville & Passumspic	Danville to Barnet or St. Johnsbury

1851	St. Albans & Bakersfield Plank	Between those towns
	Stamford & Readsboro	Through those towns
1852	Rutland & Chittendon Plank	Between those towns
1853	Forestdale Plank	Brandon to Forestdale
1860	Fayston	Fayston to Forestdale
1865	Bakesfield & Waterville	Between those towns
1874	Notch	Stowe to Underhill
1892	Elmore Pond	From Elmore Pond to Elmore Mountain

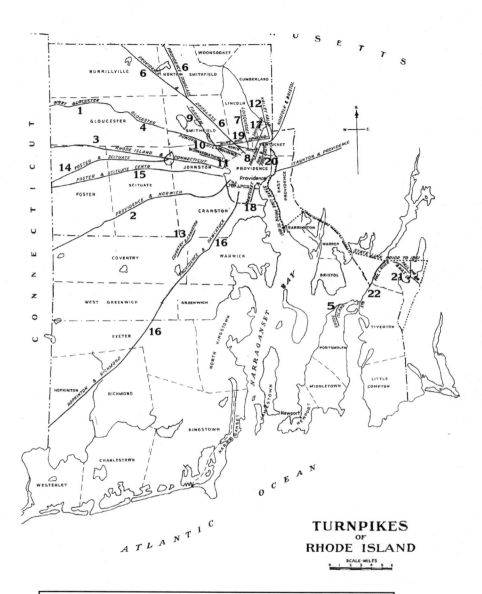

TURNPIKES
OF
RHODE ISLAND

SCALE-MILES

1. West Gloucester	12. Valley Falls
2. Providence to Norwich	13. Coventry & Cranston
3. Rhode Island & Connecticut	14. Foster & Scituate
4. Gloucester	15. Foster & Scituate Central
5. Rhode Island	16. New London (Hopkinton & Richmond)
6. Douglas	17. Smithfield
7. Loisquisset	18. Pawtuxet
8. Providence & Pawtucket	19. Mineral Spring
9. Farnum	20. East
10. Powder Mill	21. Fall River & Watuppa
11. Woonasquatucket	22. Stone Bridge & Fall River

The Turnpikes of Rhode Island

T HE first turnpike corporation in New England was created by the general assembly of Rhode Island at the February session in 1794. As in other states, the first charter has been found to be a pretty accurate forerunner of the later ones, and the following notes are given to show the usual practice in that state.

The capital stock, number, and par value of the shares was fixed in the act of incorporation (fifty shares at one hundred dollars each for the first corporation), and each share of stock carried one vote at all meetings at which its holder was present. The time and place for holding the annual meeting was specified, and provision made for calling and holding special meetings. The number necessary to constitute a quorum was established but the corporation was otherwise allowed to determine its own by-laws. The corporation was authorized to "acquire and convey" a limited amount of land, the quantity being evidently sufficient to provide for the roadway and grounds for the tollhouses and all kinds of personal property. Rates of toll were allowed as follows:

	Cents
A waggon, Cart, or Ox-sled Team, not exceeding Four Cattle	12½
A Team of more than Four Cattle	15
A Sleigh with more than One Horse	12½
A One Horse Sleigh	6
A Coach, Chariot, or Phaëton	40
A Chaise, Chair, or Sulkey	20
A Horse and Horse Cart	6
A Person and Horse	6
Horses or Mules in Droves, per head	2
Neat Cattle in Droves, per head	1
Swine in Droves, for every Fifteen	10
For any less Number than Fifteen, each	1
Sheep and Store Shoats, each	½

Exemptions from toll were allowed thus:

And that Foot Passengers be not liable to any toll nor nigh Inhabitants passing on said Turnpike Road, for the purposes of attending public Worship, Funerals, Town-meetings, or other Town Business, or going to and from Mills, or for the Purposes of Husbandry.

"To ascertain the Produce of the said Toll, a fair account shall be kept," which account was to be open at any time for the inspection of any committee which the general assembly might appoint.

The obligation of the corporation to maintain its road was plainly stated, but it seems that the act provided that the road might be abandoned whenever the company desired. Witness:

And it is further Enacted by the Authority aforesaid, That the said Corporation shall at all times keep the said Turnpike Road in good Repair, at the proper expense of the said Corporation, and their Successors and Assigns, for so long Time as they shall collect and receive the aforesaid Toll.

The usual clause appears providing that when the original investment, plus twelve per cent, had been repaid the road should become public property.

As in New Hampshire, nearly every petty detail was the subject of a special legislative act, and the Rhode Island General Statutes, compiled in 1857, contained but one chapter of four sections on the subject of "Turnpikes and Toll Bridges." It was provided that corporations of that nature could not hold land for any purpose other than that contemplated by the original charter, or amendments thereto. A justice of the supreme court, could, upon complaint of a road being in bad order, cause the gates to be opened and to remain open until the road was repaired to his satisfaction. The third section merely reiterated the provision in most of the charters that an account of tolls was to be kept and held open to the inspection of any committee of the general assembly, and section four put it up to the toll gatherer to behave himself, by making him liable to damages if he demanded toll in excess of that legally allowed. For the first offense the complainant might recover from two to five dollars, while subsequent attempts at extortion were to be followed by a twenty-dollar penalty.

In the revision of 1872 the same four sections appeared, with three additional ones, which provided that any corporation could sell its road to any town traversed by it on mutually agreed terms. Owners of land adjoining the turnpike were to be notified and a hearing given, after which the road might become a part of the public system and the corporation be relieved from responsibility for its maintenance. Such money as the corporation received was first to be applied in settlement of its debts.

The turnpike movement in Rhode Island increased rapidly, and by the year 1820 the state was crisscrossed with such roads, the town of Providence being a veritable turnpike center. Few companies were allowed to build within the town limits of Providence, nearly all being obliged to terminate their roads at the boundary. . . .

The early Rhode Island incorporations allowed the created companies to take over and repair existing roads, after which the investors were to recoup themselves by collecting tolls, but we soon find corporations chartered for the purpose of building entirely new thoroughfares. The number of gates at which toll was to be collected was specified in the charters, but the location of such gates was left to the discretion of the companies, subject sometimes to restrictions within a certain number of miles.

Persons desiring the privilege of building turnpike roads made petition for a charter to the general assembly, which petition was invariably referred to the next session, with an order to advertise giving notice to all parties interested. At the same time a committee would be appointed by the assembly to view the route proposed and report on the same, such committee being usually instructed to present a "plat" to illustrate its report. Many more petitions have been found in the legislative records than acts of incorporation, which may indicate that the general assembly weeded out the unnecessary schemes.

Late in the sixties the people became restless under the imposition of tolls on certain of the roads over which they had to travel, a feeling which we find reflected in the legislative acts at that time. A joint special committee, which had been appointed to make an investigation of the toll bridges and turnpikes of the state and to devise some method by which all could be freed, made its report to the May session of 1870. This committee had found two toll bridges and six turnpikes, and its report was little more than a tabulation of such with a few comments on each. In conclusion, inability to formulate any plan by which the roads and bridges could be made free was confessed.

In January, 1871, Edward Darling was elected commissioner of turnpikes under authority of an act passed a few days earlier by which such an office was created. His term of office was one year and his duties were to annually examine each turnpike and order such repairs as he found necessary. If the corporation failed to obey the orders of the commissioner, he was authorized to use the familiar weapon of opening the gate for free passage of all. If that persuasion failed for three years the road thereupon was to become forever free. Annual reports were required but only one appears to have been made. That was submitted to the general assembly at its January session in 1872 and reported five turnpikes, on all of which repairs had been ordered. The commissioner hoped that all those roads would have become free before he fell under the necessity of writing another report.

The comments of the commissioner and of the special committee on the respective roads will be mentioned in connection with each road later.

Every Rhode Island turnpike was established on the American principle of private investment, but a precedent must have been derived from the English turnpike trust system when the assembly enacted that the inability of the Proprietors of the Providence and Norwich Turnpike to keep their road in repair should be met by an obligation imposed upon the towns to expend money and labor on that road. This will be mentioned at greater length later.

1. The West Glocester Turnpike

The official name of the corporation by which this road was operated for many years was "The Society for establishing and supporting a Turnpike Road from Cepatchit Bridge in Glocester, to Connecticut Line," but the road was generally known as above indicated. The corporation was created at the February session of the general assembly in 1794, and was the first turnpike corporation formed in New England. For a year or two prior to the incorporation of this company, the old Mohegan Road from New London to Norwich, and the section in Greenwich, Connecticut, of the New York Post Road, had been operated as toll roads, but not by incorporated companies. Commissioners had been appointed to manage such roads in behalf of the counties within which they were located, and the receipts from tolls were used entirely on repairs of the road. Hence the West Glocester Turnpike was the first of what we have chosen to call "commercial turnpikes" in New England.

The charter allowed the company to build its road "from Cepatchit Bridge in Glocester to Connecticut Line, on the great Road leading from Providence

West Glocester Turnpike: In North Central Gloucester

to Killingly." One gate was allowed at any place within four miles of the Connecticut line.

In the petition for a charter the subscribers had set forth that they had subscribed eight hundred and fifty pounds for the purpose of repairing the road which they desired for their turnpike, one hundred and fifty pounds for repairing the road toward Providence from "Cepatchit Bridge," and various stated sums for repairs on other connecting roads in Massachusetts and Connecticut, as well as in Rhode Island. So the total of the sums subscribed was made the amount of the capital stock of the company, and the amount which was to be earned, with twelve per-cent interest, before the road was to become free. Work must have been commenced promptly, for the company appeared at the October session in the same year, stating that its original estimate of eight hundred and fifty pounds was not sufficient to accomplish the necessary repairs on the old road, and asking that it might expend an additional one hundred and fifty, the same to be included in the amount for which reimbursement was to be allowed. This was granted by an act passed at the same session.

In February, 1800, this company made a rather comprehensive and amusing petition. Strange to say differences of opinion had arisen with the assessors of taxes for the town of Gloucester, and the turnpike corporation appealed to the general assembly to enact that its capital stock, land, and buildings be exempted from taxation and relieved from past assessments. Either for the sake of getting good measure or to befog the issue, it was further asked that the toll gatherer of the company should be allowed to sell intoxicating liquors without the formality of obtaining a license; and the trivial privilege of holding the corporation meetings in the tollhouse was solicited. Evidently the forces of temperance were on the alert, for all that

West Glocester Turnpike: Entering Chepachet from the west

West Glocester Turnpike: Chepachet, R.I.

was granted of the prayer was that meetings might be held in the tollhouse, and that Gloucester should not tax any shares of stock owned by residents of other towns.

The length of the road operated by this corporation was about seven miles, so the thousand pounds which we have seen available for its repair spread out about seven hundred dollars a mile, which we have seen was sufficient to build certain of the Massachusetts roads of a similar grade. But an insufficient sort of work must have been accomplished on this Rhode Island road, for after the company had had it under its control for six years, a committee of the general assembly, appointed for the purpose of examining the road, reported that it had been found "in very bad order," but that the necessary repairs had been made. Again, in 1817, complaint was made of the condition of the turnpike, which had been bad for several years.

Very little has been found in local Rhode Island histories on the subject of turnpikes, and only two of the books consulted are free from serious errors. A historian of Gloucester speaks of the tavern kept by Hezekiah Cady, in the west part of that town, and says that a tollgate stood opposite it. As Colonel Joseph Cady lived on the West Glocester Turnpike, about two miles from the Connecticut line, in 1815, it seems probable that the gate in question was located on that turnpike. Only one other turnpike was ever built in the west part of Gloucester, and that was so close to the line of Foster that it was not known to be in the former town until steps had been taken to make the road free in 1875.

The joint committee of the general assembly, reporting at the May session of 1870, had found the West Glocester Turnpike in good condition, but no dividends had been declared for three years and the receipts were not exceeding the expenditures. In spite of such a discouraging situation the corporation continued to operate its road for another eighteen years.

At the May session of 1888 nine hundred dollars of the state's money was appropriated to compensate the town of Gloucester for assuming the care and responsibility of the turnpike, which was thereby declared free. The corporation received nothing beyond the relief from obligation to maintain the road and thus closed its ninety-four years of corporate existence.

2. The Providence to Norwich Turnpike

The old Post Road between Boston and New York passed through Providence and then followed the old Pequot Path which ran along practically the lines of the present Weybosset and Broad streets, through East Greenwich and over Kingston Hill, to Westerly, where it crossed the Pawcatuck River into Connecticut, and continued thence to the ferry at New London. That ferry, being of great width, must have been a serious obstacle in the days when a canoe was all the business demanded, and by the beginning of the eighteenth century complaints were freely made of its inconvenience. In 1711 the general assembly of Rhode Island ordered that a road should be laid out and built from Providence to the state line in the proper direction for Norwich, Connecticut, the intention being to reach the head of the Thames River, where it could be more easily crossed than at New London. The Connecticut general assembly passed a similar order at its October session in 1712, and the road throughout was completed in 1714, being provided with a "safe and sufficient bridge" at the point where the Moosup had previously been forded. The road thus built was a portion of the route over which the mail riders, at

Providence and Norwich Turnpike: Thornton Avenue, Johnston, R.I.

the close of the Revolutionary War, were able to average only about forty miles a day in the best season, so it is not surprising that this main line of travel was the subject of early efforts at improvement.

In October, 1794, action for that end was taken in both Rhode Island and Connecticut, the latter state endeavoring to establish a tollgate on the Post Road, with nominal tolls, the entire receipts to be expended for repairs on the road. In the same month the Rhode Island general assembly incorporated "The Providence and Norwich Society for establishing a turnpike-road from Providence to Connecticut line, through Johnston, Scituate, Foster, and Coventry."

This corporation was allowed to take over the Post Road as far as the Connecticut line and, when it had expended eighteen hundred pounds in repairing and improving the road, it was to be allowed to erect its tollgate at any place within nine miles of the Connecticut boundary, and to proceed with the collection of tolls. By an act of the January session of 1795 the location of the gate was permitted two miles nearer Providence.

A curious situation developed at the January session in 1798, when certain citizens resident along the Post Road recited their grievances. Prior to the acquisition of the road by the turnpike company those citizens had " worked out their taxes" on the town highways, and a reasonable proportion of their labor had been expended on the road which was most used by them. Now that the corporation was responsible for the maintenance of the road the town's energies were entirely given to other sections and, the turnpike company neglecting to properly fulfill its duties, the road and the abutting owners suffered accordingly. Therefore those citizens, having in mind the English turnpike trusts which, failing to properly maintain their roads, devised their obligations to the municipalities, petitioned that the towns of Johnston and Cranston might be obliged to include their portion of the Providence and Norwich Turnpike as a road district and keep it in repair.

This petition was twice referred, and it was two years before action was finally taken upon it. Then in February, 1800, it was enacted:

That the Town Councils and Surveyors of the towns of Johnston and Cranston be and they are hereby directed to cause a just proportion of highway taxes and highway labour to be expended and done in and upon the said turnpike road, by the inhabitants living upon or near the same, who usually paid taxes or laboured upon the said road before the charter of incorporation was granted to the turnpike company.

Upon first thought such a law seems to be most unjust as apparently it imposed the burden upon the two towns named of maintaining a highway for the use of which their citizens were obliged to pay toll, but upon second consideration the reader will remember that only one tollgate was allowed on this road, and that at a considerable distance west of either of the towns named. As the greater part of the travel over the road in Johnston and Cranston, by the citizens of those towns, was to and from Providence, it is seen that in reality such citizens had the free use of the road while contributing largely to its destruction.

But the fact that the road was owned by a corporation which was supposed to be deriving revenue therefrom was a point not to be overcome, and the law remained upon the statute books only one year. The two towns concerned entered their remonstrance at the next October session, and the act was repealed in the following February.

For two years longer the corporation struggled along and in October, 1803, secured the passage of an act by which it was allowed to raise ten thousand dollars by a lottery, the proceeds "to be laid out and expended in the repairing and amending the turnpike-road of said society." Three managers for this lottery were appointed and, since the state stood sponsor for the scheme, they were to give bonds with sureties to the satisfaction of the general treasurer.

Originally the company was allowed one gate within nine miles of the state line. This was changed so that the gate might be anywhere within eleven miles of that boundary, and again to make the eastern limit fourteen miles away. In February, 1805, the western gate was placed within five miles of Connecticut's jurisdiction, and another gate was allowed within eight miles of the bridge in Providence when the road was properly repaired. Many other acts have been found making changes in the manner of holding meetings, altering locations of the gates, and revising the location of the road, until, in 1841, the name was changed, or perhaps it is better to say abbreviated, to "The Providence and Norwich Turnpike Society," and the charter generally revamped to match those issued to later companies.

The portion of the road lying within the town of Johnston was deeded to that town by the corporation on August 27, 1852, but the town apparently did not appreciate the gift, as its acceptance did not materialize until September 9, 1865, over thirteen years later. Scituate accepted the deed of the portion within its territory in 1866. A petition was made in January, 1857, that the charter of the company might be annulled and, although no action was taken on the petition, it seems that the whole road was given up to the public about that time or soon after. In any case none of it was found in operation as a toll road by the committee of 1870.

The road which we have been considering commenced at the westerly line of Providence, at the present corner of Westminster and Stokes streets in Olneyville, and followed southwesterly along the present lines of Plainfield Street westerly, forming the boundary between Johnston and Cranston, to South Scituate and Richmond. Thence, it bore southwesterly again, crossing corners of Foster and Coventry, and entered Connecticut near the little village of Oneco.

The length in Rhode Island was about twenty-one miles, and its continuation to Norwich added about nineteen miles more.

3. The Rhode Island and Connecticut Turnpike

This road formed the direct connection between Providence and Hartford, and it was quite often called the "Hartford Turnpike." The petition for a charter was made to the assembly at the May session of 1802, and asked the franchise to build a turnpike

from tar bridge (so called) near Colonel Christopher Olney's, in Providence, by the south end of Moshanticutt pond . . . and on the direc*test* rou*t* to the northerly part of John Colwill's hill in Foster and from thence on the most direct rou*t* to Connecticut line.

The petitioners stated that they were willing to spend fifteen thousand dollars on the construction of the road in return for the privilege of collecting tolls.

Tar Bridge was the name given to the bridge over the Woonasquatucket River where Manton Avenue now crosses, and the reference to Colonel Olney's place suggests the origin of the name of the Olneyville section of Providence.

The charter was granted in February, 1803, and gave the corporation the imposing name of "The Rhode Island and Connecticut Society for establishing a turnpike-road from or near the west line of the town of Providence to Connecticut line, through Johnston, Scituate, and Foster." Fortunately for the treasurer national banks had not then been established, so he was not

Rhode Island and Connecticut Turnpike: Hartford Avenue, Providence

obliged to sign that name to checks. It was provided that, when the company had expended the stated sum of fifteen thousand dollars, it might erect two gates and proceed with the collection of tolls.

Apparently the promoters had not waited for the formality of being incorporated but had gone ahead with the preliminaries for opening their road, for the next act passed by the assembly, after that of incorporation, provided for the appointment of a committee to appraise the damages on land where the company's agents had not been able to make an agreement, and empowered such committee to give possession to the corporation after payment or tender of the award.

A complete report of the location and of the awards of damages was rendered in October, 1804, from which it is seen that the road commenced in Providence at a point on the Providence and Norwich Turnpike. Damages had been awarded to twenty-one owners with a total of twelve hundred and sixty-one dollars.

In 1805 an extension of two years was granted on the time within which the road must be completed, as the corporation had been unable to finish within the required limit.

Proceedings were commenced in the next year, 1806, for carrying the turnpike through to a connection with the Boston Turnpike over which connection with Hartford was to be had. In that year the Connecticut and Rhode Island Turnpike Company was created by the Connecticut legislature to connect with the Rhode Island company's road at the state line, and to build through Killingly, Pomfret, and Ashford. Evidently these two corporations were really one, but the distinction between states was more sharply drawn than in the case of the Providence and Boston, which we have just noticed. It is clear that both roads were under one management in 1816, for permission was then obtained to treat the two roads as one and to locate a gate in Connecticut at which collections would be made for the use of the westerly miles of the Rhode Island road. The Connecticut section of the road was made free about 1840, but the remainder continued under the imposition of tolls for another thirty-one years.

The management of this road offered to sell, through the joint committee of 1871, all the property and franchise of the corporation for two thousand dollars. The road was reported to be in good condition, and the gross receipts were stated to be about twelve hundred dollars per annum. The report of the turnpike commissioner, which was made to the general assembly a year and a half later, stated that he had found the road very bad and had ordered repairs. But the assembly had enacted that the road should be free, and the towns were then engaged in the necessary work.

In May, 1871, such action had been taken by the assembly. Five hundred dollars was awarded to the corporation, and one thousand to be divided proportionally between the towns of Johnston, Scituate, and Foster, provided the terms were accepted by all interests. The terms were accepted and the road became free, but soon a peculiar fact was brought to light. The course of the road across the town of Foster had borne a little too far to the north, and for about a mile it lay just over the boundary line and in the town of Gloucester. Now that town had not been consulted, and its citizens showed no avidity to take over and maintain a mile of road that was hardly in the town at all, so an act was passed in 1875 appropriating two hundred dollars to be paid to Gloucester if it would accept the road. But the town still held off and in May of the same year the two hundred dollars was raised to five hundred, to which the town agreed.

This turnpike commenced in Providence at the present corner of Hartford Avenue and Plainfield Street, the latter being the old Providence and Norwich Turnpike. Hartford Avenue was the old Rhode Island and Connecticut Turnpike, which crossed the town of Johnston, passing through Pocasset and Elmdale in Scituate, and entered the town of Killingly, Connecticut, about a half mile south of Killingly Pond.

4. The Glocester Turnpike

The first wagon which reached Providence from Connecticut by any road north of the Norwich Post Road arrived in that town in September, 1722, and so poor were all the northern roads for many years after, that, it is said, one traveler between Providence and Pomfret, in 1776, consumed two days in covering the necessary thirty-six miles. The route followed was probably over the old Killingly road, a part of which we have already seen improved under the name of West Glocester Turnpike. A farther section of that road is now in line for development.

"The Glocester Turnpike Company in the State of Rhode Island and Providence Plantations," was created at the June session of the general assembly in 1804, and was given the old road through Johnston, Smithfield, and Gloucester, ending at Chepachet Bridge, a length of seven miles. The corporation was to be allowed to straighten the road, if it could purchase the necessary land, but was required to keep the location to the southwest of Chestnut-Oak Hill.

This company seems to have had an uneventful, although long career. Unlike most of the others it bothered the general assembly very little, only three acts being found subsequent to that of incorporation. Miss Perry's *History of Gloucester* notes the location of the gate opposite the tavern of Richard Aldrich in the eastern part of the town, although she erroneously

Glocester Turnpike: Approaching Wawaloam Lake from the east

attributes the toll collecting to a turnpike corporation which did not carry out its plans and which was not authorized to build in that end of Gloucester. There was no other turnpike than the Glocester which could have had a gate in that section. The road evidently appeared to be prosperous, for a petition was made in 1837 to have the corporation accounts examined to see if the collections had not repaid the original investment with interest. Commencing in 1839 the gate was leased for a fixed price per annum, the lessee to have the gross collections for his own. The committee of 1870 found this practice in force and reported that, for the year 1869, the gate had been leased for the sum of thirteen hundred dollars, from which the net receipts had been four hundred.

The business done in 1869 had enabled the corporation to finally pay its last debts and declare a dividend of six per cent, which excellent showing

Glocester Turnpike: Between Chepachet and Harmony

Glocester Turnpike: Wawaloam Lake from the west

caused the stock to be held at thirty-five dollars a share. The committee found the road in good condition, but the town was averse to assuming its maintenance, which later events make us suspect was a matter of business shrewdness rather than satisfaction with turnpike conditions. When the town did finally assume the care of the three roads within its limits, it was paid a goodly sum by the state for so doing. The commissioner, in 1871, deemed it necessary to order repairs to be made on this road.

At the May session of 1888, fifteen hundred dollars was appropriated to make the Glocester Turnpike a free public road, three hundred and seventy-five going to the town of Smithfield and eleven hundred and twenty-five to Gloucester, the corporation getting nothing.

The Glocester Turnpike extended from the village of Greenville in the town of Smithfield, northwesterly through Harmony, to the easterly end of the West Glocester Turnpike at Chepachet Bridge. Aldrich's Tavern must have been in Harmony, if Miss Perry's story of the gate is well founded, for there the sign giving rates of toll was hung. The same may be seen to-day in the rooms of the Rhode Island Historical Society in Providence.

5. The Rhode Island Turnpike

The petition for a charter to build this road was entered with the February session of 1804 and was followed by an amusing method of procedure. At the corresponding session of 1805 an act was passed upon the foregoing petition. First it was voted that a charter, as prayed for, should be granted. The second section provided for appeals from any awards of damages which might be made under authority of the charter which was about to be issued. The third told the expected corporation that, when it had its charter it must not lay out its road through any land for which it had not paid or tendered payment; and the fourth provided that the charter should be void in two years unless utilized. Then, in an entirely separate act, the charter was enacted.

Authority was granted to build a road "in Portsmouth, on the island of Rhode Island," and the route was defined as

beginning at the fork of the cast and west roads near Mr. Job Durfey's, and from thence on a southeasterly course, until it shall meet with the east road near the corner of the orchard late belonging to Mrs. Bathsheba Fish.

This corporation bothered the general assembly but little, but signs of life are visible, for it secured an act in 1840 by which its charter was revived. From this it is not to be assumed that the corporation had temporarily given up business, but rather that some trifling formality in the holding of its annual meeting had been omitted. The corporation laws of Rhode Island were so narrow that failure to hold an annual meeting to elect officers has been observed, in another case, as invalidating the charter. According to the index of special laws, William Anthony made some petition regarding this road in 1853, but the matter referred to could not be found by the pages indicated. However, it seems likely that the road was in operation at as late a date as that.

The Rhode Island Turnpike is locally known as such on the island of Rhode Island to-day by the older residents, at least. It commenced near the Bristol Ferry at the northerly end of the island, where the old roads, running up the east and west sides thereof, came together, and from thence it ran southerly and southeasterly, about a mile and three quarters, to a point in the old East Road, now called the Newtown Road, near the present village of Portsmouth.

This Bristol Ferry was an ancient institution, being the ferry of which mention was made in an earlier page in quoting an advertisement issued in 1720. It first appears in the Portsmouth records under date of November 1, 1642, when a ferryman was appointed and a "necke of land" was granted to help him eke out a living.

6. The Douglas Turnpike

The petition for this road was made in October, 1803, but it was not until February, 1805, that the charter was issued. The original name of the corporation was "The Smithfield Turnpike Company" and its authorized route was "from Providence to the line of Massachusetts in the town of Douglas or Uxbridge." Construction evidently proceeded slowly, as the layout and award of damages had not been completed in May, 1807. In that month the corporation made petition to be allowed to build a branch of its turnpike

Providence and Douglas Turnpike: South End, near Orms Street, Providence

from Providence over common land, by the south-west corner of the North burying ground, from thence north-westerly nearly two miles till it shall open into said turnpike-road as already established.

This petition was granted at the June session of 1807 and the work then proceeded promptly. Clearly a better entrance into Providence than that originally laid out was needed to justify the project, and the branch, allowed in 1807, provided it. The first layout began at the North Providence line near Orms Street, and was on the back side of the old Cove, not at all convenient for access from the old compact parts of Providence.

At the October session of 1808 the name of the company was changed to

Providence and Douglas Turnpike: Branch Avenue, Providence

Providence and Douglas Turnpike: Passing the Geneva Mills, Providence

"The Providence and Douglas Turnpike Company," and another branch was authorized to be built "near the cotton factory lately erected by Almy and Brown in Smithfield." Under the name of Smithfield the corporation had then opened its road from Providence through North Providence, Smithfield, and Burrillville to "the country road" in Douglas, Massachusetts. Three gates were allowed, but none of them could be placed on any portion of an appropriated old road.

Although the road had been completed and was earning money, payments for stock subscriptions were slow in coming in, and in May, 1810, authority was secured to sell "at public vendue" any shares for which payment had not

Providence and Douglas Turnpike: South of Branch Avenue

been made.

Although permission to build the branch in Smithfield had been obtained in 1808, nothing was done toward that end until late in 1820, when the assembly appointed a committee to appraise the damages consequent upon the layout. The branch was built within the next nineteen months but, on account of the long interval between 1808 and 1820, doubts were raised regarding the legality of the proceedings, and legislation was sought to legalize what had been done. Although the layout of the road was made legal it does not seem to have been made satisfactory, for alterations were found necessary within three years.

In June, 1839, it was enacted that the gates might be moved to any location the company desired provided (1) none were placed within a mile and a half of the state house, (2) none on any old road, and (3) none within four miles of another. Three whole or six half-gates were allowed to be placed on the main road and one whole or its equivalent in half-gates could bar travel on the Slater branch.

The main road of this corporation commenced at the present corner of Douglas Avenue and Goddard Street in what was then North Providence, and ran thence northwesterly, following the lines of Douglas Avenue and continuing in a course easily picked out on the map by its straightness, through Smithfield, North Smithfield, and the northwest corner of Burrillville, to the Massachusetts line in Uxbridge, at which point it joined the road of the Douglas, Sutton, and Oxford Turnpike Corporation in Massachusetts. The branch provided for by the act of 1807 was the present Branch Avenue in Providence, while the branch built in 1820-21 left the main road at the village of Smithfield and ran northerly through Primrose to Slatersville.

The eight miles of the main road, north of Smithfield Village, was turned over to the public by permission of the assembly in 1845, the remainder of the road continuing in operation for another year. The town council of North Providence laid out the turnpike and its branch as public roads August 24, 1846.

A road of earlier date traversed the country covered by the lower section of this turnpike, but the new road, while it seems to have been superimposed for part of the way, left the line of the old road for quite a portion of the distance. Although abandoned many years ago, portions of the embankments of the early road still exist in places.

In Providence and North Providence this road is to-day a busy street, but northerly to the Massachusetts line it is a sorry old road, except when occasionally a state highway enters it from the northeast and, after following the old turnpike for a short distance, bears off to the southwest.

7. The Loisquisset Turnpike

Loisquisset was the old Indian name for the region around the village of Lime Rock in the present town of Lincoln, so it was quite appropriate that the turnpike which was to serve that section should bear the name given by the original inhabitants. The Loisquisset Turnpike Company was created by the general assembly at the October session of 1805, and was allowed to take over and improve the old road from "near John Mann's," in Smithfield, to the Providence line. Smithfield, at that date, comprised the whole region on the west bank of the Blackstone River, north of North Providence, but the Loisquisset was in that part which was later set off as the town of Lincoln. By some it is thought that this turnpike reached as far north as Union Village, but the fact that only one full gate was allowed prevents our concluding that a road as long as that was contemplated. Rather, we think the northerly termination was at the village of Lime Rock.

A petition to be allowed to resurvey the limits of the road was made by the company in 1824, in consequence of which an act was passed the following year permitting it to be done. This proceeding was not as trivial as appears at first thought, for the committee appointed to supervise the work also had authority to make alterations and new locations in the road.

It seems that this road bore a heavy traffic in lime from the quarries and kilns at Lime Rock, which was formerly the center of a thriving industry. In 1830 the corporation was allowed to impose extra tolls on loads of lime exceeding a specified weight.

The joint committee of 1870 found this road in operation and reported that it could be bought for one thousand dollars, adding that negotiations were then under way between the corporation and the town of North

Loisquisset Turnpike: Charles Street, Providence

Providence for the public opening of the turnpike. In consequence thereof the corporation conveyed its road to the town of North Providence on the twenty-ninth of June, 1870, the town having previously voted to accept it if offered.

The old turnpike commenced at what was then the town limit of Providence, on the present Charles Street, near the corner of West River Street, and followed northerly along the Charles Street of to-day, and over the continuation thereof, through North Providence and Lincoln to Lime Rock.

8. Providence and Pawtucket Turnpike Corporation

The road of this corporation served as an important link in a busy line of travel, and it is to-day an interurban avenue teeming with traffic. North Main Street, from the southerly end of the North Burying Ground in Providence, and Pawtucket Avenue in Pawtucket, date from the opening of this road.

The petition for incorporation was entered at the October session of 1806, and a committee was at once appointed to view the route. Most expeditiously did the committee work, for its report was made in a very few days, and then the whole matter was referred to the next session, with an order for a public advertisement.

In 1807, at the June session, the act of incorporation was passed, giving a franchise from

the north line of the town of Providence, near the dwelling-house of the late Jeremiah Dexter, and run from thence northerly, on the east side of the old road, and passing by the westerly end of Jeremiah Sayles' dwelling-house, extend to such part of Pawtucket village as the committee hereinafter named shall direct.

The road was to be three rods in width, and it is interesting to note that, while originally the entire length was in the town of North Providence, the nearest point in that town to-day is nearly a mile from the road.

This corporation does not appear very frequently on the legislative records, only four acts being passed in relation to it during its twenty-six years of corporate life, two of these being for the purpose of determining if the state would be justified in taking the road, on account of sufficiency in its earnings.

In consequence of the two acts just mentioned, another act was passed at the June session in 1833, by which the state asserted its rights, appointed a committee to take possession of the road and all the corporation's property, and to operate the same in behalf of the state. The committee was instructed at the same time to offer the turnpike to the Boston and Providence Railroad Company, which was then in the process of formation, which is interesting as showing the transition from turnpike to railroad, and how people generally regarded the railroad as merely an improved form of turnpike. But the railroad people fought shy of the alluring morsel, as we learn from the committee's report in 1834, giving noncommittal replies to two propositions

Providence and Pawtucket Turnpike: North Main Street, Providence

from the state's representatives, after which the committee gave it up, assumed the management of the road, and appointed Thomas Burgess as the agent of the state. A certain history asserts that the purchase of this turnpike by the railroad company was contemplated in the original charter of the railroad but, if so, the compiler of Rhode Island's special laws failed to include such section in the published records.

While, as corporation property, the road made little legislative fuss, as a state turnpike it required thirty-nine separate acts of the general assembly during its thirty-six years under state control.

In 1841 it was enacted that the turnpike should be extended to the Massachusetts line, thus including what is now Pleasant Street and a portion of Main Street, in the heart of Pawtucket, with the Pawtucket Bridge, within the limits liable to toll.

The Massachusetts line was a sore subject between the two states, as it had been a matter of controversy since the charter granted to Rhode Island by Charles II in 1663. Under its charter granted in 1629 Plymouth Colony seemed to be entitled to the territory as far west as the center of the Narraganset, Seekonk, Pawtucket, and Blackstone rivers up to the present south line of the state of Massachusetts, but the charter granted by Charles II was so vaguely worded that the Rhode Islanders were able to put a far different interpretation upon it. According to their version, their easterly boundary ran due north from the ocean to a point in the present town of Lakeville, three English miles east-northeast from the head of Assonet Bay in the town of Freetown; thence in a straight line to Fox Point at the mouth of the Seekonk River; thence northerly along the easterly bank of that river to Pawtucket Falls, and thence due north to the present northeast corner of the state. With such a large area in dispute the parties could not come to an agreement and the matter was made the subject of an appeal to the Crown.

The commissioners appointed to adjust the matter made their finding known in 1741 and, while bringing the extreme eastern line much farther to the west, still upheld Rhode Island's contention that the line followed the easterly bank of the Seekonk River as far north as Pawtucket Falls. This decision, which was confirmed by the Crown in 1746, remained in force, although the subject of much contention between the states, until the present boundary was established by the decree of the supreme court of the United States in 1861. This boundary question has been treated in greater detail on account of several turnpikes and bridges falling within the disputed area. Of these Pawtucket Bridge was one.

The first bridge was erected at the joint expense of the two colonies in 1713, and was demolished by legislative order in 1730, after which it was renewed again jointly. Down to this time Massachusetts had asserted her claim to the center of the river and, therefore, was willing to assume one half of the cost of bridging the same, but after the finding of the commissioners in 1741, she was obliged to accept the easterly bank as the line, and when further repairs became necessary in 1772, the Bay Colony declined to share the cost of the bridge and only paid for the repairs on the eastern abutment. Hence the authority of the Rhode Island assembly to include the ancient bridge site within the turnpike limits.

The turnpike agent's report for 1843 shows a regard for the æsthetic and practical value of trees, for he reported that shade and ornamental trees had been grown along almost the entire road. In seeking a supply of gravel he had contracted with the town of North Providence to obtain that material by making the excavation for a desired street, agreeing to complete the work in four years. In the year and a half during which the arrangement had been in operation, the gravel thus obtained had cost the state two hundred and thirty dollars. The extension to the Massachusetts line had cost a large sum, including, as it did, "two of the principal streets and the bridge in Pawtucket." The bridge had been rebuilt and the streets put in proper condition.

Much trouble arose about 1848 over encroachments which abutting owners had made upon the turnpike right of way, and a committee appointed to deal with such cases compiled a list of twenty such offenses and notified each offender to move off. Two sets of cellar steps seem to have given the most trouble, and the attorney general was instructed to institute proceedings against those responsible for them, but one set was finally allowed to remain after the owner had inclosed them with an iron railing.

The march of progress is seen in the history of this road, for when gas was introduced into Pawtucket in 1848, permission was given to lay pipes along the turnpike, and the agent was authorized to erect eight lanterns, using the new illuminant along the road.

In 1849 the salary of the agent was substantially increased, being raised from fifty to seventy-five dollars per annum. How often it is seen that prosperity ruins a good man; the next year we see the final settlement with Thomas Burgess, "late agent."

A new tollhouse was provided for in an act of June, 1853. It was to be erected on the site of the old one and was not to cost in excess of one thousand dollars. The location of this house and the gate was opposite the present location of Pidge Avenue, where the old road to Pawtucket, now known as Main Street, branched off.

In 1857 Pawtucket Bridge demanded further attention. The agent in that year reported that the bridge was then fourteen years old and that many of its timbers were in so decayed a condition as to be unsafe. He was much worried because the bridge was high above the rocks and, if the under part should give way, "the whole structure would fall with fearful ruin."

July 6, 1858, the old bridge was closed and at once demolished. Timber bridges had been found so short-lived that the opinion was general that some more substantial form of construction should be used, and the present stone arch bridge was commenced immediately, and opened for public travel on the fourth of November following.

In the days of the Indians the remains of an old channel of the river existed on the westerly bank, extending from above the falls around the same, and into the river again a short distance below. In the effort to provide the towns on the Blackstone River with an annual supply of herring and such other fish as seek the sources of our rivers, this old channel was deepened, in 1714, to provide a runway through which the fish might pass around the falls. After the construction of the first dam, in 1718, which was built just below the point where the old channel left the river, the advantages of the fishway for the utilization of power were soon observed, and in 1730 a dam was thrown across its lower end and an anchor mill established, to be followed by several other industries, all driven by the water power from this old fishway. By 1790 a hive of industry was located on the bank and we find the old run known by the name of "Sergeant's Trench." In its course of but a few rods it passed the westerly end of the Pawtucket Bridge, and hence the road approaching the bridge had to pass over it. In 1854 we find the trench occupying the attention of the general assembly in connection with the Providence and Pawtucket Turnpike, and an appropriation was voted for two hundred and fifty dollars to be used in repairing the trench under the turnpike, if the mill owners would contribute an equal amount. But the mill men held off and petitioned the assembly, at its June session in the same year, to bear the whole expense, now increased to six hundred dollars, which the assembly graciously consented to do.

A diligence running between Pawtucket and Providence was established by Horace Field about 1823, Goodrich tells us, and was sold to Simon H. Arnold in December, 1825. Arnold at once issued the usual form of announcement, notifying the public that the round trip would be made twice each day, leaving Pawtucket at nine and two o'clock, and Providence at twelve and four. Commencing in 1836 Wetherell and Bennett ran an omnibus line for eighteen years, selling out to Sterry Fry, who operated the same until the advent of the horse cars.

The death knell of the turnpike was sounded October 25, 1847, on which day the Providence and Worcester Railroad was opened. The convenience of this route and the low fares which were, offered gave it a monopoly of the travel between the neighboring cities, and the turnpike earnings soon became too small for profit.

The march of progress again appears in 1863, this time in the shape of one of the agencies which were working the turnpikes into the past. The Providence, Pawtucket, and Central Falls Street Railway Company was then projecting a horse railway to connect those cities, and in the year named was granted permission to lay its tracks "over and along the whole or any part of" the state's turnpike. Specified payments were to be made for this privilege and, for the next six years travelers on the horse cars had the novel experience of passing through a tollgate.

The general assembly, at its January session in 1869, instructed the general treasurer to quitclaim the state's interest in the road to Providence, North Providence, and Pawtucket. The agent was instructed to spend no more money on the road unless absolutely necessary, and to throw the gate open forever when properly notified. The road became free on April 24, 1869, on which occasion the Tower Light Battery fired a salute of twenty-five guns, while a general celebration was being held at the tollhouse.

The Pawtucket and Providence was by far the most remunerative turnpike which has come under our observation. Reports of the business done may be seen in the Rhode Island State Library, and show through the period of the state's control to about 1847 that the earnings ran at an average of nearly eighteen hundred dollars a mile per year, while the net receipts paid to the general treasurer held close to twenty-five hundred dollars a year.

The road formed the Rhode Island continuation of the Norfolk and Bristol Turnpike in Massachusetts, and over it passed the extensive traffic between

Boston and Providence, including that between the first-named city and New York.

9. The Farnum Road

At the February session of 1808 the Farnum and Providence Turnpike Company was created for the purpose of building a road from "Tripptown," in North Providence, to Appleby's Road in Smithfield. Evidently the route thus specified was not enough to encourage the prosecution of the work, for the company petitioned the next year to be allowed to extend its road northeasterly to the line of the state of Massachusetts near Allum Pond, meanwhile delaying the construction of its main line of road. The petition was not granted, and it was renewed in 1811 and again in 1812, after which the project of the extension seems to have been abandoned by the promoters of this enterprise, and the corporation proceeded with the road which was allowed it.

The report of the locating committee was rendered in October, 1812. One full gate or two half ones was the allowance for this road, and the committee decreed that one should be placed near the powder mill, and if that was a half-gate, the other should be erected "north of the old road over Wolf Hill."

Work then proceeded, but at the end of seven years the road was uncompleted and the corporation was in financial difficulties. In consequence of an execution issued against the company the property was sold at auction, and was bought by Stephen and Elisha Steere. At the June session in 1819 those men obtained a renewal of the charter in their own behalf, with authority to finish the road. The Powder Mill Turnpike, which had been incorporated after the one under present consideration, had been con-

Farnum and Providence Turnpike: Waterman Avenue, Centerdale, R.I.

structed in the meantime, and that road was now made the southerly termination of the Farnum and Providence. The road was then completed as originally proposed north of the Powder Mill Turnpike, and became one of the successful and long-lived Rhode Island turnpikes. A revision of the charter was secured in 1828 whereby the privileges accorded to the later companies were bestowed on this one.

The joint committee of 1870 found the officials of this company an uncommunicative lot, and reported that it had been able to learn nothing of the road's affairs. So the report merely stated that the road extended from Centerdale to Smithfield, and was five miles long, which brought the northerly end to the present village of Smithfield. But the turnpike commissioner, according to his report in 1872, found only four miles of road.

The Farnum and Providence Turnpike was made free by act of the general assembly at the January session in 1873. Five hundred dollars was then appropriated to compensate the corporation.

The southerly end of the old turnpike in Centerdale is known to-day as Waterman Avenue.

10. The Powder Mill Turnpike

The petition for a charter for this utility was first made in 1807 and was renewed in 1808 and 1809. The prayer was finally granted by the general assembly of February, 1810, which created the Powder Mill Turnpike Corporation and allowed it to build a three-rod road which was to

begin at Sprague's tavern (formerly owned by the widow Waterman) at the southeasterly end of the Glocester turnpike-road in Smithfield; from thence eastwardly until it reaches the westerly line of the town of Providence on the plain near Fenner Angell's.

By the construction of this turnpike improved roads were provided all the way from Providence to the state line, on the way to Putnam, and over the route thus provided a daily stage between Providence and Pomfret struggled along for many years.

The road was completed and opened for travelers in 1815, according to Angell in his *Annals of Centerdale*. Two gates were established, one at the present corner of Smith Street and Fruit Hill Avenue, and the other at the corner of the road to Spragueville, about halfway between Centerdale and Greenville, where George Mowry once kept a tavern. The southerly end of the turnpike was near the corner of Smith and Holden streets, well within the present limits of Providence, and almost under the shadow of the state capitol. The road through Providence and North Providence is now called Smith Street, which name was applied to it in 1874. Beyond North Providence it is still known as the "Powder Mill Pike," and has been improved of late years with the help of the state until it is now a fine stretch of road. The

Powder Mill Turnpike: Terminus at Holden Street, Providence

Chepachet line of the Providence Street Railway system follows the old turnpike for its entire length.

In 1816 permission was granted to move the gate but not toward Providence. If it was located on any portion of an old road anyone was to be allowed to pass free upon declaring that no portion of his journey had been, or was to be, made on any part of the road which the corporation had built. In 1829 an excess toll of a half-cent per hundredweight was allowed on loads exceeding five thousand pounds, if the vehicle was furnished with tires less than five inches in width.

The Powder Mill is mentioned by the joint committee and by the turnpike commissioner in the respective reports, but no detailed statement is made by either.

The road was made free by act of the general assembly at the January

Powder Mill Turnpike: Centerdale, R.I.

Powder Mill Turnpike: West of Centerdale

session of 1873, one thousand dollars being appropriated and paid to the corporation. March 3, 1873, the town council of North Providence voted to accept the turnpike within the town limits "under the terms and conditions fixed by the general assembly" at its January session.

11. The Woonasquatucket Turnpike

Atwells Avenue, in Providence, is of mongrel birth, originally being both turnpike and public road. About 1809 the Providence town council laid out and built a four-rod road extending from Aborn Street almost due west to the Woonasquatucket River, which then formed the westerly limit of the town. At the February session in 1810 the Woonasquatucket Turnpike Corporation was created, with authority to continue that road northwesterly "till it shall come to the road leading from Tar Bridge to the village of Tripptown." Tar Bridge, we have already seen, was the bridge which carried the street, leading northerly from Olneyville Square over the river of the long name. Tripptown was the old name given to the modern village of Manton, and the road recited as the northwesterly terminus of the new turnpike is now known as Manton Avenue.

Financing the enterprise must have been difficult, for in 1812 permission was obtained to levy an assessment, not exceeding five dollars, on each share of stock. Instances of the fussiness of the Rhode Island laws are found in 1814 and 1815, in each of which years the corporation had to appeal to the general assembly for a renewal of its charter. The first time the franchise had been invalidated because the corporation had failed to elect its officers for the ensuing year. No provision existed that officers should hold office until their successors were qualified, consequently the company found itself without any official heads, and no business could be done. The second time the difficulty arose from the failure to hold the annual meeting. As the company secured authority again in 1815 to levy an assessment on the shares, we may imagine that the trouble was due to lack of enthusiasm, and that the building of the road was a slow process. But it was finally completed and operated for probably thirty-five years.

A petition having reference to this turnpike was entered at the state house by Andrew Williams in 1852, but no action has been found in consequence of it. It is easy to see, however, that it had for its object the freeing of the road, and that action was rendered unnecessary by the action of the town.

In 1854 the town of North Providence took over the turnpike, making it a part of the public system, and by the annexation of 1874, the whole length of the old toll road was included within the city of Providence. The plan prepared at the time the road was surrendered to the town shows the tollgate at the corner of Valley Street with the toll gatherer's house on the north-easterly corner. Atwells Avenue, from the Woonasquatucket River to the junction with Manton Avenue, was the Woonasquatucket Turnpike.

12. The Valley Falls Turnpike

This road was the beginning of the present Broad Street in Pawtucket and Central Falls. It was first built by the Valley Falls Turnpike Company, under a charter granted in February, 1813, by which authority was conferred to build from the northwesterly part of Pawtucket on the old road from Pawtucket Bridge to Providence, "northerly crossing the new bridge, now building at the valley falls, across Blackstone River," and on to an intersection with the Diamond Hill or Old Mendon Road. According to Grieve in his *History of Pawtucket*, the northerly terminus was at the crossroads at the Catholic Oak in Lonsdale.

The road was built by Isaac Wilkinson, the son of the Oziel Wilkinson who was so prominent in the construction of the Norfolk and Bristol Turnpike. This family, in addition to being among the pioneers of Pawtucket's manufacturers, was prominent in several of the turnpike developments in their neighborhood.

In 1842 the corporation made petition for the privilege of having its turnpike resurveyed, but a counter-petition was made by certain citizens who alleged that the charter had been forfeited, and secured the appointment of a committee to investigate their charges. Curiously enough the same committee was authorized to make the asked-for survey. The committee reported in January, 1843, giving the details of the new lines which had been determined as the boundaries of the road, and the assembly enacted that "said turnpike be, and the same is hereby, established and confirmed" as reported, which plainly enough disposed of the petition for annulment of the charter.

The turnpike was laid out, under the name of Broad Street, by the town of North Providence in 1864.

13. The Coventry and Cranston Turnpike

The hustling little group of factory villages along the boundary line between Coventry and Warwick were fairly well supplied with transportation over the river roads, except the ones called Anthony and Washington in the eastern part of Coventry. Being located well up the south branch of the Pawtuxet, and around a long bend in the same, the mill owners of those places found themselves at a decided disadvantage when it came to shipping their goods.

An early road had been built by the colony in 1737, which came over Natick Hill, passing Edmond's gristmill, which has given way to the Lippitt Mills, and up the river valley to the southeast corner of the town of Scituate; and this road, while offering no service to Anthony and Washington, was all that the needs of the other villages seemed to require until about 1810. Until then the villages on the upper river had been obliged to reach Providence by an old road through Apponaug.

In 1811 the mill owners of Washington and Anthony joined with the proprietors of the Roger Williams and the Lippitt mills, in a petition to the general assembly for a new and direct road, connecting all those manufacturing villages. At the February session, 1812, a road as desired was laid out and established by the assembly, but it was required that the petitioners should construct the same at their own expense, which did not appeal to the mill men as attractive, without the privilege of collecting tolls. So they next asked for a turnpike charter.

So the Coventry and Cranston Turnpike Company was formed in February, 1813, with a franchise "from the factory of the Coventry Manufacturing Company, by the Lippitt and Roger Williams Manufacturing Companies' factories, towards Monkeytown and Providence."

The mill of the Coventry Manufacturing Company was located in Anthony, and was one of the first cotton mills in the state, having been built in 1805-06, and substantially enlarged in 1810. The Lippitt factory was located in the village to which it gave its name, and the Roger Williams gave employment to the men of the village later called Phenix. In the month of May, 1821, fire laid the Roger Williams factory low, and another building promptly rising, as from the ashes, recalled the mythical bird and named the place.

From Fuller's *History of Warwick* we learn that the turnpike was three miles, one hundred and three rods, and twenty-two links in length, reaching from Anthony, through Phenix and Lippitt, to an already existing highway in the southerly part of Cranston.

The location of the road must have been a difficult matter, for the corporation returned to the general assembly three months after receiving its charter to ask permission to make alterations in its prescribed route. That was granted, and in less than two years they were back, stating that they had bought the land over which they desired to build an alteration of their road, and would the assembly allow them to so build. Naturally no objection was offered, and the road was changed accordingly.

Fuller says that the tollgate stood near the Lippitt Mills, and that the toll gatherer at one time was Caleb Atwood, who was also the landlord of the tavern near-by.

The gate has been gone so many years that no one has yet been found who dares hazard a guess as to the date when the road became free, even the insistent questioning of the lawyers in a case tried in Coventry many years ago failing to bring it out.

14, The Foster and Scituate Turnpike

The petition for this road was first made in June, 1811, at which time the petitioners desired to build from the Rhode Island and Connecticut boundary, through Hopkins Mills, to the Rhode Island and Connecticut Turnpike in the easterly part of the town of Scituate. But the assembly, doubtless having in mind the delays and difficulties of the Farnum and Providence, deferred action, finally granting a charter at the October session of 1813 to the Foster and Scituate Turnpike Society. The length of road, however, was curtailed, and a franchise was granted only from the Connecticut line to Hopkins Mills, a place in the northeasterly part of the town of Foster.

An unusual privilege was allowed in the charter of this company which was designed to meet the difficulty of raising ready money. The proposed road was to be divided into two hundred sections of equal length or cost to build, and whoever would undertake to construct and maintain one or more of such sections could be paid in stock, one share for each section. As the allowed road was about four and a half miles in length, the sections would average about one hundred and ninety feet, for the building and maintaining of which thirty dollars in stock at par value was to be paid. How much difficulty would a modern corporation find in recording that that amount of cash had been received from sale of stock and at once paid out on account of work performed? But such a detail had to receive the sanction, in advance, of the general assembly a century ago.

Even with the special privilege outlined above, the construction of the turnpike seems to have been a slow matter. The first meeting was appointed for a day in April, 1814, but the promoters failed to gather on that date and had to apply for a legislative act authorizing them to meet on October 16. By that time the corporation seems to have established a reputation for ability to carry out its plans, for the assembly then granted it permission to extend its route easterly to its originally desired connection with the Rhode Island and Connecticut Turnpike.

The promoters of this enterprise expected that another turnpike would be chartered in Connecticut, over which they would have direct connection with Hartford by way of Danielson and Windham. But that hope was long deferred for the expected corporation, the Providence Turnpike Company, was not formed until 1825. The Connecticut legislature then granted a franchise, but only from the state line to Danielson.

The Rhode Island road started from a point on the state line, "near the house of Captain George Baker," about midway on the westerly line of the town of Foster and opposite the village of South Killingly in Connecticut, and proceeded directly to Hopkins' Mills, where Jonathan Hopkins was then operating the saw and grist mills which he had established about twenty-four years before. Thence it bore nearly due east through the villages of Chopmist, Trimtown, and North Scituate to a junction with the Rhode Island and Connecticut Turnpike at the southern end of Moswansicut Pond, in the northeast corner of Scituate.

That the turnpike was not profitable is seen from an act passed in January, 1848, by which the rates of toll were revised, being substantially increased on the common classes of traffic.

The road was still in operation in 1858, in which year it appeared in the assembly halls, asking for certain amendments in its charter, but it was given up in 1866, in which year the portion in Scituate was deeded to that town. That portion was an old road which was first laid out in 1731.

15. The Foster and Scituate Central Turnpike

The corporation responsible for this road was first formed by the June session of 1814, and promptly commenced work, although it did not carry it to completion. All that we know about the first chapter of this road's history is what is told us in the preamble of the act creating the Foster and Glocester Appian Way Society. . . .From that we learn that enough of the Foster and Scituate Central was finished in a year to justify listing it among the turnpikes of the state. But the work languished and the corporation's rights expired before all was done. At the October session of 1822 a new act of incorporation, creating the same company, with the same name and the same franchise, was passed, and by this corporation the road was pushed to completion. Six gates were allowed, the most westerly to be within six miles of the

Connecticut line, and the next within twelve miles thereof. Alterations were made in the location between Scituate and Knapp's Hill in Johnston in 1824, and an increase of stock was allowed in 1828.

This road touched Connecticut three eighths of a mile south of where the Foster and Scituate met that state. It is shown on the road maps as the "Central Pike" and as "Saundersville Pike," and swings in a semicircular course across the towns of Foster, Scituate, and Johnston, crossing the north end of Barden Reservoir, passing through Saundersville and entering Providence over Sunset Avenue to its connection with Plainfield Street, the old Providence and Norwich Turnpike.

In 1842, in response to a petition, it was enacted that unless the corporation repaired its road properly within twelve months the charter should stand repealed. Under conditions as serious as this indicates, it is doubtful if the terms were met, and this probably marks the end of the turnpike operation.

16. The New London Turnpike

When one considers the importance of the railroad division between Providence and New London and observes the tremendous traffic which daily passes between those cities, it indeed seems strange that the turnpike which preceded the railroad was so late in being built. Not until 1815 was a petition entered for a franchise covering this route.

Before the European saw this region the Indians had their well-beaten path leading from Providence to Westerly and thence to New London. Later, known as the Pequot Path, this trail developed into the early colonial Post Road, over which a post was established as early as 1690, and which was used by Madam Knight in 1704. Starting in Providence at what was then the head of the bay, the path crossed a ford at the foot of what is now Steeple Street, and followed the lines of the present Weybosset and Broad streets and Elmwood Avenue, through East Greenwich and over Kingston Hill, passing on the north of Charlestown Pond, and entered Connecticut by a ford of the Pawcatuck River where the town of Westerly now stands. In subsequent development of the post route, the Providence and Norwich road was opened, but it is significant of the engineering instincts of the Indians that the highly developed railroad returned to the primeval location. But from 1795 to 1820 the line of improved highways between Providence and New London lay through Norwich; and Westerly and Stonington, with all the east side of the Thames River, were left on a side route.

In May, 1816, the Providence and Pawcatuck Turnpike Society was incorporated with the privilege of building from Providence to the Nathaniel Arnold Bridge in West Greenwich, and thence southwesterly to Pawcatuck

Bridge in Westerly. Promising as the route seemed the corporation had hard work in constructing its road and in raising the money therefor. Three years after the incorporation the company secured the passage of an act by which it was allowed to erect a gate as soon as it had completed six miles of road, and additional gates as fast as more six-mile sections were finished. In 1820 it was provided that the gates might be spaced four miles apart instead of six, which all shows that every little addition to the finances was welcome.

Pawcatuck Bridge was an old establishment connecting the villages of Westerly, Rhode Island, and Pawcatuck, Connecticut, so we see in the first turnpike proposal a return to the way of the Indian. A public stage road was built about 1815 from the head of the Mystic River, across Stonington to Westerly, and this was at first intended to form a part of the improved route. But some insurmountable force was in opposition to a road through Westerly. The Providence and Pawcatuck never built its road beyond to-day's village of Wyoming in the town of Richmond, and another corporation took up the burden from that point. The Hopkinton and Richmond Turnpike Corporation was formed by an act of the February session of 1820, its franchise extending from a point on the Connecticut line southwesterly from Hopkinton City, and at the end of a Connecticut road from New London, thence northeasterly to a connection with the Providence and Pawcatuck. The Connecticut road just referred to was the Groton and Stonington Turnpike, which had been chartered in 1818 and built from Groton Ferry, which crossed the Thames River, to the Rhode Island line. It was expected that the Connecticut road would follow the new stage road to Westerly, but a sudden change in the plans threw it up through North Stonington, and the Hopkinton and Richmond bridged the space to the Providence and Pawcatuck, completing the turnpike connection from Providence to the ferry by which New London was entered.

The opening of this route revolutionized travel between Boston and New York, which now proceeded to New London by stage, and thence to New York by a steamship which lay overnight at New Haven. Not until about this time was it considered practicable for any form of boat to make regular trips around Point Judith, but soon we find a scheduled line from New York to Providence, which superseded the New London Turnpike for through travel about 1830. By the opening of the railroad from Providence to New London, it would seem that the turnpike had been dealt its deathblow, but it lasted many years longer, although not a prosperous enterprise.

The attorney-general was instructed, in 1857, to examine the charter under which the turnpike was operated, and advise the general assembly how the same could be amended so that the corporation could be compelled to keep its road in good condition during the winter.

To follow the New London Turnpike to-day one should start at the corner of Elmwood Avenue and Parkis Street, that being at the old Providence town line, and follow out Elmwood and Reservoir avenues to Blackmore Pond. From there to the Sockanosset Reservoir the old road has been changed and does not now appear on the map, but the turnpike is found again in the road which skirts the reservoir estate on the southeast side; thence through Natick, Centerville, and Crompton, in Warwick, and Wyoming and Hope Valley, in Richmond, to Hopkinton "City" and straight ahead to the limits of the state. A glorious view is to be had when passing over Prospect Hill, midway between Natick and Centerville, sweeping the bay from Rocky Point to Pawtuxet.

There seems to be no record of the transfer of the turnpike to the town of Cranston, and we have been unable to determine when the road became free of toll.

That there was a test of strength over the location of the new turnpike route from Providence to New London, and that the advocates of a road through Westerly fought to the last ditch may be inferred from the incorporation of another company soon after the formation of the Hopkinton and Richmond. That was the Wickford and Pawcatuck Turnpike Company, chartered at the May session of 1822 to build from the village of Wickford to Pawcatuck Bridge. If the new turnpike would not pass through Westerly, the interests of that town would build a turnpike of their own with a parallel entrance into Providence. But this must have been the last card of the Pawcatuck Bridge advocates, for no such road was built, and apparently the opposition to the Providence and Pawcatuck's connection with the Hopkinton and Richmond was heard no more.

17. The Smithfield Turnpike

This proposition was first heard in 1818 when the petition was made which resulted in the creation of the Cumberland and Smithfield Turnpike Corporation. Nothing was done by this company, but in May, 1823, a new petition was made for a franchise over the same route, and in June of the same year a charter was granted creating the Smithfield Turnpike Corporation. The route allowed was "from the Friends' meeting-house in Smithfield southerly, to the branch of the Douglass Turnpike at the Moshassock Bridge."

Friends' meeting-houses in Rhode Island seem to have been as thick as the proverbial thieves, and the reference above to one of them helps us but little. It seems, however, from reading both the act and the petition that it was intended to have the road terminate about at the village of Lonsdale, but it was never built that far. Steere's *History of Smithfield* tells of a Quaker church which stood on the river at Lower Smithfield, and which was

Smithfield Turnpike: Smithfield Avenue, Providence

mentioned in a deed given in 1708. That may have been the one mentioned in the charter for the Smithfield Turnpike, although the fact of its being "on the river" is hardly consistent with our conclusion that Lonsdale was the northerly objective point.

An additional franchise to build a branch of the turnpike was secured in 1826, by which the corporation was authorized to build from its road northeasterly to the Smithfield Road at the southerly end of Scott's Pond. This was clearly constructed, as was the main turnpike from the junction southerly. Together the road and its branch formed the street known to-day as Smithfield Avenue in Providence, Pawtucket, and Lincoln.

With the authorization for the branch, permission was given to increase the capital to provide the sinews for its building, and the company was allowed to collect extra tolls on heavily loaded teams. Lime was here a favored industry as is indicated by the easier tolls imposed upon its carriage.

The Providence and Worcester Railroad, which had been opened to Pawtucket in 1847, was seen pushing its way northward in 1848, when it encountered the Smithfield Turnpike at an angle awkward for crossing. On the petition by the railroad company the general assembly authorized the supreme court to relocate the turnpike to provide a proper crossing. That was in June, 1848, and a later act in January, 1849, causes a smile. The first act had put it up to the court to personally relocate the turnpike, and another act was necessary before three commissioners could be appointed to do the detail work. The result of these proceedings is to be seen to-day in the sharp bend made by Smithfield Avenue where it crosses the railroad in the northerly part of Providence.

The town council of North Providence laid out the Smithfield Turnpike as a public highway April 4, 1870.

18. The Pawtuxet Turnpike

Eddy Street, in Providence, is another thoroughfare which has been in part a turnpike. The portion from the junction with Broad Street, in the Edgewood District, to the corner of Richmond Street by the coal wharves, was built by the Pawtuxet Turnpike Corporation, which was formed at the January session of 1825. In the franchise the route was thus described:

from the Providence and Pawtuxet road, about two miles northerly of Pawtuxet, northerly, between the two hospitals, until it enters the compact part of said town [Providence] at Eddy's Point.

Three rods was to be the width of the road, and one gate was allowed provided that it was not placed within two miles of the state house, which was then on the east side of the river. At the June session in the same year the corporation was allowed to include the portion of the old road from its junction therewith to the present corner of Berwick Lane, which was "within half a mile of Pawtuxet Bridge." Before this was done, however, the village of Pawtuxet was required to put the portion of the road thus to be given to private interests in satisfactory repair. No gate was to be erected on such portion of the old road.

The map of Providence, prepared by Daniel Anthony in 1803, shows the two hospitals mentioned above well out of town and to the south. A road, apparently the predecessor of the modern Plain Street, is indicated as the "Road to New Hospital," while another, about on the lines of the present Hospital Street, is marked "Road to Hospital." The two hospitals gave place some fifty years ago to the present efficient Rhode Island Hospital. Eddy's Point we find on the same map at the foot of Ship Street, and we can see by the present-day maps that Eddy Street points straight for that section.

The life of the corporation was uneventful as far as written records show for many years, although it is easily to be seen that a great deal of internal quarreling and external bickering must have gone on. But in 1841 a storm broke, and the corporate skeleton in the closet came out in full view. With the January session of that year was filed a petition by certain of the stockholders in the corporation, asserting that they were not properly treated in the management of the company's affairs, that money which should be devoted to the payment of dividends or repairs on the road was spent in a manner detrimental to the stockholders' interests, and that the management of the business was improperly conducted in other particulars. They prayed that a committee might be appointed with power to examine the corporation's books, inspect the road, and issue such orders as would best conserve the interests of the investors. Another petition was presented by the owners of land adjacent to the turnpike, many of whom had built their dwellings on its side. These complained that the road was not built in conformity with the franchise requirements, being in the wrong location, that the gate had been erected, notwithstanding the prohibition, within two miles of the state house, and that toll was exacted from persons engaged in agricultural work and who were exempt from such demands. It was further set forth that the form of construction of the road was such that water would not flow from the adjoining lands but was held back in standing pools. The corporation would neither place culverts across its road nor allow others to do so. To those dwellers along the road who asked permission to lay sidewalks at the side of the street in front of their houses, invariable refusals had been given. So they, too, begged for the appointment of a committee with power to remedy their grievances.

To the complaint of illegality in the location of gate and road the assembly gave prompt and complete answer, which must have raised little hope among the petitioners of any further favor. It was enacted that, however illegal, the gate and the road should remain where they were, and their locations were confirmed and established. But the committee was appointed as asked, and upon its recommendation a further act was passed at the same session, which required the corporation to be more human.

That part of the turnpike within the city limits of Providence was deeded to that municipality April 7, 1846, but the city advisers seem to have doubted the legality of the transfer, and acceptance of the road was delayed until the general assembly could be asked to sanction the same. At the January session of 1847 the desired sanction was obtained, conditional upon the consent of the city and all the adjoining property owners, and on July 3, 1847, the city made formal acceptance of the road.

Complaints again arose in 1853, when another committee was appointed to examine the books and inspect the road. Adverse action on account of any report which this committee might make, was forestalled by the corporation's completing negotiations with the town of Cranston to take over the balance of the road. Hence in April, 1855, the Cranston portion of the turnpike was deeded to that town, which had already voted to accept the same if it was offered.

By the two actions noted above, the entire turnpike became free, but apparently the corporation continued to maintain its existence and transact some kind of business, for in 1862 the attorney-general was instructed to ascertain if the company was still legally doing business and if its rights had not been forfeited.

19, The Mineral Spring Turnpike

The Smithfield and Glocester Turnpike Corporation was created in June, 1825, to build from the village of Pawtucket westerly to the Powder Mill Turnpike and thence to the Connecticut line. The westerly end of this proposed route was open to the same criticisms as the Rhode Island and Connecticut Central, as it was to pass halfway between the Rhode Island and Connecticut, and the Glocester turnpikes. It is hard to see, at this day, why so many were anxious to provide direct connections from Providence to the eastern part of Connecticut, and we must remember that, at that time, many of the waterfalls of the Quinebaug and Shetucket valleys had been utilized for small textile mills. Small as was the output of these mills it must have been the prospect of the freight from them that raised such hopes of turnpike prosperity. But the section east of the Powder Mill Turnpike had other reasons for rosy hopes, which seemed sufficiently well-founded to enable the promoters to build that part.

Near the mineral spring which has given a local name to the northwest part of Pawtucket, a deposit of bog iron was found by the early settlers, and by the beginning of the eighteenth century a rough cart path ran from Pawtucket Falls over the route now followed by Mineral Spring Avenue. Ironworks were in operation at Pawtucket Falls before the erection of the Pawtucket Bridge, and a forge stood on the banks of the Moshassuck River where the iron was converted into blooms to be carted to the works at the falls. The installation of the first carding and spinning mill in America at Pawtucket in 1790, and the rapid growth of that industry gave a tremendous impetus to the ironworks, which were called upon to provide the wear-resisting parts of the new machinery. For it must be borne in mind that England, jealously seeking to maintain a monopoly of the textile trade, prohibited the exportation of any of the machines or plans thereof. Hence the early carding and spinning machinery in Pawtucket was constructed from the memory of Samuel Slater who had operated such in the old country.

As long as the turnpike corporation was burdened with the obligation to build clear to the Connecticut line, it was found impossible to make any headway, and the promoters were obliged to return to the general assembly in October, 1826, for a revision of the charter. Then the name of the corporation was changed to the Mineral Spring Turnpike Corporation, and the franchise was cut down so that it only covered that part of the original route which lay east of the Powder Mill Turnpike. That was a more business-like proposition and the road was built during the next year, 1827. Under an agreement made with the first corporation, the town of North Providence contributed for ten years the receipts of the town landing at Pawtucket toward the construction and maintenance of the turnpike.

Mineral Spring Turnpike: Lorraine Mills, Mineral Spring Avenue, Pawtucket, R.I.

Angell's *Annals of Centerdale* speaks of this road as running through a district not previously served on east and west lines, but as being handicapped by being laid over long hills, a fault with so many turnpikes. A glance at the map will show how well the road, as finally constructed, met the needs of the community. Pawtucket now, as well as Providence, was provided with direct and improved connections with the rapidly opening textile districts in eastern Connecticut and central Massachusetts, as the new road intersected both the Douglas and the Powder Mill turnpikes.

North Providence purchased the turnpike from its owners in 1867 and named it Mineral Spring Avenue. It commenced in Pawtucket at the southeasterly corner of Mineral Spring Cemetery, and at the present corner with Main Street.

20. The East Turnpike

This road was built by the Pawtucket and Providence East Turnpike Corporation which was chartered in October, 1825. It is the present East Avenue, in Pawtucket, and Hope Street, in Providence, and to one familiar with the congested city conditions now found along the greater part of its borders, the description of the route as given in the charter must be amusing. It reads: "from the village of Pawtucket, in North Providence, through the farms of Timothy Greene, Thomas Arnold, and others, and ending at Olney's line, so called, in said Providence."

The end in the village of Pawtucket was at what is now the corner of East Avenue, Church, and Pleasant streets, and the Providence termination was then as now at Olney's Lane, at a point which was then the highest point in the town, being later selected as the location of the Hope Reservoir of the city's waterworks. . . The College Hill section of Providence was then the larger part of the town and, owing to the unhealthy influence of the old Cove, which occupied the site of the present Union Station, seemed likely to be the coming center. Even so, the promoters of the East Turnpike must have anticipated pleasure driving and the teaming of store stocks rather than a heavy traffic, and it does not seem possible that, as late as 1825, anyone could have figured remunerative returns from the investment.

Although we may criticize their judgement on turnpike locations, to the owners of the East Turnpike we must give credit for ability to see when their investment was doomed. For this corporation, in 1837, secured the passage of an act by which it was authorized to make a railroad of its turnpike and to extend the same to India Point, to which the Boston and Providence Railroad had been built in June, 1835. At the time of this act the New York, Providence, and Boston Railroad was pushing its construction between Westerly and the Providence River, intending to connect with the Boston and Providence by means of a ferry, and to have its terminus at a convenient point on the opposite side of the harbor. In addition to the right to extend its turnpike and convert it into a railroad, the Pawtucket and Providence East Corporation secured a franchise for a full-fledged railroad to be built from some point on the line of the New York, Providence, and Boston Railroad to Central Falls, and thence up the valley of the Blackstone River to the Massachusetts line, a clear anticipation of the Providence and Worcester Railroad.

Pawtucket and Providence East Turnpike: Hope Street, Providence and East Avenue, Pawtucket

It has already been pointed out that the early conception of a railroad was that it was to be an improved form of turnpike, on which any private party was to be at liberty to drive his own horse attached to his own vehicle, and on a schedule of his own improvisation. Section six of the amended charter of this company allowed the collection of toll from all passengers and on all property, at such rates as the directors might establish. The directors were further empowered to make rules regulating the form of cars and wheels and limiting the loads, always:

PROVIDED, that no regulation shall be adopted by said corporation that shall exclude individuals residing on said road, from travelling on the same in private cars; conforming in all things to such regulations, and paying such tolls as may be required by said corporation.

Warehouses were to be erected and tollhouses built, and tollgates were to be swung across the tracks.

In 1839 the name of the corporation was changed to the Providence and Boston Branch Railroad Company, not appropriate at all for a road reaching toward Worcester, and it was allowed until 1844 to complete its railroad. The expiration of its rights was followed promptly by the incorporation in May, 1844, of the Providence and Worcester Railroad Company, and construction by that company ended all hopes of extensions by the East Turnpike.

In October, 1843, the portion of the East Turnpike between the crossing of the Providence and Pawtucket Turnpike and the end at Church Street, in Pawtucket, was thrown open for free passage, but collections continued for passing over the balance of the road. In May, 1850, the corporation secured authority to erect an additional gate on the southerly side of Harrington's, or Herrendon's, Lane, at which half tolls were to be assessed.

Nothing further has been found concerning this road until 1872, and apparently it gradually died away. The committee which reported in May, 1870, had not discovered such a turnpike at all, but the turnpike commissioner had had it called to his attention. He reported that he had found no one conducting the affairs of the road and had been unable to learn the names of any stockholders or officials of the corporation. Providence and North Providence were then acting with the object of laying out the turnpike as a free public highway. So the East Turnpike became such in 1872.

21. Fall River and Watuppa Turnpike

This is the only turnpike which has been noted as being entirely transferred into another state by a change in boundary lines. Originally chartered by the Rhode Island assembly and built in Rhode Island territory, this road, by the adjustment of the state line which was made in 1861, became throughout its length subject to Massachusetts laws, and was finally made free in accordance with them.

Previous to 1861 the state line passed almost through the center of the present city of Fall River and crossed the narrow neck between the two Watuppa Ponds, leaving a considerable section east of the ponds in Rhode Island. Hence the authority of Rhode Island to grant the franchise for this road.

At the May session of the general assembly in 1827, the Fall River and Watupper Turnpike Company was incorporated with the franchise to build a turnpike from the line between Massachusetts and Rhode Island at the corner of the "first great lot and the mill share of the Pocasset purchase," thence "southeasterly to the Narrows on the road that divides the Watupper Ponds "; and thence eastwardly to the line of the town of Westport. In 1838 it was enacted that the erection and maintenance of the bridge across the Narrows, should be forever incumbent upon the turnpike corporation.

In consequence of the charter just recited the present Pleasant Street in Fall River was built, and it was operated as a toll road until September, 1864, when the city acquired the turnpike and made it free. The western end of the turnpike was the corner of what is now Plymouth Avenue and Pleasant Street, while its eastern terminus was a short distance east of the ponds.

This road is well known to trolley tourists, as over it the high-speed electric cars to New Bedford enter and leave Fall River.

22. The Stone Bridge and Fall River Turnpike

This road was the original of the present Bay Street in Fall River, extending from what was then the state boundary, at the corner with William Street, to the Stone Bridge; mostly along the shore of Mount Hope Bay. It was built by the Stone Bridge and Fall River Turnpike Company, which was created at the January session of 1838.

Stone Bridge was then about thirty years old, having been commenced in 1806 and completed about the end of the following year. Its total length was one thousand five hundred and twenty-four feet, of which eight hundred and sixty-four feet were between the abutments of an old and insecure bridge. Parallel walls, filled between, were built across the entire distance with the exception of sixty-five feet over the river channel which was provided with a drawbridge. Originally the cost was estimated at eighty thousand dollars. Passengers between Newport and Boston previously needed two days for the trip by way of Providence but, after the bridge was opened, could go in one day by way of Fall River and Taunton.

This corporation had a good idea of the conditions necessary to produce business, for it early proposed the construction of a public road to connect its turnpike with the Tiverton Print Works, only asking in return that it might include the cost of such road in its capitalization. That construction was slow is seen from the act passed in June, 1839, by which it was provided that, when the road was finished as far south as the "old road by Earl B. Anthony's store," and the branch to the Print Works was completed, one gate might be erected and tolls collected. But no dividends were to be paid until the whole turnpike was finished.

Anthony's store stood on the southwest corner of the present Globe and South Main streets, and the Tiverton Print Works were on the northerly side of Globe Street, from which it appears that the building of a public road as a feeder really meant the: repairing and maintaining of Globe Street, which had probably existed as an old lane for many years.

The portion of the turnpike within the present limits of Rhode Island, lying close along the shore of the Bay, occupied the natural location for the coming railroad, and was appropriated for the laying of its track by the Newport and Fall River Railroad Company in 1862. The Fall River city records, under date of March 2, 1863, show a peculiar disposition of the Massachusetts portion of the turnpike, it being ordered:

That so much of the road, known as the Fall River and Stone Bridge Turnpike, as is within the limits of the city, be regarded as a Public Highway so long as for public travel, its free use is allowed and that it be in charge of the Superintendent of Streets and Highways, and repaired as are others of the city.

A satisfactory disposition, no doubt, and one not likely to be disturbed, but it makes Bay Street interesting as a street which is "*regarded* as a Public Highway," without being definitely so laid out.

This road, too, was affected by the adjustment of the boundary between Massachusetts and Rhode Island in 1861, the same being shifted from the northerly end of the turnpike to a point about two miles farther south.

The following turnpikes are reported by Wood to have been chartered but never operated as toll roads:

1800	Providence & Boston	Providence to Wrentham, Mass.
1803	Greenwich	East Greenwich to Connecticut line at Coventry
1806	John & Phlip Browns' Road	Massachusetts line, Gloucester, to Wallum
1807	Wickford	Wickford to Connecticut line at Beach Pond
1813	Burrillville	Burrillville to Farnum & Providence Turnpike
1815	Foster & Glocester Apian Way	Vernon to Connecticut line at Gloucester

1824	Cumberland	S. Arnold's in Smithfield to Manville thence northerly to Mendon Road
1825	Rhode Island & Connecticut Central	Johnston to Connecticut line at Gloucester
1827	Providence & Warren	Between the towns named
	Worcester	Friend's meeting-house in Smithfield to Massachusetts line near Blackstone Village
1828	Foster Branch	Connecticut line northeasterly about 4 miles to Foster & Scituate Turnpike
1830	Providence & Norwich City	Providence to Connecticut line at West Greenwich
	Woonsocket Falls	Woonsocket Falls to Loisquisset Turnpike
	Foster Valley	From Foster & Scituate Turnpike at Hopkins Mills to Connecticut line
1836	Worcester	Massachusetts line in Cumberland to the Blackstone River; down that river to Crook Fall River Valley; through said valley to the Great Road in Smithfield
	Moshassock	Southerly end of the Worcester Turnpike to Scott's Pond
1842	Peacedale	Peacedale to Narrgansett Pier
1853	Pawtuxet Plank Road	Providence to Pawtuxet Village
1856	Silver Hook Road	Near the present Silver Hook Bridge
1859	The River Road	From High Street in Central Falls northerly through Valley Falls, Lonsdale, Ashton, Albion, and Manville, to the road from Manville to Woonsocket. A branch to Granite Ledge on Sayles Hill in Smithfield.

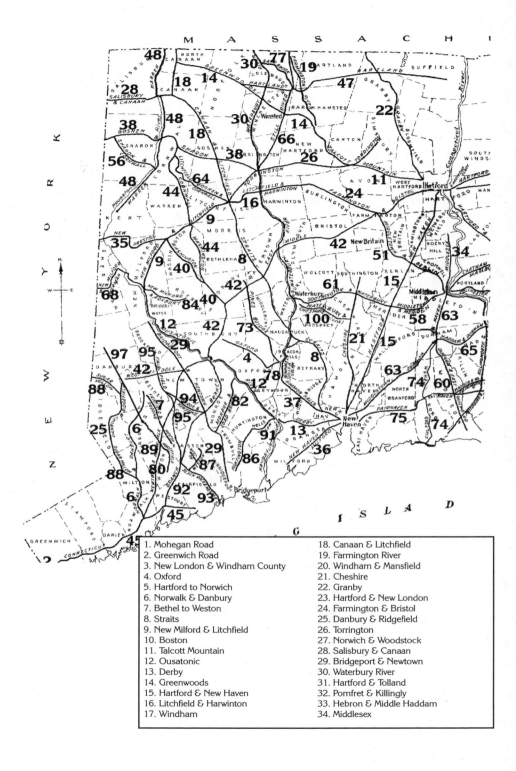

1. Mohegan Road
2. Greenwich Road
3. New London & Windham County
4. Oxford
5. Hartford to Norwich
6. Norwalk & Danbury
7. Bethel to Weston
8. Straits
9. New Milford & Litchfield
10. Boston
11. Talcott Mountain
12. Ousatonic
13. Derby
14. Greenwoods
15. Hartford & New Haven
16. Litchfield & Harwinton
17. Windham
18. Canaan & Litchfield
19. Farmington River
20. Windham & Mansfield
21. Cheshire
22. Granby
23. Hartford & New London
24. Farmington & Bristol
25. Danbury & Ridgefield
26. Torrington
27. Norwich & Woodstock
28. Salisbury & Canaan
29. Bridgeport & Newtown
30. Waterbury River
31. Hartford & Tolland
32. Pomfret & Killingly
33. Hebron & Middle Haddam
34. Middlesex

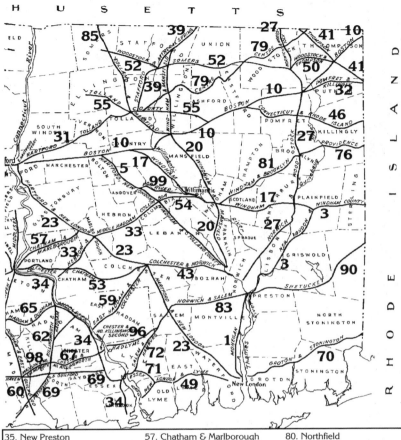

35. New Preston	57. Chatham & Marlborough	80. Northfield
36. New Haven & Milford	58. Middletown & Meriden	81. Windham & Brooklyn
37. Rimmon Falls	59. East Haddam & Colchester	82. Monroe & Zoar Bridge
38. Goshen & Sharon	60. Durham & East Guilford	83. Norwich & Salem
39. Stafford Mineral Spring	61. Southington & Waterbury	84. New Milford & Roxbury
40. Washington	62. Killingworth & Haddam	85. Tolland & Mansfield
41. Thompson	63. Middletown	86. Huntington
42. East Middle-West Middle	64. Litchfield & Cornwall	87. Weston
43. Colchester & Norwich	65. Haddam & Durham	88. Sugar Hollow
44. Cornwall & Washington	66. Still River	89. Newtown & Norwalk
45. Connecticut (Old Boston Post Road)	67. Chester & North Killingworth	90. Shetucket
46. Connecticut & Rhode Island	68. New Milford & Sherman	91. Wells Hollow
47. Hartland	69. Pettipauge & Guilford	92. Branch
48. Warren	70. Groton & Stonington	93. Black Rock & Weston
49. New London & Lyme	71. Essex	94. Monroe & Newtown
50. Woodstock & Thompson	72. Salem & Hamburg	95. Fairfield County
51. Middletown & Berlin	73. Pines Bridge	96. Hadlyme-Chester & North Killingworth Second
52. Woodstock & Somers	74. Guilford & Durham	97. Sherman & Redding
53. Colchester & Chatham	75. Fairhaven	98. Madison & North Killingworth
54. Columbia	76. Providence	99. Hop River
55. Tolland County	77. Sandy Brook	100. Waterbury & Cheshire Plank Road
56. Sharon & Cornwall	78. Humphreysville & Salem	
	79. Center	

The Turnpikes of Connecticut

ALL PARTS of the state being within easy distance of the salt water, Connecticut was settled throughout its extent at a very early date and, according to the census of 1790, then possessed a density of population which had not been equaled in 1910 by Maine, New Hampshire, or Vermont. Such being the case it is but natural that roads existed in all directions, connecting all the towns with each other and leaving little room in which a new route for a turnpike could be projected. Previous comments on early New England roads are fully applicable here, and the wretched condition of such roads as were in use is amply demonstrated by the fact that, in this small state, one hundred and twenty-one franchises for turnpike improvement were granted between the years 1795 and 1853, the larger part of which resulted in development. In consequence of there being roads of some quality wherever needed, nearly all the turnpike charters issued in Connecticut were for the improvement of a road previously existing but which the neighboring inhabitants were unable to maintain in proper order. Owing to the lack of turnpike characteristics due to the new roads following the lines of the old, it has often been difficult to determine which of various roads was the one improved by the turnpike system.

Connecticut in its early efforts tried the method of Charles II, under which the maintenance of a road was sought from those using it, and erected tollgates at two places on the Old Post Road from Boston to New York, vainly hoping that the receipts thus collected would be sufficient for the annual repairs of the road. Only in the case of the Mohegan Road was this method continued.

Next the plan of granting the right to make such improvements to private investors under the form of corporations was adopted, but in this Connecticut failed to realize the great improvement made in America over the English practice and formed its turnpike corporations along the lines of the English turnpike trusts.

Under the idea that the turnpike companies, like the English trusts, assumed a road already laid out and were not bound to build anything but a road, the towns through which turnpikes were projected were obliged to purchase and pay for the land needed for a new road, or for alterations in an old one, and to build all the necessary bridges. Consequently much hostility was caused against all turnpike companies, and many towns were seriously strained in their financial resources.

In some cases a new turnpike was laid out on petition of the local residents who needed it. Then a committee would be appointed by the assembly to view the route and lay out the road, reporting the same with recommendations as to the method of building it. If the assembly saw fit to accept the report it would do so, and then declare the road laid out as a public highway "subject to a bill," which meant that the layout was not to take effect until a turnpike corporation was formed which would undertake the construction. Many of these layouts are recorded in the office of the secretary of state in Hartford. Often a layout covers much more ground than the subsequently formed corporation was willing to assume, and sometimes one has to look for two corporations to account for one committee's action.

Similar procedure was followed when a group of investors had themselves selected a route over which they wished to open a new road. Upon their petition a committee would be appointed, which would lay out the road and advise as to the number and location of the tollgates which were to be allowed upon it. The corporation then was usually formed immediately after the acceptance of the report.

When a group of turnpike promoters had selected an old road on which they desired to make their investment, they would petition the assembly asking that that road might be given them in return for their advancing the money to put it in sufficient repair and that they might have the further privilege of collecting tolls from all traveling over it. If the road was recorded as a properly laid out public highway the charter of the new company would describe it as it appeared upon the records, and then declare it discontinued as a public road. Next a corporation would be formed for the purpose of reconstructing the route and opening a turnpike and operating the same thereafter. A bond was usually required to guarantee that the promoters would proceed in good faith and carry out the purposes of their incorporation.

In many cases the old road, or roads, were so crooked that the alterations due to building a direct route practically constituted new locations, and in such cases the county court, and sometimes the assembly, would make the layout in the form customary for public roads, describing the new route and declaring the same laid out as a public highway. Then the assembly would undo the public dedication, declare the road discontinued, and give it to the turnpike company.

Except as above the Connecticut practice differed little from that of the other New England states. Every corporation was the result of a special legislative act and the tolls of each were prescribed separately. The usual list of exemptions is found in all cases, favoring the churchgoers, the members of the militia, and those doing business with the local mills. No general laws were ever enacted for the organization of turnpike corporations nor to simplify their incorporation, but early acts established laws for the government of companies operating roads.

The first of these, enacted in 1803, was apparently experimental, as it was only to remain in force for three years, but with slight modifications it was permanently renewed at the expiration of that time. For each turnpike in the state three commissioners were to be appointed for the purpose of watching that road and seeing that it was kept in good order. As found in the Revised Statutes of 1835 this law provided for two commissioners appointed by the senate, who were required to inspect their road at least once a year. When they saw fit to order repairs they were empowered to open the gates until their orders had been obeyed. They could fix a limit of the time within which compliance with their orders should be made and, if the corporation neglected for a month after that to make the repairs, the general assembly could declare the charter forfeited. The commissioners had to examine the books and accounts of the company and make report to the assembly on a form prescribed by an act of 1804. For their arduous labors they were allowed the sum of two dollars per diem, paid by the corporation over which they were set. These laws are interesting as being the first instances of public-service commissions.

The early Connecticut corporations were chartered with no other limit to their corporate lives than the one which provided the repeal when the original investment, plus twelve per cent, had been repaid. As the failure of turnpikes became evident it was realized that those companies were perpetually chartered, and an effort was made by the assembly of 1835 to secure the right to repeal such franchises. An act was then passed which allowed:

(1) All existing gates might remain where they were with the consent of the road's commissioners and one court judge.

(2) The location of gates which had been moved was confirmed and collections of accounts at such gates was allowed.

(3) The commissioners and a judge might change any gates after having given a public hearing.

(4) The charter of all companies which accepted the terms of this act were made subject to repeal by the assembly; and all companies which did accept were obliged to formally vote to do so and file a record of such vote with the secretary of state.

It is hard to see that any additional privileges were granted by this act, and one wonders why any company should have seen fit to accept it at the price specified, but ten companies are on record in the secretary of state's office as having so voted.

Several more sections of general law for turnpikes are found in the compilation made in 1835, among them the wise provision that any corporation could enter upon adjoining land for the purpose of making such drains as were necessary to keep the roadbed dry. Contracts with frequent or heavy travelers were allowed as might be mutually agreed. Double tolls might be recovered in action against anyone who had evaded payment, in which event double costs of court were also assessed. Many disputes had arisen over the responsibility for the bridges, in cases where the company had gone ahead with the erection of one, looking to the town to pay later. To settle such it had been enacted that, wherever a company had built a bridge which was not definitely stated in the act of incorporation as one which the town should build, such bridge should be the corporation's, and the corporation should maintain it.

The early exemptions from toll had included all those "going to or returning from mill for the use of their families, or passing to attend their ordinary farm business. . . ." This also had caused disputes and a law had been passed by which no one traveling a distance in excess of four miles could lay claim to exemption under that clause. Seven dollars' penalty was laid upon a toll gatherer who collected excess tolls.

In 1837 it was provided that executions against a turnpike, or toll-bridge, company might be collected by the judge's putting a receiver in charge of one or more gates to collect the tolls for the benefit of the creditor until the debt was canceled.

An improvement over the laws of other states was secured in 1844 when it was enacted that any town might, upon the neglect of a corporation to keep its road in repair, do the necessary work itself and collect the cost from the company. To hasten payment no tolls were allowed while the debt was unpaid.

A law by which any corporation could unload its road upon the towns traversed was passed in 1854, and forfeiture of the franchise was established as the penalty for neglecting repairs about the same time. Various modifications of the same appeared in the next twenty years.

1. The Mohegan Road

The road through the Mohegan's country, connecting New London with Norwich, was first laid out in 1670 by Joshua Raymond, who was paid for opening the highway by the grant of a farm on the route. Miss Caulkins' *History of Norwich* tells us that it was little more than an Indian trail for over a century, having numerous windings, fords, and precipitous hills. The travel

Mohegan Road: Montville, Connecticut

over it was chiefly by those on horseback or in oxcarts. In 1789 an association was formed to effect improvements in the old road, and a lottery authorized by the legislature was drawn in Norwich in June, 1791, to assist in the work. Evidently a great deal of work was accomplished, for the distance between the two towns was materially reduced, and where the journey twice over the road had seldom been performed in a single day, after the improvements it could easily be done in four hours.

Such blessings seemed to the general assembly worth paying for and, in May, 1792, an act was passed establishing a tollgate, the second in America and the first in New England, on the newly made old road. Tolls were specified

Mohegan Road: Montville, Connecticut

Mohegan Road: Montville, Connecticut

in old currency, ninepence being levied on a four-wheeled pleasure carriage, and threepence on a loaded wagon or cart, while a "man and horse" paid only a penny. The proceeds of the tolls were to be devoted to the repair and maintenance of the road, chiefly in the Mohegan Reservation. The road soon became an important thoroughfare and a heavy traffic in cattle and produce passed over it on the way to the deep water docks of New London, there to be shipped abroad.

Early repairs seem to have been needed, for we find that the commissioners had felt obliged to advance from their own funds four hundred dollars in addition to the toll collections, and an act in 1805 allowed them to practically

Mohegan Road: Montville, Connecticut

double the tolls until they were repaid.

The road under charge of the commissioners and subject to toll was extended in 1806 to "Norwich Landing," from a point a little southerly from "Trading Cove Bridge," and in 1812, to the courthouse in Norwich.

In 1824, for some reason, it was enacted that three tenths of the net proceeds of the toll collections at the gate in Montville should be paid to the town of Waterford. By this it need not be inferred that there was more than one gate, for the indications are that there was not. Apparently on account of the strangeness of giving money collected in one town to another, it was made clear that such was the intention. This division continued until about 1837, after which all net proceeds were required to be spent on repairs, chiefly on that part passing through the reservation.

The New London, Willimantic, and Palmer Railroad, now the Central Vermont, opened its iron road parallel to the Mohegan Road in 1849, with the usual result that toll collections ceased soon after.

By act of the general assembly the gate was abolished July 3, 1852.

About 1900 the Montville Street Railway opened its line between New London and Norwich, following in large part the lines of the old Mohegan Road. The trip over this line has ever since been deservedly popular for, aside from the historic associations, the pilgrim is well repaid with beautiful scenery.

The Mohegan Road was never owned by a corporation but was managed throughout by commissioners in the interest of the road itself. In this it stands alone among all early American roads as the only one operated throughout in accordance with the principles established by Charles II, in 1663.

2. The Greenwich Road

In October, 1792, the general assembly established a gate on the "main County or stage road in the town of Greenwich," the same to be erected by commissioners acting in behalf of the county and the proceeds to be applied to the maintenance of the road. Thus was created the third tollgate in America. This was an effort to improve the conditions which we have already noticed in the New York *Advertiser's* statement of the road along the Sound being "rough, rocky, and uncomfortable" and often impassable for wheeled vehicles. The road affected was a part of the Old Post Road between Boston and New York, a route which had been in use then for over a century, and which formed a part of the journey of Madam Knight. As nothing was required beyond the erection of the gate, the road already being there, it seems certain that the road promptly became a toll road, although further information has not been found.

The Connecticut Turnpike Company, formed in 1806, was a much more extended proposition and was allowed to absorb the Old Post Road and its tollgate, of which more in its turn.

3. The New London and Windham County Turnpike

This road followed the Old Post Road and formed a continuation of the road of the Providence and Norwich Society, etc., of which we have already read as existing in Rhode Island. In the effort to improve the condition of traveling over this route, the Connecticut assembly in October, 1794, at the same time that the Rhode Island corporation was chartered, authorized the county to erect a tollgate on the road, the proceeds from which were to be devoted to the proper maintenance of the highway. But a condition was attached that the gate should not be erected until the road was first put in good repair. That proved too much of a burden and improvements waited until the next spring, when a corporation was formed to do the work.

In May, 1795, the New London and Windham County Society received a franchise to build a turnpike from Norwich to the Rhode Island line, through Norwich, Lisbon, Preston, Plainfield, and Sterling. One gate was allowed within ten miles of Norwich courthouse and another within five miles of the Rhode Island line. That the road was improved in reasonably prompt time is seen from the passage of an act, in 1801, by which changes in the rates of toll were allowed.

The New London and Windham County Turnpike evidently started from Norwich and followed up the westerly bank of the Shetucket River as far as the confluence with the Quinebaug, above which it crossed the first-named stream, and on the bridge thus necessitated erected its tollgate. Thence it followed up the valley of the Quinebaug to Plainfield Center, from which place it struck an easterly course and joined the Rhode Island road at what is now Oneco Station on the railroad between Providence and Willimantic.

Sometime prior to 1808 the gate near the Rhode Island line was moved to another location without formality and the assembly, at its October session in 1808, ordered it put back at once and forbade the collection of tolls until it was done.

In May, 1836, the right to collect tolls from those passing over the Shetucket River bridge was taken from the company.

Operation as a turnpike was continued for fifty-five years at least for, in 1849, a relocation around Bundy's Hill, in Lisbon, was approved by the assembly and a new gate location was allowed, but no record has yet been found to show when the entire road became free to the public.

4. The Oxford Turnpike

The Oxford Turnpike Company was formed at the May session of 1795 and given authority to open a road from Southbury to Derby. This was clearly a privilege of improving a previously existing road for the charter stated that the incorporators were to be allowed to erect their gate as soon as they had expended seven hundred pounds' lawful money.

In considering the territory which this road was to serve it must be borne in mind that Derby, at that date, was a much larger town, territorially, than it is to-day. Old Derby included the present towns of Seymour, Beacon Falls, and Oxford, and the terminal proposed for the turnpike was not the present village of Derby, but one of the villages of the old town, which is now known as Seymour, and then was called Chusetown. But a change was made in the plan, for Orcutt and Beardsley tell us in their *History of Derby*, that when first constructed the turnpike did not come quite to the village of Chusetown, but turned from the Little River some distance above its mouth, over the hill and up the Naugatuck River, crossing at Pines Bridge and joining the turnpike from Naugatuck to New Haven on Beacon Brook. As constructed the turnpike seems to be about the same as the present main road to Southbury.

This road was built about the time that New Haven was building the long wharf by which it was hoped to make that city a port of entry, and soon after there was a large trade for many miles around, much of it coming over the Oxford Turnpike.

An act of 1797 allowed the company to pass free "the stage to Massachusetts," which leaves rather a confused idea of the route followed by that stage, and the terminal town in Massachusetts, for the location and direction of the turnpike do not seem favorable for such traveling.

Tolls were collected on this old road for nearly ninety years, and the turnpike was finally made free sometime between 1880 and 1887.

5. Hartford to Norwich Turnpike

The Hartford, New London, Windham, and Tolland County Turnpike Society was the full name of the corporation which built this road, receiving its charter from the October session in 1795. Its route was thus described: "from the city of Hartford to the city of Norwich, from the court-house in Hartford to the court-house in Norwich." It may be interesting to note that Hartford and Norwich, with three other Connecticut towns, were incorporated as cities in January, 1784, thirty-eight years before that degree was conferred upon Boston.

On this road of about twenty-seven miles' length, two tollgates were allowed, to be located between East Hartford and Joshua Hyde's house in Franklin. The first meeting was to be held in Coventry. Consideration of the

Hartford to Norwich Turnpike: Broadway, Norwich

project during the succeeding winter evidently showed the promoters that they had a difficult problem on their hands, for they sought the assembly in the following May and secured a modification of their franchise so that they were only bound to build from White's Monument in Bolton to Joshua Hyde's in Franklin, thus avoiding the question of a means of crossing the Connecticut River at Hartford and being relieved of construction through the compact portions of the two terminal cities.

The road was built, by which term in Connecticut we mean that it was improved from its pioneer crudity to a form to justify the collection of tolls,

Hartford to Norwich Turnpike: Southeast from Lebanon Green

Hartford to Norwich Turnpike: Site of Joshua Hyde's house in Franklin

but built in rather a shoddy way, for we learn that in 1800 complaint was made to the assembly that the corporation was not keeping it in proper repair. A committee was appointed to investigate, but the company got busy and had its road in satisfactory shape when the legislators arrived, so a favorable report was made.

Joshua Hyde was born in Norwich in 1756, and after his marriage with Cynthia Tracy, in 1779, settled in that part of Norwich which was later set off as Franklin. His house stood about a mile above Yantic, where the Franklin and the Lebanon roads come together, and almost on the boundary line between Franklin and Bozrah. He was a prominent man in his day, repre-

Hartford to Norwich Turnpike: Split of roads at Lebanon Green

Hartford to Norwich Turnpike: Ten Mile River Bridge, Chestnut Hill, Conn.

senting his town in the assembly and serving as a member of the constitutional convention of 1818. He died in Franklin in 1830.

6. The Norwalk and Danbury Turnpike

The turnpike connecting Norwalk and Danbury extended from Semi Pog Brook in Danbury to Belden's Bridge in Norwalk, the improvements being made by the Norwalk and Danbury Turnpike Company which was created by act of the October session of 1795. This road is known to-day as the old turnpike and extends almost directly from one terminal to the other, passing through South Wilton, Wilton, Georgetown, and Topstone.

In 1800 the company was permitted to make contracts "to pass by the year" with anyone living within three quarters of a mile of a gate. Apparently the business had not prospered by 1802, for the privilege of taking tolls had been taken away and the assembly came to the relief of the harassed corporation by decreeing that it might renew collections when it had repaired the road.

The Norwalk and Danbury was about eighteen miles in length, but only one gate was allowed to be erected.

7. Turnpike from Bethel to Weston

In May, 1797, the Fairfield, Weston, and Reading Turnpike Company was incorporated to improve the road from the meeting-house in Bethel in Danbury to a point in Weston. An act relative to tolls shows that the road was in operation in 1801.

This turnpike continued in active life until 1834, when the portion between Bethel and Wild Cat Road was thrown open to the public. The balance continued in private control for four years longer, when the charter was repealed in May, 1838.

8. The Straits Turnpike

The thirty-six miles between New Haven and Litchfield were covered by the road built by the Straits Turnpike Company, which was incorporated in October, 1797, the franchise reading from courthouse to courthouse. Watrous, in his contribution to the *History of New Haven*, says that the road ran through the westerly part of New Haven and the village of Westville, then called Hotchkisstown, where it was later joined by the Rimmon Falls Turnpike.

The name of "Straits" was derived from a section along the road which had long borne that name and which was thus described by a writer in the early thirties.

About fourteen miles from New Haven the main road to Waterbury passes by Beacon Mountain, a rude ridge of almost naked rock stretching south-west. At this place is Collins' tavern, long known as an excellent public house, and the Straitsville post office. About half a mile south of Mr. Collins's the road passes through a narrow defile formed by a gap in the mountain, barely sufficient in width for a road and a small but sprightly brook which winds through the narrow passage. On both sides the cliffs are lofty, particularly on the west; on the east, at a little distance from the road, they overhang in a threatening manner.

The first meeting of the corporation was held in the house of Irijah Terrill, in Waterbury, in November, 1797. Much controversy arose over the location of the turnpike as Waterbury citizens wanted it to pass through the center of their town, while the people of Watertown made similar demands for their district. Anderson's *History of Waterbury* tells that a great deal of bitterness was bred of the contention, which we can imagine was not appeased when the final construction left Waterbury well to one side. The turnpike crossed Naugatuck River on Salem Bridge, so called from its location in Salem Society, the early name of Naugatuck. The town of Salem is in a part of the state remote from the Naugatuck River and had no connection with the naming of this bridge.

Bronson's *History of Waterbury* recites that the first bridge over the Naugatuck at Salem Society was built by the town of Waterbury in 1736 and was washed away in the winter of 1740-41. In 1743 the town, groaning under the expense of maintaining the structure, petitioned the assembly to be allowed to collect tolls for passage across the river. Whether that was allowed or not is not known, but if not, it was conceded later, for the bridge was a toll bridge in 1761. Repairs at a cost of eighty pounds were made in 1748-49.

The Salem Bridge, known as the Naugatuck Bridge in later years, soon became a bone of contention between the town of Waterbury and the turnpike corporation. First the company, tiring of waiting for the town to act, made some necessary repairs and then vainly tried to collect pay from the town for the same. After several years the bridge was washed away and the town, considering the fact that the turnpike company sent all its travelers over the bridge and collected its tolls on or near it, refused to rebuild and sought to put that expense on the corporation. But this was one of the old turnpikes, and its franchise had not placed the burden of bridges or land upon it, so the town was obliged to provide a new bridge. That in its turn soon followed its predecessor downstream, and again the town sought to shift the burden of rebuilding.

Claiming that the cause of the last catastrophe was a dike which the corporation had built a short distance above the bridge for the purpose of protecting its road where it crossed the low ground, the town brought suit to compel the company to pay the damages. It was claimed that the dike had so diverted the current of the river that it had undermined one of the abutments, causing it to tip and launch the bridge structure into the river. But again the town was a loser and had to rebuild the bridge and pay the costs.

It seems remarkable that permission should have been necessary for such an ordinary matter, but we find that in May, 1806, the company secured an act of the assembly allowing it to erect houses at its gates. Each house was allowed a lot of land not to exceed five acres, but the total cost of house and land was not to be more than seven hundred dollars in each case.

The Straits Turnpike was operated in its entirety until May, 1821, when all that portion between Westville and New Haven was made free. How long the balance remained a toll road we have not ascertained.

9. The New Milford and Litchfield Turnpike

The charter granted to the New Milford and Litchfield Turnpike Company in October, 1797, allowed it to open its road from the Friends' meeting-house in New Milford to some forgotten point in Litchfield, and to erect two gates for its collections. Construction was not rapid, as we find an act passed in 1798, allowing collections to begin at one gate when the road was completed in Litchfield, but by the end of 1800 the entire road was in service. The allowed tolls were found at that date to be insufficient, so an act was secured by which they were doubled.

The original turnpike was built over Mount Tom in Litchfield, and we can imagine that the resulting grade was a trial for all concerned, but it was endured for nearly half a century. Then, about 1841, the towns of Litchfield and Washington laid out a section of road passing east and southeast of Mount Tom and having the turnpike on each end. This they asked the corporation to construct, take over as a part of its road, and discontinue the old section over the mountain. An accommodating assembly gave its sanction, but the corporation was slow to act, legislative proceedings being observed in 1843 and 1844, extending the time within which the relocation should be made.

10. The Boston Turnpike

The middle route from New York to Boston, over which President Washington traveled on his trip in 1789, ran from Hartford to the northeasterly corner of Connecticut, where it entered the neighboring Commonwealth of Massachusetts. Travelers over this route were obliged to cross the Connecticut River between Hartford and East Hartford by means of an old established ferry.

Goodwin's *East Hartford History and Traditions* gives a complete story of this ferry, and from it we learn that it was first authorized by a lease given by the town of Hartford, in 1681, to Thomas Cadwell, who operated it, collecting tolls fixed by the town for seven years, after which his widow continued the business for an equal length of time. In 1728, apparently to make the operation more legal, Hartford secured from the assembly a charter under which to continue the ferry. In 1737 the charter was renewed, this time with the provision that the assembly was to fix the rates of toll. That the business was good is seen from the fact that the proceeds of the collections were sufficient in 1748 to provide firewood for the town schools.

East Hartford was established as a separate town in 1783 and one half of the rights in the ferry was granted to it. The ferry continued to be controlled by the two towns until the opening of the Boston Turnpike, and for eleven years after provided the only means of crossing the broad river at that point.

The Boston Turnpike Company was formed by an act of the October session of 1797. It was granted a franchise over the roads "from Hartford, through East Hartford, Bolton, Coventry, Mansfield, Ashford, Pomfret, and Thompson, to Massachusetts line." Four gates were to be allowed—one within two miles of the state boundary; one within one mile of Mashamaquet Brook in Pomfret; one within one mile of the line between the towns of Mansfield and Willington; and one at the notch of the mountain in Bolton. The capital stock of the corporation was fixed within the elastic limit of four thousand eight hundred pounds and more.

The project was bitterly opposed, especially in East Hartford and Pomfret. The former town succeeded at first in keeping the turnpike out, as an act of May, 1798, deprived the company of the right to build its road west of "White's Monument" in Bolton, but that advantage was reversed in 1812 and the toll road entered the town. But Goodwin says that the people

Boston Turnpike: Britt Tavern, Willington, Conn.

succeeded in keeping the tollgates out of the town at all times. Pomfret folks fought the enterprise at all points and when beaten sought to have changes made in the route, but they had to submit and were forced to levy a heavy tax to pay for the land.

The Boston Turnpike, as finally constructed, commenced at the corner of Burnside Avenue and Tolland Street in East Hartford Village, where it formed a junction with the Hartford and Tolland Turnpike which was built in 1802 and over which the Boston travelers continued their journey to the ferry. Thence it ran easterly through Burnside and past the old powder mills to Manchester Green, from which place it continued directly to the pass

Boston Turnpike: Fenton River Bridge

through the mountain range at Bolton Notch, where the present-day trains between Willimantic and Hartford wind their way around a sharp curve, cut through the solid rock, with perpendicular walls seventy feet in height. Continuing its easterly course the turnpike passed across the foot of what has since become the Willimantic Reservoir, and into Quarryville, which long had an established reputation for its production of smooth thin layers of beautiful slate which served for flagging in many of our towns and cities.

After leaving North Coventry the old road proceeded directly to its crossing of the Willimantic River where now the Central Vermont Railway trains stop at Mansfield Depot. A change in the course occurred here and the road went northeasterly across the towns of Mansfield and Ashford, passing the villages of West Ashford and Ashford before reaching the point where the Connecticut and Rhode Island Turnpike, to Providence, later joined it. From that point it went easterly again through the towns of Eastford and Pomfret and northerly and northeasterly across the town of Thompson to the northeast corner of the state where it joined the road of the Ninth Massachusetts Turnpike Corporation in the town of Douglas.

The journey to Boston was continued over the roads of the Ninth Massachusetts, the Hartford and Dedham, and the Norfolk and Bristol, after which the traveler pursued his way toll-free over Boston Neck and into the town of Boston.

The *Old Farmer's Almanac*, in 1802, gave the distance from Boston to Hartford as one hundred and six miles, with taverns from one to seven miles apart. Those on the Boston Turnpike were Jacobs' Tavern in Thompson, seven miles from the last tavern in Douglas, and Nichols' in Thompson two miles from Jacobs'. Another seven miles brought the traveler to Grosvenor's

Boston Turnpike:Easterly in the Valley of the Fenton

Boston Turnpike: Fuller Tavern, Mansfield Four Corners, Conn.

in Pomfret, and seven miles farther to Spring's in Ashford, which town maintained two other hostelries, Perkins' and Clark's, three and five miles respectively beyond Spring's. Covering four miles from Clark's, Utley's in Willington came into view, and another four miles revealed the sign displayed by Dunham in Mansfield. The only chance to obtain accommodations between Mansfield and East Hartford was at Kimball's Tavern in Coventry, six miles from Dunham's, and it was six miles thence to Woodbridge's in East Hartford. Woodbridge must have kept his house well in the eastern part of the town, for another tavern is noted in East Hartford, nine miles farther west, kept by Little. One mile farther, over the ferry, the pilgrim could rest his weary bones in the bed provided by Bull of Hartford. As the distance from the center of Hartford to the eastern line of Manchester along the old turnpike is but little over eleven miles, it is evident that one looking for the site of Woodbridge's Tavern should wend his way to Manchester Green. To the antiquary such a pilgrimage would be well worth taking, for see what Goodwin has to say on the subject.

One of the older public hostelries was that kept by the Wells family. This tavern [noted as still standing] was in its day one of the most resorted to in town. It was kept in 1811 by the Woodbridge family and in 1817, by a Mr. Buckler. It has a low spacious bar room with a slat enclosed bar, until recently intact, with a large fireplace on one side. The "best chamber" was until lately complete in its ancient furnishings; with flowery blue wall-paper, and two high post bedsteads canopied with large figured blue curtains. It had curtain rests like rosettes of brass, and brass andirons in its fireplace, over which hung old-time prints of historic scenes, cheaply colored and nearly a hundred years

Boston Turnpike: Along the Willimantic River

old. The other chambers were as bare as barracks. A low ceiled hall with two corner fireplaces and a bench around the wall was kept for dancing parties which used especially to resort here in sleighing time, having gay times and racing their horses, with tremendous jangling of bells up and down the street. Their sleighs were large high-backed green and yellow affairs with yellow or red linings.

The barns and sheds that stood north of this tavern, close to the road, were burned down a number of years ago.

It is further recorded that Woodbridge's was one of the stopping places of President Monroe on his eastern tour in 1817.

Boston Turnpike: Willimantic River Bridge

Boston Turnpike: North Coventry, Conn.

After ten years of turnpike operation the tolls were found insufficient and an act was secured in October, 1807, by which they were increased by about one third. In 1812, as already mentioned, authority was obtained for the extension of the road westerly from White's Monument in Bolton to a junction with the Hartford and Tolland Turnpike, and another whole or two half gates were allowed.

Four years previous to this, however, the ferry had become subject to the competition of a toll bridge which was allowed by a charter granted in 1808, and which no doubt greatly increased the popularity of the Middle Route.

On account of its position the Boston Turnpike was often locally called the "Middle Turnpike" and as such it is marked on one of the maps published

Boston Turnpike: Burnside Avenue, East Hartford, Conn.

to-day. It continued subject to toll along its whole length until 1845 when all that part in Pomfret was made free. Similar action was had in reference to Eastford in 1850, and by 1879 all rights to collect toll had ceased.

Just west of Mansfield Four Corners a road branched off to Springfield over which the stages from that city to Norwich used to come, continuing their journey southward over the Windham and Mansfield Turnpike, whose intersection with the Boston formed the Four Corners. Fuller's Tavern is still standing in the northwesterly of the four corners, and the ell of the house opposite is the old tollhouse, which formerly stood about halfway to the Springfield road on foundation stones which are still to be seen. At the summit of the next hill easterly may be seen one of the old milestones telling off twenty-three miles from Hartford courthouse.

Farther east, where the turnpike crosses the Fenton River, is the old Mason mill where an old-time cart is yet occasionally turned out. The old "up-and-down" saw is still in use, a relic of the days ere circular saws were known.

11. The Talcott Mountain Turnpike

This road extended from the west line of Hartford through Farmington and Simsbury to New Hartford and was opened by the Talcott Mountain Turnpike Company under authority of a charter granted in May, 1798. Apparently an expert bookkeeper was not employed in the early days for the assembly of 1799 deemed it necessary to appoint a committee to "liquidate the accounts" of the company, determine the amount of stock, audit the accounts, and thereafter report yearly to the assembly.

A change of location was made in the year 1807 across the town of Farmington, and the responsibility for a bridge over the Farmington River was imposed upon the company. Further alterations in the route were made in 1816.

The Talcott Mountain Turnpike connected in New Hartford with the Greenwoods Turnpike, which continued the journey to the Massachusetts line in Sheffield, where it joined the road of the Twelfth Massachusetts Turnpike Corporation. These three turnpikes, with their extension in New York, formed the great highway between Hartford and Albany and a heavy traffic passed over them for over half a century. Apparently the system was much more extended than we have outlined for Dr. Timothy Dwight, in his travels, mentioned a continuous turnpike to Wattles' Ferry on the Susquehanna River, and he amusingly calls it a "branch of the Greenwoods."

The Greenwoods Turnpike was made free in 1872 and as this one was so closely linked with it, but nearer the developed parts of the state, it is probable that the Talcott Mountain was given up but a few years earlier.

12. The Ousatonic Turnpike

The turnpike thus named extended from New Milford to Derby on the northeast bank of the Housatonic River, following close to the shore and winding in and out as the river changed its course. The corporation which provided this utility was formed in May, 1798, and named the Ousatonic Turnpike Company. Three gates were authorized, but even with that frequency it became necessary to secure increased rates of toll within nine years. Owing to some clerical error the franchise did not clearly specify that New Milford was to be the northerly terminus, so an amending act was passed in May, 1800, in which the corporation was plainly allowed to build to the meeting-house in New Milford.

A peculiar effect of Connecticut laws, which has been often noted, first appears in connection with this road. It seems that a turnpike corporation, although obliged to remove stones and cut trees from its route, did not have any title to the material thus partly prepared for sale. The Ousatonic Turnpike Company petitioned the assembly of 1807, asking that it might be the owner of such timber and stone, but the matter was referred to the next assembly.

In October, 1813, the portion between Southbury and New Milford, about a third of the total mileage, was discontinued as a turnpike and, in addition to the loss of that much road, the corporation was obliged to deduct from the amount of its capital stock the recorded cost of making that part of the road, which was three thousand seven hundred dollars.

The River Turnpike Company was incorporated at the May session of 1834 and given the northerly half of the Ousatonic Company's road. The division was made at Zoar Bridge in Oxford, all southerly of that point remaining the road of the Ousatonic. Whatever this deal may have been the Ousatonic seems to have kept a string on the property, for after seven years of the experiment, as the River Turnpike Company had abandoned the effort to make both ends meet, that corporation was dissolved and the road which it had tried to operate was restored to its original owner, the Ousatonic Company.

One year more saw the finish. In 1842 the road was reported as out of repair and the corporation took the poor debtor's oath. So the Ousatonic's charter was repealed and its road given to the public.

Scanning the map in 1916, the prospects for a road located along the Housatonic valley seem to have been as good as any in the state. In connection with the New Milford and Litchfield and the Derby turnpikes, this road offered an improved route all the way from Litchfield to New Haven and on the easy grades of a river location. Following down the valley it served the large territory tributary to it with its yields of produce from fertile farms.

The Housatonic Railroad Company was not incorporated until shortly after the turnpike had been abandoned, and when it built its railroad it did not follow the river along the route of the turnpike but left the valley at New Milford and bore straight for Bridgeport. That the turnpike management should have been in financial difficulties during the years which we have seen to be the most prosperous for other such enterprises, that is, the decade preceding the introduction of railroads, is hard to understand.

13. The Derby Turnpike

About 1836 the Connecticut assembly made an appropriation for the purpose of having compiled all the special and private laws which had been passed since the establishment of the Union. The learned gentleman to whom was intrusted the work contemplated acquitted himself well, arranging the laws under subject headings and not chronologically as was done in most of the other states. But he made one peculiar error in treating acts establishing turnpike companies. If the charter of a company had later been repealed, even if it was after many years during which the road had been built and operated, he omitted the act creating that company from his compilation, merely citing its heading with a note that the act had been repealed. Thus we read of the Derby Turnpike Company only that it was created in May, 1798, and that its charter was repealed in May, 1832.

But another error appears here, for the Derby Turnpike was the last in Connecticut to surrender its privileges, collecting its tolls until 1895, so the charter could not have been revoked on the date given. Even had the canceling of the franchise taken effect in 1832 the fact that the road was built and had then been in operation for over thirty years entitled the company to have its act of incorporation printed in full with the others.

The Derby Turnpike is known as such to-day, although no longer are tolls collected. It ran from the center of New Haven to Derby Landing, a distance of eight miles. It is now known, also, as West Chapel Street in New Haven and as New Haven Avenue in Derby.

Watrous in the *History of New Haven* says that although there were other roads to Derby the turnpike was the best. The capital stock for this eight-mile road was $7520. The gate stood a few miles from New Haven, just west of Maltby Lakes. The easterly end was at York Street.

The expectations which prevailed in Derby of the results which the turnpike would produce are most amusing in the light of later knowledge of the tendency of commerce. The *History of Derby* by Orcutt and Beardsley recounts that great expectations were had of the amount of New Haven trade which would come to Derby, little realizing that the larger place would inevitably draw the business from the smaller.

Previous to the opening of the Derby the Oxford Turnpike had been completed in the northerly part of Derby, passing close to the village of Chusetown, now Seymour, about four and a half miles up the Naugatuck River from the end of the Derby Turnpike. The Derby people interested themselves most strangely in having turnpike connection made between these two roads, apparently little appreciating that such an improvement would make of their town nothing more than a way station, past which the commerce of the upper valleys would flow uninterruptedly to New Haven.

At a town meeting in 1803 Derby voted "to do something" relative to a turnpike from the Oxford to Derby Landing. But the assembly could nor be convinced of the need of that particular utility and, after two years of fruitless effort to have a franchise issued, the town laid out and built the road.

New Haven, which became a city in 1774, by 1847 had laid out so many improvements near the line of the Derby Turnpike that the operation of the easterly portion became unprofitable, so in the latter year the company secured the passage of an act releasing it from responsibility for the road between York and Kensington streets in New Haven.

In 1895 the last turnpike in Connecticut passed out of existence, as the Derby was then made free. Eight thousand dollars was awarded to the corporation in compensation and the city of New Haven and the towns of Orange and Derby became the owners of the turnpike.

14. The Greenwoods Turnpike

As already mentioned in the account of the Talcott Mountain Turnpike, that road, in connection with the road of the Greenwoods Turnpike Company, formed the Connecticut portion of an important and much-traveled route from Hartford to Albany, and by New York extensions, to the Susquehanna River. The Greenwoods Company was incorporated at the October session of 1798 and allowed to build "from Eldad Shepard's in New Hartford to Sheffield line."

Crissey's *History of Norfolk* and Boyd's *Annals of Winchester* give pertinent facts about this old road, from which the following has been gathered.

Through Winchester it passed along the easterly and northerly edge of Mad River, passing through what later became the borough of Winsted. A new and more direct route was thus opened, and the travel was diverted from the old north road over Wallen's Hill and the old south road, through old Winchester, to the more favorable grades of the road along the bottom of the river valleys. The turnpike was finished in 1799 at a cost of nineteen thousand five hundred dollars, and for many years paid a good dividend and was somewhat sought as an investment. The first gate was located in West Norfolk and was a primitive swing affair. Later, when it became necessary to

Greenwoods Turnpike: Tollgate in Norfolk, Conn.

construct a second gate, the site was shifted farther cast, on which ground the third and last gate was built, which continued its collections until the road was finally dedicated to the public good.

An alteration was made in the location of the road in 1811, by which land was taken from eight owners, the total award for such damages being $48.87. Further alterations were made in 1842, when recommendations which had been made in 1830 were carried out. In 1853 a portion of the road in Norfolk was made free.

The last of the old turnpike came in 1872 when, on the first of October, the gate ceased to obstruct travelers. During the last years the collections had run between eight and twelve hundred dollars each year. The length of the turnpike was about twenty-four miles so, accepting Crissey's statement of the cost, this road was built at the rate of about eight hundred and fifteen dollars a mile, which accords with the costs of similar Massachusetts roads of that period.

15. The Hartford and New Haven Turnpike

The Connecticut Colonial Records show that in 1717 Captain John Munson had set up a wagon and was granted the exclusive privilege of being a common carrier between New Haven and Hartford for seven years. He was obligated to make the trip once a month at least except during the winter months of December, January, February, and March, starting on the first Monday of the month and making the round trip within a week. The early road passed through Wethersfield, Farmington, Middletown, and Wallingford, and does not seem to have caused complaint until 1759 when the general assembly was advised that its condition was bad. A committee reported to the 1760 session, advising certain changes which were ordered and assessed upon the towns. Such a road served until the turnpike march of progress.

The Hartford and New Haven Turnpike Company was created by another act of the October session in 1798, and seems to have been one of the first corporations to disregard the old roads and lay out a new route on turnpike fallacies—the straight line. This road went about as straight from one city to the other as it could be laid out, passing through the northerly part of New Haven over what is now Whitney Avenue, thence through the southeast part of Hampden, the westerly part of Wallingford, and the center of Meriden. Crossing the easterly part of Berlin, the southeast corner of Newington, and the northwest quarter of Wethersfield, it entered Hartford over the street now known as Maple Avenue.

Watrous has recorded that the first meeting of the corporation was held in November, 1798, at which time the stock was offered for subscription. The outlook must have seemed promising, for by December 6 it was announced that all shares had been taken with an overflow list of those anxious to buy. The southerly termination in New Haven was at Grove Street, at which street a branch later authorized also ended.

Blake, in the *History of Hampden,* says that the original road crossed Mill River just above where the dam now impounds the waters of Whitney Lake. When in 1861 the level of the lake was raised, it became necessary to move the turnpike, and the bridge which had carried the stages over Mill River was moved about a quarter of a mile up the lake where it was again put in service on another road which crossed a narrow part of the lake. This bridge was one of those ever interesting old structures—a covered timber-latticed truss, such as are so familiar even yet in northern New England. The one on the turnpike was built in 1823 by Ithiel Town, the originator of such bridges, and was composed of oak planks three inches thick and eight and a half to nine inches wide. These, arranged in a lattice form, were fastened at their intersections with wooden treenails. . . . The expense of moving the bridge on Whitney Lake was two hundred and fifty dollars, and it remained in its new location at least as late as 1886, and doubtless much longer. For a quarter of a century after the changes in the old road the early roadbed could plainly be seen along the north shore at the lower end of Whitney Lake.

A Century of Meriden by Curtis states that "as much joy and excitement" attended the opening of the turnpike in 1799 as greeted the railroad thirty-eight years later. The record of damages paid by the corporation enabled that historian to draw a most interesting description of Meriden at the beginning of the nineteenth century, which, however, is not of general interest. One item, however, is interesting. Samuel Yale occupied a house in the center of the town facing on what had previously been the main street. The turnpike,

Hartford and New Haven Turnpike: View of Maple Avenue, Hartford

reverencing nothing which stood in its direct path, cut its way so close to the rear of Mr. Yale's dwelling that the house stood like a precipice above the roadway and soon became an eyesore and a source of so much mortification to the town that the citizens bought the house and moved it away. It is hoped that his neighbors were generous and gave Mr. Yale a good price, for he only received fifty-seven dollars for damages from the corporation.

The turnpike is now Meriden's Broad Street, and at the corner of East Main Street a tavern built by Dr. Insign Hough in 1792 long served the travelers as a halfway stop for dinner. The *Old Farmer's Almanac* tells us that this tavern was kept by one Robinson in 1802. Other bonifaces along the Hartford and New Haven Turnpike in that year were Wright of Wethersfield, Riley of Worthington, Carrington of Wallingford, and Ives of North Haven, while Nichols and Butler provided the comforts demanded by the traveler who had completed the long trip to New Haven.

Hartford and New Haven Turnpike: View of Maple Avenue, Hartford

This was the turnpike of which Secretary Gallatin reported that its thirty-four and three fourths miles had cost $79,261, or about $2280 a mile, and that the net income of the entire road did not exceed $3000 a year. By which we have reason to believe that the investment paid about three and eight tenths per cent previous to 1807. Captain Bailey of Connecticut, who built the first section of the First Massachusetts Turnpike from Western, now Warren, to Palmer in 1796 and 1797, found the business sufficiently good to encourage him to take the contract to build the Hartford and New Haven Turnpike. His price in Massachusetts had been three dollars a rod, so it is to be supposed that he tried to get the same figure on the later job, but the Massachusetts men thought that they had paid too much by half, so perhaps he had to shade his figure.

In 1815 a branch was authorized in New Haven by which Temple Street was extended to the northerly end of Church Street, after which two entrances into New Haven were available.

16. The Litchfield and Harwinton Turnpike

In October, 1798, the charter for this road was given to the Litchfield and Harwinton Turnpike Company. The route was described as from Litchfield courthouse to the corner of the Simsbury and Hartford roads. It is evident from the further sections of the act that the road was to pass through the town of Harwinton and into that portion of the town of Bristol which was later set off as Burlington. Just where the road ran is anybody's guess, so here is ours. Let us say that the turnpike started from Litchfield, near the courthouse, and proceeded in a semicircular course to East Litchfield, thence easterly across Harwinton and about a mile into the present town of Burlington, at which point it was later joined by the road of the Farmington and Bristol Company. It is probable that the franchise covered a greater distance and reached into the town of Farmington, as we have to go that far to find conditions which justify the description of "the corner of the Simsbury and Hartford roads," but it is clear that the road was not built east of the point named above. When the Farmington and Bristol was laid out its route was specified in precise detail and it defined the easterly end of the Litchfield and Harwinton as stated.

No mention of this road has been found in any history. In 1803 it was allowed to collect toll from passing mail carriages, and in 1820 permission was granted to move the gates. Again, in 1827, the assembly took notice of the corporate existence, confirming certain proceedings and allowing changes in the road.

Commencing in 1844 general laws successively appeared as a result of which the abandonment of a road, or the freeing of the same by a town, might be accomplished automatically and without formality. Hence the end of many Connecticut turnpikes is veiled in obscurity.

The Farmington and Bristol, which must have been an integral part of the scheme by which the Litchfield and Harwinton was of use to the community, gave up the struggle in 1819, reporting its entire investment a loss, and it seems strange that this road should have done business as much as eight years longer. It does not seem possible that it could have continued many years alone.

17. The Windham Turnpike

The first white settlers in Windham County found an old Indian trail leading from Canterbury through Plainfield to Greenwich on Narragansett Bay, and they soon developed it into a road which was then considered passable. Soon after 1699, when Major Fitch had established his home at Peagscomsuck in Canterbury, a road was cut out to that point from Windham. These, offering the best route then available by which the Windham County colonists could reach Providence, became a road of importance which was later known as the "Great Road." It seems that the act of 1712, to which reference was had in speaking of the Providence and Norwich Turnpike in Rhode Island, contemplated the improvement of a part of this road and that some work was actually done in the town of Plainfield in consequence, but generally the "Great Road" appears to have, like Topsy, "just growed."

Under date of September 28, 1795, a report was made to the assembly by a committee which had been appointed to view this road, make alterations, and advise regarding the establishment of tollgates upon it when completed. It had been found possible to improve the road by changing its layout at six places in Plainfield, seven in Canterbury, and two in Windham, each of which was described by a surveyor's record, after which the report continued:

> We would further observe that upon a view of said road we find it proceeds in a very direct course from Windham to Providence; that it is a road of great travelling but extremely rough and out of repair in many places; that it is capable of being made a pleasant road for carriages; but in some of the most parts of it the inhabitants are the thinly, settled and the least able to repair it and it is the opinion of your committee that after suitable repairs are made upon said road there ought to be a Turnpike Erected and Established on said road in the town of Canterbury . . . and that the avails thereof will probably be sufficient to support and maintain said road with a reasonable toll.

The report was accepted and the alterations declared laid out and established, and then the whole matter was laid aside until capitalists with sufficient courage should appear to undertake the work. They were slow in coming forward, but finally in May, 1799, the Windham Turnpike Company

Windham Turnpike: Canterbury Green

was incorporated for that purpose, with the additional privilege of extending the road to the Boston Turnpike in North Coventry.

Windham, being on the "Great Road," had for many years seen the tide of western emigration flowing past its doors to the new settlements in Wyoming County, New York, western Massachusetts, and southern Vermont, and consequently had been at great expense in maintaining its roads and the several bridges over the three large rivers which crossed its territory. In 1771 a destructive flood carried away nearly every bridge, in the town and the poor inhabitants rebelled, refusing to rebuild bridges for the accommodation of strangers who were merely passing that way. In this they were

Windham Turnpike: Old house and church in Windham

overruled, the assembly directing the town to rebuild the bridge over the Shetucket on the road from Windham to Hartford, called the Old Town Bridge, and one over the Willimantic, known as the Ironworks Bridge. The first bridge across the Shetucket was built in 1722 and was probably on the site of the Old Town Bridge, and the Ironworks Bridge was first erected in 1727 on the site of the present stone arch bridge in Willimantic over which the trolley cars pass as they leave for Norwich. Each of these bridges figured in the turnpike layout.

That over the Shetucket evidently did not fall within the mathematical situation required for an ideal turnpike, and the road builders refused to utilize it and called upon the town to provide another in a different location. The town being loaded with the burden of providing the bridges and land for the new road naturally wanted the turnpike to pass over such bridges as were already provided, and strenuously objected to building another bridge within a short distance of the older one which it had been forced to build. But again the town was overruled and until 1806 two bridges threw their shadows on the Shetucket. The turnpike was the original of the Plains Road from Windham to Willimantic, and the turnpike bridge was on the site of the present Bingham Bridge. The Ironworks Bridge was acceptable to the corporation and the turnpike crossed the Willimantic on that. Again, between Mansfield and Coventry, the turnpike crossed the Willimantic, but there the burden was put upon the company and the towns were free from that expense.

Besides the gate recommended by the committee in Canterbury another was allowed which was to be "somewhere between the dwellinghouse of

Windham Turnpike: East to Bridge Street, Willimantic

Windham Turnpike: Junction with the Hop River Turnpike

Stephen Turner and the iron works bridge over the Willimantic river." By the best information obtainable to-day Stephen Turner lived in what is now South Coventry Village, so the management was not very closely confined in locating its gate.

Main and Union streets, which are really one, in Willimantic were laid out in 1707 to enable the first Windham settlers at the Horseshoe to carry home the meadow hay which they cut on the banks of the Willimantic River. The turnpike entered this old road at the point where the name changes, and occupied it from there westerly.

Windham Turnpike: South Coventry, Conn.

The Windham Turnpike when finally completed commenced on the New London and Windham County Turnpike in Plainfield Center and led westerly, crossing the Quinebaug River and passing through Canterbury Center, Westminster, and Scotland to Windham Green, where the courthouse stood. Thence, as already described, through Willimantic and, along the road now followed by the South Coventry trolley cars to that village. There it provided the main street on which South Coventry later concentrated and passed to the north of Lake Wamgumbaug to a junction with the Boston Turnpike in North Coventry. A glance at the map will show that this road offered as direct a road from Providence to Hartford as could be made through the, hills of eastern Connecticut. It was an important route before the day of the turnpike, and it continued so until the railroad took the burdens from the horse.

It was several years before the entire project was completed, as is seen from an act passed in 1804, which allowed two additional gates when the road was finished.

A breaking away from the old conceptions which placed the cost of providing the land for turnpikes on the towns is seen in an act of May, 1835. The corporation had petitioned for an alteration in its road from the bridge across the Willimantic River between Mansfield and Coventry to Joseph Talcott's in Coventry and asked that the cost of the land should be imposed upon the town. The alteration was allowed but not the share of the expense. The corporation had to buy its own land, the only concession being that it might increase its capital by the amount of that cost.

The Hop River Turnpike was built about 1835 and entered the Windham at the westerly end of the present city of Willimantic opposite the poor farm.

Windham Turnpike: Skunkermaug River Bridge

Willimantic by this time was becoming a place of importance, and travelers bound there over the Hop River objected to paying another toll for passing a mile over the Windham. So an act passed in 1838 provided that such persons might pass the gate which stood on Willimantic's main street for half toll.

The Windham Turnpike passed into history in 1852 when its corporation was dissolved.

18. The Canaan and Litchfield Turnpike

This road was authorized from Litchfield courthouse to the Sheffield Massachusetts line, but it is unlikely that it was ever built over that whole distance. At Canaan Village the Greenwoods Turnpike was encountered, it having been under construction when the charter now being considered was granted, and since that road gave access to the Massachusetts line it was useless to build another over the same ground. The Canaan and Litchfield Turnpike Company was enacted into life at the May session in 1799.

The turnpike commenced in Litchfield near the courthouse, and ran directly to Goshen Center, thence it bore northwesterly, cutting off a small corner of Cornwall and passing through Cornwall Hollow into the town of Canaan. Another northwesterly bearing carried it through Huntsville and South Canaan, from which place the road headed northerly to Canaan Village, where it joined the Greenwoods Turnpike. The turnpike was the means of giving to Cornwall its first blessing of a daily mail, the post-office being established in Cornwall Hollow, we read in Gold's *History of Cornwall*.

Apparently established credits and book accounts were not recognized as legitimate in those early days, for this company had to apply to the assembly for permission "to contract for tolls by the year or less term," which was granted at the May term in 1801.

The life of this corporation must have been a quiet, uneventful one, for it lasted for many years. In connection with the Straits Turnpike it offered a long-distance route from New Haven to Albany and beyond to the valley of the Susquehanna, and it is probable that much heavy teaming passed over it for many years.

In 1853 the corporation, representing that by the opening of railroads up the Housatonic and Naugatuck valleys its business had been seriously reduced, was released from its obligations to maintain the road.

19. The Farmington River Turnpike

The opening of the nineteenth century was marked by the incorporation of three turnpike corporations, of which the Farmington River Turnpike Company was one, being created by the assembly in its May session of 1800.

The road of this company started in New Hartford at the junction of the Talcott Mountain and Greenwoods turnpikes, and followed up the east bank of the Farmington River to the Massachusetts line, where it joined the Tenth Massachusetts Turnpike, thus providing another through route from Hartford to Albany by way of Lee and Lenox. It passed through the Connecticut towns of Barkhamsted, Hartland, and Colebrook. The length was but twelve and a half miles and two gates were allowed, at one of which could be collected only half the rates allowed at the other.

About 1803 the town of Barkhamsted built a bridge across the Farmington River at Pleasant Valley, and so much of the travel over the Farmington River Turnpike was diverted to the Greenwoods by this bridge that the assembly was petitioned to allow the abandonment of all of the turnpike south of the point of diversion. Hence no road is found to-day on the east bank between Pleasant Valley and New Hartford. In consequence of the same act the corporation was allowed to improve a new road from the bridge to the Greenwoods Turnpike and include the same in its turnpike system.

An addition to the road was provided by an act of 1813, since which time no mention of this corporation has been found. Local histories are also silent.

20. The Windham and Mansfield Turnpike

The Windham and Mansfield Turnpike Company was another product of the 1800 May session and its route was defined as running from Joshua Hyde's in Franklin to the meeting-house in Stafford. The layout had been made by a committee which made its report at the same time that the act of incorporation was passed, and the description of the route teems with references to the houses of old-time residents. First it passed Joshua Hyde's house, then Samuel Hyde's Tavern and the houses of Daniel Ladd, Levi Gager, and Ephraim Browning, after which the route reached Manning's Bridge, an old-time structure which crossed the Shetucket River at the northwesterly corner of the town of Franklin. Then in Windham it passed Colonel Thomas Dyer's house and climbed Sawyer's Hill to Windham Green. Gilbert's Bridge carried the turnpike over the Natchaug River into Mansfield, in which town it passed Major Crocker's, Roswell Eaton's, and Captain Barrows' houses and Samuel Thompson's Tavern, crossing the Boston Turnpike at Bardsley's Corner. Thence it passed through the center of Willington to Stafford meeting-house.

Windham and Mansfield Turnpike: In the southern part of Franklin, Conn.

To-day the old road is still in use as the main road across the town of Franklin north and south, but the mile adjacent to the Shetucket River crossing has long been discontinued. Near where the Willimantic-Norwich trolleys cross on an overhead bridge and the highway turns sharply to the left to cross the Central Vermont Railroad at grade, an old wood road can be seen bearing straight ahead to the north. That is the old turnpike and a mile along it will bring one to the site of Manning's Bridge. The bridge disappeared many years ago, but the roads on each side leading to it can still be traced. Gilbert's Bridge, too, has long been gone, and its site is covered by the impounded waters of the Willimantic waterworks.

In May, 1806, authority was secured to extend the turnpike from Stafford Center toward the Massachusetts line. The Stafford Pool Turnpike Company,

Windham and Mansfield Turnpike: Intersection with the Boston Turnpike

Windham and Mansfield Turnpike: South of the Connecticut Agricultural College

which later changed its name to the Stafford Mineral Spring, assumed the management of a portion of this road under permission given in an act of October, 1813.

No more has been found concerning the Windham and Mansfield except that it occupied the attention of the assembly occasionally until May, 1828, when certain alterations in the road. were allowed.

21. The Cheshire Turnpike

On this road we have more definite information, for it is mentioned in Timlow's *History of Southington*, Beach's *History of Cheshire*, Blake's *History of Hampden*, and by Watrous in his New Haven contribution. The Cheshire Turnpike Company was also formed in May, 1800, its franchise reading "through Hampden near the meetinghouse as reported by the committee." The committee's report is accessible in the office of the secretary of state and shows the route beyond any question. It commenced in the center of Temple Street in New Haven and followed the Hartford and New Haven Turnpike for 178.71 chains, or to the Gun Factory Dam, and it extended northerly for a total distance of twenty-four miles, one quarter, sixty-two rods, and eleven links to the south line of Farmington. Two gates were allowed—one between New Haven and Hampden and the other between Cheshire and South- ington. A bond for fifteen thousand dollars was required to secure payment of the damages and assure the proper maintenance of the road.

The joint use with the Hartford and New Haven seems to have been a matter of controversy for several years until 1815, when it was enacted that the expenses of the Hartford and New Haven in keeping up that section since the Cheshire commenced using it should be one half repaid by the Cheshire Company, and afterwards equally divided.

It was only a few years prior to the opening of this turnpike that Eli Whitney, tiring of the vexatious lawsuits in which his invention of the cotton gin had involved him and despairing of obtaining justice, had turned his attention to the manufacture of muskets. At this time he was engaged in filling his first contract for ten thousand stand for the United States government for the purpose of which he had erected his factory at the foot of East Rock, now the village of Whitneyville. "Whitney's Gun Factory" is mentioned often in the acts concerning the two turnpikes.

In Hampden the Cheshire had the familiar trouble over a gate barring travel over an old highway. Passing Mount Carmel an old road had been appropriated which did not seem to worry anyone until the corporation erected its gate on that portion. A town meeting in August, 1803, instructed the selectmen to request the removal of the gate and, in case of refusal, to retaliate by taking away a fence belonging to the town. Request and threat alike failed to move the corporation, so in September the town voted to petition the assembly to order the gate taken off the town's old road. What the result was has not been learned, but it can be safely surmised that the corporation had its own way.

Cheshire's history contains an old map on which the turnpike is shown, so we are left in no doubt as to its location in that town. Here the turnpike project was hotly opposed, but corporate influence prevailed and certain citizens of the town had the grace, in submitting, to become stockholders. In Southington the road was cut through a ridge of ground which extended across the Common from the northeast corner to the south end.

That the road was in operation as late as 1856 is shown by an act passed in that year allowing the substitution of two half-gates for one whole one. The road became, free within the next twenty years.

When the New Haven and Northampton Railroad was laid out in 1875 the engineers made the location along the old turnpike from "The Steps" in Mount Carmel to Centerville, and proceeded with the construction. Before the rails were laid the assembly intervened and decreed that the town should buy and grade a new right of way in another place, for which the railroad company should pay thirteen thousand dollars and give up its location on the turnpike.

22. The Granby Turnpike

The Granby Turnpike Company was incorporated in October, 1800, for the purpose of opening a turnpike "from the Massachusetts line in the county of Hartford to the Talcott Mountain Turnpike near the city of Hartford."

Within these limitations the road was built from a corner with the Talcott Mountain Turnpike near the boundary line between Hartford and West

Hartford, northwesterly through Bloomfield Center, North Bloomfield, Tariffville, Granby, Pegville, and North Granby to the northwest corner of Granby town. The road was about twenty miles long and the company had the privilege of erecting two gates on it.

In May, 1821, the location of the road was confirmed by the assembly, but this must not be taken to mean that the road had only then been completed. More likely some irregularity had occurred in the original layout which had been allowed to slumber until someone, brooding over the tolls he had been obliged to pay, sought to obtain revenge by a complaint. Several such cases have been observed, in all of which the assembly disposed of the case by legalizing the corporation's position.

This turnpike was a part of a scheme for another through route from Hartford to Albany, but the Massachusetts section failed to materialize. We have already seen how the Eleventh Massachusetts Turnpike Corporation secured a franchise in 1801 and how, eight years later, the Granville Turnpike Corporation received a charter to build over identically the same route. Their plan was to connect at the state line with the Granby Turnpike and to continue the route through the Massachusetts towns of Granville and Blandford to a junction with the Hampden and Berkshire Turnpike at Blandford Center. The Hampden and Berkshire, by its connections with the Tenth Massachusetts and the Housatonic River turnpikes, led by at least two different improved routes to the Hudson River. But as we have said, the link from the Hampden and Berkshire to the Connecticut line was ever missing.

The turnpike corporations were held strictly in hand even as late as 1845, for we find an act by which the location of the Granby's gate in Bloomfield was legalized. Some detail in the formalities required in changing the location of a gate had not been observed and complaint had been made, but the assembly disposed of the matter by making the gate lawful and confirming all past doings thereat.

The Granby Turnpike continued in business until 1854 when its charter was annulled.

23. The Hartford and New London Turnpike

This road was built by the Hartford and New London Turnpike Company, which received the right to operate a turnpike from the assembly of October, 1800. As originally built the turnpike ran from East Hartford, five miles down the river along the road now followed by the South Glastonbury trolley cars, as far as Glastonbury; thence southeasterly through Marlboro Mills and Marlboro to Colchester. From there it turned more to the south and passed through Salem and Chesterfield Village, across the town of Waterford, and entered New London over what is now Broad Street. Miss Caulkins, in her

History of New London, says that the corporation improved an old highway from State to Hempstead streets and then built a new road to Colchester, passing more to the north than by the old route.

All of the road northerly of the "two mile stone" in East Hartford was made public in May, 1807, and in May, 1829, all east of Huntington Street in New London was discontinued as a turnpike and made a part of the city's streets. In 1839 the company represented to the assembly that for five miles, at the northerly end, its road was the main street of East Hartford and of Glastonbury, and that over it was hauled "large quantities of coal, wood, and other heavy articles," which wore out the road. Inasmuch as the corporation was not allowed to maintain a gate on that section and therefore collected no tolls from such traffic, its petition to be relieved of that portion of its road was granted. Authority to transfer to New London all of the road between Pound and Huntington streets was given in 1845. The balance of the turnpike was collecting tolls in 1852 and probably for many years longer.

From *Famous Old Taverns of New London* we learn that the stage for Hartford left New London on Tuesdays and Thursdays at eight in the morning in the year 1818, returning Wednesdays and Fridays. The New London terminus was at the Dutton House, a tavern so old that it had been built by John Richards, who died in 1720. H. G. Broome, a veteran stage driver, was the proprietor and rein manipulator of this line, and his business must have seemed precarious for he appears to have been easily discouraged. In the fall of 1823 a biweekly steamship line was started from New London along the Sound and up the Connecticut River to Hartford, and Broome issued an announcement under date of October 5, 1823, that he feared that the competition of this steamer, which was named *The Experiment*, would

Hartford and New London Turnpike: The Main Street of East Hartford and Glastonbury

Hartford and New London Turnpike: Glastonbury Center, Conn.

prove disastrous to his business and therefore he withdrew his stages. But Broome continued driving for many years longer on the shorter runs to Norwich, Colchester, and Lyme.

24. The Farmington and Bristol Turnpike

In the published acts of Connecticut we read only that the Farmington and Bristol Turnpike Company was incorporated in May, 1801, and that its charter was revoked in May, 1819; but the reader interested in turnpike history is entitled to know more.

This company received in its act of incorporation the right to build a road from the end of the Litchfield and Harwinton Turnpike in Bristol, now Burlington, to Thompson's Corner at the north end of the town street in Farmington and thence to Hartford. The committee appointed to make the layout of the road commenced its labors at the west door of the courthouse in Hartford and laid out the present Asylum Street, Farmington Avenue, and Main Street in Farmington. Thence it continued to the east end of the Litchfield and Harwinton Turnpike in the northwest part of Burlington, which was then a part of Bristol.

The Hartford courthouse stood on Main Street at the corner of State and nearly opposite the end of Asylum Street. The first building was erected in 1719 but the present building, which for many years served as Hartford's city hall, was built in 1796. During the life of the turnpike the old courthouse sheltered the delegates to the Hartford Convention in 1814, that famous gathering of pacifists who sought to end the War of 1812. Recently the city has erected a much more pretentious office building two blocks farther south on Main Street and has vacated the old brick house.

Construction of the turnpike was evidently slow, for the company was back in May, 1802, asking for a revision of the layout. In yielding to the direct-line obsession a saving of eight rods had been made by cutting across some valuable land, and permission was given to make a desired detour. That the road was finished in 1805 is seen from an act by which alterations were allowed in the location of certain gates which were being avoided by the familiar device of a shunpike.

In May, 1819, the company petitioned the assembly to be released from its obligations. The road had never paid and the investment of $15,232.10 was a total loss. In compliance the corporation was released from its burden of maintaining the road and its charter was *"disannulled."*

The portion between Hartford and Farmington formed a part of the so-called Hartford and Danbury Turnpike, the Middle Road Turnpike Company, incorporated in October, 1803, maintaining a road from Farmington to Danbury.

The layout committee reported the entire length of the Farmington and Bristol Turnpike as nineteen miles, fifty-six rods, and twenty-one links, which we have seen was later increased by eight rods. Thus we are enabled to compute that the road cost at the rate of $793.23 a mile.

At the time this charter was granted, Hartford was a small city mostly along the river front, but to-day Asylum Street is a crowded city thoroughfare with the up-to-date rule of one-way traffic in force. On Farmington Avenue, over a mile out, the author had difficulty in exposing for photographs on

Farmington and Bristol Turnpike: Old Hartford Courthouse, built 1796

Farmington and Bristol Turnpike: Farmington Avenue, Hartford, Conn.

account of the constant passing of automobiles, trolley cars, and other vehicles. If the old corporation could collect its tolls to-day it would be but a few days before it had recouped its $15,232.10.

25. The Danbury and Ridgefield Turnpike

This was a short road connecting the two adjoining towns named. It was built by the Danbury and Ridgefield Turnpike Company which was chartered in May, 1801. The route proposed is so indefinitely described that one cannot pick out the road followed, but apparently it was the Sugar Hollow Road of southwest Danbury. An alteration was made in 1832, and the turnpike continued to be operated until June 23, 1860, when its charter was repealed.

In 1829 another corporation, the Sugar Hollow Turnpike Company, was formed, which continued the Danbury and Ridgefield on each end. On the south it made connection with the Norwalk and Danbury and over that to the sea at Norwalk, while on the north an extension to the New York line was provided.

26. The Torrington Turnpike

The Torrington Turnpike Company, chartered in May, 1801, had a right to build from West Simsbury to Litchfield courthouse, and the road built in accordance passed through the intervening towns of Torrington, New Hartford, and Canton, crossing both the Waterbury and Farmington rivers. This was the company which found itself in ill favor with the assembly on account of an early anticipation of "excess land condemnation." The locating committee, finding that the intersection which they had made with the Talcott Mountain Turnpike was at so slight an angle as to make the land between of little value, had made a taking of the entire triangle from Samuel Humphrey, Jr., of Canton. This was subsequently represented as illegal, inasmuch as by that action a layout in excess of four rods in width had been made at that point. The assembly of 1805 was convinced of the illegality and ordered the land to be restored to the former owner.

The town of Torrington did not welcome the turnpike with cordiality according to Orcutt's history, as it was obliged to buy the necessary land and build a bridge over the Waterbury River for the use of the company. A tax of five cents per thousand dollars was voted to pay for the land in 1801 but the building of the bridge was flatly refused until twice ordered by the courts. In the end the town was more benefited by the turnpike than the stockholders.

Of the bridge over the Farmington River in Canton we hear nothing until 1857, when it met a common fate of bridges in being swept downstream. The town did not see fit to replace it but did erect another bridge about one hundred rods farther up-stream which left certain stub ends of useless turnpike. Consequently the company secured the passage of an act in 1859 by which it was allowed to build connecting sections of road, giving access to the new bridge, and abandon the parts of no further use to it.

In 1838 all of the turnpike east of Luther Higley's in Canton was given over to the public, and in 1861, Orcutt says, the company surrendered its charter.

27. The Norwich and Woodstock Turnpike

The story of this road is all in legislative acts. The act of incorporation was passed in May, 1801, forming the Norwich and Woodstock Turnpike Company for the purpose of building from Norwich Landing through Lisbon, Canterbury, Brooklyn, Pomfret, Woodstock, and Thompson. The route was described and the layout declared a public highway and immediately given to the newly formed corporation on its agreement to make and maintain the same. Three gates were to be allowed—one near the Norwich-Lisbon line, one in the south part of Brooklyn, and one in Woodstock.

By the inclusion of Thompson among the towns to be crossed, it seems that the intention was to make a connection with the Ninth Massachusetts Turnpike and to open a route from Norwich to Boston, but, if so, that idea did not hold long, for an amendment was enacted in 1803 by which the road could be built from Woodstock to the Massachusetts line in the direction of Sturbridge. By building on this line no connection was made at the state line with any Massachusetts turnpike but the journey to Sturbridge was continued over public highways. The decision to bear northwesterly instead of heading for a direct connection with the Ninth Massachusetts was a wise one and avoided an error too often made by early turnpike promoters, who were far too apt to duplicate facilities. We have seen in Rhode Island how certain parties sought to build a road between two turnpikes already in operation and but a few miles apart, and in Massachusetts the multiplicity of propositions for reaching Boston from southern New Hampshire. In this case the Norwich traveler wishing to reach Boston was fully as well served by going on to the Boston Turnpike at Pomfret Center as if the road had gone directly to the northeast corner of the state, while the great tendency of travel, which then existed in a northwesterly direction, was also accommodated.

An additional gate was allowed in 1827 which calls for comment, on account of so many years elapsing before this sign of distress appeared. Generally the extra gate was found necessary within a very short time. In 1829 it was provided that no carriage should be entitled to reductions in toll because it carried the mail. The question of exemption for mail carriers was one which cropped out frequently and in many places, being finally settled, as we have seen, in connection with the Maysville Turnpike in Kentucky.

The Woodstock portion of the road was made free in 1836, but the rest of the turnpike continued as such for another ten years.

In 1846 the corporation represented to the assembly that the cost of the road had been over fourteen thousand dollars and that no "considerable profit" had ever been realized; that since the operation of the Norwich and Worcester Railroad the income had not been sufficient to provide for the necessary repairs and that no dividends had been paid for six years. Consequently the corporation was relieved of the balance of its road which thereafter was free.

Norwich and Woodstock Turnpike: Burdick Tavern, Brooklyn, Conn.

Norwich and Woodstock Turnpike: General Putnam Inn, Brooklyn, 1767

The Norwich and Worcester Railroad was authorized by legislative acts in Massachusetts in April, and in Connecticut in May, 1836, although earlier charters had been granted in 1832 and 1833. It is to be noted in connection with the northerly and southerly trend of commerce at that time, that this railroad was projected while the first railroads in New England were yet under construction.

From the above figures we see that the turnpike, being about thirty-eight miles in length, cost at the rate of about three hundred and seventy dollars per mile, the lowest figure we have yet noted. Connecticut roads naturally

Norwich and Woodstock Turnpike: Old farm in Canterbury, Conn.

Norwich and Woodstock Turnpike: Canterbury Green

cost much less than those in other states, where a more equitable method of providing for land and bridges prevailed, but even allowing for that the cost is very low.

28. The Salisbury and Canaan Turnpike

This was a turnpike away up in the northwest corner of the state and apparently it did quite an amount of business during its twenty-eight years of existence. The published acts deal more harshly with this road than with the others, for, besides merely noting its discontinuance, they give its name wrongly. In them you will find a reference to the Salisbury Turnpike Company but only the date of the revoking of the charter.

The Salisbury and Canaan Turnpike Company was created by act of the October session of 1801, when it was authorized to open a road from the Canaan and Litchfield Turnpike near Simeon Higley's dwelling-house, by way of Burrall's Bridge and the furnace in Salisbury, to the New York line.

Burrall's Bridge was the first bridge built over the Housatonic River and was erected about the year 1744. It was later called the Falls Bridge and occupied the site of the present bridge at Falls Village. Although later there were several furnaces in Salisbury, at the date of this charter there was but one and it stood in what is now the village of Lakeville. A grade of ore somewhat better than the average found in New England gave encouragement for the establishment of an iron industry, and a forge was built there about 1748. This was supplanted in 1762 by a blast furnace, said to have been the first in Connecticut, which was sold in 1768 to Richard Smith of Boston. On account of his loyalty to his sovereign in England Smith found it advisable to leave the country with the British troops when Boston was evacuated, and his ironworks were confiscated by the state. With the royalist's plant many cannon were cast for the Continental army, and it is said that the guns which belched defeat for the opponents of the *Constellation* and the *Constitution* were also products of this same Furnace Village.

The road was completed promptly, for in one year from the date of incorporation, trouble had been found on account of an omission in the rates of toll. Sleds and single horse carts had not been considered, and an act passed in October, 1802, provided what tolls such should pay.

An instance of the ample protection given to the public interests is found in the proceedings for the changing of the position of a tollgate. In May, 1806, upon petition of the company, a committee was appointed to consider a change and report to the next session. In October the committee asked for more time and was continued, and in May, 1807, one year from the first action, the western gate was allowed to be moved.

In May, 1829, the assembly accepted the surrender of the charter, dissolved the corporation, and imposed the maintenance of the turnpike upon the towns of Salisbury and Canaan.

29. The Bridgeport and Newtown Turnpike

The Bridgeport and Newtown Turnpike Company was incorporated in October, 1801. Its franchise read from the north line of Bridgeport to the south line of New Milford, but the road was built and operated farther south and within the town of Bridgeport without any other authority as far as we have learned.

The turnpike extended from Bridgeport northerly, practically along the route later occupied by the Housatonic Railroad, and passed through the towns of Trumbull, Monroe, Newtown, and Brookfield to the line of New Milford.

An interesting feature connected with land ownership where the towns had paid for the same is to be noted here, as in the twenties the corporation was allowed to sell what land it wished as long as the width of the road was not reduced below three rods.

In May, 1835, alterations were permitted by which the road could be located so as to "avoid two considerable hills," one of which was known as "Pine Swamp Hill."

In 1848 all of the road in Bridgeport and all north of the crossing of the Housatonic Railroad, including about two miles in Newtown and all in Brookfield, was declared free, the corporation being directed to pay Brookfield two hundred and fifty dollars, to compensate that town for the burden imposed upon it. A toll house and gate with a quarter of an acre of land were situated upon the Newtown portion thus discontinued and this the corporation was allowed to sell for its own benefit.

March 24, 1886, marks the end of the Bridgeport and Newtown Turnpike, as on that day the assembly made provision for the discontinuance of the balance of the road.

30. The Waterbury River Turnpike

This road was, originally projected "from Woodbridge through Plymouth . . ." to the Massachusetts line and was so specified in the charter, which also designated the crossing of the Waterbury River as in Plymouth, but in May, 1802, alterations in the route were allowed which placed the turnpike in a far different and more logical place.

The Waterbury River Turnpike Company was chartered in October, 1801, and built its road from a point near Naugatuck Center up the east bank of the Naugatuck River through Waterbury and Thomaston as far as Thomaston Center, where it crossed the Naugatuck and continued up the west bank through Litchfield to Torrington. Thence it bore northerly across Torrington and Winchester to Colebrook Center, from which place it ran northwesterly to the Massachusetts line at the corner of Colebrook and Norfolk, where it joined the road of the Fifteenth Massachusetts Turnpike Corporation and opened another route to Albany. Orcutt's *History of Wolcott* speaks of a turnpike project to connect Torrington with New Haven, which was much favored by the town but did not succeed. Probably that refers to the Waterbury River proposition which was diverted from Wolcott to the more favorable location in the valley of the Naugatuck.

Anderson tells, in the *History of Waterbury*, that the turnpike was built through the cemetery above Salem (Naugatuck) Bridge and that graves were ruthlessly opened and the bones scattered about. Tradition has it that all of the stock at one time was owned by Victory Tomlinson, a man so rich that he could be careless in his dress. Seated one day by the side of his turnpike he was arrested for vagrancy and haled before a justice who acquitted him upon his plea that he was occupying his own land.

Boyd's *Annals of Winchester* describes this turnpike and says that it was given up in 1850. That is true regarding most of the road, but about eight miles in Naugatuck and Waterbury remained subject to toll collections until July, 1862, when, upon representations that even that small section was out of repair and unsafe, the assembly repealed the charter of the corporation.

An ancient highway between Plymouth and the Naugatuck Bridge was deprived of its public character and given to the corporation, and of it Bronson has this to say in his *History of Waterbury*:

The present turnpike from Plymouth to Salem [Naugatuck] bridge, there to unite with the Straits turnpike connecting New Haven with Litchfield by Watertown, was finished in 1702. It was an open highway and a great undertaking.

31. The Hartford and Tolland Turnpike

From the courthouse in Tolland to the state house in Hartford seemed sufficiently promising for a turnpike to justify the incorporation of the Hartford and Tolland Turnpike Company in October, 1801. At that time the only means of crossing the Connecticut River at Hartford was the ferry of which we have already read. So at that ferry the turnpike was made to terminate. Goodwin, in *East Hartford History and Traditions*, wrote that the turnpike followed the "road coming from the ferry landing to Bigelow Hall Building and thence over Main Street to Burnside Avenue," whence it ran straight to Bucklands Corner. In the eastern part of East Hartford it followed the old road called "the road east near Gilman's Brook," which was laid out in 1734.

On account of an error in the original survey a corrected description by metes and bounds was confirmed by an act of May, 1804, and further acts authorizing the moving of gates are found in 1836 and 1852.

For the first seven years of turnpike operation its travelers were wafted across the Connecticut River by the ferry until, in 1808, the Hartford Bridge Company was incorporated for the purpose of providing a toll bridge a short distance above the ferry.

The first bridge built by this company was a low uncovered structure which, while it lasted, was obliged to compete with the ferry for the scanty pickings offered by travelers. But the bridge was soon washed away, and to encourage its rebuilding the assembly suppressed the ferry on condition that

Hartford and Tolland Turnpike: Governor Street, East Hartford, the old road to the

Hartford and Tolland Turnpike: Burnside Avenue, East Hartford

the bridge should be replaced by a more substantial construction. The subsequent bridge or bridges continued to serve the public on consideration of tolls until 1879, when it was thrown open to the public.

East Hartford persistently appealed to the assembly for the restoration of the ferry until 1836, when success met its efforts, but the privilege was finally taken away, never to be restored, in 1841.

A monumental masonry structure now occupies the site of the old toll bridge.

Hartford and Tolland Turnpike: Tolland Street, East Hartford

The Hartford and Tolland Turnpike became later, when the Stafford Pool Turnpike and the Worcester and Stafford Turnpike were opened, a part of a through route to Boston by way of Worcester, and the indications are that a heavy travel passed over the road for many years.

The old road to the ferry is now known as Governor Street, but the portion south of the bridge has disappeared from the sight of man. The traffic requirements of late years demanded the construction of the present straight boulevard from the bridge to Church Corner, and Governor Street ends at the intersection. The site of the eastern ferry landing is now occupied by the shipyard of the Hartford and New York Transportation Company.

Turning sharply to the left where the Bigelow Hall Building now stands the turnpike followed the lines of Main Street to Burnside Avenue, over which it continued to the present corner with Tolland Street. Over Tolland Street it went and crossed the northerly part of Manchester, through Vernon Center, to Tolland courthouse.

32. The Pomfret and Killingly Turnpike

In Larned's history we read that the citizens of Killingly gave much consideration in the early years of the century to the matter of transportation, finally deciding, in 1801, to support a turnpike proposition to connect the Norwich Turnpike in Pomfret with the Glocester Turnpike in Rhode Island. It seems that such a vote must have been secured by some old-time parliamentary trick, for the town was in no position to aid in construction and later showed a decided disinclination to do so.

The Pomfret and Killingly Turnpike Company was created in May, 1802, but, since the charter was revoked in 1819, the compiler of the special laws gave no details of the act of incorporation and access must be had to the spacious vault in the basement of the Hartford capitol, where the manuscript records of the assembly are kept. There we find the route described—from the Boston Turnpike in Pomfret through Killingly eastward to the Glocester Turnpike at the Rhode Island line. Eight and one quarter miles was the length and, following the precedent set in the formation of many Rhode Island companies, the corporation was allowed to hold land not in excess of thirty acres. The petitioners had estimated that their road would cost at the rate of five hundred dollars a mile, but their ultimate opinions are not available.

Miss Larned says that the road was completed in 1803 and that it passed over Killingly Hill by the meeting-house. Killingly, exhausted by previous heavy expenses, refused to build any part of the new bridge demanded by the corporation until cited to court for its neglect. Then the town grudgingly gave in and appointed a committee which performed the work in the same grudging spirit, doing the construction so poorly that the structure was soon washed away. Then Killingly had to do it over again. A bridge over the Quinebaug in Pomfret was built at divided cost by the corporation and town after a controversy.

In 1809 the Glocester Turnpike Company of Rhode Island joined with various Connecticut citizens in protesting the location of a gate on the Pomfret and Killingly, which had been erected within one hundred and sixty rods of the Rhode Island line and in such a place that it intercepted such travelers as journeyed easterly over an old road which entered the turnpike forty rods west of the offending gate. Thus, it is seen, the Pomfret and Killingly was collecting full tolls from people who were using its road for a distance of only two hundred rods. The protest being laid before the assembly resulted in the appointment of a committee charged to change the gate to another location.

The road was abandoned by its proprietors about 1817, and the bridge in Killingly was taken down. In May, 1819, the charter was revoked.

33. The Hebron and Middle Haddam Turnpike

The Hebron and Middle Haddam Turnpike Company was chartered in May, 1802, and built its road from the meeting-house in Hebron through Hebron, Colchester, and Chatham to Middle Haddam Landing on the Connecticut River. A portion of this old road appears on the road maps to-day with the label of "Turnpike" against it, but very little has been found regarding the operations of the company.

Much trouble seems to have been met in collecting tolls, for the moving of a gate was allowed in 1830, 1844, and 1846. From this we see that the turnpike enjoyed a life of at least forty-four years.

34. The Middlesex Turnpike

The Middlesex Turnpike Company, which was incorporated in May, 1802, built a road from the sixth milestone from Hartford, at Goff's Brook, in the town of Wethersfield, to the stage road in Saybrook, passing through Middletown and over Walkley Hill in Haddam. The corporation was required to file a bond for thirty thousand dollars, guaranteeing to complete its road before the first of November, 1804.

In May, 1804, the company was allowed to make an alteration in its layout, taking for that purpose a section of old public highway. Following the custom the assembly proceeded to take from this piece of road its public dedication, which it did by resolving that it *"be and the same hereby is not a highway."*

The ride along this turnpike must have been one of the most inspiring in Connecticut, for it followed closely along the bank of the Connecticut River from a point six miles below Hartford, nearly to the mouth. Until 1871, when the Connecticut Valley Railroad's first trains disturbed the valley, the traveler was free to contemplate Nature's undisturbed beauty, and it must have been with a jar that he was brought back to earth by the demand for toll.

The turnpike did not give up business with the advent of the railroad but struggled along for several years, although doubtless under discouraging conditions. When its Saybrook tollhouse was burned in April, 1874, circumstances did not warrant its being rebuilt. Tolls were finally discontinued on the whole road on March 29, 1876.

For sixteen years the Saybrook gate was tended by Robert Rankin and later by Henry Safferry. Tolls collected after nine at night were allowed to the gatherer for his own, a clever device of the company to prevent the tollman from going to sleep and making it an object for the public to postpone its traveling until after his bedtime.

35. The New Preston Turnpike

This road was built to accommodate the emigrant travel which was then beginning to "the western settlements," and connected the New Milford and Litchfield Turnpike with the New York boundary on the way to Fishkill and Poughkeepsie. The New Preston Turnpike Company was chartered in May, 1802, and evidently built its road soon after.

Leaving the New Milford and Litchfield at the village of New Preston the new turnpike ran westerly into and about halfway across the town of New Milford, thence northerly into the town of Kent, and then westerly again through the village of South Kent to the Housatonic River at Bulls Bridge in the southwest corner of Kent. Thence a short run brought it to the New York line.

The turnpike enjoyed nearly a half-century of existence, the charter being repealed in 1851. For over a year previously the corporation had neglected and refused to repair its road and had taken down its gate. The necessary repairs had therefore been made by the towns traversed, and their reasonable request to own the road which they had to maintain was granted.

36. The New Haven and Milford Turnpike

Another product of the May session in 1802 was the New Haven and Milford Turnpike Company, which was allowed to build a road from the courthouse in New Haven to the meeting-house in Milford. By its charter the company might take the old road or make such alterations as would meet the approval of the county court. The road as it stretches from one city to the other to-day shows plainly that the corporation availed itself fully of the privilege of making changes in the crooked sections. Lambert's *History of the Colony of New Haven* testifies to that, for it records that the town of Milford clashed with the new enterprise and sought to make it keep in the bounds of the old road, objecting to the company's "running the turnpike-road through peoples' land."

August 26, 1802, the New Haven county court approved the location desired by the corporation, each variation from the old road being described by metes and bounds, and referred to various trees and houses designated by their occupants' names. For good measure the court allowed a few more than were asked, and appointed a committee to make the formal layout and appraise the damages.

In October, 1804, the assembly designated the portion of the turnpike which was to be in New Haven as being the old road from West River Bridge to the southerly end of Church Street where the market then stood. This had previously been thrashed out in the county court and a decision rendered there to the same effect.

A friendly arrangement between New Haven and the turnpike was made in 1836 by which the turnpike west of the hospital was exchanged for a city street on the east side of that institution.

About a quarter of a mile near the hospital was given up in 1847, as the city improvements were advancing so fast as to require refinements not in a turnpike corporation's line of business.

The "Milford Pike" is easily detected by the tourist to-day, as it forms a most direct route between its original terminal cities and, moreover, is locally known by that name.

37. The Rimmon Falls Turnpike

With the opening of the Oxford, Straits, and Derby turnpikes intercourse between New Haven and the country northwest of it would seem to have been amply provided with facilities. But the route over the Oxford and the Straits was roundabout and repugnant to turnpike conceptions, while there was quite a space of undeveloped country to be passed over between the Oxford and the Derby. Efforts by certain Derby citizens to bridge the latter difficulty, by forming a turnpike company to build across the intervening space, were defeated by some of their neighbors, who insisted that any company should pay for its own land and bridges. Hence a deadlock ensued.

The Rimmon Falls Turnpike Company, chartered in May, 1802, was first projected in 1798, apparently, to connect with the Derby at Derby Landing, but after years of strife finally located its road straight across country from Chusetown, now Seymour, to New Haven, leaving Derby off on one side.

In Sharpe's *History of Seymour* we read that the limits of the road were Thompson's Bridge in New Haven and the Falls Bridge in Chusetown. Pearl and Main streets in Chusetown were straightened in turnpike development so as to lead straight to the bridge. A large cut on Hill Street below Washington Avenue was taken out by diverting a near-by brook and sluicing the gravel into the river.

The Falls Bridge was found to be insufficient for the increased travel which would follow the turnpike, so it was rebuilt by the turnpike corporation. Although a short section of public road was between the corner of the Oxford Turnpike, where it turned away from Little River to go to Pines Bridge, and the Falls Bridge, the proprietors of the Oxford seem to have realized the value of a connection with the new Rimmon Falls road enough to cause them to share in the expense of rebuilding the Falls Bridge.

The Rimmon Falls Turnpike, as finally located, went directly southwest from Chusetown across the town of Woodbridge to Westville, then called Hotchkisstown, where it entered the Straits Turnpike over which its travelers continued to New Haven.

The last reference to this road which has been found is an act passed in 1838 by which the management was allowed to move a gate.

38. The Goshen and Sharon Turnpike

This road was built by the Goshen and Sharon Turnpike Company under authority of a franchise granted them in May, 1803, to build from Goshen meeting-house, through Sharon, to "York State line." Although the charter plainly specifies Goshen meeting-house as the easterly limit there seems little doubt but what the road was actually built and maintained as a turnpike farther east to Torrington, where it united with the Waterbury River Turnpike. Orcutt speaks of it in his *History of Torrington*, saying that it was "made mostly" in 1805 and that the town, seeing no other way, voted at once that it would build and maintain four bridges if the corporation would release it from further bridge obligation.

Gold's *History of Cornwall* has permanently recorded the location of the road in that town. It says that it crossed the river at West Cornwall, led through Cornwall Center, and with true spirit of liberty, "climbed Bunker Hill." One tollgate was at the bridge in West Cornwall and another stood near Tyler Pond in Goshen.

In May, 1825, the portion from the foot of Riley Hill in Sharon to the New York line was made free, and the same procedure was had upon all west of Pine Swamp Road in Sharon, while whatever was left in that town followed suit in 1846. Ten years later the charter was repealed and the entire Goshen and Sharon Turnpike passed into history.

39. The Stafford Mineral Spring Turnpike

The Stafford Pool Turnpike was chartered in October, 1803, to build from Tolland courthouse to the Massachusetts line through Stafford, passing by the mineral spring in that town. In 1814 its name was changed to Stafford Mineral Spring Turnpike.

By the construction which this corporation carried out, with that later done in Massachusetts by the Worcester and Stafford Turnpike Corporation, a through route from Worcester to Hartford was opened, using the already built Hartford and Tolland Turnpike for the westerly section. Reference to the map will show at once the idea back of these combined roads. The "northern route" from Boston to New York passed through Worcester, Springfield, and Hartford, and by the cutting of a route through Stafford the distance was much reduced, for almost a direct line from Worcester to Hartford was thus developed, although leaving away off on one side the growing town of Springfield. That long-extended through-routes traversing unproductive districts were not remunerative was well demonstrated by the experience of these roads which "gave up the ghost" at the time when other turnpikes were at the height of their prosperity. The Massachusetts road ceased its efforts in 1835 and the Stafford Mineral Spring Turnpike was abandoned about that time by its owners.

In 1839, upon information that the corporation had abandoned its road through Tolland, Ellington, and Stafford as far as the Massachusetts line, and that the corporate organization itself had not been kept up, the assembly annulled the charter and the road became a public charge. Part of it was not even of local use, for in 1853 that between a new highway and Number Nine Schoolhouse was discontinued as a highway.

40. The Washington Turnpike

This ran from the

centre of Woodbury to the centre of Washington, thence across the New Milford and Litchfield Turnpike, to meet at the east end of the New Preston Turnpike Road.

Built by the Washington Turnpike Company, which was incorporated in October, 1803, it seems to have been one of those useful but little known facilities which served its own community for many years.

The charter was repealed in 1843.

41. The Thompson Turnpike

An important old road leading from Providence to the northeast part of Connecticut was improved in 1794 and operated as the West Glocester Turnpike for ninety-four years. In the beginning it was but a section of a rough country road and really of but local importance, but with the continuation of turnpike improvements to Providence and the prospects of business from farther northwest it soon assumed considerable importance, and a continuation through Connecticut was demanded. So the Thompson Turnpike Company was created in October, 1803, with a franchise to build "through said town of Thompson." The gate was to be within three miles of the Rhode Island line.

Miss Larned's *History of Windham County* tells of the opposition of unwilling taxpayers who objected to being saddled with the cost of land for the benefit of private investors. But their opposition only served to postpone the coming of the improvement for a few years, the road's completion quickly following the granting of the charter.

The new road intersected the Boston Turnpike on Thompson Hill, soon transferred business and population to the hilltop, and caused a flourishing village to be built.

The Thompson Turnpike became the main thoroughfare between Providence and Springfield, and it was not long before daily stages passed over it.

In 1814 a gate was authorized within three miles of the Massachusetts line. As the Rhode Island connection of this road was operated until 1888 there would seem to have been no reason why the Thompson Turnpike should not have been a paying investment for that long also, but we have not learned when it ceased its collections.

It is to be noted that no turnpike in Massachusetts connected with the Thompson at the state line and that the entire distance to Springfield was completed over public roads.

42. The East Middle and West Middle Turnpikes

Communication between Hartford and Danbury about the year 1802 must have been difficult and also desirable, for strenuous efforts were then made to secure a satisfactory road, a committee being appointed by the general assembly to lay out such a route and also to submit their recommendations as to the advisability of establishing the same as a turnpike. The first report of the committee, covering the section from Danbury to Newtown, was made in October, when the committee was continued and instructed to continue its labors to Poland Bridge in Plymouth. That done and reported in May, 1803, the scheme was still unsatisfactory and the patient committee was further required to continue its labors to Farmington, where the Farmington and Bristol Turnpike would be met, over which the journey to Hartford could be finished.

The committee's full report, containing certain alterations in the older part of the route, was accepted in October, 1803, and the road declared laid out as a public highway, with the proviso that the part between Poland Bridge and Farmington should only attain that status when a turnpike corporation had been formed to construct it.

The Middle Road Turnpike Company was formed at the October session of 1803 and given the newly created public road, with the obligation to build the section from Poland Bridge to Danbury. The influence which had prevented the part from the bridge to Farmington from being accepted in full was either absent or met defeat, for the towns of Bristol and Farmington were obliged to build that section for the corporation.

The turnpike, as recorded in the secretary of state's office, commenced on the Farmington and Bristol Turnpike in the Main Street in Farmington and went nine miles, seventy-two rods, and seven links to the bridge over the Poland River in the easterly part of the town of Plymouth. Thence it continued generally westerly, passing Plymouth meeting-house, to the Waterbury River Turnpike, which it followed for a distance of eighty chains or one mile. It then crossed the towns of Watertown, Woodbury, and Southbury, to the Main Street in Newtown after which it continued directly to Danbury. The road was commonly known as the Hartford and Danbury Turnpike, although after 1823 the journey between those places took one over the roads of three distinct corporations. In its length it intersected the Middletown and Berlin, Waterbury River, Straits, Pines Bridge, Washington, Housatonic, and Bridgeport and Newtown turnpikes which, with its two important terminals, doubtless seemed to justify the building of forty-six miles of road.

After twenty years of operation in May, 1823, the road and corporation were divided; the East Middle and the West Middle Turnpike companies being formed and given respective sections of the old Middle Road Turnpike. The part from Danbury to a point ten miles east of the crossing of the Housatonic River was given to the West Middle Turnpike Company, the East, Middle taking the balance. The point of division was about where the Washington Turnpike crossed the Middle Road.

The East Middle secured permission to make changes in its gates in 1834, 1840 and 1844, but in the last year suffered the repeal of as much of its charter as applied to the towns of Woodbury and Watertown. When the balance through Plymouth, Bristol, and Farmington became free has not been learned.

All franchise rights of the West Middle were revoked by the assembly at its May session in 1839.

43. The Colchester and Norwich Turnpike

The turnpike from Bacon Academy in Colchester to Fitch's Ironworks in Bozrah was built by the Colchester and Norwich Turnpike Company under a franchise granted in October, 1805, two years having then elapsed since such a charter had been granted. In 1807 the corporation was allowed to extend its road to an intersection with the Lebanon Road at Backus' Ironworks in Norwich.

That the turnpike was in operation in 1814 we know from an act which provided a revision in the rates of toll, but further we have not been able to learn.

This corporation was allowed to hold fifty acres of land in connection with its tollhouse, a decidedly liberal allowance as compared with the privilege of the Straits Turnpike Company, which had to ask the assembly, in 1806, for permission to erect houses at its gates and was then only allowed five acres with each house.

44. The Cornwall and Washington Turnpike

A committee reporting to the assembly in October, 1803, gave a description of a comprehensive road which it had laid out from Nathaniel Loury's in Canaan to Derby Landing, and recommended that it should be built as a turnpike and specified where the gates should be located. The report was accepted and the assembly waited for a corporation to appear.

Two years later certain parties signified that if they could be incorporated as the Cornwall and Washington Turnpike Company they would undertake the construction of a part of the route. In consequence the corporation was formed in October, 1805, to build from Loury's to the Washington Turnpike in the northerly part of Woodbury, of which privilege it did not take advantage for several years. The corporation occupied the attention of the assembly in May, 1806, when certain alterations in the route were permitted. In October, 1812, it again appeared at the capitol. Its road was not completed

Colchester and Norwich Turnpike: In Yantic, Conn.

and the management tried to blame it on the committee in spite of the late date. All was forgiven, however, and it was enacted that the company might complete the road and do business when it had done so. When the collection of tolls commenced is not known.

In May, 1829, all of the turnpike between "Lory's" gate in Canaan and the south line of Cornwall was made free, and in 1839 the entire charter was revoked.

45. The Connecticut Turnpike (The Old Boston Post Road)

The Old Post Road from Boston to New York, after crossing the Connecticut River, followed as close to the shore as the numerous indentations would allow and, west of New Haven, took a fairly direct course. We have already seen that the portion in Greenwich was made a turnpike under county control in 1792. In 1798 an act was passed under authority of which the towns of Fairfield and Norwalk built a toll bridge across the Saugatuck River, which was in use before 1800. The road continued with only those improvements until May, 1806, when the Connecticut Turnpike Company was formed to improve the Old Post Road from the house of Jonathan Sturges in Fairfield to the Byram River, which is the boundary between Connecticut and New York. This franchise is thus seen to include the section in Greenwich which then passed from county to corporation control.

Four gates were allowed "including the toll at Saugatuck Bridge." The other gates were to be located in Greenwich; in Stamford, at least eighty rods west of the Noroton River; and in Fairfield, between Mill River and the old road from Greenfield.

Ye Historie of ye Town of Greenwich by Mead is our authority for saying that the gate in Greenwich was located just west of Horse Neck Brook and about halfway up the hill, which is still known as Tollgate Hill.

Huntington's *History of Stamford* says that the proposition for this turnpike was received with much dissatisfaction in all the towns along the route except Stamford. The people of that town had evidently little knowledge of turnpike methods and failed to realize the dawn of the day of "soulless corporations," for they welcomed the improvement until they saw what was to be done in their midst. War broke out when they learned that the commissioners proposed to straighten the road even to the extent of cutting directly through the center of the village and dividing their cemetery. The town fought desperately to prevent this desecration but lost on the final appeal, and construction commenced. Tradition credits the corporation with proper care in opening the graves and handling the bodies, but Stamford was not appeased by that. Following the first day's grading operations in the cemetery, large numbers of citizens with many yoke of oxen gathered in the early darkness and labored all night, hauling large rocks into the opening at each end and blocking the entrances. But what man could put in, man could take away, and for three days Stamford piled rocks in by night and the corporation's forces removed them by day, until the money power finally prevailed. Many of the good people of the town, it is said, were so wrought up by the invasion of their sacred precincts that they never afterwards would pass over that portion of the road which is now Main Street.

The Connecticut Turnpike continued to demand its tolls until 1854, when the corporation gave it up.

The continuation of the Old Post Road in New York was improved about the year 1800 by the Westchester Turnpike Company, which collected tolls on the old road from Sawpits, now Port Chester, nearly to New York City.

Stephen Jenkins, in writing of the Old Boston Post Road, gives some interesting data on the road of the present day. He says that in leaving Greenwich for Stamford in the olden days, the stagecoach would have taken us out by way of Dumpling Pond, but the trolley car of to-day follows a more direct route, as the various inlets of the Sound have been bridged and much distance saved. The entrance into Stamford was the same, and the route was lined with beautiful shade trees, as it is to-day. Further along he writes:

"Turnpike" seems to be the favorite term in this section to apply to the Post Road which, after leaving Stamford, passes through many fine estates. At Noroton is the Wee Burn Country Club with its famous golf course. A detour of half a mile at this point takes us to the old Gorham Tide Mill near the shore. The old inhabitants will tell you of the time when this was a busy place, with stores, taverns, mill, and post-office; for here the farmers brought their grain to be ground, and their produce for shipment by vessel to New York.

The Connecticut Soldiers' Home is located at Noroton but sets back from the old turnpike. The final soldiers' home, to which so many of the veterans have retired, Spring Grove Cemetery, abuts on the turnpike' and many of the trim regular stones may be seen in passing.

46. The Connecticut and Rhode Island Turnpike

The Rhode Island and Connecticut Turnpike extended from a point on the Providence and Norwich Turnpike at the westerly line of Providence to the state line at a point about half a mile south of Killingly Pond in the town of Killingly. The corporation which built this road was formed in May, 1802, and carried out its purposes within a few years. As a part of the same general scheme and to continue the route to Hartford, the Connecticut and Rhode Island Turnpike Company was formed in Connecticut in May, 1806, to extend the Rhode Island road to an intersection with the Boston Turnpike, over which access to Hartford could be had.

The Rhode Island Company seems to have had some difficulty in prose-cuting its work and only succeeded in the final completion when assurance came of the supplemental work to be done in Connecticut. In fact, it may fairly be surmised that a reorganization was effected in 1806, and that the men connected with the Connecticut enterprise became interested in the Rhode Island portion. It is certain that joint ownership prevailed in 1816, for then authority was secured to treat the two corporations as one, and a gate on Connecticut soil was used to collect tolls for traveling over Rhode Island miles.

Two gates were allowed in the original Connecticut allotment and the corporation was obliged to build its own bridge over the Quinebaug River. In 1813 an alteration was allowed, which apparently had already been made, as confirmation was given to the construction across the Natchaug River at the foot of Snow's mill pond in Ashford, in a part of the town which became Eastford in 1847.

Miss Larned tells in her *History of Windham County* that poor Pomfret put up its usual fight to escape being saddled with heavy expense for improve-ments not locally needed, and failing to shut out the turnpike sought to have it located in a less expensive section. So heavy had been Pomfret's expenses in fighting turnpikes and then bearing costs and paying damages, that it had been seriously proposed to convert the new town house into cash to relieve the depleted treasury. What a change a century has brought! Now Pomfret is the summer home of millionaires with palatial estates, and has a railroad station worth many times the cost of that town house.

Ashford, on the other hand, regarded all turnpikes as harbingers of prosperity and willingly paid for the expected benefits.

The route opened by the two corporations just considered and the Boston Turnpike became at once an important channel of traffic, and for many years a heavy teaming travel passed between Hartford and Providence, with daily stages interspersed.

The Rhode Island section passed into public control in 1871 and 1875, but the Connecticut road was assumed by the towns in 1851.

47. The Hartland Turnpike

This road was built by the Hartland Turnpike Company which was formed in May, 1806. The franchise covered from the Greenwoods Turnpike east of the pond in Norfolk to the Green at the East meeting-house in Suffield.

The road had been laid out by a committee which reported to the assembly in September, 1805, and from the report it appears that it passed one mile north of Newgate Prison, that notorious underground mine which in later years had been used for the confinement of criminals. The towns through which the turnpike was built were Norfolk, Colebrook, Barkhamsted, Hartland, Granby, and Suffield, but it seems that construction was slow, as in May, 1809, an extension of time to October 1, 1810, was secured. That was undoubtedly sufficient, for in 1812 we find the corporation making petition for a change of gates. The petition was continued, and a year later was taken up, when the commissioners on that road were instructed to investigate and report. Such slow action must have been too much for the company. At any rate the charter was revoked in October, 1814.

48. The Warren Turnpike

No description whatever is given in the act of incorporation of the route which this road was to follow and only by certain references is it seen that it was confined to Litchfield County. The Warren Turnpike Company was chartered in May, 1806. An act passed in October, 1809, shows that the northerly terminus was at what is now Falls Village in Canaan, where a large hydroelectric plant has recently been installed, and Gold, in his *History of Cornwall*, says that the Warren Turnpike is still an important public road. So we know that the road ended at Falls Village and that it passed through Cornwall. It seems probable that the Warren Turnpike was the original of the present East River Road, along the east bank of the Housatonic River, from Kent to Falls Village.

By the act of 1809, above mentioned, an extension was granted from Falls Village to the Massachusetts line, where connection was made with a branch of the Twelfth Massachusetts Turnpike which had been authorized by an act of the Massachusetts legislature in 1803.

Gold's history, published in the early eighties, speaks of this road as if it had been free for many years.

49. The New London and Lyme Turnpike

Another section of the Old Post Road was marked for improvement when the New London and Lyme Turnpike Company was chartered in May, 1807, to improve that road between New London and Killingworth through Waterford and Lyme. The improvement in Waterford consisted in making a new road which extended from the end of Bank Street, across Bream Cove, and over "the Neck," to an intersection with the old road in the westerly part of the town.

A bridge over Bream Cove was first established in 1712, according to a contributor to the New London Historical Society, and then only foot passengers were accommodated. In 1766 a pile bridge sufficient for vehicles replaced the earlier structure, and in 1807, under turnpike incentive, a substantial stone construction, since known as Long Bridge, was erected.

That was built by the new corporation, New London contributing five hundred dollars and the materials from the old bridge toward the cost. The section of new road was named Shaw's Avenue in 1815.

One of the milestones set up by Benjamin Franklin along the post roads, when he was postmaster general, is still standing on this old turnpike on Dorr's Hill between New London and Lyme.

The westerly terminus of the turnpike was at the Connecticut River where it connected with the old Saybrook Ferry, which had been in operation since 1662, and over which the stages were carried to Connecticut River Village in Old Saybrook. Thence to New Haven the journey was continued over public roads, for no turnpike was ever provided along the Sound from Saybrook to that city.

In 1849 all in Lyme south and west of the main street was made free, and in 1853 all in New London came under the control of that city.

Apparently the company never utilized its franchise west of the Connecticut River.

In 1824 the Connecticut River Steamboat Company commenced the operation of a line of steamers from Connecticut River ports to New York, its first boat being named *Oliver Ellsworth* after Connecticut's distinguished jurist. The next year marked the death of Commodore McDonough, the hero of Tripoli and of Plattsburg Bay, and the second boat bore his name.

These steamers were met at Calves Island Wharf in Lyme by stages which took passengers to New London over the New London and Lyme Turnpike. The short piece of road by which access was had to Calves Island from the turnpike is still open to the investigating tourist.

The Connecticut River Steamboat Company continued in business until 1834, at which time many other steamers were running up and down the river.

50. The Woodstock and Thompson Turnpike

This road was built by the Woodstock and Thompson Turnpike Company which was chartered in May, 1808, and it ran northeasterly from the Woodstock meeting-house to the line of the town of Thompson and then easterly to Grosvenor Dale, where it met the Thompson Turnpike which had been built some five years earlier.

Miss Larned speaks of this road as being laid out on turnpike principles, straight through all obstacles including the "granite hill range of western Thompson."

The turnpike was operated for several years but was finally abandoned by its owners, and in May, 1832, the charter was repealed in order to allow the towns to repair and maintain the road, which seemed to be a public necessity.

51. The Middletown and Berlin Turnpike

Travel between Middletown and Farmington by way of Berlin and New Britain was the next to receive attention, the Middletown and Berlin Turnpike Company being chartered in May, 1808, to cover that district.

The *History of New Britain*, by Camp, states that this road was constructed about 1810 and passed through the west part of that town. As New Britain's manufacturing importance had not then developed it is not surprising that the road passed on one side of it.

Alterations were made in the location in 1809 and again in 1810, and in 1841 a gate which had been moved without the required formalities was confirmed in its new position, after which no more legislative acts were passed on this road.

52. The Woodstock and Somers Turnpike

The prospects of the Woodstock and Thompson Turnpike must have seemed rosy during the first six months of its corporate life, for in October, 1808, the Woodstock and Somers Turnpike Company was chartered for the purpose of continuing the good work of the Woodstock and Thompson as far as the village of Somers.

The road had previously been laid out, as may be read in the manuscript records in the Hartford capitol, through Woodstock, Ashford, Stafford, and Somers, a distance of twenty-six miles and 59.25 chains. On the easterly end it connected with the Woodstock and Thompson Turnpike, and it reached 180.62 chains into Somers, which brought it to Somers Street, as the center was called.

Alterations were allowed in the location in 1813 and the turnpike was operated for several years. Conditions in the northern tier of Connecticut towns must have been radically different a hundred years ago from what they are to-day or such a project would have proved a vain dream. Indeed it is hard to see how the corporation managed to pick up a fraction of its expenses, and very likely it did not.

Like the Woodstock and Thompson it was abandoned by its owners and for several years was neglected. Finally in May, 1832, the assembly revoked the charter, and the road became an obligation of the various towns traversed by it.

53. The Colchester and Chatham Turnpike

Throughout the turnpike era there were no bridges across the Connecticut River below Hartford, and the only means of crossing was by ferries, of which there were several, and naturally any turnpike leading to that river planned to make one of the ferries its terminal.

A ferry was established between Middletown and Portland in 1726, and thither the promoters of the Colchester and Chatham Turnpike projected their road. This company was formed at the October session of 1808 to build from Colchester to Middletown. The Hebron and Middle Haddam was already in the field, but it is hard to see that the two propositions conflicted with each other. Nevertheless, sufficient opposition was put up by that company to compel the new proprietors to enter into an elaborate agreement as to division of tolls in the region where the two roads were to cross each other, and the full text of that agreement was inserted in the act of incorporation of the Colchester and Chatham.

The report of the laying-out committee of this road is interesting because the surveyor, whenever he could see two church spires at once, read a compass bearing on each. Those notes would be of great assistance in locating the road if we could be sure of the location of the various churches.

This turnpike commenced in Colchester Center and ran a little south of westerly to the head of Babcock Pond, thence through the village of Westminster and the town of Chatham, passing close to the present Cobalt and Middle Haddam Station of the Air-Line Division, and across the town of Portland to the Middletown Ferry, just below where the railroad now crosses.

54. The Columbia Turnpike

Under date of August 27, 1808, a committee reported to the assembly that it had laid out a road from a point on the Hartford and Windham Turnpike, 4.04 chains southerly from the south end of a bridge near Clark and Gray's paper mill to the meeting-house in Hebron, at the easterly end of the Hebron and Middle Haddam Turnpike. The report was accepted, and the road declared established, provided a corporation was formed to build it. But the investigation had been urged in good faith, for the men with capital stood ready and the Columbia Turnpike Company was formed in October of the same year.

The bridge mentioned in the above-quoted report was the old Ironworks Bridge in Willimantic, and the paper mill of Clark and Gray stood about where the Number One Mill of the American Thread Company's Willimantic plant now stands. The Hartford and Windham Turnpike will not be found in our list of companies, as that was a name which could have been only locally applied. The road from which the survey started was that of the Windham Turnpike Company which, by its connection with the Boston Turnpike in North Coventry, led to Hartford.

By its turnpike connections on either end the road of the Columbia Company offered a direct route from Providence to Middle Haddam on the Connecticut River, and it is easy to see that the promoters believed that they

Columbia Turnpike: Easterly end, junction with Windham Turnpike

were opening a road which would be of great use to long-distance travelers. The river was reached at a point accessible by boats from the Sound, and it was not a wild dream, at that date, to picture a heavy commerce transferring at Middle Haddam to boats for New York. But there is no evidence that such dreams were ever realized.

Pleasant Street, which lies "over the river" in Willimantic and its continuation as Willimantic Road across Columbia to Hebron, is the old Columbia Turnpike. Willimantic at that date was still the "Old State," so called from the location there of an arsenal during the Revolution, and its future greatness as a manufacturing center was not anticipated. So the Columbia

Columbia Turnpike: Pleasant Street, Willimantic, Conn.

Columbia Turnpike: Site of gate at Bridge Street, Willimantic, Conn.

Turnpike made no effort to cross the Willimantic River but continued down its southerly bank to the intersection with the Windham Turnpike, which it might have joined a mile farther to the west with a great saving in cost and distance. But "Old Windham" was then the county seat and a place of much more importance than Willimantic, so the turnpike committee proceeded toward it as directly as they could.

State highway improvement has corrected that error and the modern road from Columbia to Willimantic branches off from the old turnpike about a half mile east of Columbia Green and crosses over to the Hop River Turnpike.

Columbia Turnpike: Columbia Green, junction with Hartford and Norwich Turnpike

Between the point of divergence and Willimantic the old road is but a woods lane, kept open only on account of a few residents along its borders.

A tollgate stood in Willimantic where the corner of Bridge Street is now and opposite Burnham's carriage shop. Mr. Burnham in his seventy-ninth year could just remember when tolls were collected and so judged that the road became free about the year 1845. When he built his shop he removed the foundations of the old tollhouse in preparing the site for the new building. An old plan found in the Windham town office also showed the location of the tollgate, as above stated.

55. The Tolland County Turnpike

The Tolland County Turnpike Company was chartered in May, 1809, and opened its road in about a year from that date. Its route was easterly through Ellington, Tolland, and Willington to the Boston Turnpike in Ashford, and Miss Larned says that it met the latter road two miles west of Ashford Village.

Business was poor and the company petitioned for extra gates in October, 1810. According to rule the petition was continued, and in the next May was practically denied, as all that was allowed was to change one of the gates into two half-gates.

The company's charter was revoked in May, 1834.

56. The Sharon and Cornwall Turnpike

The Sharon and Cornwall Turnpike Company, formed in May, 1809, built from the Warren Turnpike in Cornwall to Swift's Bridge and thence to Amasa Beebe's in Sharon. A subsequent act shows that the said Beebe's place was close to the meeting-house in Sharon, and Swift's Bridge may be found on the maps of to-day across the Housatonic River near the southerly boundaries of both Cornwall and Sharon.

This was another of the useful but little known utilities, and apparently it filled an important niche in its community, for it continued to quietly collect its tolls for thirty-six years. In 1845 all of the road in Sharon was made free and the gate was moved to a new location, probably on the bridge. There could not have been any length of road in the town of Cornwall, so it is probable that the corporation continued its existence for a while longer as a toll-bridge company. But of that we have found no data.

57. The Chatham and Marlborough Turnpike

In early September, 1809, a committee of the assembly was engaged in surveying the line for a new route by which the Connecticut River could be reached from the western part of Windham County. Its report, dated September 16, 1809, is to be commended for the definite location of the terminal points of the survey. The beginning was on the Hartford and New

London Turnpike, south 34° east, 1.60 chains from the thirteenth milestone, and the ending was at Pistolpoint Bar, where a line drawn south 80° west from the north end of the meeting-house in Middletown Upper Houses intersected the easterly bank of the Connecticut River.

In October, 1809, the Chatham and Marlborough Turnpike Company was incorporated to open the road, which duty it performed within the next two and a half years at least, for in May, 1812, an alteration of the westerly three miles was made.

Of the further history of this road nothing has been learned.

58. The Middletown and Meriden Turnpike

In October, 1809, the Middletown and Meriden Turnpike Company was formed to connect those towns, and, according to Curtis's A Century of Meriden, the road was built the same year. It was a short road, only about eight miles long, so it is possible that it was completed in the few months remaining in that year after incorporation.

The turnpike passed through Middlefield and East Meriden, swinging in a big bow to the south and followed the street now used by the East Meriden trolley cars.

A gate was moved, with proper consent, in 1841, but further information has not been forthcoming. But that shows an active life of over thirty years.

59. The East Haddam and Colchester Turnpike

The road running southwesterly from Colchester to Goodspeed's Landing in East Haddam was built by the East Haddam and Colchester Turnpike Company, which was chartered in October, 1809. The single gate allowed was located in East Haddam town.

The life of this road was too quiet to attract the notice of local historians and no items regarding it have been found. It was in operation as a turnpike as late as 1852, for in that year a change of gate was allowed.

The Connecticut River terminus of this road was determined by the presence of a ferry, or opportunity for one, at East Haddam. Provision was made for the maintenance of means of crossing at that point as early as 1664. In 1741 a new grant was made, and a ferry was operated intermittently after that until 1811, when a ferry charter was secured from the assembly, presumably by the turnpike interests.

60. The Durham and East Guilford Turnpike

This road was commonly and more properly called the Durham and Madison Turnpike, for it ran to Madison and not to Guilford at all. But the official name of the corporation responsible for it was the Durham and East Guilford Turnpike Company, which was chartered in May, 1811. One of the provisions in the charter was that only half tolls should be charged for vehicles having rims over seven inches in width.

The capital stock of the company was ten thousand dollars, according to Steiner's *History of Guilford and Madison*, which gives a pro rata of about seven hundred and forty dollars a mile. This accords with costs of the Massachusetts roads of which we have data.

The turnpike started at Durham Street and ran through the center of North Madison to Madison Green, following like a backbone down the center line of the long narrow town of Madison. In its thirteen and a half miles it was allowed one gate, which was changed for two halfgates by the assembly of 1830.

Thirty-four years did this turnpike last, the surrender of its charter being accepted in 1845. The corporation was allowed six months longer which to close its affairs and sell its property.

61. The Southington and Waterbury Turnpike

October, 1812, was the date of incorporation of the Southington and Waterbury Turnpike Company which built the road from Meriden to Waterbury between the years 1812 and 1815.

To follow the road to-day one should go to the corner of Meriden Road and South Main Street in Waterbury, then follow Meriden Road along the southerly boundary of Wolcott and through the south part of Southington, then over Southington Avenue, along the trolley line of the Meriden, Southington, and Compounce Tramway Company, to the corner of Blackwood Road in Meriden. One tollgate stood in the south part of Wolcott, according to Orcutt's history of that town. In that we are also told that a large part of the stock in this corporation was owned by the Upson family of Wolcott.

The franchise of this company also contained the provision that only half tolls should be collected when the tires were over seven inches wide.

62. The Killingworth and Haddam Turnpike

A connection with the Middlesex Turnpike at Higganum in the north corner of Haddam, and leading thence to Killingworth Center, was made by the Killingworth and Haddam Turnpike Company under a charter issued in October, 1813. In October, 1815, a branch road was authorized to connect with the Middlesex at another point. A change of gates has been noticed in 1825.

This was another of those country roads which seem to have filled a useful niche in the local development but which have not left any indelible records for history. It rounded out an even thirty-seven years of life, the charter being repealed in 1850.

Four years later it appeared that there was still some property in real estate owned by the defunct corporation, and it became necessary for the assembly to appoint an agent, giving him power to sell such. The proceeds, after satisfying any outstanding indebtedness, were to be divided among the stockholders.

The branch above mentioned was locally known as the "Beaver Brook Turnpike" and seems to have extended from the crossroads known as Duncan, in the south part of Haddam, to Haddam Street on the river. It was a little over four miles in length and the main road was about ten.

63. The Middletown Turnpike

The Middletown, Durham, and New Haven Turnpike Company was granted a franchise in October, 1813, for a road from Middletown to New Haven through Durham, Northford, and North Haven.

In New Haven an old road, early known as Negro or Neck Lane, was utilized for turnpike purposes, which in later days was called Hancock Avenue and is now the State Street of that city. In Middletown the modern name of the turnpike is Durham Avenue, and as the Durham Pike it is known through the intervening towns.

This road does not seem to have its mark in history. Watrous, who has noted many interesting points in connection with other roads, found nothing to say about the Middletown Turnpike except that it was chartered in 1813.

That it was in operation as late as 1846 is proved by the passage of an act in that year making an alteration in the road.

64. The Litchfield and Cornwall Turnpike

Under a charter issued in October, 1814, the Litchfield and Cornwall Turnpike Company built a road from Litchfield through Goshen into Cornwall, where it probably joined the road of the Goshen and Sharon Turnpike Company, which was built in 1803.

This road was not much of a history maker, but undoubtedly served its rural communities for many years. It was in operation in 1834, for in that year an act was passed by which a change of gates was allowed. Gold's *History of Cornwall*, which had something to say about other turnpikes, is silent regarding the Litchfield and Cornwall.

65. The Haddam and Durham Turnpike

The Haddam and Durham Turnpike Company was incorporated in May, 1815, and built its road from Higganum, in the northeast part of Haddam on the Middlesex Turnpike, to Durham Street, a distance of less than eight miles.

This was practically a branch of the Middletown, Durham, and New Haven Turnpike with which it connected at Durham Street. That hamlet must have presented a hustling aspect in stage-coach days, with four turnpikes intersecting there. On the other end the Haddam and Durham connected with the Middlesex Turnpike, but at such an angle that it is hard to see how either derived any advantage from the junction. The Killingworth and Haddam Turnpike made the intersection at Higganum a three-cornered one.

Higganum owed its distinction as a turnpike terminal to the Higganum Ferry, between that village and the Middle Haddam, which was established in 1763.

66. The Still River Turnpike

In May, 1815, the Still River Turnpike Company was formed to open a road from the Farmington River in Colebrook to Wolcottsville, now known as Torrington.

This is a busy street to-day, being the main street in both Torrington and Winsted, while over the section between, the cars of the Torrington and Winchester Street Railway pass frequently. North from Winsted the road skirted the easterly edge of Colebrook, crossing the Farmington River and uniting with the Farmington River Turnpike in the northeast corner of that town.

By that connection access was had over the Tenth Massachusetts Turnpike to Albany by way of Lee and Lenox, while on the south a route, as direct as could be expected, was had to New Haven over the Waterbury River Turnpike and the Straits or Rimmon Falls.

By all indications the Still River should have been an important and successful road.

Its charter was repealed in 1844 after twenty-nine years of corporate existence.

Another corporation, the Wolcottsville Turnpike Company, was formed in May, 1826, with a franchise from the meeting-house in Winsted to Wolcottsville in Torrington, "and running near Still River." Whether the Still River Company had failed to develop this lower section of its franchise and the second company was organized to complete it, or the second effort was for the purposes of competition with an already established road, we are unable to state. Nothing further has been found regarding the Wolcottsville Company.

67. The Chester and North Killingworth Turnpike

In May, 1816, the Chester and North Killingworth Turnpike Company was formed to build between the places named. Chester and the north part of Killingworth being adjoining towns, the road was but a short one and of only local importance. That it was opened and operated for several years is seen from two acts relating to it which were passed in 1817 and 1827, but nothing more is known on the subject.

By the construction of the Hadlyme, and Chester and North Killingworth Second turnpikes, which were chartered in 1834, an effort was made to make this road a part of a through route from Norwich to New Haven. The Chester and North Killingworth Second extended its parent company's road on the east to the Connecticut River and on the west to a connection with the Fairhaven Turnpike. The Hadlyme Turnpike started from the opposite side of the Connecticut River and ran to the Salem and Hamburg Turnpike in Salem.

Probably the whole system was given up in 1846 and 1847, when the two roads just described were made free.

68. The New Milford and Sherman Turnpike

This adventure was disappointing at the outset. The New Milford and Sherman Turnpike Company was formed in May, 1818, when the Philipstown Turnpike Company of New York was busy with its preliminaries. Connecting with that road the Connecticut corporation would have been able to offer a route to Cold Spring Landing on the Hudson River, from Hartford by way of Litchfield, and from New Haven over the Derby and Ousatonic River turnpikes. But the Philipstown Turnpike was an air castle, according to the petition filed by the New Milford and Sherman Company in 1837, and that corporation faced an unprofitable business for nineteen years, at the end of which time its bridge over the Housatonic River was carried away by "a big ice flood."

The company had expended about five thousand dollars which it considered a total loss, as the receipts had never been sufficient to keep the road in repair, and now that it was called upon to lay out some fifteen to eighteen hundred dollars more to rebuild the bridge, the stockholders were in despair. A petition was therefore made asking to be relieved from responsibility for the road, offering in return to rebuild the bridge.

Consequently an act was passed in 1837 by which the New Milford and Sherman Turnpike Company was relieved of all its obligations "except the bridge place across the Ousatonick river in New Milford at the place commonly called Boardman's bridge and the approaches thereto." The company was allowed until January 1, 1839, to comply with the conditions.

69. The Pettipauge and Guilford Turnpike

This road ran from Petti-paug, on the Middle Cove, in Essex, easterly and northerly along the Middlesex Turnpike and then to Killingworth Center, from which place it went directly to the stage road in the southeasterly corner of Guilford. It was built by the Pettipauge and Guilford Turnpike Company under a charter granted in October, 1818.

The length of the road is stated by Steiner to have been sixteen miles and the cost $10,000, or $625 a mile.

In May, 1839, the charter was repealed and the towns were obliged to assume the care of the road. Madison offered strenuous objections but was compelled to submit.

The entire road was ready for business seven months after the franchise was granted. That the investment was not a good one is seen by the frequent acts by which rates of toll were altered and gates changed.

70. The Groton and Stonington Turnpike

"From the River Thames to the state of Rhode Island," including from Groton Ferry to the Head of Mystic, was the next franchise granted, which was given to the Groton and Stonington Turnpike Company in October, 1818. By this link was completed the turnpike anticipation of the New Haven Road's Shore Line from Boston to the Connecticut River, for this road continued the line of the Providence and Pawcatuck and the Hopkinton and Richmond turnpikes in Rhode Island, the three making a continuous turnpike from Providence to the shore opposite New London.

We have seen, in Rhode Island, the efforts put forth by Westerly to retain for itself a place on the through route between Providence and New York. In pursuance of that desire a new stage road was built west from Westerly for the purpose of drawing that form of travel, and it was confidently expected that the new turnpike would see fit to absorb that piece of new road. But the same idea prevailed in Connecticut as elsewhere and, carrying out the conception of a turnpike, the route was made direct without regard to grades or important centers left off the line.

Wheeler's *History of Stonington* tells us that the project was first broached in 1816 by the stage interests which appear to have favored Westerly, but if so, the control must have changed by the time of incorporation. Stonington did not oppose the turnpike charter but did object to the corporation being fettered to any particular route, preferring that the location should be left to the judgment of the men responsible, and that request prevailed, we can imagine, to Stonington's ultimate mortification.

Starting from Groton Ferry the new road followed the Old Post Road through Groton, with several improvements, to the Head of Mystic, but from there the locating surveyors cut loose and showed their independence. Instead of continuing on the new stage road to Westerly they took an old country road, which led to North Stonington as far as Wolf Neck, and then blazed a way of their own easterly through Stonington and North Stonington to the line of Rhode Island in the town of Hopkinton, where they connected with the southwesterly end of the Hopkinton and Richmond Turnpike, which was undoubtedly surveyed at the same time.

The length of this turnpike was about seventeen miles and it cost, according to a statement made by the corporation, $12,000, which makes about $710 a mile. Upon completion it immediately became the through stage and mail route between New London, Providence, and Boston.

An interesting light upon conditions of travel from Boston to New York at the time of the opening of this road is thrown by the following announcement which appeared in a New London paper in November, 1818:

The steamboat "Fulton" will discontinue running after December 5, for the present season; the stage with the mail on the New London route from Boston will be extended to New Haven during the winter for the accommodation of such passengers as wish to join the Connecticut, Captain Bunker, at that place on their way to New York.

The ferry across the Thames at New London is described by Miss Caulkins as "one of the standing embarassments of the town." From earliest times the policy of the town had been to lease the right on the best terms it could exact. One Robert Bartlett, dying in 1673, devised property to the town, the income from which was to be used for the support of a free school for the children of New London's poor. In consequence of neglect by the authorities the property seriously depreciated, and to make good the town voted from 1702 to 1875 that the ferry proceeds should be applied to that end. Down to 1821 the propelling force was applied by means of sails or oars, but in that year horses were used. Steam power was tried in 1835 but was found too expensive. Ten years, however, showed such improvement that steam was permanently installed, and in 1849 the famous steamer *Mohegan* was put in service. Even in the present year of grace the traveler desiring to go that way may be ferried across the river to Groton.

The opening of the New York, Providence, and Boston Railroad, which in spite of its pretentious name only ran from New London to Providence, occurred in 1839 and does not seem to have troubled the turnpike business a great deal, but when the Shore Line from New Haven to New London was completed in 1852 and rail connection made continuous from New York to Boston, the deathblow was struck.

In the next year, 1853, the corporation asked to be dissolved, stating that "in consequence of the entire change of travel by the facilities offered by steamboats and railroads along the Sound and between Connecticut and Rhode Island" its turnpike had become "unproductive." The assembly acquiesced and the road became free.

71. The Essex Turnpike

We have traced the New London and Lyme Turnpike to the east bank of the Connecticut, and we have seen how travelers were accommodated on their western continuation of that journey by a turnpike running from Petti-paug in Essex. But quite a gap was left between those roads, and the ferry across the mouth of the large river must have had serious disadvantages. Now comes a turnpike to make a short connection from the New London and Lyme and the Pettipauge and Guilford.

The Essex Turnpike Company was enacted into life in May, 1822, for that purpose, provided that it should maintain a ferry over the Connecticut River at the North Cove in Essex. Its road was to run through Essex and Lyme.

This turnpike appears to have been the road running from Ely's Wharf Ferry, southeasterly to the New London and Lyme Turnpike at the foot of Rogers Lake in the north part of Old Lyme. On the other side of the Connecticut it had a short section from the ferry to Petti-paug with a drawbridge over the mouth of North Cove.

In 1825 the assembly made free all of the road east of its crossing with the Salem and Hamburg Turnpike. Apparently what was left of the Essex, with the Salem and Hamburg, and another road from Salem to Norwich, were later consolidated and known by various names, such as Essex, Salem, Salem and Norwich, and Norwich and Essex.

Under this combination the Essex later got into trouble with the maritime interests, for it appears that, in 1853, its draw in the bridge over North Cove was too narrow for the demands upon it. The assembly of that year ordered the company to make the draw wide enough for any vessel, equip it for easy operation, and put in charge some person living within half a mile of the bridge.

This road is said to have been relinquished about 1860.

The steamers *Oliver Ellsworth* and *McDonough,* which have been noticed in connection with the New London and Lyme Turnpike, made regular stops at the wharf at Ely's Ferry, where passengers for Norwich transferred to the waiting stages and were rushed over the Essex, Salem and Hamburg, and Norwich and Salem turnpikes to the city at the head of the Thames.

72. The Salem and Hamburg Turnpike

The Salem and Hamburg Turnpike Company was formed in May, 1824, with a franchise very indefinitely worded, so that it is difficult to determine from it just what route was intended. But from its later consolidation with roads on either end of it, it seems clear that the Salem and Hamburg started from Salem Center, ran through North Lyme and Hamburg, and joined the Essex Turnpike a very short distance east of the ferry of that road. As stated in connection with the Essex this road became a part of a through route from Norwich to Essex, which seems to have been regarded at the time as one road, although we have no evidence that a consolidation of corporations was really made. Probably not, as such a proceeding would have called for elaborate legislative action.

It is said that Andrew Jackson, on his presidential tour, passed over this turnpike on his way to Norwich.

It has been noted in connection with the whole road from Norwich to Essex that it was discontinued about 1860, so we will take a chance on that date being the one for the end of the Salem and Hamburg Turnpike.

73. The Pines Bridge Turnpike

Another of the radial feeders for New Haven was projected by the Pines Bridge Turnpike Company, chartered in May, 1824, to build from the northeast part of Woodbury to the west abutment of Pines Bridge in the east part of Oxford, in which length of road of about thirteen miles one gate was allowed.

Starting from Pines Bridge the road followed a northwesterly course into the town of Woodbury, after which it turned northerly, skirting the east side of Quassapaug Lake and running on the boundary between the towns of Watertown and Woodbury. Then it turned into Woodbury, ending in the northeast quarter of that town.

Twelve years was long enough to try the experiment in the town of Oxford and in May, 1836, the assembly allowed all in that town to be turned over to the public. In 1841 the charter was repeated and that marked the end of the whole turnpike.

74. The Guilford and Durham Turnpike

For the purpose of building a road "from Durham to the public square in Guilford and thence to Sachem's Head Harbor in said Guilford," the Guilford and Durham Turnpike Company was chartered in May, 1824, filing a bond for ten thousand dollars to carry out its plans before November 1, 1828.

Steiner knew of this road when he wrote his *History of Guilford and Madison*, for he says that it followed the West, or Menunkatuck, River to Lake Quonepaug and then ran along another West River to Durham Street where it connected with the road of the Middletown, Durham, and New

Haven Turnpike Company. In the borough, above Guilford Green, the road is now known as Church Street.

At an 1831 town meeting Guilford voted to bear the expense of repairing the road, if its inhabitants might use the same toll free, but it does not appear that the offer was accepted, for it would have meant practically the giving up of the whole road.

The turnpike management was still in control in 1855, for then a revision of tolls was enacted by the assembly.

75. The Fairhaven Turnpike

From Killingworth to Dragon Bridge was the next section to receive attention and the Fairhaven Turnpike Company was incorporated in May, 1824, to provide a turnpike over such a route.

Steiner again helps us out, for he has noticed that this road branched from the Pettipauge and Guilford Turnpike in the center of Killingworth and ran by the North Madison meeting-house, through North Guilford, North Branford, and the northerly section of the town of East Haven to Fairhaven Village. It was nineteen and a quarter miles long and cost $7500, making a pro rata of about $390 a mile, a very low figure. Clearly this company did nothing beyond the repairing of an old road.

A portion of the turnpike was surrendered to the towns in which it lay in April, 1843, but some of it was in operation in 1846, when confirmation was given to the location of a gate which had been moved.

76. The Providence Turnpike

When the Foster and Scituate Turnpike was projected in Rhode Island in 1811, it plainly was the intention to open a road into Connecticut as far as Danielson. That road was chartered in 1813, but the part in Connecticut was a long time coming.

In May, 1825, the Providence Turnpike Company was incorporated in Connecticut for the purpose of enabling the Foster and Scituate to realize its ambition. The franchise covered "from the Foster and Scituate Turnpike at the Rhode Island line to Danielson in Killingly." The road as built ran southeasterly from Danielson about one and a half miles, then easterly through South Killingly to the state line and the Foster and Scituate.

It seems improbable that this corporation was formed or financed by any other interests than those in control of the Rhode Island connecting road. The length in Connecticut was only a little over five miles, which of course only allowed one gate, but that was stipulated as not "to be in addition to the last one in Rhode Island." In other words, if the Rhode Island gate was within the usual gate interval from Danielson, no gate could be erected in

Connecticut. Unless the same interests benefited by the collections in each state such an arrangement would not have been equitable.

The Rhode Island road became free in 1866 and, as the Providence Turnpike seems to have been a part and parcel of the same scheme, we will assign the same year for its demise.

77. The Sandy Brook Turnpike

A cross turnpike leading from the Waterbury River Turnpike in the north-westerly part of Colebrook, across the Still River Turnpike to the Farmington River Turnpike in Barkhamsted, was built by the Sandy Brook Turnpike Company under a charter granted in May, 1825. The layout of the road had been made by the towns, but the assembly saw fit to make the road a private one and gave it to the turnpike company.

The road made a short jump from the Waterbury River Road to the upper valley of Sandy Brook and then followed the course of that small stream until it came to the Still River Turnpike, which it crossed, and continued south-easterly for a short distance to its junction with the Farmington River.

This corporation never bothered the assembly after its incorporation, an unusual record.

78. The Humphreysville and Salem Turnpike

We have previously seen how the residents of Derby Landing were dissatisfied with the turnpike connection whereby the Oxford turned to the north and connected with the Straits, going thence to New Haven by a route remote from Derby; and how efforts were made to have a turnpike come down the Naugatuck River, connecting the Oxford with Derby Landing, after which the journey to New Haven would be made over the Derby Turnpike; and of the building of the Rimmon Falls Turnpike which did not go north of the Falls Bridge in Chusetown.

Now comes a corporation which desires to fill the gap left in the river valley when the Rimmon Falls was laid out, without connecting with the Oxford. So the Humphreysville and Salem Turnpike Company was formed in May, 1825, with a franchise to build "on both sides of the Naugatuck River from said Salem Bridge to said Falls Bridge."

Salem, as has already been mentioned, had no reference to the town of Salem, which is in the easterly part of the state adjacent to Norwich, but referred to Salem Society, the ancient name of Naugatuck prior to its separation from Waterbury, and Salem Bridge was the Main Street Bridge of Naugatuck. The Falls Bridge was at the old village of Chusetown, now Seymour. It does not appear that the corporation exercised its power to build on both sides of the river but that it kept wholly on the east side.

In that appears an apparent discrepancy, for we have already observed that the Oxford Turnpike built up the east side of the river almost to Beacon Brook, and now that section seems to be given to the new turnpike. We will not attempt to explain this but will state that it was quite common for a corporation to be given a franchise allowing it to run for certain distances along the road of another company. Sometimes a division of tolls was prescribed, and in one case an elaborate agreement, which had been made in advance, was incorporated into the charter. But nothing of that sort appears in this case and we are left in doubt as to what really occurred. At any rate the Humphreysville and Salem had a clear field along the east river bank after entering the town of Naugatuck, as now divided, and we learn from Anderson's *History of Waterbury* that some heroic work was done there, for the road was "cut into the foundations of the hills along the east side of the river."

Sharpe's *History of Seymour* tells us that the company did not get down to work until 1832, and the assembly records show that the charter for the road was repealed in 1856.

79. The Center Turnpike

In June, 1824, the Central Turnpike Corporation was formed in Massachusetts to build from the Worcester Turnpike in Needham to the Connecticut line in Dudley, and in May, 1826, the Center Turnpike Company was chartered in Connecticut to continue the work as far as Tolland courthouse. The Worcester Turnpike, leading out from Boston, had long been built and a turnpike from Tolland to Hartford had been in operation for a quarter of a century, so it is seen that by the opening of the Central and the Center a new route from Boston to Hartford was provided. What need could have been imagined or what encouragement found to build another route is hard to conceive. Turnpikes by this time were known to all to be very poor investments, and connection between the two important New England centers was amply provided. But sufficient faith or credulity was found and the roads were built. Immediately a new line of stages appeared, and residents along the Center had the daily pleasure of watching for the passage of the "Boston and Hartford Telegraph" coaches.

The Massachusetts road was completed and opened for travel in the early part of 1830, and in 1836 the corporation gave it up and had its road made free. The Connecticut company however held on until 1853, when its charter was repealed and the corporation dissolved.

The Connecticut road is known to-day as the old Hartford and Boston Turnpike and may be easily followed. Entering the state in the northwest corner of Thompson at Quinebaug post-office, it runs across Woodstock, skirting the northerly slopes of Child, Pigeon, and Tommy Lyon hills, the southerly edge of Winthrop Swamp, and the north shore of Black Pond, and passes over the corner of Union, Woodstock, and Eastford. Thence it passes through North Ashford and Westford, northerly of Sharpe's Hill and into Willington, crossing that town by northwesterly and southwesterly courses, and passing over the Willimantic River about a mile up-stream from Tolland Station on the Central Vermont Railroad.

The road is crooked, like any ordinary country highway, and it is hard to reconcile it with the idea of a turnpike.

80. The Northfield Turnpike

The Northfield Turnpike Company was chartered in May, 1826, with the right to build from a point in Redding near a gristmill, southerly near the Saugatuck River, through Redding into Weston as far as the "second cross road from the front, so called." It was a short road as is seen from the allowance of but one gate, or two with half rates of toll.

That the road was completed is shown by the act passed in May, 1828, which recited that the turnpike had been built and corrected an error in the record of the layout. It is also referred to in 1841, in an act in connection with the Newtown and Norwalk Turnpike, and in 1851 in the charter for the Danbury, Redding, Weston, and Westport Plank Road.

Except for the facts mentioned above no information has been found. The road evidently came down the valley of the Saugatuck into the present town of Weston.

81. The Windham and Brooklyn Turnpike

This road extended from the courthouse in Brooklyn to an intersection with the Windham Turnpike in Windham about a mile east of Windham Green and near the scene of the famous Windham Frog Fight. It was built by the Windham and Brooklyn Turnpike Company under a charter granted at the May session of 1826, and was probably completed during the following summer. It is now the direct road from Brooklyn through Howard Valley and the northerly part of Scotland to Windham Green, or Old Windham.

The corporation endeavored to make money for nineteen years, moving its gates and altering its location in the effort, evidently with some success for, in 1845, it was willing to take over the road from Brooklyn to the bridge over the Quinebaug at Danielson, and bear one half the expense of the bridge. Probably the bridge had been recently washed away and the town was willing to make such a trade to secure a new one. On this new road the company was allowed to erect a gate with half tolls.

Windham and Brooklyn Turnpike: Site of a gate in Scotland, Conn.

A gate at one time stood in Scotland where a cellar hole in the bushes now marks the site of the tollhouse. The corporation owned an acre and a quarter of land there and subsequent sales of the surrounding land have had to take notice of the adverse ownership.

By extending to Danielson, the Windham and Brooklyn made a connection with the Providence Turnpike, and can easily be seen to have thus opened a through and improved route from Providence to Hartford. But how, in 1845, with railroads already well demonstrated and plenty of the old-time turnpikes filling the need, could anyone have seen merit in opening

Windham and Brooklyn Turnpike: East, through Scotland, Conn.

such a through route?

82. The Monroe and Zoar Bridge Turnpike

Two corporations were formed at the May session of 1826 for the purpose of opening turnpike connection from Bridgeport to Zoar Bridge over the Housatonic River between the towns of Monroe and Oxford. One of these was the Zoar Bridge Turnpike Company, which aspired to build an independent line all the way to tidewater at Bridgeport, notwithstanding the fact that the Bridgeport and Newtown Turnpike, then in operation, would be practically paralleled for several miles. The second was the Monroe and Zoar Bridge Turnpike Company which had a much more sensible proposition to build from the bridge to the nearest point on the existing Bridgeport and Newtown Turnpike.

It is hard to understand how the assembly could have seen it consistent with the public good to thus charter a company to parallel an existing road, compelling it to divide a revenue which probably was none too much anyway, or how it could have deemed it advisable to charter two companies to cover the same ground and leave them to fight for possession. The routes were identical from the bridge to Monroe Center. But protection of invested capital in public utilities was then far from realization and many other cases of parallel franchises have been observed in turnpike charters.

Apparently the Monroe and Zoar Bridge Company was the only one to carry out the intention, and that company did build its road on a southwesterly course from Zoar Bridge to a point on the Bridgeport and Newtown in the town of Trumbull about halfway between Stepney Depot and Long Hill stations on the Bridgeport Branch of the New Haven Road.

Operations continued until 1852, when the company was relieved of all its road between Zoar Bridge and the town house in Monroe Village. Permission was granted to sell the tollhouse, and the company was allowed to retain the balance of its road with one gate at which half-rate collections could be made. How long this short piece remained a toll road has not been ascertained.

83. The Norwich and Salem Turnpike

In May, 1827, the Norwich and Salem Turnpike Company was created, its franchise reading "from the Wharf bridge in Norwich Landing to Salem to meet the road leading from Essex to Salem."

The Salem we meet this time is the real town of Salem, which is in New London County and about halfway between the Thames and Connecticut rivers. The road "leading from Essex to Salem" was the consolidation, which we have already noticed, of the Salem and Hamburg, and the Essex turnpikes.

As previously stated this corporation, the Norwich and Salem, formed, with the Salem and Hamburg and a portion of the Essex, one continuous road from Norwich to Essex, which was generally regarded as a single turnpike, although there is no evidence of the corporations ever having been actually merged.

The Norwich and Salem started from the Wharf Bridge, which stood across the estuary of the Yantic River on the southwesterly side of Norwich, and ran directly to the southwest corner of the town. Thence it passed across a small tip of the town of Bozrah, through the northerly part of Montville, and entered Salem by the old Willoughby Tavern near the south end of Gardner Lake.

In the early summer of 1833 President Andrew Jackson, on his official trip to New England, passed over the Essex, Salem and Hamburg, and Norwich and Salem turnpikes on his way to Providence and Boston.

In an act passed in 1856 the assembly recited that the Norwich and Salem Turnpike had been out of repair for many years and proceeded to suspend the charter of the corporation. The towns of Norwich, Bozrah, Montville, and Salem were directed to repair the road, and it was provided that, if the corporation should repay them for the amounts expended, its rights under the charter should be renewed. This indefinite condition seems to have existed for about four years, for Miss Caulkins says, in her *History of Norwich*, that the rights in the road were relinquished in 1860.

84. The New Milford and Roxbury Turnpike

A proposition to connect New Milford with Woodbury, running from a connection with the West Point Turnpike in New York to the Middle Turnpike in the town of Woodbury, was chartered by the assembly in May, 1823, under the name of the New Milford and Woodbury Turnpike Company. It is to be noted in connection with this late charter that the towns were to be obliged to pay the land damages. But for some reason or other, this project of 1823 does not seem to have materialized.

In May, 1827, the New Milford and Roxbury Turnpike Company was chartered to build from the east end of the New Milford and Sherman Turnpike to the meeting-house in Roxbury, and all portions of the route granted to the New Milford and Woodbury which conflicted with the newly granted rights were declared void.

Orcutt's *History of New Milford* tells us that that town opposed the granting of the charter, but unsuccessfully. The road was built and was in operation in 1831. Probably it continued a great many years longer, for this was one of those local roads which, we have observed, pursued a quiet and) moderately profitable career.

85. The Tolland and Mansfield Turnpike

Some calculating mind, in which distances to be traveled by stages were not seriously considered, conceived a plan about 1820 by which the stage travel over the Northern Route from Boston to New York was to be diverted at the westerly end of the First Massachusetts Turnpike and carried to Hartford by way of Tolland. As parts of this scheme the Wilbraham Turnpike was chartered in Massachusetts in 1820, and in Connecticut efforts were made to have the Burbank Road completed. This road had been laid out from the Massachusetts line through Somers, Stafford, Ellington, and Tolland to the Tolland courthouse, by the towns involved, in 1805, but the cost seemed prohibitive, so the project languished for many years. Finally, in May, 1828, the Tolland and Mansfield Turnpike Company was formed for the purpose of building the Burbank Road, with an additional section running from Tolland Street to Daniel Fuller's in Mansfield. Had the whole plan been carried out, a roundabout route between Worcester and Hartford would have been provided, but the need of it is not evident to the present generation. Apparently it was not to the people of a century ago, for the Wilbraham was never built.

But the Tolland and Mansfield was and, by its southerly connection at Daniel Fuller's with the Windham and Mansfield Turnpike, undoubtedly provided for some business between Norwich and Springfield. This corporation was obliged to build its own bridges, except those over the Willimantic and Skunkermaug rivers. The freedom from this obligation seems to have troubled the town of Somers, for it voted to assume the burden of the three bridges within its limits, an arrangement which the assembly sanctioned in May, 1834.

The charter of the Tolland and Mansfield was repealed in 1847.

86. The Huntington Turnpike

A short time previous to May, 1828, the Fairfield county court made a layout of a highway from the center of Huntington to the borough of Bridgeport, for the purpose of having the same built as a turnpike. The assembly of the month named deprived the road of its public character and formed the Huntington Turnpike Company to take over the location and build the road. In 1830 authority was given to extend the turnpike to the west bank of the Housatonic River, thus giving a through route from Bridgeport to Derby Landing.

The road as finally built started from the river opposite Derby Landing and ran westerly and southerly to Huntington Center, thence southwesterly through Trumbull into Bridgeport, where it intersected a new road which led into the center of the borough.

In 1852 all of the road west of the easterly abutment of the Berkshire Bridge was made free. This, it is seen, included the bridge which Bridgeport was loath to take on account of its condition. So the corporation was obliged to pay the town four hundred and fifty dollars toward the needed repairs.

The rest of the road continued under the imposition of tolls until March 24, 1886, when an act was passed authorizing the corporation to relinquish its rights and make the road free.

87. The Weston Turnpike

This turnpike was built from Philo Lyons to the Black Rock Road in Fairfield with a branch from Fairfield to the Academy in Weston.

From Barber's *Connecticut Historical Collections* we learn that the academy mentioned was in the village of Easton, which was then a part of Weston, and that it was possessed of a fund that rendered it a free school. It was presented to the town by Samuel Staples, who included in his gift sufficient land in the vicinity to support it.

A revision of the tolls was made in 1861 and the road was made free on the day on which Fairfield County had a clearance of turnpikes, March 24, 1886. The Weston Turnpike Company was incorporated in May, 1828, and had a life of fifty-eight years.

88. The Sugar Hollow Turnpike

The Sugar Hollow Turnpike was remarkable because it provided for extensions on each end of a previously established turnpike, using the older road for a connection for its two sections, and further because it derived its name from the particular section traversed by the road first built. One would say that the charter really was an amendment of the first one, but additions to or alterations of existing roads were commonly provided by amending acts and could easily have been so secured in this case. Evidence favors the idea of two separate companies.

The road commenced in Wilton on the Norwalk and Danbury Turnpike and then passed through the Mountain Gap to Ridgefield Center, where it met the southerly end of the Danbury and Ridgefield Turnpike. The layout is then described as "on said turnpike-road through Sugar Hollow." At a point almost at the end of the Danbury and Ridgefield in Danbury, the new road branched northwesterly and, crossing the outlet of Mill Plain Pond, extended to the New York line.

The Sugar Hollow Turnpike Company was formed at the May session of 1829, and nothing appears regarding it after 1836, when a change of gates was allowed. The Danbury and Ridgefield's charter was repealed in 1860 and, since the two roads were so interwoven, it seems probable that the Sugar

Hollow became free at the same time, although no act to that effect has been found.

89. The Newtown and Norwalk Turnpike

The franchise under which this road was located allowed it to be built from the foot of Main Street in Newtown, passing near the Episcopal Church in Redding, through the westerly part of Weston, with the option of passing through the easterly part of Wilton, to the Great Bridge in Norwalk at the head of Norwalk Harbor. It was granted to the Newtown and Norwalk Turnpike Company in May, 1829, a late date for so long a road. Financing evidently was not easy, for the company was obliged to apply for an extension of time, which was granted in 1830.

Apparently this turnpike is the Newtown Avenue of to-day in Norwalk, and the road in continuation, which twists through the southeast corner of Wilton and then passes northerly through Weston and Redding and into Newtown, where it reaches Newtown Center after going near Hattertown and Dodgingtown. It intersected the Northfield Turnpike near where it crossed the Saugatuck River in the northeast corner of Weston.

All of the road north of the Northfield Turnpike was made free in 1841, and the balance, through the towns of Weston, Wilton, Westport, and Norwalk, passed into public control in 1851.

90. The Shetucket Turnpike

Although by the building of the Providence and Norwich Turnpike in Rhode Island, and the New London and Windham County Turnpike in Connecticut, travel between Providence and Norwich had been accommodated to a greater extent than it was able to pay for, certain optimists found encouragement to believe that a rival route, having no advantages beyond the saving of a mile or two, would prove a paying investment. We have already seen how Duty Green labored in Rhode Island to promote the Providence and Norwich City Turnpike but failed to interest the necessary capital. We will now consider the efforts to carry out the Connecticut end of the same scheme.

The Shetucket Turnpike Company received from the assembly of May, 1829, a charter to build a road from the toll bridge over the Shetucket at Norwich Landing through Preston, Griswold, Voluntown, and Sterling, to the Rhode Island line, and, although obliged to secure an extension of its time in 1831, managed to have its turnpike in operation by 1832. Miss Caulkins' *History of Norwich* says that the capital invested was eleven thousand dollars, and that during its thirty years of existence the corporation paid an average of only one and one third per cent in dividends. Considering that the Rhode Island part of the plan contemplated a road running straight from the state boundary to Providence, and that that part failed of consummation, leaving practically no connection at all with Providence, it is a wonder that the management was able to make both ends meet. But the Shetucket Turnpike connected at Voluntown Center with the old "Ten Rod Road," which led by Beach Pond on the state boundary to Wickford on Narragansett Bay, and since over that road large numbers of cattle were driven for shipment abroad, it is possible that the Shetucket may have shared that business.

The cost of this road appears to have been about $610 a mile, and the average of its net earnings, according to Miss Caulkins, was about $8.15 per mile per year.

By 1859 the corporation had had enough and it then asked for an additional gate, or that a portion of its road might be assumed by the towns. Another gate was too much, but the assembly obligingly allowed the company to unload on to the town of Voluntown that part of its road between the east line of that town and the highway at Robbins Tavern. As long as tolls were collected in Voluntown on the remainder of the road, the corporation was obliged to pay forty dollars annually to Voluntown to make repairs on the part given up.

In June, 1860, provision was made for the surrender of the entire road, upon such terms as might be agreed. If agreement was found impossible the superior court of New London County was to appoint commissioners to fix the price, but acceptance of their award was dependent upon a vote of the town implicated, so that law did not amount to anything.

In July, 1861, the same act was renewed but without the provision that the towns might vote on acceptance. They were then forced to take the road and pay the commissioners' award for it, and Voluntown lost the forty dollars which it had been collecting yearly.

Under this act Preston, Griswold, and Voluntown assumed the Shetucket Turnpike and made up the price of $1375 between them.

91. The Wells Hollow Turnpike

Incorporated in May, 1830, the Wells Hollow Turnpike Company built its road from the west side of the Housatonic River, where the Leavenworth Bridge Company was about to erect a bridge, toward Bridgeport, through the valley called Wells Hollow, and joining the Huntington Turnpike near Elan Hawley's store in the center of Huntington.

The Leavenworth Bridge Company was first incorporated in May, 1804, when Gideon Leavenworth and others received a charter to bridge the Housatonic at Derby Landing. In May, 1830, an act was passed by which the company was allowed to sell its bridge, tollhouse, and all other property, dividing the proceeds among its stockholders. Then a new corporation was to be formed, or rather new stock of the old corporation was to be created, which was to be sold, preference being given to former shareholders. From the capital thus raised a new bridge was to be erected at Hawkins Point in Derby or farther north at "the point of rock." That was the bridge referred to in the charter of the Wells Hollow Turnpike. In 1833 the name of the Leavenworth Bridge Company was changed to Derby Bridge and Ferry Company, and under that name the bridge was operated as a toll bridge until 1872, when it was sold to the towns of Derby and Huntington and by them made free.

The Wells Hollow Turnpike, in connection with the Huntington Turnpike, formed nearly a direct route from Derby Landing to Bridgeport. In the final clean-up of Fairfield County on March 24, 1886, both the Huntington and the Wells Hollow turnpikes were made free.

92. The Branch Turnpike

The Branch Turnpike Company was incorporated in May, 1831, and built a road from Bennett's Bridge over the Housatonic River between Newtown and Southbury, through Newtown, Monroe, Weston, Fairfield, and Westport. In 1836 an alteration was allowed from a point in Monroe to Bennett's Bridge.

Apparently this is the road which now starts a little south of Westport Village and runs northeasterly, forming the boundary between Weston and Fairfield, across the town of Easton and the northwesterly part of Monroe to Bennett's Bridge.

In 1837 all of the road, about one mile, which lay south of Westport Village was made free, and the balance of the road was similarly treated in 1851 when the charter was repealed.

93. The Black Rock and Weston Turnpike

The road running northwesterly from Black Rock Harbor across the town of Fairfield and to some point in Weston, north of the Branch Turnpike, was built by the Black Rock and Weston Turnpike Company under a charter granted in May, 1832.

The lower end between Fairfield and Black Rock was made free in 1844, with the apparently unreasonable provision that no gate should be maintained on the remainder for which the corporation still was held responsible. The rest within Fairfield's limits was discontinued as a turnpike in 1847, and all in Easton became public in 1851.

The reason for selecting Black Rock Harbor for the terminus is learned from Barber's *Historical Collections*, which were published soon after the opening of this road. We there read:

BLACK ROCK harbor, about 1½ miles from Fairfield court house, is, with the exception of New London, one of the best harbors in the Sound, being safe and commodious, and having 19 feet of water at summer tides, below what is called the middle ground. There is a lighthouse on Fairweather's Island, which forms the easterly chop of the harbor. Vessels can enter and depart from this harbor at any time of the tide.

94. The Monroe and Newtown Turnpike

This was a short road which led from the Bridgeport and Newtown Turnpike at Upper Stepney and ran northwesterly close to the line between Monroe and Easton across the southwesterly corner of Newtown to Dodgingtown, where it ended at the line of Bethel, then a part of Danbury.

In 1847 the company was allowed to move a gate and was authorized to sell the tollhouse and the connected land.

The Monroe and Newtown Turnpike Company was chartered in May, 1833.

95. The Fairfield County Turnpike

The Fairfield County Turnpike Company was formed in May, 1834, with a franchise to build a road from the northerly end of the Black Rock and Weston Turnpike, through Weston and Newtown to the intersection of the Brookfield Road with the Middle Road Turnpike, and thence to Meeker's Mills in Brookfield.

The location was changed in 1836 and again in 1837, and the charter was repealed in 1848.

96. The Hadlyme, and Chester and North Killingworth Second Turnpikes

By the opening in 1816 of the Chester and North Killingworth Turnpike a short local road was provided between two country centers, but it happened that the road lay in almost a direct line between Norwich and New Haven, although far from both cities and without turnpike connection on either end in their direction.

In May, 1834, various parties who were subject to the turnpike delusion regarding the value of shortened distances, and who failed to realize the approach of the railroad, saw in the route along the line of the Chester and North Killingworth a desirable opening for turnpike investment. Consequently the Hadlyme Turnpike Company was chartered in that month for the purpose of building from Warner's Ferry through Lyme and East Haddam to a junction with the Salem and Hamburg Turnpike in the westerly part of Salem; and the Chester and North Killingworth Second Turnpike Company was formed at the same session to continue the route westerly, starting from Warner's Ferry and running to the easterly end of the Chester and North Killingworth. The Chester and North Killingworth Second's charter further allowed that company to build westerly from the west end of the older road to a junction with the Fairhaven Turnpike, but it does not appear that that part of the franchise was utilized by this company.

Warner's Ferry had been in operation across the Connecticut River between Chester and Hadlyme for sixty-five years at this time, having been established in 1769.

On account of the well-known inability of turnpikes to pay on their investment and the agitation for railroads which had been under way for several years, it can be imagined that the promoters of this turnpike enterprise found it difficult to persuade moneyed men to join them. Nevertheless as the time limit of the Hadlyme neared expiration that corporation found itself with a road seven eighths completed and mostly paid for, so the assembly of 1837 saw fit to grant an extension of time for completion.

The Chester and North Killingworth Second must have proceeded with as much promptness and built its road from Warner's Ferry to Chester, but since another corporation was formed in 1835 with a franchise covering the same ground as the Second's western section it is plain that that portion was not built at this time. In a petition filed by the Chester and North Killingworth Second the investment is given as twenty-three hundred dollars, about enough to pay for two miles with ferry approaches and improvements. The same petition gave the "total dividends" as 1.3 per cent. That covered a period of about ten years, and it is quite possible that "total" was properly used and that the average dividend yearly had been about 0.13 per cent.

In 1846 the charter of the Chester and North Killingworth Second was annulled, and that of the Hadlyme was repealed in 1847.

It may be remarked that a charter for a railroad was passed at the same session which granted the two turnpike franchises here considered.

97. The Sherman and Redding Turnpike

The Sherman and Redding Turnpike Company was formed at the May session in 1834 and allowed to build from Sherman to either the Newtown and Norwalk Turnpike in Redding, or to the Northfield in Weston. It is clear that the plans, were carried out, but it is impossible to-day to pick out the location of the road.

A petition filed in 1846 declared that the turnpike was never demanded by public necessity or convenience and that for six years it had been "wholly and entirely abandoned," and consequently was impassable and useless. From that it appears that the life of the turnpike had been less than six years and that the corporation had practically made its road free. But some form of public dedication seems to have remained and the assembly, therefore, discontinued a section between the Danbury and Brookfield line and the highway leading from Danbury to Newtown, which thereby ceased to be a road at all, and the land reverted to the former owners. In 1852 similar action was taken with reference to several disconnected parts of the road, so that all that could be expected to exist to-day are a few short pieces of country road in separate places.

98. The Madison and North Killingworth Turnpike

It has been noted that the Chester and North Killingworth Second Turnpike Company did not improve its franchise on the westerly end, but that that was left for another corporation. A year later, in May, 1835, the Madison and North Killingworth Turnpike Company was incorporated with a franchise reaching from the west end of the Chester and North Killingworth Turnpike to the Fairhaven Turnpike in North Madison. By the construction of this road the short line of turnpike communication between Norwich and New Haven was completed, but it was a disappointment to its projectors.

We have noted the demise of the Hadlyme and of the Chester and North Killingworth Second in 1847 and 1846 respectively. The Madison and North Killingworth preceded them by four years, its charter having been repealed in 1842.

99. The Hop River Turnpike

The Hartford, New London, Windham, and Tolland County Turnpike, which extended from Bolton Notch to Norwichtown, must have gone out of business, at least on its westerly end, before 1835, for on that date in May, the Hop River Turnpike Company was formed and granted a franchise which covered the road of the long-named company from Andover to Bolton Notch. The rest of the Hop River route carried it to the village of Willimantic, where it entered the Windham Turnpike over the street which now forms the westerly boundary of the Willimantic Cemetery and terminates opposite the almshouse.

This company invested over five thousand dollars, according to its own statement in a petition filed in 1851, which makes an average cost of about three hundred and sixty dollars a mile.

The Hartford, Providence, and Fishkill Railroad commenced operations in 1842 and paralleled the turnpike, close by, for its entire length. Poor enough before, the business of the Hop River then became absolutely

Hop River Turnpike: Approaching the Windham Turnpike

valueless, but the company held on until 1851 when it sought to be relieved of the responsibility for the road. The assembly allowed that it might be so relieved, if no one of the towns interested made protest, but apparently one did, for the act was of no effect.

In 1853 outside parties made petition that the road might be made a public obligation. The road was very much out of repair and one of the bridges was broken down and impassable. The corporation had vanished, and no process could be served on it, but the road was a public necessity.

So the Hop River Turnpike was legislated into the past, and the towns of Windham, Columbia, Andover, and Bolton were obliged to assume its maintenance.

Hop River Turnpike: In Andover, Conn.

Connecticut's Plank Roads

Plank roads had been thoroughly demonstrated for about sixteen years before the venture was made in Connecticut. The first company was the Danbury, Redding, Weston, and Westport Plank Road Company which was incorporated in 1851. In this charter a mild form of specification for the road was included : "The track of which plank road shall be made of timber, plank, or other hard material, so that the same shall form a hard and even surface."

The authority given the corporation for laying out its road and taking land was comprehensively expressed and has since been followed in its language in railroad franchises. The capital stock was fixed at one hundred thousand dollars, divided into shares of a par value of fifty dollars each, which shares were declared to be personal property. Gates could be erected where the management saw fit, provided they were not less than three miles apart. Tolls were to be fixed by the corporation but were not to be in excess of the following schedule:

Any vehicle drawn by two animals . . . . 2 cents a mile
Each additional animal . . . . 1½ cents a mile
Any vehicle drawn by one animal . . . . 1 cent a mile
Each horse and rider, or led animal . . . . ½ cent a mile
Each mule, cattle, sheep, or swine . . . . 1/10 cent a mile

No mention of this road has been found in local histories and only the act of incorporation appears in the publication of special acts. On account of its late date it is unlikely that it could have escaped the notice of the historians if it had been built. The distance was about thirty-four miles and, since the Danbury and Norwalk Railroad was even at the date of the charter under construction and commenced operations in 1852, an investment of one hundred thousand dollars in a decadent type of road would have been injudicious. It seems safe to say that the road was not built.

The Stamford, New Canaan, and Ridgefield Plank Road Company was created in the same year to build from Stamford through Darien to New Canaan "with permission to extend said plank road to and into the town of Ridgefield." Nothing more has been found regarding this effort.

Two roads to lead into New Haven were authorized. The New Haven and Seymour Plank Road Company and the Wallingford, North Haven and New Haven Plank Road Company received their charters in 1852 and 1853 respectively. In the *History of New Haven*, written by George H. Watrous, a successful attorney of New Haven and president of the New York, New Haven, and Hartford Railroad Company for several years, is found a thorough summary of transportation affecting that city. Since he included every other form of roadway, pioneer paths, turnpikes, railroads, and canals, his omission of any reference to plank roads seems to remove them from the history of New Haven. Sharpe, in his *History of Seymour*, refers to the formation of the New Haven and Seymour Company but leaves the reader with an impression that it did nothing.

The Woodbury and Seymour Plank Road Company was chartered in 1852 to build from some point in Woodbury through Southbury, Oxford, and Seymour to Seymour on the Naugatuck River.

Although Sharpe, in his *History of Seymour*, mentions this as the only company collecting tolls in 1879, positive assertion is made by competent Woodbury authority that no such plank road ever existed. Perhaps a short section was built and operated in Seymour only.

In 1853 another company, the Salisbury Plank Road Company, was incorporated to build from the New York line across the town of Salisbury, through Lime Rock, and to end at Falls Village in Canaan. The New York and Harlem and the Housatonic railroads were then crossing the ends of this proposed route in parallel directions and only about nine miles apart, so the need of an investments of about fifteen thousand dollars is hard to see. An old resident of Falls Village who said, "I knew them all," when the names of the incorporators were read to him, had never heard of the Salisbury Plank Road and was very certain that nothing of the kind was ever built.

But one charter was granted which was not issued in vain.

100. The Waterbury and Cheshire Plank Road

The Waterbury and Cheshire Plank Road Company was formed in 1852 to provide plank-road communication between the towns named. Its road was built and is mentioned in Bronson's *History of Waterbury*, published in 1858, as "the new plank road." Anderson also mentions it, but in a casual way. It ran from Waterbury Village easterly and entered the old Cheshire Road just north of Spectacle Pond.

Besides the companies which have been mentioned in the preceding pages the following, of which we have been able to glean no further facts, were incorporated by the Connecticut general assembly.

1797	Stratfield and Weston Turnpike Company	Apparently wholly in the town of Weston.
	Saugatuck Turnpike Company	Dragon Bridge to Byram River
1802	Greenwich and Ridgefield Turnpike Company	Mostly within New York State.
1812	Farmington and Harwinton Turnpike Company	Between those towns.

1817	Dragon Turnpike Company	New Haven to Connecticut River. Was not built.
1818	Granby and Barkhamsted Turnpike Company	Was never finished.
	Wolcott and Hampden Turnpike Company	Through Plymouth, Wolcott, and Hampden.
1820	Pleasant Valley Turnpike Company	River Head to Warner's Ferry.
1823	Woodbridge and Waterbury Turnpike Company	Waterbury to Woodbury.
1830	Moosup Turnpike Company	Union Factory Village to Rhode Island line.
1832	Simpaug Turnpike Company	In Ridgefield.
1834	Kent and Warren Turnpike Company	New York line, through Kent, to Litchfield.
1836	Litchfield and Plymouth Turnpike Company	Between those towns.
1839	Millington Turnpike Company	East Haddam to Colchester.

Index